Reconsidering Science Learning

Reconsidering Science Learning looks at science learning in a wide range of contexts. A variety of issues are explored in terms of curriculum and science provision in both schools and universities and for adult learners in distance education settings.

The reader is divided into four parts. Part 1 deals with the arguments put forward for studying science and includes a discussion on what science learners need to know about the nature of science and how decisions about what forms science curricula are made. Part 2 includes chapters on the processes by which science is learned. Part 3 focuses on opportunities for developing science learning for all students, including extending access to science knowledge and increasing students' motivation for learning science. The fourth part deals with researching science education.

Reconsidering Science Learning will be of particular interest to teachers on masters courses in science education and academics with an interest in science education.

This is a companion book to *Mediating Science Learning through Information and Communications Technology*, also published by RoutledgeFalmer.

Eileen Scanlon, Patricia Murphy, Jeff Thomas and **Elizabeth Whitelegg** are all members of The Open University MSc in Science team.

SEH806 Contemporary Issues in Science Learning

The companion volume in this series is *Mediating Science Learning Through Information and Communications Technology (ICT)* by Richard Holliman and Eileen Scanlon.

Both of the Readers are part of a course, **Contemporary Issues in Science Learning** (SEH806), that is itself part of an MSc in Science Programme at the Open University and also counts towards the MA in Education and the MA in Online and Distance Education.

The Open University MSc in Science

The MSc in Science at the Open University is a relatively new 'distance-taught' programme that has been designed for students who want to explore broad scientific topics at postgraduate level. It provides opportunities to pursue some of science's most pressing issues using the innovative teaching methods pioneered at The Open University.

Structure of the MSc in Science

The MSc in Science is a modular programme that allows students to select modules that best fit with their interests and professional goals. The Programme has two main themes or 'strands': Science Studies and Frontiers in Medical Science.

Modules currently available

> Science and the Public
> Communicating Science
> Imaging in Medicine
> Molecules in Medicine
> Issues in Brain and Behaviour
> The Project Module

It is also possible to count other OU modules towards the MSc in Science and to count MSc in Science modules towards other OU awards such as the MA in Education.

OU supported learning

The MSc in Science Programme, in common with other OU programmes, provides great flexibility. Students study at their own pace and in their own time, anywhere in the European Union. They receive specially prepared study materials and benefit from tutorial support (electronically and at day schools), thus offering them the chance to work with other students.

How to apply

If you would like to register for this Programme, or find out more information, visit our website http://www.open.ac.uk/science/msc. If you would like to find out more general information about available courses, please contact the Course Information and Advice Centre, PO Box 724, The Open University, Walton Hall, Milton Keynes MK7 6ZS, UK (Telephone 01908 653231). Details can also be viewed on our web pages: http://www.open.ac.uk/courses

Reconsidering Science Learning

Edited by Eileen Scanlon,
Patricia Murphy, Jeff Thomas
and Elizabeth Whitelegg

RoutledgeFalmer
Taylor & Francis Group

LONDON AND NEW YORK

The Open
University

First published 2004
by RoutledgeFalmer
11 New Fetter Lane, London EC4P 4EE

Simultaneously published in the USA and Canada
by RoutledgeFalmer 29 West 35th Street, New York, NY 10001

RoutledgeFalmer is an imprint of the Taylor & Francis Group

© 2004 The Open University

Typeset in Goudy by
Bookcraft Ltd, Stroud, Gloucestershire
Printed and bound in Great Britain by
CPI Group (UK) Ltd, Croydon, CR0 4YY

British Library Cataloguing in Publication Data
A catalogue record for this book is available from the British Library

Library of Congress Cataloging in Publication Data
A catalog record has been requested

ISBN 0-415-32831-4 (pbk)

ISBN 0-415-32830-6 (hbk)

Contents

Illustrations

Figures

Tables

Sources

Where a chapter in this book is based on or is a reprint or revision of material previously published elsewhere, details are given below, with grateful acknowledgements to the original publishers.

Chapter 1.1   This is an edited version of a chapter originally published in Amos, S. and Boohan, R. (eds) *Teaching Science in Secondary Schools*, pp. 40–54, Routledge-Falmer (2002).

Chapter 1.2   Reprinted from *International Journal of Science Education* 21(7), pp. 703–10, Taylor and Francis (1999).

Chapter 1.3   This is an edited version of a chapter originally published in Levinson, R. and Thomas, J. (eds) *Science Today*, pp. 119–36, Routledge (1997).

Chapter 2.1   This is an edited version of Chapter 3 in *The Private Life of the Brain*, pp. 51–76, Penguin (2000).

Chapter 2.2   This is an edited version of an article originally published in *Educational Researcher* 23(7), pp. 5–12, ©American Educational Research Association (1994).

Chapter 2.3   This is an edited version of an article originally published in *American Psychologist* 52(4), pp. 399–413, ©American Psychological Association (1997).

Chapter 2.4   This is an edited version of Chapter 6 in *The Culture of Education*, pp. 115–29, Harvard UP (1996).

Chapter 2.5   This is an edited version of an article originally published in *Educational Researcher*, 28(3), pp.14–24, ©American Educational Research Association (1999).

Chapter 2.6   Adapted from a paper presented at National Association for Research in Science Teaching, New Orleans, April 2002.

Chapter 2.7   This is an edited version of Chapter 3 in Wallace, J. and Louden, W. (eds) *Dilemmas of Science Teaching: perspectives and problems of practice*, pp. 36–55, RoutledgeFalmer (2002).

Chapter 3.1   This is an edited version of an article originally published in *Research in Science and Technological Education* 17(1), pp. 45–66, Carfax Publishing Ltd, (1999).

Chapter 3.2   This is an edited version of a chapter originally published in Ogawa, M. (ed.) *Effects of Traditional Cosmology on Science Education*, pp. 15–21, Faculty of Education, Ibaraki University, Japan (1997).

Chapter 3.3   This is an edited version of an article originally published in *Science Education* 85(1), pp. 50–67, ©Wiley (2001).

Chapter 3.4   This is an edited version of an article originally published in *Journal of Research in Science Teaching* 37(5), pp. 426–40, ©Wiley (2000).

Preface

This collection of readings has been chosen to complement the Open University's course on contemporary issues in science learning, which is part of a Master's degree. This is the first of two volumes which together provide our students with a set of readings for their use in the course. The other reader deals with the impact of new technology on science learning.

These two volumes of readings form a small part of the Master's module on Contemporary Issues which is part of a Master's course in Science being produced in the Science Faculty of the Open University by a team from the Faculties of Science and Education and Language Studies and the Institute of Educational Technology. It is followed by students aiming for the Master's degree in the Studies of Science, but it also can act as a subsidiary course aiming for other Open University Master's awards in Education and Open and Distance Learning. Study materials provided by the University also include a study commentary, set texts and CD-ROMs with a library of additional paper and video material produced by the BBC. Students also have access to the Internet and receive tutorials using computer conferencing.

Some of the material in this reader has been newly commissioned by the editors for use in our course. Some chapters have been adapted and edited from previously published papers in journals, conference proceedings and books. As a result, a range of styles has been used by the authors which were appropriate for the original contents. A range of referencing styles is in use in this volume so students of our course may notice that they do not all conform to our course referencing style.

This is a collection of readings dealing with contemporary issues in science learning, and issues and debates in extending access to science knowledge and research in science education. It is divided into four parts which cover issues of what science should be taught, theories of learning which have an implication for science education, opportunities for developing science learning for all and research in science education. The first part includes a discussion of the nature of science and the relationships between science, citizenship and the public under-standing of science and interactions between school science and its problems with scientific literacy. The second part draws on a wide range of writing on learning from biologists, educationalists, psychologists and science educators. It includes discussions of learning communities for science, learning science in the workplace and laboratory work. The third part explores different aspects of extending access to science knowledge. This examines the implications of cultural perspectives on learning science and the role of context in learning science, multicultural and gender-inclusive approaches. The fourth part on researching science education reflects on the status and methods used in such work.

The editors would like to thank the other members of the course team for their help in selecting the articles. We would also like to thank Cheryl Newport, Carol Johnstone, Gillian Riley and Pat Forster for their invaluable help in the production of this volume. Opinions expressed in the articles are not necessarily those of the course team or the Open University.

The editors of the volume would also like to thank the authors who produced newly commissioned articles: Peter Chin, Hugh Munby, Nancy Hutchinson, Jenny Taylor and Francis Clark, Queen's University, Canada; Edgar Jenkins, University of Leeds; and Susan Barker, University of Warwick, UK.

Eileen Scanlon

Part 1

What is science?

Jeffery N. Thomas

Those anxious about contemporary representations of science in the media dwell on the presumed disparity between the image of science and the reality as imagined by insiders. A concern with the representation of science in the classroom surely needs to occupy as significant a place within the current educational debate. The impressions of science acquired in early education are presumably especially durable, shaping perceptions more fundamentally than the ephemeral and mixed messages that often comprise informal learning. For this reason, the beguilingly simple questions of 'what science?' and 'for what purpose?' need to preface any contemporary debate about science education.

The readings in the first section provide this curtain-raiser to what follows, touching on the heavily contested topics of the nature of science and the purposes of science education. Their aim is to challenge and to energize the reader. Michael Reiss's stimulating and wide-ranging article 'What is science?' sets the scene, by exploring how the richness, complexity and occasional contradiction that is contemporary science might be represented in the classroom. In his view, today's science is far from rule-bound, unsullied and standardized; he argues for science that is located within a cultural milieu, with the boundaries of the subject blurred and tolerant of leakage.

Edgar Jenkins's elegant article brings together two disciplines that have usually occupied separate territories and traditions – educational and sociological perspectives on how science understanding is handled. His pioneering work with David Layton and colleagues showed that citizens lacking a formal knowledge base can be wonderfully adept self-learners when they have the motivation and opportunity to find out about aspects of science that have a particular bearing on their lives. The plea that the science that young people learn has clearer social purpose and relevance therefore seems unarguably clear. But the fact that many such science issues are entwined with a host of attendant social contexts – including issues of trust, expertise, media representation and institutional interests – requires of young people a sensitivity to forms of knowledge and thinking far removed from the narrow world of science. A science curriculum rich in 'citizen science' requires an approach and content far removed from the insular and fact-rich lessons that are still widespread today.

Anxieties about 'what science?' and 'for what purpose?' have a global relevance and timeliness. Peter Fensham's account of efforts urging the abandonment of traditional curricula and the introduction of a genuine 'science for all' reports more frustration than it does achievement. Given that the type of curriculum he advocates shows a 'warts and all' science – richer for example in 'the subjective, irrational … (and) social construction' – resistance to change might be expected from the scientific community. His observation that the forces of educational conservatism run much deeper is enlightening. Science educators themselves are seen to have an ambiguous role. Our lack of research understanding about how students experience the type of socio-scientific issues that characterize the new-style curriculum suggests that moving ahead will itself be far from risk-free.

If readings are meant to inspire, provoke and unsettle, then these few chapters will reveal how great is the need for change and how uncertain is the uncharted path ahead.

1.1 What is science?

Teaching science in secondary schools

Michael Reiss

I have found Ms … has had to deal with another problem: the history of science is almost entirely the history of *Western* science, and Ms … has almost no knowledge of European history since classical times. This is obviously a considerable drawback in coming to a general view or coming to grips with many broader problems in the development of science …

(Copied from a 1981 end-of-term supervision report of a student from Pakistan doing the second-year undergraduate course in History of Science at Cambridge University)

Who are scientists?

A while ago, I happened to see a new set of postage stamps produced in the UK, entitled 'Scientific achievements' (issued 5 March 1991). It's worth spending a few moments imagining what you might expect (or hope!) to see on these stamps. Well, whatever you thought, the Royal Mail produced four stamps under the heading Scientific achievements' with the captions 'Faraday – Electricity', 'Babbage – Computer', 'Radar – Watson-Watt' and 'Jet Engine – Whittle'. I find it difficult to imagine a narrower conception of what science is and who does it. The image seems to be that real science is hard physics, with military applications, done by males who are white and worked on their own between about 1820 and 1940. No wonder so many students drop science at school as soon as they have the chance! Children come to school science lessons with clear impressions of what science is, how it operates and who does it (Driver *et al.* 1985; Osborne and Freyberg 1985). There is a limit to what science teachers can realistically be expected to achieve in terms of challenging social perceptions and changing received wisdom.

It seems sad that the Royal Mail could produce a set of stamps that portrayed such a biased view of science. Stamps to feature scientists could convey the notion that women do science, that science didn't start in the nineteenth century and finish around the time of the Second World War, that it isn't a Western construct, that it is done by people working in groups and that it permeates every area of life. […]

The nature of science

The popular view of what science is and how it proceeds probably goes something like this:

> Science consists of a body of knowledge about the world. The facts that comprise this knowledge are derived from accurate observations and careful experiments that can be checked by repeating them. As time goes on, scientific knowledge steadily progresses.

Such a view persists, not only among the general public, but also among science teachers and scientists despite the fact that most historians of science, philosophers of science, sociologists of science and science educationalists hold it to be, at best, simplified and misleading and, at worst, completely erroneous (Latour 1987; Woolgar 1988; Wellington 1989; Harding 1991).

It is not too much of a caricature to state that science is seen by many as *the* way to truth. Indeed, a number of important scientists have encouraged such a view by their writings and interviews (e.g. Peter Atkins and Richard Dawkins). It is generally assumed that the world 'out there' exists independently of the particular scientific methodology used to study it (Figure 1.1.1). The advance of science then consists of scientists discovering eternal truths that exist independently of them and of the cultural context in which these discoveries are made. All areas of life are presumed amenable to scientific inquiry. Truth is supposed to emerge unambiguously from experiment like Pallas Athene, the goddess of wisdom, springing mature and unsullied from the head of Zeus. This view of science is mistaken for a number of reasons, which I now want to discuss.

Scientists have to choose on what to work

What scientists 'choose' to work on is controlled partly by their background as individuals and partly by the values of the society in which they live and work. Most scientific research is not pure but applied. In particular, approximately one half of all scientific research funding is provided for military purposes. To give just one specific example of the way society determines the topics on which scientists should work: the 1980s saw a significant reduction in Great Britain in the level of research into systematics, taxonomy and nomenclature (the classification, identification and naming of organisms). This was a direct result of changes in government funding which, for instance, required the Natural History Museum in London, the major UK centre for such research, to generate much of its own income. As a result, the number of scientists working there in these disciplines more than halved as such scientists generate very little income.

Now, my point is not specifically to complain at the demise of systematics, taxonomy and nomenclature in the UK, but to point out that society and individual scientists have to choose on what to work. To a very large extent that choice is not determined on purely scientific criteria (if such criteria exist), but by political machinations and by the priorities (some would describe them as quirks) of funding bodies.

Scientists do not discover the world out there as it is

Scientists approach their topics of study with preconceptions. There is no such thing as an impartial observation. In the classroom, this is seen to be the case every time a group of pupils is asked, for the first time, to draw some cells or sulphur crystals under the microscope. It isn't possible until you know what to draw. Unless you know that a leaf of pondweed consists of numerous small, brick-like structures, all you can see is a mass of green with lines and occasional air bubbles. [...]

Instances are legion where we can look back and see how scientists have unconsciously interpreted what they have seen in the light of their cultural heritage. In his book *Metaphors of Mind*, Robert Sternberg points out that much of the present confusion surrounding the concept of intelligence stems from the variety of standpoints from which the human mind can be viewed (Sternberg 1990). The geographic metaphor is based on the notion that a theory of intelligence should provide a map of the mind. This view dates back at least to Gall, an early nineteenth-century German anatomist and perhaps the most famous of phrenologists. Gall investigated the topography of the head, looking and feeling for tiny variations in the shape of the skull. According to him, a person's intelligence was to be discerned

Figure 1.1.1 What is the relationship between science and that which it describes? (Copyright: Chris Madden.)

in the pattern of their cranial bumps. A second metaphor, the computational metaphor, envisions the mind as a computing device and analogizes the processes of the mind to the operations of a computer. Other metaphors discussed by Sternberg include the biological metaphor, the epistemological metaphor, the anthropological metaphor, the sociological metaphor and the systems metaphor. The point is that what scientists see and the models they construct to mirror reality depend very much on where their point of view is.

A clear example of how the work that scientists do is inevitably affected by who they are is provided by Jane Goodall's seminal (if that is not too sexist a term!) research on chimpanzee behaviour. When she first arrived to study the chimpanzees on the banks of Lake Tanganyika, the game warden who took her round made a mental note that she wouldn't last more than six weeks. She has stayed for forty years, producing the definitive accounts of chimpanzee social organization and behaviour in her fascinating and moving books *In the Shadow of Man* (van Lawick-Goodall 1971) and *The Chimpanzees of Gombe: Patterns of Behavior* (Goodall 1986).

An important point about Jane Goodall is that she had no formal training in ethology (the science of animal behaviour), having trained as a secretary after leaving school. As she herself wrote, 'I was, of course, completely unqualified to undertake a scientific study of animal behaviour' (van Lawick-Goodall 1971: 20). However, she spent some time with the celebrated palaeontologist Louis Leakey and his wife, Mary, on one of their annual expeditions to Olduvai Gorge on the Serengeti plains. Louis Leakey became convinced that Goodall was the person he had been looking for for twenty years – someone who was so fascinated by animals and their behaviour that they would be happy to spend at least two years studying chimpanzees in the wild. Leakey was particularly interested in the chimpanzees on the shores of Lake Tanganyika as the remains of prehistoric people had often been found on lake shores and he thought it possible that an understanding of chimpanzee behaviour today might shed light on the behaviour of our Stone Age ancestors.

Goodall couldn't believe that Leakey was giving her the chance to do what she most wanted to do – watch chimpanzees in their natural habitat. She felt that her lack of training would disqualify her. But, as she later wrote:

> Louis, however, knew exactly what he was doing. Not only did he feel that a university training was unnecessary, but even that in some ways it might have been disadvantageous. He wanted someone with a mind uncluttered and unbiased by theory who would make the study for no other reason than a real desire for knowledge; and, in addition, someone with a sympathetic understanding of animal behaviour.
>
> (van Lawick-Goodall 1971: 20)

Now the point, of course, is not that Jane Goodall could approach chimpanzees with a mind 'uncluttered and unbiased by theory' but that the clutter and theory in her mind was crucially distinct from that in someone who emerged from a university course in ethology. In the 1960s, one of the great heresies of academic ethology was to be anthropomorphic – to treat non-humans as if they had human attributes and feelings. That is precisely what Jane Goodall did and it allowed fundamentally new insights into chimpanzee behaviour. A flavour of her approach can be obtained by reading the following quote:

> One day, when Flo was fishing for termites, it became obvious that Figan and Fifi, who had been eating termites at the same heap, were getting restless and wanted to go. But old Flo, who had already fished for two hours, and who was herself only getting about two termites every five minutes, showed no signs of stopping. Being an old female, it was possible that she might continue for another hour at least. Several times Figan had set off resolutely along the track leading to the stream, but on each occasion, after repeatedly looking back at Flo, he had given up and returned to wait for his mother.
>
> Flint, too young to mind where he was, pottered about on the heap, occasionally dabbling at a termite. Suddenly Figan got up again and this time approached Flint. Adopting the posture of a mother who signals her infant to climb on to her back, Figan bent one leg and reached back his hand to Flint, uttering a soft pleading whimper. Flint tottered up to him at once, and Figan, still whimpering, put his hand under Flint and gently pushed him on his back. Once Flint was safely aboard, Figan, with another quick glance at Flo, set off rapidly along the track. A moment later Flo discarded her tool and followed.
>
> (van Lawick-Goodall 1971: 114–15)

Other writers at the time did not give names to their animals; nor did they use language like 'getting restless', 'wanted to go', 'set off resolutely' and 'pottered about'; nor did they impute to their subjects the ability consciously to manipulate one another.

Apart from her lack of formal training, there is another factor about Jane Goodall that may well be significant. She is a woman. The longest-running studies on animal behaviour have all been carried out by women including: Jane Goodall on chimpanzees (1960 to present); Dian Fossey on gorillas (1966 to 1985 when she was murdered, probably because of her dedication to the gorillas); and Fiona Guinness on red deer (1972 to present). All three worked/work quite exceptionally long hours with what can only be described as total dedication. In 1978 and 1979, I spent a couple of months working alongside Fiona Guinness. On average, she worked fourteen hours a day, seven days a week.

My point is not that research scientists ought to work this long, nor that only women can show the empathy with animals that these three did or do. Rather, it is that the personal and social pressures that shaped Jane Goodall, Dian Fossey and Fiona Guinness were crucial to the type of science that they carried out or do carry out. And this is true for all scientists. It's just that it is easier to see in these three cases. Donna Haraway, in her book *Primate Visions: Gender, Race and Nature in the World of Modern Science,* argues that scientific practice is story-telling. The work that primatologists do is moulded by the environment in which they operate and by the sort of people they are, so that the stories that they tell reflect the social agendas that surround them (Haraway 1989).

It is possible to suppose from the above that only bad science is affected by the presuppositions of the individuals that carry it out, influenced by the hidden assumptions of the society in which they live and move and have their being. Indeed, most practising scientists are happy with the notion that this is the case. However, many sociologists of science want to go much further than this. They argue that every science inevitably reflects the interests, the values, the unconscious suppositions and the beliefs of the society that gives rise to it (Longino 1990). For an example of how even what is almost universally acknowledged as being among the best of science may have critically been influenced by what might be described as extra-scientific forces, consider some of Newton's thinking in his *Principia* (Freudenthal 1986; discussed by Chalmers 1990).

One of Newton's key advances was to argue that the properties of wholes are to be explained in terms of the essential properties of their parts. For instance, Newton asserted that the extension, hardness, impenetrability, mobility and force of inertia of the whole result from the extension, hardness, impenetrability, mobility and force of inertia of the parts. From this, he concluded that the smallest of particles are also all extended, hard, impenetrable and moveable and are endowed with their proper forces of inertia.

Newton's assertion that the whole is simply the sum of its component parts provided the crucial foundation stone for his pivotal work on gravity, but from where did he get the idea? The assertion cannot, of course, be proved. Indeed, every biologist knows that the properties of an organism (say, a giraffe) cannot be deduced from the properties of the molecules of which it is comprised. Biology is all about understanding that the properties that one level of organization possesses are not necessarily apparent from studying lower levels of organization.

Freudenthal traces Newton's assumptions back to the individualistic understanding of society that emerged in the seventeenth century as European feudal society came to be replaced by early forms of capitalist society. He points out that, while the various new conceptions of society formulated in the seventeenth century by Thomas Hobbes, John Locke and others differ from each other in significant respects, they have one thing in common. They all attempt to explain society by reference to the properties of the individuals that make up society. Further, individuals are assumed to have these properties independently of their existence in society.

At this point, it may be worth drawing attention to the fact that accepting the essential premise of sociologists of science that science and society are inevitably, inexorably intertwined, does not necessarily require one to abandon all belief in the objectivity of science. As Alan Chalmers puts it: 'The natural world does not behave in one way for capitalists and in another way for socialists, in one way for males and another for females, in one way for Western cultures and another for Eastern cultures' (Chalmers 1990: 112). This seems reasonable. However, a scientist's *perceptions* of the natural world, as well as his or her interpretations of it, come through their senses, themselves as a person and their culture. What is of significance for science education is that there can be no single, universal, acultural science. Rather, every sort of science is an ethnoscience, as I shall now argue.

Science as a collection of ethnosciences

The term 'ethnoscience' first became widely used in the anthropological literature of the 1960s (Bulmer 1971). It has been used in two ways:

> It refers first to the 'science', in the sense of modes of classification of the material and social universe, possessed by societies unaffected or little affected by modern international scientific thinking and discoveries. Second, it refers to a particular anthropological approach which has as its objective the systematic scientific investigation of ways in which particular societies classify the universe …

Such ethnoscientific research has contributed much that is of value to those hoping to fashion a science education for a pluralist society, but we need to broaden this definition slightly. To restrict the term 'ethnoscience' to societies 'unaffected … by modern international scientific thinking and discoveries' is both to misunderstand the nature of science and to risk adopting a patronizing and racist attitude to such ethnosciences. It misunderstands the nature of science because, as I have argued above, all science is set in a cultural milieu, so that we cannot validly distinguish a number of ethnosciences from a single international non-ethnoscientific science. It risks being patronizing and racist because accepting such a definition of ethnoscience inevitably makes it likely that a writer, however impressed she or he is with a particular ethnoscience, ends up comparing it with 'modern international scientific thinking and discoveries', which then act as a benchmark against which the particular ethnoscience is judged.

Further, we should not assume that, within a particular society, all scientific thinking operates within the same paradigm. By virtue of differences between individuals in such important characteristics as gender, religious beliefs, ethnicity, age and disability, individuals may differ significantly in their scientific understanding and conception of the world. There are two extreme ways in which a teacher may react to such differences. The more common is to adopt, implicitly, what we can call a 'deficit' model of science. Here all inter-individual (and inter-cultural) differences in scientific understanding and practice are held to exist because individuals and cultures differ in the extent to which they understand and practise the one, true science. The role of a science teacher clearly is to remove obstacles to the understanding of this single true science and then teach it (cf. Layton 1991).

The second extreme way in which a teacher could react to inter-individual and inter-cultural differences in scientific understanding and practice is to adopt what we can call an 'all sciences are equal' model. Here, there is no objectivity in science. All scientific methodologies and findings, however much they differ, are of equal validity.

I suspect it is because this second model leads to conclusions which, to practically every science teacher, are so manifestly absurd, that the first model – with its assumptions of the one, true science – is so often adopted.

What I will attempt to argue is that there is a middle ground between these two models, a middle ground which genuinely allows for inter-individual and intercultural differences without abandoning all claims to real scientific progress.

Published or be damned

Once a scientist or group of scientists has discovered something or produced a new model to interpret a phenomenon, it is necessary for their work to be disseminated in some form, usually through publication. Getting work published, read, recognized and cited depends greatly on the personalities of the individuals involved and on what society values.

As a single example of the importance of society's world view in accepting a scientific theory, consider the circumstances that surrounded the publication of William Harvey's ideas on the circulation of the blood. Although the circulation of the blood had been established in China by the second century BCE at the latest, in Europe the idea was proposed by Michael Servetus (1546), Realdo Colombo (1559), Andrea Cesalpino (1571) and Giordano Bruno (1590). These men had read of the circulation of the blood in the writings of an Arab of Damascus, Ibn Nafis (died 1288) who himself seems to have obtained at least some of his ideas from China (Temple 1991). Harvey published his 'discovery' in 1628. It is possible that the early seventeenth-century accounts of a huge diversity of pumping engines for mine drainage and water supply caused the scientific community and general public to be in an appropriate frame of mind to accept the notion of the heart as a mechanical pump (cf. Russell 1988). In other words, most people remember Harvey as the person responsible for the discovery of the circulation of the blood because earlier proponents of the idea published their announcements at times when the understanding and acceptance of them were more difficult for people.

Mention can also be made of the importance of the language that scientists use. Some scientists are simply much better at writing up their work so that it is more likely to be published, read and cited. What people then remember is the language used as well as the science. Indeed, the two cannot be separated. We cannot sift out the language of corruption to reveal a pure, unsullied science.

An illustration of the intimacy of the relationship between language and science is provided by the attempts of newspapers and magazines in the UK, on 24 April 1992, to describe the reported discovery by a NASA satellite of radiation from the Big Bang. The word most often used was 'ripple'. The first two paragraphs of the *Independent* report (which dominated the front page of the paper) were as follows:

Fourteen thousand million years ago the universe hiccuped. Yesterday, American scientists announced that they may have heard the echo.

A NASA spacecraft has detected ripples at the edge of the Cosmos which are the fossilised imprint of the birth of the stars and galaxies around us today.

Even the *Sun* weighed in. Under a headline 'We find secret of the creation' (page 6) the ripples were said to 'look like wispy clouds'. The publicity attending the news was heightened by Stephen Hawking, who was reported on the front page of the *Daily Mail* as describing the finding as 'the discovery of the century, if not of all time'.

It's easy to make fun of reports which talk of wispy clouds and the universe hiccuping, but my point is that all science has to be reported in a language, even if it is the language of mathematics. And all languages, including the language(s) of mathematics, are human constructs.

Changing conceptions of science

The notion as to what constitutes science differs over time and between cultures (Hiatt and Jones 1988; Brooke 1991). Attempts by certain historians and philosophers of science to identify a distinctive 'scientific method' which demarcates science absolutely from other disciplines have not proved successful. Though certain principles, such as testability and repeatability, may be central to modern science, it is now widely held that the question 'What is science?' can only be answered: 'That which is recognized as such by a scientific community'. Although this answer, being somewhat tautologous, may appear distinctly unhelpful, its truth may be seen by examining what other times and cultures include in science. [...]

In England and Wales, successive versions of the Science National Curriculum Attainment Target 1 have had a model of science which, while there is much that is good about it, would disqualify the inclusion, for instance, of much of the work done by astronomers, taxonomists, palaeontologists and theoreticians. Mayr has argued that after the time of the Middle Ages (in Western Europe), the physical sciences were the paradigm of science:

> As everyone was willing to concede, the universality and predictability that seemed to characterize studies of the inanimate world were missing from biology. Because life was restricted to the earth, as far as anyone knew, any statements and generalizations one could make concerning living organisms would seem to be restricted in space and time. To make matters worse, such statements nearly always seemed to have exceptions. Explanations usually were not based on universal laws but rather were pluralistic. In short the theories of biology violated every canon of 'true science', as the philosophers had derived them from the methods and principles of classical physics.
>
> (Mayr 1988: 9)

Sadly, it is still the case that much school science has too narrow an understanding of the *methods* of science. This, I suspect, is one reason why pupils too often find their school science unsatisfying. They know that it's too restricted a way of looking at the world. And they're right.

References

Brooke, J. H. (1991) *Science and Religion: Some Historical Perspectives*, Cambridge: Cambridge University Press.

Bulmer, R. N. H. (1971) 'Science, ethnoscience and education', *Papua and New Guinea Journal of Education* 7 (1): 22–33.

Chalmers, A. (1990) *Science and its Fabrication*, Milton Keynes: Open University Press.

Driver, R., Guesne, E. and Tiberghien, A. (eds) (1985) *Children's Ideas in Science*, Milton Keynes: Open University Press.

Freudenthal, G. (1986) *Atom and Individual in the Age of Newton*, Dordrecht: Reidel.

Goodall, J. (1986) *The Chimpanzees of Gombe: Patterns of Behavior*, Cambridge, MA: Belknap Press of Harvard University Press.

Haraway, D. (1989) *Primate Visions: Gender, Race and Nature in the World of Modern Science*, London: Routledge, Chapman and Hall.

Harding, S. (1991) *Whose Science? Whose Knowledge? Thinking from Women's Lives*, Milton Keynes: Open University Press.

Hiatt, L. R. and Jones, R. (1988) 'Aboriginal conceptions of the workings of nature', in R. W. Home (ed.) *Australian Science in the Making* (pp. 1–22), Cambridge: Cambridge University Press.

Latour, B. (1987) *Science in Action: How to Follow Scientists and Engineers through Society*, Milton Keynes: Open University Press.

Lawick-Goodall, van, J. (1971) *In the Shadow of Man*, Glasgow: Collins.

Layton, D. (1991) 'Science education and praxis: the relationship of school science to practical action', *Studies in Science Education* 19: 43–79.

Longino, H. E. (1990) *Science as Social Knowledge: Values and Objectivity in Scientific Inquiry*, Princeton, NJ: Princeton University Press.

Mayr, E. (1988) *Towards a New Philosophy of Biology: Observations of an Evolutionist*, Cambridge, MA: Belknap Press of Harvard University Press.

Osborne, R. and Freyberg, P. (1985) *Learning in Science: The Implications of Children's Science*, Birkenhead, Auckland: Heinemann Education.

Russell, N. (1988) 'Teaching biology in the wider context: the history of the disciplines as a method 2: worked examples', *Journal of Biological Education* 22: 129–35.

Sternberg, R. J. (1990) *Metaphors of Mind: Conceptions of the Nature of Intelligence*, Cambridge: Cambridge University Press.

Temple, R. (1991) *The Genius of China: 3000 Years of Science, Discovery, and Invention*, London: Prion/Multimedia.

Wellington, J. (ed.) (1989) *Skills and Processes in Science Education: A Critical Analysis*, London: Routledge.

Woolgar, S. (1988) *Science: The Very Idea*, Chichester: Ellis Horwood.

1.2 School science, citizenship and the public understanding of science

Edgar W. Jenkins

Quantitative and qualitative studies of the public understanding of science have been conducted in many countries. They provide important insights into the extent to which lay citizens understand a number of important scientific concepts and into the ways in which they seek and use scientific knowledge. This chapter draws upon the outcomes of these studies to identify some of the dimensions of 'citizen science', and to examine their implications for the form and content of school science education.

School science education, citizenship and the public understanding of science are linked in a number of ways. One of the functions of schooling is the development of an informed citizenry and this, at the end of the twentieth century, is widely assumed to require that all students receive an education in science. 'Science for All', an old rather than a new slogan (Brock 1996), now has a global resonance, with many countries revising or reforming school science curricula towards this end, although the impulse for doing so is often principally economic, rather than democratic. Where the latter is invoked, the rhetoric is that citizens need to be 'scientifically literate' in order to be able to contribute to decision-making about issues that have a scientific dimension, whether these issues be personal (e.g. relating to medication or diet) or more broadly political (e.g. relating to nuclear power, ozone depletion or DNA technologies).

Studies of the public understanding of science, however, suggest that achieving a scientifically literate citizenry will require more than the reform of school science curricula, although the importance of such reform should not in consequence be underestimated. In general, quantitative measures of the public understanding of science from a variety of countries and, in some instances, extending over time, present a disappointing picture (Jenkins 1997), although such measures are open to the obvious criticism that they report the extent to which the public knows the science which the scientific community thinks ought to be known. In contrast to these quantitative approaches to measuring the public understanding of science, qualitative studies have focused attention on the needs which different social groups have for scientific knowledge and understanding and on the use that they make of them. These studies (e.g. Irwin and Wynne 1996) reveal that the relationship of lay citizens and other non-experts to science is much more complex than that normally captured by quantitative surveys of the 'public understanding of science'. In particular, the relationship is interactive, rather than one that can be conceptualized in the beguilingly simple terms of ignorance or rejection of scientific knowledge. In the everyday world of the citizen, science itself emerges not as coherent, objective and unproblematic knowledge, but as uncertain, contentious and often unable to answer many important questions with the required degree of confidence. In some instances, expert scientific knowledge is marginalized or ignored as irrelevant to the problems being addressed. In addition, such knowledge, assuming it exists, is not separated from its social or institutional source and it is weighed alongside other more personal or local knowledge in establishing a basis for action. 'Citizen thinking', i.e. everyday thinking, turns out to be much more complex and less well understood than scientific thinking and, as might be expected, well adapted to decision-making in an everyday world which, unlike science itself, is marked by uncertainty, contingency and adaptation to a range of uncontrolled factors. It is important to note that the implication here is that in many everyday situations 'citizen thinking' may offer a more comprehensive and effective basis for action than scientific thinking, not that the former is in some general way always to be preferred to the latter.

In the context of a scientifically literate citizenry, 'citizen thinking' is intimately related to the notion of 'citizen science', i.e. science which relates in reflexive ways to the concerns, interests and activities of citizens as they go about their everyday business. This chapter draws upon research in the public understanding of science to identify some of the dimensions of 'citizen science' and to examine their implications for the form and content of school science education.

For most citizens, interest in science is linked with decision-making or action. The underpinning notion here is that of science for specific social purposes (Layton *et al.* 1986). These purposes may relate to a variety of contexts and issues, and range from personal matters (e.g. health or child care), employment (e.g. safety at work, risk assessment), leisure (e.g. choosing the best fishing rod, fabric, mountain bike), to individual or organized protest (e.g. at a proposal to irradiate food or flood a valley). A citizen who wishes, individually or as part of a group, to engage seriously in a debate about an issue which has a scientific dimension sooner or later has to learn some of the relevant science. For example, informed opposition to extending an airport runway is likely to demand, as a minimum, familiarity with the logarithmic basis of the decibel scale, the procedures for measuring, recording and monitoring sound levels, and the effect of noise on human health and well-being, together with an understanding of the degree of confidence that can properly be placed in the various relevant measurements. However, matters are rarely as straightforward as simply seeking the relevant scientific knowledge. That knowledge may not be in a form in which it can be used (Layton *et al.* 1993), it may be unavailable (Wynne 1996) or, as in the case of the thalidomide tragedy, not in the public domain. In addition, even when scientific data are available, there may be argument about the methods by which the data were obtained, about the extent to which generalizations may be sustained, or about the significance to be attached to the findings. The protracted controversy over the harmful effects of lead in petrol involving the Ethyl Corporation and the Environmental Protection Agency in the USA, displays all these features. This has been well described by Collingridge and Reeve (1986), who also discuss its implications for the interaction of science and public policy.

When it is available, the scientific knowledge may also be unnecessarily sophisticated and over-elaborate for the purposes in hand. For example, it is usually more convenient for heating engineers to think of heat as something which 'flows' rather than in terms of the 'more correct' kinetic theory of matter. In much the same way, lay citizens choose a level of explanation which meets their needs. Workers in a computer company, chained to their benches by an earthed metal bracelet in order to prevent damage to sensitive electrical components by the build-up of static electricity, regard electricity as a fluid which can either pile up (static electricity) or be discharged to earth, where it is dispersed or 'lost' (Caillot and Nguyen-Xuan 1995). This 'unscientific' model of electricity enables the workers to function safely and to make sensible decisions when confronted with problems. These scientifically incorrect understandings or misconceptions should not be lightly dismissed. They have been well tested in the context of experience and action and, in those contexts, have served people well. Those, like science teachers, seeking to remedy these misconceptions, might do well to recognize that the tenacity with which they are held outside the classroom probably owes less to cognitive ability than to the proven usefulness of these ideas in the world of everyday experience.

During the course of their personal, working and social lives, all citizens construct a body of practical knowledge, tested and validated against their individual and collective experience. In deciding how and when to act in practical matters that have a scientific dimension, scientific knowledge is considered alongside this other, experiential and personal knowledge base. Wynne (1996) has reported how, in the aftermath of the Chernobyl disaster, the scientific advice offered to sheep farmers in the north west of England failed to accommodate several factors recognized by the farmers as essential to any valid examination of the problem of how long the soil would remain contaminated. These included differences between individual farms even within the same valley, and farmers' own expert knowledge of how and where sheep graze on high ground and about how field experiments could be conducted reliably. Likewise, a study of how elderly people respond to well-intentioned advice about energy conservation revealed that they do so in ways that are much more subtle and complex than might be understood – or even dictated – by a consideration of the nature of energy itself. For these elderly people, the purchase, consumption and use of energy cannot be reduced to a matter of conservation: it is a commodity which has personal, social and financial dimensions (Layton *et al.* 1993). Citizens may also make a positive choice to ignore scientific knowledge that seems, to an outsider, to be of direct relevance to them. Apprentice electricians working at a nuclear power plant, for example, judged it unnecessary to know anything of the nature of ionizing radiation and its associated risks as this was properly regarded as the responsibility, not of the electricians, but of the health physicists employed at the plant (Wynne

1991). What is being stressed here is that, where necessary, citizens construct, from the sources available to them, syncretic bodies of practical knowledge which are well adapted to specific everyday situations. It is, of course, important to acknowledge that while such practical knowledge may be adequate in many contexts, such knowledge can, in other circumstances, be misleading or even dangerous.

It is also important to acknowledge that citizens see the scientific knowledge relevant to an issue with which they are engaged as intimately linked with its social or institutional connections. Citizens ask questions such as: 'From whom?', 'From where?' and 'From what organization or source?' does the knowledge come. Many of the science-based issues with which citizens are concerned are controversial, contentious and at the heart of policy decisions by government, industry or other organizations. The BSE crisis in the UK illustrates very clearly the relationships between the scientific tale and the teller. In a field in which many basic questions surrounding the nature and transmission of the disease remain unanswered and the subject of ongoing scientific debate, government advice about the safety of beef and about how to deal with the problems facing the livestock industry was viewed with considerable scepticism. In a survey conducted in Britain in March 1996, 80 per cent of those surveyed judged that government ministers were more concerned with party politics than with the well-being of consumers (Marris and Langford 1996).

Central to the BSE debate and, more particularly, to the hazards to health associated with eating beef, is the notion of risk. Risk lies at the heart of many science-related policy issues and there are several ways of estimating it. Many of these are both sophisticated and quantitative, and different measures of risk, calculated in different ways, are not always easy to reconcile. In addition, psychological and sociological studies of adults' perceptions of risk do not point towards simple generalizations about how citizens perceive the risks associated with some activity or issue with which they are engaged (e.g. MacGill 1987, Price 1996). Most citizens understand that guarantees of 'absolute safety' cannot be given and they are not, therefore, usually sought. In offering reassurances about contentious issues, such as childhood vaccination or the safety of nuclear waste, the relevant authorities may, therefore, be undermining rather than strengthening the case they wish to promote. What constitutes an acceptable risk depends on many factors. Studies suggest that the risks which people find most acceptable are those which they see as self-imposed or having an immediate impact (e.g. driving a car, consuming alcohol). Conversely, the least acceptable risks are those associated with issues that are seen as the result of the actions of others and as having long-term, perhaps unknown but potentially catastrophic, consequences, e.g. ozone depletion, the storage of nuclear waste.

It will perhaps be clear from the above that it makes little sense to treat 'citizens' as though they were a homogeneous group, or to regard 'science' as an undifferentiated field of activity. At a general level, surveys suggest that in most industrialized countries, adults are more interested in, and more attentive to, medical and environmental rather than other scientific matters, and that the level of attentiveness correlates positively with the duration of formal education. Often, there are also gender differences, especially in the field of attitudes. In a study of eighteen nation-wide surveys in the USA from 1972 to 1990, Trankina (1993) revealed that, irre-spective of their educational background, adult women consistently displayed less confidence in science than men. While the confidence of both genders increased with educational level, it also widened as the extent of formal education increased. In another American study, Hornig (1992) explored the responses of men and women to stories of hypothetical new developments in science and technology. In general, women saw less benefit and more risk than men, their concerns focusing upon the social implications of the innovation. It is important to note here that both men and women agreed that increasing scientific knowledge was desirable and that careful control was necessary. Hornig's response to her findings was that they should be interpreted not as a rejection of male-dominated science, but as an affirmation of other aspects of life, notably personal and social relationships, family life and the home. These findings may, of course, be less valid or even invalid in other social contexts.

What are the implications of this complex picture of 'citizen science' for the form and content of school science curricula that seek to promote Science for All? It is important to begin answering this question by recognizing that the *raison d'être* of a science curriculum is science itself. At the end of the twentieth century, this implies more than helping students to acquire an understanding of a number of major scien-tific ideas, e.g. those relating to the origin of the universe, the theory of evolution and the nature and transformation of matter and energy. It also means more than helping students acquire some insight into how scientific investigations are conducted, a task that is commonly presented as central to school science education but that might be better undertaken by reading Richard Feynman (e.g. Feynman 1998) than by any of the more familiar, if unconvincing, pedagogical strategies that encompass, on the one hand, formal, algorithmic and ritualistic accounts of 'scientific method' and, on the other, highly contrived, expensive and time-consuming laboratory activities, e.g. those associated with the 'experimental and investigative science' that constitutes Attainment Target 1 of the science component of the current national curriculum in England and Wales. Any characterization of the scientific endeavour as the new millennium approaches must take into account that science is now intimately related to production and profit in ways that have allowed Redner (1987) to identify a signif-icant break with the ways in which science has been conducted in the past, and Gibbons *et al.* (1994) to refer to a 'new system of knowledge production' character-ized by, among much else, transdisciplinarity, new criteria for quality control and the generation of knowledge within the context of its application. It is this 'new system' that has done so much to transform the social context of science education, and to confront citizens and experts alike with the complex and difficult problems that mark the interface of science and society. School science education needs to respond to this changed social context and to help prepare young people to contribute as citi-zens to shaping the world in which they will live.

This means constructing science curricula that enable young people to engage in the reflexive ways referred to above, with science-related issues that are likely to be of interest and concern to them. Accepting this entails a number of consequences. First, school science will need to give somewhat less attention to the minutiae of established physics, chemistry and biology in order to make way for the consideration of issues where the science is less than secure or controversial. The science relating to any long-term physiological or other effects of cannabis, the possession and sale of which is illegal in most but not all countries, is an interesting example. Any consideration of issues such as those surrounding the use and control of cannabis quickly exposes the distinction between knowledge and action, and illustrates the complex interrelationship of science with social policy. It also serves to highlight the need for science teachers to develop some of the skills more commonly associated with other subjects of the school curriculum, e.g. English or History, in which debate and controversy constitute more familiar territory. Equally, it will provide an opportunity to examine several of the significant features of 'citizen science' referred to above, including the social and institutional connections of scientific knowledge, and to explore and promote students' understanding of 'risk' and how it may be assessed.

Second, it is likely that school science curricula in different countries will show a greater degree of variety than is presently the case. Not all science-related issues are global and, if the school science curriculum is to be sensitive to the interests of students, regional or other in-country variations will need to be accommodated. The case of BSE within the UK is an obvious example. It may also be necessary to recognize different interests on the part of boys and girls and to respond appropriately. Central to any response, however, is a degree of flexibility in curriculum control. Unless carefully framed, statutory science curricula, often buttressed by statutory provisions for assessment designed to raise standards and/or enhance accountability, are unlikely to allow schools and science teachers the freedom they need to work in this way.

A third consequence is that the contribution that science can make to education, and thereby to citizenship, is reassessed. Many of the benefits associated with studying science can be exposed as somewhat exaggerated. In 1985, science teachers in England and Wales were advised officially that the 'characteristic of education in science is that it introduces pupils to the methods of science' and informed that 'Each of us needs to be able to bring a scientific approach to bear on the practical, social, economic and political issues of modern life' (Department of Education and Science/Welsh Office 1985: 2, 3). It is perhaps time to acknowledge that science is successful at solving problems only when those problems are scientific or can be cast in a scientific form. As the British Association for the Advancement of Science (BAAS) recognized as long ago as 1917, scientific method, the sine qua non of investigative teaching, is appropriate only when dealing with scientific problems (BAAS 1917: 134). To acknowledge the limitations of science is not in any way to undervalue the scientific endeavour. Rather, it opens the door to a richer understanding of the nature of a profoundly creative and imaginative activity tempered by a scrupulous honesty in the face of experimental evidence. It also permits a re-examination of the relationship between scientific knowledge and other forms of knowledge, whether the latter be the particular local knowledge of a small community or the more general cosmological theories of non-Western cultures (Pomeroy 1994).

More is involved here than the now familiar courses encompassed by the label 'Science, Technology and Society' (STS). This is partly because many STS courses seem to be attempts to rescue science curricula that are in difficulty and partly because such courses lack a recognizable and legitimate theoretical underpinning (Cozzens 1990). The dimensions of citizen science outlined above offer the rudiments of such a theoretical underpinning, although other models are, of course, possible (see, e.g. Cross and Price 1992).

It is also perhaps important to acknowledge that the notion of citizen science has implications for the research agenda in the public understanding of science. As examples, questions can be asked about the nature, location and effectiveness of the mechanisms involved in the transfer of scientific knowledge between research and other communities, about the articulation of expert and lay understandings of science, and about the ways in which the public understanding of science is understood by science teachers and others.

Finally, a little history and a note of caution are appropriate. Attempts to link school science with citizenship are not new. In the UK, for example, they have surfaced from time to time in a variety of forms that range from the general science movement to the science education for citizenship associated with the political radicalism of J. D. Bernal and Lancelot Hogben. These earlier attempts to steer school science education into significantly new directions have not succeeded in the longer term. In questioning whether contemporary attempts to develop science curricula that will empower future citizens are likely to be any more successful than those of the past, it is perhaps also important to ask whether school science education can any longer encourage the view that the world is much simpler than it really is and, thereby, promote unsustainable claims about the power of science to explain and control. Students are wiser than this, and science educators should not be surprised, therefore, if fewer and fewer of them seem content to embark on a voyage to the idealized, mathematical world created by Newton and Galileo. As Feynman shrewdly observed, 'We have to understand how to handle uncertainty' (Feynman 1998). 'Citizen science' and the school science curriculum seem an appropriate place to start.

Note

Interestingly, a recent report on citizenship in England and Wales confines itself to commenting that 'Science and Technology subjects commonly raise ethical issues of social policy' (Advisory Committee on Citizenship 1998:53).

References

Advisory Committee on Citizenship (1998) 'Education for citizenship and the teaching of democracy in schools', Final Report of the Advisory Group on Citizenship, 22 September 1998, London: DfEE and QCA.

British Association for the Advancement of Science (1917) *Report*, London: Murray.

Brock, W. H. (1996) *Science for All. Studies in the History of Victorian Science and Education*, Aldershot: Variorum.

Caillot, M. and Nguyen-Xuan, A. (1995) 'Adults' understanding of electricity', *Public Understanding of Science* 4: 131–52.

Collingridge, D. and Reeve, C. (1986) *Science Speaks to Power: The Role of Experts in Policy-making*, London: Frances Pinter.

Cozzens, S. (1990) 'The disappearing disciplines of STS', *Bulletin of Science, Technology and Society* 10: 1–5.

Cross, R. T. and Price, R. F. (1992) *Teaching Science for Social Responsibility*, Sydney: St. Louis Press.

DES/Welsh Office (1985) *Science 5–16: A Statement of Policy*, London: HMSO.

Feynman, R. P. (1998) *The Meaning of It All*, London: Allen.

Gibbons, M., Limoges, C., Nowotny, H., Schwartzman, S., Scott, P. and Trow, M. (1994) *The New Production of Knowledge: The Dynamics of Science and Research in Contemporary Societies*, London: Sage.

Hornig, S. (1992) 'Gender differences in responses to news about science and technology', *Science, Technology and Human Values* 17: 532–42.

Irwin, A. and Wynne, B. (eds) (1996) *Misunderstanding Science? The Public Reconstruction of Science and Technology*, Cambridge: Cambridge University Press.

Jenkins, E. W. (ed.) (1997) *Innovations in Science and Technology Education*, Vol. VI, Paris: UNESCO.

Layton, D., Davey, A. and Jenkins, E. W. (1986) 'Science for specific social purposes (SSSP): Perspectives on adult scientific literacy', *Studies in Science Education* 13: 27–52.

——, Jenkins, E. W., MacGill, S. and Davey, A. (1993) *Inarticulate Science? Perspectives on the Public Understanding of Science and Some Implications for Science Education*, Driffield: Studies in Education.

MacGill, S. M. (1987) *The Politics of Anxiety: Sellafield's Cancer-link Controversy*, London: Pion.

Marris, C. and Langford, J. (1996) 'No cause for alarm', *New Scientist* 150: 36–9.

Pomeroy, D. (1994) 'Science education and cultural diversity: mapping the field', *Studies in Science Education* 24: 49–73.

Price, F. (1996) 'Now you see it, now you don't: mediating science and managing uncertainty in reproductive medicine', in A. Irwin and B. Wynne (eds) *Misunderstanding Science? The Public Reconstruction of Science and Technology* (pp. 84–106), Cambridge: Cambridge University Press.

Redner, H. (1987) *The Ends of Science: An Essay in Scientific Authority*, Boulder, CO: Westview Press.

Trankina, M. (1993) 'Gender differences in attitudes towards sciences', *Psychological Reports* 73: 123–30.

Wynne, B. (1991) 'Knowledges in context', *Science, Technology and Human Values* 16: 111–21.

—— (1996) 'Misunderstood misunderstandings; social identities and public understanding of science', in A. Irwin and B. Wynne (eds) *Misunderstanding Science? The Public Reconstruction of Science and Technology*, Cambridge: Cambridge University Press: 19–46.

1.3 School science and its problems with scientific literacy

Peter Fensham

From 1983 to the present day, 'Science for All', or a variant of it, has been officially espoused as the intention for school science in country after country. The Ministers of Education in the Asia Region of Unesco (from Pakistan and India to Japan and New Zealand and a dozen countries in between) determined that this goal was an urgent priority for their educational systems (Unesco 1983). In the same year, the National Science Foundation (1983) was presented with a high-level report that called for *Science for All Americans*. In 1984 in Canada, *Science for Every Student* appeared and, soon after, the Royal Society (Bodmer 1985) in Britain argued persuasively that *Science is for Everybody*.

The substance of all these reports is very similar; they can be summarized by the set of goals for school science that the report of the Science Council of Canada (1984) recommended following the most searching of these reviews.

A science education appropriate to individual needs and designed to enable students to:

- participate fully in a technological society as informed citizens
- pursue further studies in science and technology
- enter the world of work
- develop intellectually and morally.

The traditional role of school science is present in the second of these goals, but only as part of it since it (like the other three) is concerned with all students, not just the small minority (less than 20 per cent of any age cohort) who will take up science-based careers of any sort.

With such expert and official agreement about the need for school science to contribute to the scientific and technological literacy of all future citizens, one would expect to find by now that new curricula consistent with these goals would be in place and that appropriate pedagogies and assessment procedures would be practised in many classrooms. In fact, remarkably slow progress has been made; in a number of countries, promising initiatives in the later 1980s now seem less likely to be implemented or they have been stifled.

In this chapter, some of the factors that make it so difficult for school science to contribute to general scientific literacy are considered. To do this a brief account is provided of school science that pre-dated these goals and second, the circumstances in which these new goals were set.

The legacy of the 1960s

In the 1960s and early 1970s many countries reconstituted the curriculum for science in their schools. The models for these changes were a number of curriculum projects established by the National Science Foundation in the USA and in Britain by the Nuffield Foundation. In both cases these initiatives were supported by hitherto unheard-of amounts of funding. They were a response to well-justified claims that school science was hopelessly out-of-date because of the neglect of its curriculum during the world depression, the Second World War and its aftermath.

The priority for these reforms was clear when the first projects to be established were all concerned with science at the upper levels of secondary schooling which, in the 1960s, involved only that small minority of each age cohort who were aiming for university studies in science-based courses. With leadership and involvement from enthusiastic academic scientists, experienced science teachers with strong scientific backgrounds developed materials for chemistry, physics and biology. Bringing school science up to date turned out to be presenting abstract concepts that are of basic importance in each science as the primary content of significance for their study in school. It did not mean new topics that reflected the many advances, such as polymers, semiconductivity and biosynthesis, that had been made in these sciences in the previous thirty years.

This change in content discarded two social dimensions of science – the applications of science in society and the individual and cooperative processes in the scientific community that lead to these abstract concepts. As a consequence, there was no basis in school science on which to develop a critique of the role science plays in society or an appreciation of its strengths and limitations (Fensham 1973). The change did, however, mean that in the years immediately before students moved into its study at university, school science was coherent with, and a logical preparation for, such further studies.

Other projects followed that took up the issue of science at the lower levels of schooling. Their direction and character were, however, very much influenced by the conception of school science as the beginnings of an induction into science that was to be completed by studies of the disciplines in higher education. Although a few projects which originated in the USA did develop materials that could enable school science to serve other purposes, such as an understanding of technology (Engineering Concepts Curriculum Project) and creativity about the natural world (Environmental Studies Project), nowhere were these adopted as the mainstream curriculum. By the mid-1970s, the legacy of these exciting reforms was well established as the curriculum of what school science should be in most of the industrialized countries and a number of developing ones.

For the lower secondary years, there was a belief that an introduction to these specialized languages, models and processes of the sciences was good for everyone, paving the way for the accelerated treatment of this conceptual approach in the upper secondary years. For the primary years, where science had not hitherto had a significant place, the most commonly encouraged content for learning was the so-called 'processes of science' like classifying, measuring, controlling variables, and so on; practical and intellectual procedures that stemmed from a positivist and utilitarian view of what scientists do.

Roberts (1982) identified seven emphases or purposes that curriculum materials for school science had, or could have served, over time. The curriculum legacy just described had given clear priority to three of these emphases:

1   *Solid foundation*   knowledge that prepared for the scientific topics that came in the succeeding years of schooling
2   *Correct explanation*   a representation at the school level of a topic of its current description in science
3   *Scientific skill development*   practice in the laboratory of some standard scientific procedures involving technical equipment.

The other four were discarded or quite under-used as sources for content or pedagogy: *the nature of science* (philosophical and historical aspects of science) and *Self as explainer* (active involvement of the students in scientific reasoning) are interesting among these discards because a number of the scientist architects of the 1960s reforms, like Zacharias and Rogers in physics, Schwab in biology, Halliwell and Campbell in chemistry and Bruner had argued that both of these were important. *Everyday coping* (local and wider applications of science) was eliminated to make room for the new conceptual content and *science, technology decisions* (being informed and equipped to make informed judgements about socio-scientific issues) was not itself considered an issue for school science in 1960.

Unpredicted social changes

During the 1960s and 1970s, a number of changes occurred in the industrialised societies that were not apparent when the definition of school science that this curriculum legacy represented, was laid down in the late 1950s. The nuclear threat of the Cold War following the Cuban missile crisis in 1962, and the increasing recognition of the serious damage that unbridled technology causes in the biosphere, regularly gave science a bad image in the media.

The rebuilding of the totally devastated German and Japanese industries enabled these countries to incorporate the latest technologies, and hence to threaten, economically, the traditional means of production in other countries that had not had their industries destroyed. The new technologies did away with many of the less-skilled workers and required different skills from those who remained. From the middle of the 1970s, higher levels of unemployment than had been known since the 1930s became a chronic feature in many societies. In response to these pressures, students were encouraged or required to stay for more and more schooling and secondary education began to change from an elite to a mass phenomenon.

Two other social movements highlighted other inadequacies in school science. The women's movement raised questions about the participation of girls in schooling and about their access to certain professions and occupations after school. These questions of access focused attention on the participation of girls in the physical sciences which, everywhere, had become gateway subjects biased in favour of boys. The second societal change stemmed from the growth of multi-culturalism, as immigration brought in many new citizens with a variety of new ethnic backgrounds. The participation of their children in the education system was of great importance to the social mobility of these immigrants and, once again, they were often disadvantaged by the elite position that science had in the curriculum.

It was thus not surprising that evaluators of the new science curricula repeatedly found that these were not being implemented in the manner that was intended and that a decreasing proportion of the student body was being attracted to, and was benefiting from, their school science. Whatever the curriculum achieved for those who went on to further science-related studies, it was not enthusing the great bulk of students, nor providing them with a scientific basis to participate with confi-dence in societies that were increasingly influenced by science and technology. It was the recognition of these failures that prompted the reviews and reports referred to at the beginning of this chapter, with their urgent calls for alternative approaches to school science.

Search for alternatives

The difficulties in making school science more meaningful for all students as future citizens are not due to a lack of alternative approaches to the induction and prepa-ratory ones that I have described as the legacy from the 1960s. Indeed, the 1980s proved to be an extremely fruitful period, both in terms of research into the prob-lems of better and more widespread science learning and of the development of ideas and novel materials for school science. Rather, the difficulties lie in the hege-mony of school systems and science's role in them, in the place of choice of science in senior secondary schooling. These reflect the conceptions of school science that prevail in educational systems and they are reinforced by the attitudes and behav-iour of some key players in the school science scene. Academic scientists, science teachers and science educators are the main groups of players, with the first group usually maintaining the legacy and the third group contesting it, while the members of the second group are divided between the two positions.

How these structural, corporate and personal features of this curriculum scene act as barriers to 'Science for All' will become apparent as the development of some of these alternatives is described.

Uncovering alternatives

With the considerable resources that the national reviews once again released for school science, a number of projects and research studies began in many countries. These processes were greatly assisted by the fact that science education, by the early 1980s, had become an established and active field of scholarly research. This meant that the projects in the 1980s had a much sounder base for their development than the ideas from general psychological learning theory that had been almost the only theoretical underpinning for learning science in the 1960s.

Many of the new projects did not, in the first instance, set out to develop materials as the earlier ones had all done. The Learning in Science Project in New Zealand spent most of its first phase exploring children's conceptions or understanding of a wide range of natural phenomena and science concepts. Among these were the widely and strongly held ideas that motion is associated with the force *in* the moving body, that things get lighter when they burn, and that what *life* or *animal* mean is often quite different from their sense in biology. The shift of focus that Osborne and Freyberg (1985) achieved in this project, from the teacher and teaching to the learner and learning, reverberated around the world in a quite remarkable fashion. A better understanding of the needs and characteristics of young science learners and how their conception of learning science became recognized as precursor conditions for the sensible development of new materials and new curricula. The Secondary Science Curriculum Review in England and Wales brought groups of teachers together to share their experience of the problems of teaching science to the demographically different school populations of the 1980s.

Some of the projects focused on the knowledge content that could make science more relevant to students in the different stages of schooling. Others concentrated on how science learning could be a deeper, more active process than the shallow short-term learning of unconnected facts, concepts and algorithmic rules that school science was for so many. This sense of 'active learning' was quite different from the emphasis on laboratory activity that many of the 1960s projects had advocated. Now 'active' referred to the learners being active in mind, personally constructing and reconstructing meaning from their experiences of phenomena in the laboratory and from their teacher's inputs.

Yet another area of exploration related to the purposes for science at different stages of schooling and the aspects of science that could contribute most effectively to these different purposes. Roberts' (1982) work on broad categories of purpose has already been mentioned. Aikenhead (1986) and Solomon (1988) spelt out how the relationships between science, technology and society could be related to school science. Hodson (1988) did a parallel job for the philosophy of science and Fensham and May (1979) provided an epistemology for a science education that set out to make students environmentally aware and responsible.

A number of projects did produce materials, many of which claimed a place within Science-Technology-Society (STS), a slogan that became shorthand for moves to extend school science to purposes such as Roberts's *nature of science, everyday coping* and *science, technology decisions* and to *science in applications* and *science in making*, two other categories of purpose that are needed to cover some of the new materials from the 1980s.

Salters' Chemistry and Salters' Science, two British projects based at York, set as a guiding principle that the science concepts (required for course approval in England and Wales in the mid-1980s) would be introduced only when the need for them could be rooted in material and phenomena familiar to 13–16-year-olds from their own experiences or from television and books (N. Smith 1988). This principle called for radical new foci and reordering of traditional content in school science. It can be contrasted with the earlier and very popular Science and Technology in Society (SATIS) project, which produces short modules about applications of science that can be added, if a teacher wishes, to topics in the existing science curriculum.

In the Netherlands, the PLON Physics project evolved materials slowly through the 1980s, learning from the classroom trials of one unit the aspects to strengthen and delete in subsequent units (Eijkelhof and Kortland 1988). One of these, 'Ion-izing Radiation', included some topics and concepts in pure physics such as the characteristics and measurements of short-wave forms of electromagnetic radia-tion that are not part of traditional school physics in many countries. While academic physicists are attracted to this advanced physics in the PLON materials, they are not, however, comfortable with the biology that is included to make sense of the interactions between these radiations and human beings, or with the socio-scientific concepts like 'radiation damage' and 'social risk' that this unit introduces as society's ways of quantifying and regulating such phenomena.

These selections of STS materials and a number of others from Germany, the USA, Australia and Canada are examples of Concepts in Contexts – an approach to curriculum that is strongly supported by research on how students learn and are attracted to learn science. It uses familiar and motivating contexts from the students' world outside school to provide meaning and interconnectedness for the science concepts, and the concepts, in turn, provide the students with powerful new insights of the contexts (Lijnse 1990).

While the materials mentioned so far do not avoid 'decision-making' about socio-scientific issues, they do not emphasize it. This educational objective for school science is, however, quite prominent in the rhetoric of national reports, for example 'the scientific knowledge necessary to fulfill civic responsibilities' (National Science Foundation 1983: 44) and of politicians, 'to grapple with envi-ronmental issues' (Gillian Shephard, UK Secretary of State for Education, February 1995). Chemicals in Public Places (Thier and Hill 1988) and *Logical Reasoning in Science and Technology* (Aikenhead 1991) are two examples of curric-ulum materials that have made such decision-making a quite explicit learning outcome.

The issue of girls and science led on to comparative studies of the interests of boys and girls. Smail (1987), for example, found an interest in nurturing more strongly, but not exclusively, in girls. However, a number of studies found that the differences in interest of topics for study were less than had been thought. In many countries there are differences in participation and in achievement in the physical sciences in senior secondary schooling. These may be more due, in that attenuated remainder of the original cohort, to the subgroup of boys who, for extrinsic and intrinsic reasons choose to continue with these subjects, than to evidence that boys as a whole are more interested in them than girls.

'COMETS: career orientated modules to explore technology and science' (W. Smith 1987), *Girls into Science and Technology* (Kelly *et al.* 1984) and Chemistry from Issues (Harding and Donaldson 1986) are examples of materials that were developed to incorporate the nurturing interest in various ways. It may be reasonable to include as also expressing this interest the many materials that have been developed with an environmental concern. Together they would then fall in yet another purpose for school science, namely Science for Nurturing, in which care for people, society or the environment is explicitly present.

There is thus no shortage of alternatives to meet the official calls for Science for All: new purposes for school science have been spelt out and new content and new pedagogies devised and invented to serve them. As yet, however, there has been very little decisive will at the educational system level.

Contradictions in intentions

In discussing why it is so difficult for school science to make serious contributions to general scientific literacy, I will draw on a number of specific examples from the debates and efforts that have occurred in Australia (and especially in the State of Victoria). I do this partly because of my knowledge of these scenes and because there are now enough similar reports from other countries that suggest these are, indeed, examples of factors and conditions that have very widespread currency.

Education systems in general are well known for their in-built properties of benefiting the children of rich and well-educated parents more than disadvantaged children from poor backgrounds. Despite repeated attempts to compensate disadvantage, the basic hegemonic effects of these systems and their curriculum of schooling are rarely disturbed (see Bourdieu and Passeron 1973; Lundgren 1981; Connell *et al.* 1982).

Earlier in the twentieth century, science (with advanced mathematics as a concomitant partner) began to take over the hegemonic role that the classical languages had played for so long. This accelerated with the coherence reforms of the 1960s brought about between the content of the science disciplines in schooling and their counterpart parent disciplines in the universities. The study of the sciences, particularly the physical sciences, became the most powerful factor in sustaining the differentiating function of schooling (see Fensham 1980; Scriven 1987).

Science (plus mathematics) was well placed to assume this mantle. Its history in schooling is quite different from that of mathematics itself. Until very recently – the 1960s – it had no place in primary schooling, whereas elementary mathematics has always had a central and expected role from the earliest levels of schooling. David Layton (1973) described the failure of an attempt in the middle of the nineteenth century to introduce science in the primary schooling of rural children before it was established in elite schooling in England. In the USA, a similar suggestion from the philosopher, Spencer, failed and it was late in the nineteenth century when science began to appear in the US upper secondary years as part of the selection process for university entrance.

Parents, secondary teachers, school authorities, employers and society quite generally expect pupils to learn elementary mathematics. No such consensus exists about an elementary science. The current pressure for it comes much more from the compelling logic confronting educational and societal leaders, that it would be irresponsible in late twentieth century technological society if science was not part of all levels of schooling.

So, science entered the school curriculum in the form of senior secondary subjects associated with the separate disciplines of science in the universities. Indeed, until as late as the 1970s, it was not uncommon to find botany, zoology and physiology as subjects in the school curriculum, rather than biology. The combination of their content to form a single subject was made possible by the shifts in emphasis in universities from the whole organism to the micro-biological level of cells, biochemicals and genes and to the macro-level of ecology and hence to the reorganization, in the 1960s, of first-year teaching in universities to a common year of biology.

A number of university courses that led to prestigious and financially rewarding professions like medicine, engineering, dentistry, veterinary science and, to a lesser extent, science itself, expected or required entering students to have high achievement in the physical sciences (with mathematics) at school. Many of these professional fields also involve biological sciences, but if science faculties in the universities, and even biological science departments themselves, have to choose between the physical sciences and biology as a prerequisite study, they usually choose the former. This purchasing power of the physical sciences for university entry is further strengthened by the fact that, in many countries, students with high achievement in these subjects are also looked on favourably for highly selective courses like law and economics, which have little need of specific prerequisite knowledge.

The expansion of higher education everywhere since the 1960s has done nothing to lessen the discriminating power of these science subjects. Rather, it has served to heighten the competition (fundamental to hegemony) to gain a place on the exclusive courses at the higher-status universities that lead to the greatest social rewards. Universities increasingly draw their status from the research success of their scientific and technological academics and the academic quality of their entering students. Identification of its name and content with a university discipline that is recognized as important is a major factor for gaining status. It is not, however, a sufficient condition, as the differential status between school chemistry/physics and biology indicates. With status comes constraint and chemistry and physics were more constrained to include only preparatory content in the 1960s than was biology, into which more frontier topics were allowed (Fensham 1980).

When Araos (1995) asked secondary school teachers in Victoria to list the subjects in the final years of schooling in order of academic status and difficulty, physics, chemistry and advanced mathematics invariably occupied the top positions, followed usually by literature and economics. At the low-status end were found the interdisciplinary subjects, like home economics, physical education, environmental studies, and the integrated forms of science that have been developed and adopted in the last few years in some systems. By academic status, teachers mean quite simply the purchasing power that a subject has, vis-à-vis university selection. To maintain their own reputation, schools tend to encourage only students with high achievements in middle-school mathematics and science (separate or combined) to undertake the 'difficult' physical sciences. Students with lower achievement levels will be discouraged from taking these subjects or encouraged to study the 'less demanding' interdisciplinary science subjects, if these are available. It is this sort of hegemonic pattern that leads teachers to the contradictory position of agreeing that environmental science ought to have a very high priority but not insisting on it being in the school's curriculum or, if it is, ascribing only the weakest students to it.

Van Berkel (1995), in a study of the structure of school chemistry, has been concerned with a subject's maintenance of status as well as gaining it. One of the conditions his international set of respondents emphasized is demarcation. Three demarcations are reported – from common everyday thinking about substances, from technological applications and from treatment in other sciences. The problem with many of the alternative approaches to Science for All outlined above is that they deliberately set out to blur these demarcations. Van Berkel's categories correspond almost directly with Society, Technology and Science – the STS movement's favoured bases for scientific literacy. If school science is to be about real-world situations and issues it will inevitably involve content from a number of sciences. Furthermore, these situations also involve technological or science knowledge for 'practical action' (Layton 1991), that is as much of society's making as it is of the academic scientific community. [...]

Conceptions of school science

I have argued that the dominant conception of school science in the 1960s reforms and in the curriculum legacy that still prevails in most countries, is one of induction into the scientific disciplines – a process that can, at best, be achieved only to a limited extent in schooling. The fact that so few science teachers, even with a tertiary degree in science, think of themselves as scientists, testifies to the extended nature of this induction process.

As part of a national review of the education of mathematics and science teachers in Australia, Speedy *et al.* (1989) asked the staff in the science departments of universities and institutes of technology – the two types of tertiary institutions involved – what image of a graduate scientist determined their curriculum. A future secondary teacher spends three years in science studies and one year in education.

The replies from the institutes were readily forthcoming as 'an applied chemist or an applied physicist, etc.', usually to fit specific niches in the Australian industrial scene. These institutes have evolved since the 1960s from senior technical colleges, with close links to industry, to degree-granting bodies, rather like polytechnics in a number of other countries. The staff in the universities, the origins of which will be familiar, have long been very explicit about their research role. At first they suggested that the question was meaningless because a chemistry (physics, etc.) course was simply self-defining, but discussion of the content included in the various years soon led to the answer, 'an academic research chemist, physicist, etc.' Since only the university staff exert a large influence on school science, it is thus not surprising that induction into this long process, stretching from school through a degree to a PhD, remains the dominant conception for school science.

Science, Technology and Society (STS) – with the addition of Personal Development (PD) – was adopted in the mid-1980s as the official curriculum framework of school science for seventh to tenth grades (ages 12–13 to 15–16) in Victoria (Malcolm 1987). The prevailing high degree of school-based curriculum development and the strangeness of these ways of conceiving of school science meant that Chan (1993), for her studies a few years later, could find only a handful of teachers who claimed strong identification with this STS-PD approach to science. When a brave attempt was made to extend the STS alternative concept to the final two years in Victoria, Fensham and Corrigan (1994) found that even the more innovative teachers had reinterpreted the STS use of contexts into pedagogical procedures that enabled them to teach the traditional concepts more effectively, rather than to see them as opportunities for new content and learning outcomes.

When some of the alternative conceptions of school science were included in draft proposals for a possible national curriculum for first to tenth grades (ages 5–6 to 15–16) in Australia in 1993, they were strongly attacked by a number of leading academic scientists and by their spokespersons in the professional institutes of chemistry and physics. 'Subjective revisionism', 'a mess shrouded under the mantles of feminism and aboriginal culture', 'hand waving descriptions of natural phenomena', 'the impact of science and technology on society is simply not science', 'a takeover of true scientific teaching by a socially motivated, pseudoscientific approach' and 'undermines the Western scientific tradition' are but some of the scornful or angry epithets that were heaped in a number of reports in the mass media on what was, in fact, a very compromised version of what some science educators and teachers had hoped for when this project began in 1989. Paul Davies, winner of the 1995 Templeton Prize for his own very popular but highly speculative writings on the religious meaning of modern physics, was a leading member of one of these groups of hard-liners. At one point in his group's article, they did seem to acknowledge that schools should cater for the majority who need some acquaintance with scientific ideas without advanced mathematical skills. They immediately, however, went on to confirm their need to maintain the *solid foundation* purpose for school science that marks the induction conception: 'one cannot start teaching real science in grades 11 and 12 (ages 16–18) – students simply would not be able to cope without prior grounding'.

A comparative analysis of science curriculum developments in Australia, England and Wales, New Zealand and Canada from 1985 to 1995 (Fensham

1995a) has revealed that educational bureaucrats have played quite decisive roles in preventing or delaying the adoption of alternative conceptions of school science. Very often, these persons have been innovative in their own, different, areas of the school curriculum but, for science, they prove to be identified with the induction conception. Whether this is because they view science (like the primary teacher students above) in terms of what they did not study when they were at school or because they assess where the power lies between the advocacy groups proposing what school science should be will require more detailed case studies to determine (see Blades 1994; Hart 1995).

The power players

The difficulties that schools face in teaching scientific literacy discussed so far arise from relative power-plays between different advocacy groups, or between individuals who can call on institutional or other supports for their case. In this last section, I describe the positions and powers of the three main groups.

Academic scientists

The most powerful and persistent of these groups is to be found among academic scientists. Traditionally, academic scientists and their acolytes among the science teaching ranks have completely controlled what counted as school science (see e.g. Fawns 1987; Layton 1984). In general, they welcomed the reforms of the 1960s and some of them played leadership roles. As has been indicated, these changes to a conceptual content for school science meant that students entering universities to study the sciences were prepared at school and selected in terms of the same type of content as university science.

Since then, a few scientists (see e.g. Gillespie 1976 in Canada; Bucat and Cole 1988 in Australia) have been concerned about the lack of experience of new students with many of the phenomena they seem able to define and handle in conceptual and algorithmic terms. However, the main complaints from academic scientists about school science stem from quantitative features of the current scene. Not enough of the high-school achievers are taking science subjects at school and too few of those who do are choosing science courses in higher education. This leads to students with weak backgrounds in physical sciences and mathematics entering science courses, to the dismay of the academics who have to teach them. This has not led many academic scientists to question the appropriateness of the curricula of the legacy type. For example, there is currently a particularly widespread concern about the shortage of students interested in physics, but academic physicists often continue to be the main opponents of any attempts to introduce alternative approaches to school science and to school physics itself that could make this subject more appealing (see Rowell and Gaskell 1986; Hart 1995; Fensham 1995b).

Another case of this support of the legacy-type content is typified by the concern that has been expressed by some academic scientists in England at the various suggestions to widen the number of subjects to be studied for the A Level examinations that precede university entry. This could be to the advantage of science students, giving them the opportunity to be more broadly educated, but it would be at the expense of studying proportionately less of the traditional content of the prerequisite physical sciences and mathematics. An even more radical move for many countries would be general acceptance by the universities that, at least for some able students from school, studies in physics and chemistry could begin from scratch at university (as is now commonly the case with the biological or earth sciences). This approach has been tried in some universities with considerable success, provided the students have a strong mathematical base.

Although some scientists were part of the reviews in the 1980s (referred to earlier) that recommended that new approaches be developed, the academic scientists, in general, have been relatively uninvolved in, or negative about, the development of the alternatives being suggested. When these alternatives reach the point when they might be implemented, there has usually been strong opposition from leading scientists, especially if changes are suggested to science in the final years of schooling. They have, of course, much to lose in these changes, namely the narrow, but concentrated, conceptual preparedness of their first-year students in the physical sciences. They may, however, gain a much broader base of able students interested in further studies in science and, overall, future citizens who are more able to differentiate those programmes of scientific work that are in the long-term interests of society, and hence be a base of support for them. At the moment, most academic scientists seem to have chosen to stay with the preparedness potential they see in the curricula of the narrow conceptual legacy (if only more of their students had succeeded in it) and they fight hard to retain it.

From the collection of quotes above, it is evident that academic scientists are vehemently against the suggestions that school science should acknowledge that the subjective, the irrational, or social construction play a part in science. Although, in their own circles, and, as Marton *et al.* (1994) found among Nobel laureates, features such as the subjectivity of much scientific work, the role of intuition in it and the importance of the various disciplinary communities are accepted and often shared, they are not to be shared with neonate science students or with non-science audiences. It is as if this would undermine an authority about their scientific knowledge that these academics need to keep and, indeed, are responsible for guarding. Bingle and Gaskell (1994) have discussed how this power and authority of science is threatened by the complexity of real-life environmental situations for which a total scientific analysis is impossible.

School science teachers

Although a growing number of science teachers are now regularly confronted by the open boredom of their students (Baird *et al.* 1991) and their inability or unwillingness to learn school science, the general response of science teachers to the new approaches has been conservative and unenthusiastic. In England and Wales, relatively few science teachers participated in the curriculum innovations made possible by the substantial funds in the Technical and Vocational Educational Initiative (TVEI) programme. In Canada and Sweden, subject groups of teachers have used their union affiliations and other means to resist changes to their science curricula. In Australia, science teachers were found to be very inarticulate about why students should study science compared with the way other teachers argued for their subjects. They were more inclined to rest with the strength of position the eliteness of their subjects gave them than to be concerned with the mass of students' education in science.

Reference has already been made to the socialization that most of today's science teachers have been through in their own education in science. Few of them experienced the very different, more concrete and social curricula that existed before the legacy of the 1960s took over. They have all been socialized in its induction approach in their schooling and in their university studies in science. Furthermore, at school they were among the most successful students in that they continued in tertiary scientific studies for a long way, albeit not far enough to feel like scientists. It is no wonder so many of them also have a stake in its maintenance and a reluctance to teach students whose academic interests are so different from their own. There are, however, growing reports in a number of countries of groups of science teachers who are working together to use as many of these alternatives as their formal curriculum will allow.

The formal professional associations of science teachers and their umbrella organization, International Council of Associations for Science Education (ICASE), have generally been more progressive and open to the exploration of alternative approaches. A number of these bodies have provided status, publicity and, in some cases, financial support, for developing or distributing material that embodies these options. There is a growing number of reports of teachers in many countries working together on alternative approaches and, indeed, using them in their classrooms.

Academic science educators

One of the lasting and more interesting outcomes of the 1960s' projects has been the emergence of a second group of academics with interests in the nature of school science. Many of the outstanding teachers who were recruited as writers and team members of these projects did not return to their classrooms when the projects ended. Rather, they took up positions in the expanding higher education scene as teacher educators. Informed by the extensive and intensive experience in the large-scale projects, they shared not only their own experience of teaching but also the range of approaches and ideas that had been learnt in the project. They also had many questions about science teaching that needed answers; quite quickly science education became established as a field of lively research and scholarly discourse that could inform and influence school science.

With the renewal of official interest and support for school science in the 1980s, a number of these science educators became very active in promoting and developing the alternative approaches that have been outlined earlier. With the responsibilities and opportunities they have in the pre-service and in-service education of science teachers, they are well placed to explain the new conceptions of school science and to contribute to teachers' ability to accept and act on them in their teaching (see Fensham *et al.* 1994; Solomon and Aikenhead 1994). Accounts are also now appearing of the way in which these science educators have also played important roles in the debates and decision-making about whether the new approaches will be implemented (see for instance several papers in the theme issue on Policy and Science Education, *International Journal of Science Education* 17(4) 1995).

The role played by science educators in the proposed changes has, however, been much more ambiguous than has so far been suggested. This stems from the results of what is their most successful area of research since the mid-1980s, and from the limitations that their positions in higher education impose.

The shift of focus from teaching to learning and some easy-to-use methodologies (see White and Gunstone 1993) unleashed what has become a flood of more than 3,000 research studies of students, alternative conceptions of natural phenomena and of basic scientific conceptions (Pfundt and Duit 1994). Almost all of these studies have been of science concepts and topics associated with the legacy science curriculum, for the obvious reason that this was what students were supposed to be learning in school. The research has been fruitful in laying bare the extent of the problem of poor science-learning and in leading to the invention of many new pedagogies that have been shown to enhance this learning. Together, these findings provide a very solid research base for the renewal and resurrection of the legacy curriculum and the induction conception of school science. 'Things are bad but we now know how to do it better' is one reasonable interpretation of this decade of research, whether this is what these science educators with their curriculum hats intend or not. If any of us had bothered to conduct the same sort of research into students' conceptions of socio-scientific issues (like the historical nature of science) or of technological and environmental concepts (like 'social risk', 'product shelf life' and 'radiation damage', etc.) we would, I am sure, have found a similarly amazing range of alternative views and misinformation, and of useful pedagogies. A parallel research base to support the social constructivist and STS alternative approaches would then exist and the reforming science educators' hands would have been much stronger. [...]

References

Aikenhead, G. S. (1986) 'The content of STS education', *STS Research Network Missive* 1(3): 18–23.
—— (1991) *Logical Reasoning in Science and Technology,* Toronto, Ontario: John Wiley.
Araos, A. C. (1995) 'Environmental education in Victorian secondary schools: constraints and possibilities', Master of Environmental Science thesis, Monash University, Victoria, Australia.
Baird, J. R., Fensham, P. J., Gunstone, R. F. and White, R. T. (1991) 'The importance of reflection in improving science teaching and learning', *Journal of Research in Science Teaching* 28(2): 163–82.

Bingle, W. H. and Gaskell, P. J. (1994) 'Scientific literacy for decision making and the social construction of scientific knowledge', *Science Education* 78(2): 185–201.

Blades, D. W. (1994) 'Procedures of power and possibilities for change in science education curriculum discourse', Doctor of Philosophy thesis, University of Alberta, Edmonton, Alberta.

Bodmer, W. (1985) *The Public Understanding of Science: Report of an* ad hoc *Group endorsed by the Council of the Royal Society,* London: Royal Society.

Bourdieu, P. and Passeron, J. (1973) *Reproduction in Education, Society and Culture,* London: Sage.

Bucat, R. and Cole, A. (1988) 'The Australian Academy of Science school chemistry project', *Journal of Chemical Education* 65(9): 777–9.

Chan, A. (1993) 'Science teachers and Science-Technology-Society (STS), Doctor of Philosophy thesis, Monash University, Victoria, Australia.

Connell, R. W, Ashenden, D. J., Kessler, S. and Dowsett, G. W. (1982) *Making the Difference: Schools, Families and Social Divisions,* Sydney: Allen and Unwin.

Eijkelhof, H. and Kortland, K. (1988) 'Broadening the aims of physics education', in P. J. Fensham (ed.) *Developments and Dilemmas in Science Education,* London: Falmer.

Fawns, R. A. (1987) 'The maintenance and transformation of school science', Doctor of Philosophy thesis, Monash University, Clayton, Victoria, Australia.

Fensham, P. J. (1973) 'Reflections on the social content of science education materials', *Science Education Research* 3: 143–50.

—— (1980) 'Constraint and autonomy in Australian Secondary Education', *Journal of Curriculum Studies* 12(3): 189–206.

—— (1995a) 'Curriculum emphases in conflict in science education', in D. Roberts and L. Ostman (eds) *The Multiple Meanings of a School Subject: Essays on Science and the School Curriculum,* New York: Teachers' College Press, Columbia University.

—— (1995b) 'One step forward …', *Australian Science Teachers Journal* 41(5): 24–9.

—— and Corrigan, D. (1994) 'The implementation of an STS chemistry course in Australia: a research perspective', in J. Solomon and G. Aikenhead (eds) *STS Education: International Perspectives on Reform,* New York: Teachers' College Press, Columbia University.

—— and May, J. B. (1979) 'Servant not master: a new role for science in a core of environmental education', *Australian Science Teachers' Journal* 25(2): 15–24.

——, Gunstone, R. F. and White, R. T. (1994) *The Content of Science: A Constructivist Approach to its Teaching and Learning,* London: Falmer.

Gillespie, R. (1976) 'Chemistry – fact or fiction? Some reflections on the teaching of chemistry', *Chemistry Canada* 28(11): 23–8.

Harding, J. M. and Donaldson, J. (1986) 'Chemistry from issues', *School Science Review* 68(242): 49–59.

Hart, C. (1995) 'Access and the quality of learning: the story of a curriculum document for school physics', Doctor of Philosophy thesis, Monash University, Victoria, Australia.

Hodson, D. (1988) 'Towards a philosophically more valid science education', *Science Education* 72(1): 19–40.

Kelly, A., Whyte, J. and Small, B. (1984) *Girls into Science and Technology (GIST),* Manchester: Department of Sociology, University of Manchester.

Layton, D. (1973) *Science for the People: The Origins of the School Science Curriculum in England,* London: Allen and Unwin.

—— (1984) *Interpreters of School Science,* London: John Murray.

—— (1991) 'Science education and praxis: the relationship of school science to practical action', *Studies in Science Education* 19: 43–79.

Lijnse, P. (1990) 'Energy between the life-world of pupils and the world of physics', *Science Education* 74(5): 571–83.

Lundgren, U. P. (1981) 'Education as a context for work', *Australian Educational Researcher* 8(2): 5–29.

Malcolm, C. K. (1987) *The Science Framework P-1 0*, Melbourne, Victoria: Ministry of Education, Schools Division.

Marton, E., Fensham, P. J. and Chaiklin, S. (1994) 'A Nobel's eye view of scientific intuition: discussions with the Nobel prize winners in physics, chemistry and medicine (1970–86)', *International Journal of Science Education* 16(4): 457–73.

National Science Foundation (1983) *Educating Americans for the Twenty First Century, Report of the National Science Board Commission on Pre-college Education in Mathematics, Science and Technology*, Washington, DC: National Science Foundation.

Osborne, R. and Freyberg, P. (1985) *Learning in Science: The Implications of Children's Science*, Auckland, New Zealand: Heinemann.

Pfundt, H. and Duit, R. (1994) *Bibliography: Students' Alternative Frameworks and Science Education*, 4th edn, Kiel, Germany: IPN.

Roberts, D. (1982) 'Developing the concept of "curriculum emphases" in science education', *Science Education* 66(2): 243–60.

Rowell, P. M. and Gaskell, P. J. (1986) 'Tensions and realignments: school physics in British Columbia', in I. Goodson (ed.) *International Perspectives in Curriculum,* London: Croom Helm.

Science Council of Canada (1984) *Science for Every Student: Educating Canadians for Tomorrow's World,* Summary of Report 36, Ottawa: Supply and Service.

Scriven, M. (1987) *The Rights of Technology in Education: The Need for Consciousness Raising,* a paper for the Education and Technology Task Force, Adelaide, South Australia: Ministry of Education and Technology.

Smail, B. (1987) 'Encouraging girls to give physics a second chance', in A. Kelly (ed.) *Science for Girls 13–18*, Milton Keynes: Open University Press.

Smith, N. (1988) 'In support of an application-first chemistry course: some reflections on the Salters' GCSE scheme', *School Science Review* 70(250): 108–14.

Smith, W. (1987) 'COMETS: career-orientated modules to explore topics in science', in K. Riquarts (ed.) *Science and Technology Education and the Quality of Life*, Kiel: IPN.

Solomon, J. (1988) 'Science technology and society courses: tools for thinking about social issues', *International Journal of Science Education* 10(4): 379–87.

—— and Aikenhead, G. (eds) (1994) *STS Education: International Perspectives on Reform,* New York: Teachers' College Press, Columbia University.

Speedy, G., Annice, C., Fensham, P. J. and West, L. H. T. (1989) *Discipline Review of Teacher Education in Mathematics and Science, Vol. I., Report and Recommendations,* Canberra: Australian Government Printer.

Thier, H. and Hill, T. (1988) 'Chemical education in schools and the community: the CEPUP project', *International Journal of Science Education* 10(4): 421–30.

Unesco (1983) *Science for All*, Bangkok: Unesco Regional Office for Education in Asia and the Pacific.

Van Berkel, B. (1995) 'A conceptual structure of school chemistry', in P. Janich and N. Psarros (eds) *Proceedings of the Second Erlenmeyer Colloquy* (pp. 141–57), Würzburg, Germany: Knöigshausen and Neumann.

White, R. T. and Gunstone, R. G. (1993) *Probing Understanding*, London: Falmer.

Part 2

Learning science

Patricia Murphy

In Part 2 we examine theories about learning and their influence on views of the goals of science education and how to achieve them. The readings selected have either had a significant influence on the direction of science learning or raise challenges for the future. Each of the theoretical perspectives considered offers a view of what is significant in understanding the nature of the human 'mind' and the teaching and learning process.

Constructivism has dominated understanding about learning in science for several decades. Greenfield's work into the functioning of the brain provides us with an understanding of the physical basis of mind that is congruent with key features of constructivist theorising. Greenfield's account of the personalised nature of mind, for example, challenges the view of human potential as genetically 'fixed' and reinforces the view that understanding is constructed and not given. The concept of neuronal plasticity provides a rationale for the belief in the lifelong learner. The evidence cited in support of the role of environment and culture in learning, however, challenges constructivist theorising in relation to the social nature of knowledge construction.

Constructivist theories taken up in science education typically see learning as an individual process and have paid scant attention to the social plane. Driver *et al.* address this, drawing on Vygotskian theorising, and advocate a social constructivist view of learning that involves both social and individual processes. The social plane, they argue, is involved when students are introduced to the concepts, symbols and conventions of science. This socialization into the practices of the scientific community, however, is seen to rely on individual meaning-making. A social constructivist perspective casts the teacher as both the expert who introduces students to the social plane, and the guide who scaffolds students' individual appropriation of meaning working in the 'zone of proximal development'. The approach of Driver *et al.* has increasing support in science education but remains a challenge to dominant practice.

Ann Brown adopts a sociocultural view of learning, which differs from social constructivism in the increased emphasis given to the social plane. In her approach, agency, i.e. the active, strategic nature of learning, which is a central tenet of all constructivist theorising, and collaboration are brought together in communities of learners. Brown also draws on Vygotskian theorising but she argues for a view of expertise as distributed and emerging between people. '*Ideas seeded in discussion migrate throughout the community via mutual appropriation and negotiated meaning*' (p. 87). For Brown, learning has to be situated in tasks that are personally authentic, i.e. have meaning and relevance to the students, and culturally authentic in that they allow learners to engage in practices that can be related to those of scientists. The concept of learning communities, while influential, is still not widely practised. The isolation of students from the social world and the perceived goals of science education are seen to limit the potential for authenticity in formal science learning.

The next three chapters focus on the implications for the goals of science education of a sociocultural view of learning. Bruner argues that it shifts learning away from answers, the outcomes of scientific endeavour, toward a concern with the process of scientific problem-solving. What students should learn, he argues, is how we construct our model of nature. In arguing for students to engage in the narrative construal of science, he provides examples of how this allows students to play with ideas and come to understand the structure of the domain. It is this structure, he argues, that allows students to go beyond what they know.

McGinn and Roth draw on studies in science and technology to make the case for understanding scientists' and engineers' ways of working, thinking and acting as embedded in a 'web of social relationships'. They therefore challenge the way science and scientists are represented currently in science education. They describe how a range of people outside the scientific community participates in science as they use it in their occupations and/or daily lives. They see this participation as one of the ways in which science is shaped and argue for this to be taken into account when reformulating what can be considered as authentic science and redefining the curriculum for scientific literacy. They make three recommendations for this redefinition. The first is to broaden the nature of scientific inquiry to engage students in social activist inquiries. The second is to consider competence in scientific discourse as scientific knowledge to be taught and assessed. Third for scientific visual representations to be taught and understood as important means of communication which can be used to develop and represent shared understanding. Their vision is for students to engage in trajectories of legitimate peripheral participation in science-related discourses and practices.

Chin and his colleagues' research into cooperative education in Canada provides a theoretical framework to understand the instructional implications for bridging science in schools and science in the workplace. They argue that students' participation in the workplace is enhanced if they understand the scientific declarative knowledge behind workplace practices. They suggest, therefore, that workplace communities need to be re-conceptualised as communities of learners as well as practitioners. The implication for formal science learning is that it should be embedded in the functional aspects of workplace practices, which is a significantly different approach to the relationships between vocational and academic knowledge from that reflected in current UK policy initiatives.

Practical work remains a contentious issue in science learning in its role in defining the domain and as a means of learning about the tools and practices of science. Students are, by the nature of educational institutions and their goals, sequestered from 'real' laboratories and their purposes. Wallace *et al.* challenge current practice and argue the need to alter the contexts, tasks, resources and techniques for formal laboratory learning to enhance its relevance and meaning, to orientate students away from answers towards problem-solving, and to better represent authentic cultural practices. These recommendations resonate closely with those of Brown, Bruner, and Chin *et al.*

2.1 The child

Susan Greenfield

[…] Small children seem to live on an emotional roller coaster. With miraculous rapidity, heart-rending sobs give way to gurgles of delight at the sight of a chocolate bar or a cat walking past. Yet at the time, the rage – or the laughter – seems so important and so definitive. Were such intense emotions displayed in an adult, they would presumably be assumed to be indicative of some inner state, such as a bereavement, so extreme that it would have to pervade the individual for far longer than the seconds for which it streaks across the face of a child.

Children can more readily abandon themselves to the joys, perhaps it is even the ecstasy, of an amusement-park ride or the sight of the sea, compared with adults, who find it virtually impossible to shake off the dripping worry of the mortgage payments. According to David Warburton, director of human psychopharmacology at Reading University, children laugh, on average, 300 times a day. By adulthood, this number plummets to 50. But, by the same, token, a child will be more readily frightened by a creak on the stair, by someone with a white sheet draped over his head, or by a train roaring into the station. Children experience emotions as strongly, perhaps even more strongly, than adults, but seemingly, for less good reason. We may call them 'crybabies', not because of the nature of the emotion itself, but because such strong feelings have been evoked by such a feeble cause.

To a much greater extent, children are passive victims of their senses, one-off experiences that have an impact by virtue only of their intrinsic physical quality: the brightness, loudness, smell, taste or touch of whatever is going on. This exaggerated emphasis on the actual sensuality of waves of sound and light and of clouds of chemicals pervading the ears, eyes, nose, skin and mouth is because, for the very young, there is nothing else. Children are less equipped to interpret the present situation against the sobering yet reassuring background of past experience, a private collection of memories that tells us that it is only an ordinary person masquerading as a ghost under the white sheet or that there are more significant possessions in life than an ice cream cone that has fallen on the sidewalk.

As we grow up and see the world more and more in the light of previous experiences, we develop a personalized inner world of private resources that increasingly act as a retaliatory buffer to the assault of the 'booming, buzzing confusion' (James 1890) that previously poured into our brains unopposed. And as we continue to live out our lives as adults, more and more associations pile on and around the objects, events and people among which we are thrown.

This rapidly expanding inner world of personal associations offers an ever-growing framework of reference, an increasing degree of meaning to ongoing experience. The most obvious type of meaning is the culturally and socially accepted identity of objects and people around us. However, these objects and people gradually acquire ever more extensive and idiosyncratic associations and hence ever more eccentric and intense degrees of significance. The more ramifying and multiple the associations, the more 'meaning' or 'relevance' an object will have.

Think of a cup.[1] A newborn child, even if it could focus on a cup, would not be able to recognize it as such; it would be just a series of curves, shades and shadows. As time went on, however, the child would begin to associate the different shapes and sizes of cups with the activity of drinking and would eventually learn the verbal label for the general concept of 'cup' so that the object could be conjured up in his or her imagination, even when a cup was not physically there. One cup in particular might become associated with a particular event or be special because it was a present from a special person, in that it, too, evoked a raft of memories. Once the child entered high school, he or she might read Freud and assign a new meaning to the cup (e.g. as a symbol of fecundity). Or the child might become an expert in eighteenth-century porcelain, so that certain types of cups would become even more finely differentiated than snow to Eskimos. Hence the object, the humble cup, would be shot through with a rich range of associations triggering all number of memories and it would thus acquire a significance it could never have had, had the child been reared in some hypothetical environment where people drank only from bottles.

Another example, perhaps the most obvious for those of us brought up in a traditional family environment, is a mother. For the infant, Mummy's face looms into view most often. It is a swimming constant in a shifting world of colours, smells and textures and quickly acquires associations of feeding, being warm, being rocked and being dry. Throughout the child's early years, such persistent involvement in much of one's daily experiences will ensure that some woman whom the rest of us would pass in the street without a glance, a woman who in psychophysical terms makes no impact on the raw senses, would nonetheless be of overwhelming significance to someone.

Following this train of thought, it is easy to see how the gradual forging and trafficking of associations equip us, first, with a simple, literal meaning for the immediate world around us. As more associations pile up, objects, people and events acquire differential degrees of importance with corresponding ease or otherwise of recall. A well-known memory trick is to attach as many associations as possible, however contrived, to the object, list or fact that you want to remember. For example, if you can visualize the items on a shopping list as distributed around a kitchen or can imagine being back on the playground with those classmates whose names were previously so hard to call to mind, then the whole business of remembering becomes easier. By stacking up associations, it is not so much that our memories get better but that they become more readily accessed through more potential routes.

As we grow, we learn to generalize across experiences, to see common patterns and themes and thus to develop generalizations such as 'cat', abstract concepts such as 'beauty', and finally to relate these concepts to one another in an original way – to have ideas. But in each case, the constellation of such associations will be as varied as an individual life and thus the understanding of the world will be different for each individual. [...] Sometimes, associations with certain objects seem to others to be excessive and baffling. When we speak of something having sentimental value, what we really mean is that an object will trigger far more extensive connections than might have been expected on the basis of its physical properties alone. A cheap, plastic, toy ring might have been the token of love used in a spontaneous marriage proposal when found in a Christmas cracker at a particular party one December. Only two people in the world share that particular memory and only for them would the subsequent sight of the ring trigger a particular state of mind. For them, the worthless object would mean a great deal at a very private level. This sort of association applies not just to objects of sentimental value. Everything around you will be imbued with a significance that is unique to you because only you have lived your life and had a particular set of experiences.

One object, one word, one glance, will act like a stone cast into a puddle, sending out ripples of memories triggering off one another. Gradually, beyond the generic concepts, the verbal label, we acquire a more sophisticated and highly personalized view, an understanding of the world that is unique to each of us. As we grow up, we are better able to understand or explain an ongoing situation in the light of previous experience and objects, people or actions with only a modest impact on the raw senses will monopolize our attention because of a far more covert, less tangible and private significance. We start to register not only the loudest and brightest in each waking moment, but the secret lover's eyebrow raised silently for a fraction of an inch over a fraction of a second across a noisy, crowded room.

Each time you hear a noise, blink at the light, have a conversation or cut another piece of cake, some small, imperceptible and unspectacular modification to the configuration of the brain occurs[2] and we interpret the world in a slightly different way. With increasing frequency, previous associations start to dominate our interpretation and response to ongoing situations. The brain becomes less of a sponge and more of a yardstick in a turning world, retaliating in an increasingly balanced dialogue with the outside world.

The critical issue here is to develop an understanding and to attach meaning to an event or person by placing it, him or her in a wider, more general context of pre-existing facts and memories, however idiosyncratic or misguided it might appear to others. For example, how often do we hear someone excuse the behaviour of a friend or colleague as 'human nature'? The very concept of human nature is one that will have evolved through a lifetime of dealing with people and seeing recurrent and common ways in people's actions and responses. If someone makes a spiteful remark, say, about a friend's new dress, a teenager might be wounded, whereas someone older might react less strongly by placing the remark in a more general context, such as the 'natural' tendency for jealousy among peers. Such understanding cannot be simply downloaded from a chip or, more prosaically, taught at the blackboard. It is only as we become older that we stand any chance at all of being described as 'wise'. However, we need to see now how the generic brain can become personalized in this way, that is, how it develops a mind.

Mind is a murky concept. It peppers our daily conversation, lurks in idioms and expressions and yet evades a clear definition. Ask most people to define *mind* and they will probably come up with one of two possibilities, neither of which is satisfactory. The first answer is that somehow the mind is the opposite of the brain. This knee-jerk response is the inheritance left to us more than 300 years ago by René Descartes, whose distinction between mental and physical, a dualism, has clung to Western thought ever since.[3] Nowadays it might seem easy to resort to the reassurance of the material world and spurn anything that smacks of the mystical. However, it is important to remember that Descartes lived in an era dominated by the church, where no theory could fly directly in the face of the religious, and thus spiritual, perspective on life. How much neater, therefore, to develop the idea of parallel systems, a concept concerned with the bump and grind of banal material things that left the sanctity of the human experience as remote and unreachable as ever. Many still like to think that there is more to our lives and to ourselves than our banal existence in our sweaty and imperfect physical bodies.

This additional but intangible special quality is seldom described or defined, but following this line of thought, it might be regarded as a 'soul'. Now, let us distinguish mind from soul. What we are dealing with here, in this chapter, is the essence of individuality, the constellation of characteristics, propensities and prejudices, that make us who we are, literally ourselves, until we die. For those who believe in a soul, the most important aspect is that it is immortal; it would survive the death of the brain. But with death, the mind, as defined here, is finished. We are dealing with the lifetime consistency of development of character that is rooted in the development of your physical brain, and therefore it terminates when your brain does. True, we refer in an everyday sense to someone 'having soul', but really we are not speaking literally. Soul, as in 'soul music', is a metaphor that encompasses more emotions and sensitivities than grey-suited crowds of commuters or, dare I say it, white-coated neuroscientists. Whereas for Descartes, immortality and character were more easily conflated, from the privileged stance of the twenty-first century, we can place considerations of immortality outside the scope of this investigation of the Self.

So, we are confronting the riddle of a mortal mind versus a mortal brain. Meticulous clinical observation over the past few centuries has revealed how the actions of drugs, head wounds and strokes modify the state of the physical brain and, at the same time, how those physical processes modify how people think and feel. The idea of something mental, divorced from the tangible grey matter, has grown increasingly unattractive.

An alternative, more modern way of defining *mind* would simply be to view it as no more than the physical brain. In the 1940s, the great behaviourist movement led by B. F. Skinner proudly brought a new age of reason to the study of the human mind by dispensing with the concept altogether and placing emphasis instead on the inputs and outputs of the physical brain.[4] Final behaviour – observable, measurable phenomena – was all that mattered. But it soon became clear that the brain was not just a receptacle for reflex responses to specific triggers or stimuli. Instead, even laboratory rats showed that something was intervening between the stimulation going in and the response coming out: thinking. So, this stark, mechanistic stance gradually gave way to the cognitive (literally 'thinking') approach where, as its name suggests, the importance of the intervening mental processes played a central role. Instead of throwing out the term *mind* altogether, advocates of the cognitive approach, such as Dan Dennett, now use it interchangeably with the term *brain* (Dennett 1998), instead.

But the old terminology and the need to separate the generic, physical brain from something else endure. Despite the clear demonstrations by modern medicine of a causality between tampering with the physical brain, say with drugs, and subsequent changes in the mental world – in one's mood – we still seem to need the two separate words, *mind* and *brain*, in everyday conversation. Even medical textbooks often describe disorders of the brain, the 'organic' dysfunctions such as strokes and epilepsy, as opposed to those of the 'mind': schizophrenia, depression or anxiety, with the treatment in each case segregated respectively to the artificial, in my view, distinctions of neurology or psychiatry. If the mind is, indeed, tied in with the brain, the nature of that relationship is far from one of a mere synonym. So Descartes's division lingers: we may legitimately reject the idea of airy-fairy stuff, a New Age alternative to matter, but we apparently need – in our vocabulary at least – a term that refers to something beyond the physical brain.

Mind still captures a subtly different concept that cannot be catered to automatically by contemplating the physical lump of tissue between the ears. All our physical brains look pretty much the same, but one's mind is quintessentially one's own. [Elsewhere I have written that] there was no uniqueness in the generic brain and that it was far from obvious where or when the individuality crept in. If mind is not airy-fairy, then it must be reflected in some special physical feature of the brain, developed as we grow up in a world that only slowly we come to understand. If our minds take shape over childhood, then we can look at the changes in the brain over this time frame to address the great question, what is the physical basis of the mind?

Imagine a room. When you first move in, you have almost infinite scope in determining what sort of room it will turn out to be. Of course, you will have to make do with its size and shape, the height of the ceiling and the number of windows, but the early stages of living in the room and decorating it from scratch will probably be the most formative. Most likely, you will immediately impose a theme, a general style, be it art deco, antique, high-tech, sloppy student or undomesticated bachelor. However, it is only as you live in the room that you will be able to evolve the most pleasing and practical configuration of furniture, and indeed discover which items you need most. With changing fashion and changing lifestyle, these needs will, of course, themselves change, albeit in the minor move of an ornament being shifted along a mantelpiece or in a more drastic manifestation, like a new overall colour. Then there will be changes that you do not control or anticipate: perhaps a window will be smashed, a rug burned, or items will wear out and need replacing with more efficient or more effective alternatives. However, whether dramatic or modest, by accident or on purpose, nothing will remain the same. Few people could be confident that the rooms in which they are currently living would never undergo the slightest modification. So it is with brains, but on an infinitely finer and faster scale.

It is in early childhood that experience has its most dramatic effects in determining our world view. 'Give me a child until he is seven,' promised the Jesuits (Lacoutere 1995) 'and I will give you the man.' It is self-evident that it is the experiences that occur after birth that will determine the language we speak first, the accent we have, the religion we adopt, the values we live by and so forth. In my case, I was born in London, the product of a mixed marriage between a Jewish father and Protestant mother. I assumed everyone in the world spoke English and that some invisible line running from head to foot demarcated the Jewish half of me from the Protestant side, although it was unclear which was which. Such is the attempted holistic view of the child, coloured wholly by the haphazard and literal inputs of the immediate environment.

Throughout life, we constantly modify our outlook and expectations, shifting the furniture around in the room, purchasing new items and throwing out the old. In imperceptible steps, we become increasingly unsurprised by and cynical about human behaviour. Or there may be some dramatic changes in perspective – a bereavement, religious conversion or, indeed, the realization that those childhood beliefs should be challenged. Some of these changes of mind will appear to be initiated by ourselves, such as deciding to have a child, having another slice of cake, going to a party or going to work in another country, whereas others will be imposed upon us, say, a car accident, a death, a lottery win, a chance encounter. Our world view, then, remains highly interactive and dynamic, but increasingly there is a theme, a continuity of style as we grow that is more personalized and more individual than any room – even for clones.

The common perception of science fiction clones is that they not only look alike but have the same personality and even the same consciousness. Yet having a clone, who is, after all, merely an identical twin, is like having an empty room of identical size and shape as your neighbour, with exactly the same number, size and position of windows. Individual differences will soon creep in. If I had a clone living in the Amazon jungle, even at the physical level, she would only partly resemble me; after all, height and weight would be influenced by diet and the stress induced by teaching medical students and running a laboratory might affect the number of wrinkles, grey hairs and facial muscle configuration, compared with my genetic counterpart luxuriating in tropical vegetation. She would have a host of rainforest survival skills that I lacked, though her views and knowledge, say, of daily life in Oxford would be zero. Nature and nurture would have interacted to produce two distinct individuals.

In the old days, the segregation of environment from genes seemed quite straightforward. The investigator studied the coincidence of traits (covariance) in human clones, namely, identical twins who had identical genetic portfolios yet had been reared apart. In this way, nurture was cleanly separated from whatever cards had been dealt from an oblivious sperm and ovum. However, a recent paper in the journal *Nature* (no bias intended) threw a spanner in the works of this dichotomy (Devlin *et al.* 1997). Devlin, Daniels and Roeder, working at the Pittsburgh School of Medicine and Carnegie Mellon University, have highlighted an anomaly over the delicate and much-debated question of the degree to which one's IQ is inherited.

For some time, this issue has presented a puzzle to behavioural geneticists. The difficulty arises from different results generated by different types of studies on twins. When the subjects have been identical twins reared apart, it has been esti-mated that the degree of IQ they inherit is about 70 per cent. Yet it is also possible to tease out the genetic component of a trait such as IQ by working with twins living together. In this case, identical twins are compared with non-identical coun-terparts. Assuming that any factor arising from a similar environment will be constant for both types of twins, any other difference in ability between identical compared with non-identical twins should presumably be genetic. Surprisingly, the degree to which IQ can be attributed to genes is much lower, only 50 per cent! What is the extra, unaccounted-for factor that was inflating the value of an inher-ited component to IQ, specifically for twins reared apart? Devlin and colleagues have an ingenious hypothesis.

For twins growing up together, the important factor is not whether they are identical: the shared environment, nurture, would be undeniably a constant factor irrespective of whether the twins came from two eggs or one. For twins growing up apart, however, only identical twins would usually be investigated, in order to distinguish the identical set of genes from the variable environment. However, for twins living in different homes all their lives, the hitch is that nurture might not be as negligible as one supposed. It is easy to overlook that there is a common shared environment *before* birth. In comparisons between identical and non-identical twins living together, this factor would be common to both groups, but it might not have counted in any final discrepancy. When Devlin and his colleagues reanalysed previous studies, they indeed found that a staggering 20 per cent of IQ could be attributed not to shared genes, nor to a shared home, but to a shared womb.

It seems truly remarkable that the developing foetal sense organs are able to transmit information reflecting specific variations in their uterine environment back to the growing brain, where there is, presumably, a sufficient influence on cerebral mechanisms to be reflected, ultimately, in differences in some kind of external performance or trait later on in life. So, if there is a wild card, the womb environment, that contributes to our mental make-up, then perhaps we are one step less near *Brave New* World eugenics. However, turbulent events are occur-ring, none the less, in the womb.

As early as four weeks after conception, the human foetus has a recognizable brain. As you might imagine, it is, of course, very different from the brain that will control its life, effectively *be* its life, for the following seventy years or so. The four-week brain consists of three swellings, like beads on a string, that develop into bulges and, in turn, become rounded brain regions that enclose a stalk. This is the brain stem, the most primitive part of the brain, [...] which is continuous with the spinal cord. As growth gets seriously under way, the cells that constitute the brain will proliferate at the staggering rate of 250,000 per minute. Slowly, this restless mass of tissue takes shape as the future brain cells, or neurons, shuttle back and forth from the innermost core of the brain to its outermost reaches. The newest cells will end up in the outermost layers, so the brain effectively grows inside out.

Once they have reached their final destination, the itinerant brain cells start to set down the neurological equivalent of roots. They will no longer be able to travel back and forth according to a preordained script, but now start to bear more resemblance to a spider in the middle of its web. In terms of the real brain, the web is actually a cosseting of support cells that form a delicate cradle for the neuron and ensure that its local environment remains benign, free of debris and harmful substances, yet rich in nutrients. And so it is that, with some 100 billion neurons in place and ten times as many support cells, we make our debut in the world.

Already, we have seen the experience in the womb might shape certain traits by influencing, presumably, certain circuitry between neurons (Purves 1994), but it is from the moment of birth that this process is about to be massively exercised and exploited. Experience now becomes completely unique: no one, however close, occupies the same identical points in time and space throughout your life as you do. And as you live, memories pile up and this accumulation of past scenarios, all stored within your brain, gives you a unique perspective from which to interpret the flood of sensations that bombard you every waking moment. Memories and mind are, therefore, inextricably linked.

One of the most remarkable differences between us and our closest simian cousins is that our brains undergo astonishing post-natal growth, doubling in size during our first two years, finally increasing by 400 per cent, from 450 cc to a maximum of some 1,700 cc by the time we are sixteen years of age (Kolb 1995). However, we are born with most of the neurons we are ever going to have, so something else must be going on within our post-natal skulls. It is not the brain cells themselves that change and continue to change so much as the *connections* between them. These neurons, which are already in place at birth, have no further room to manoeuvre; they are henceforth static, but the extensions that now grow out of them can be diverted and steered by chemicals. These extensions, some of which are established in the womb, remain highly dynamic. They are constantly being strengthened by experience or atrophying through lack of it. The neurons do not increase in number but the connections between them now become increasingly conspicuous, pushing the main bodies of the neurons ever farther apart, as though they were clasping hands with one another and then unfolding and stretching out their spindly arms. The 'arms' in the case of neurons can be tens to hundreds of times longer than their main central body and some one hundred times thinner (Levitan and Kaczmarek 1996). It is via these threadlike conduits that electrical signals buzz at speeds of up to 250 miles an hour along any of 10,000 to 100,000 connections.[5] Only once these connections are in place, networking one brain cell with another, are neurons able to communicate with one another. Only then will the brain be able to work to its full potential and start to interpret the world in the light of experience.

As we develop, as our bodies move around in the world, our brains are working incessantly on the use-it-or-lose-it principle (Purves 1994). Just like the muscles of your body, connections in the brain will strengthen and grow as they are exercised. In a general way, this phenomenon can be seen at work in all human brains. For example, the fingers and mouth are capable of highly agile movements and are particularly sensitive to touch. Despite being relatively minor, in purely anatomical terms, it is the fingers and mouth that receive the greater allocation in neuronal territory in the brain compared with, say, the upper arm or the back (Kandel *et al.* 1991). But this 'neuronal plasticity' is also at work at a much less generic, more individual level. The brain cells that are involved in the activities that occur most frequently will have extensive connections, whereas those that are used less frequently will be pushed out of the way, and their targets will be taken over by their more hardworking neighbours. [...]

Nature has at times conducted her own demonstration of the remarkable plasticity of the human brain. There are frequent stories of coma victims revived as relatives have sat by their bedside, stimulating the brain by endless talk or by playing music. Perhaps less dramatic but, to me at least, equally emotive, was what happened to my own father.

On a cold February day in 1991, my brother phoned from London with alarming news. The snow made travel from Oxford almost impossible, but I had to get home as quickly as I could. Apparently, my mother had returned from a shopping trip to discover my 78-year-old father sitting listlessly in a chair, oblivious to everything around him, including her increasingly agitated questioning. On arrival at the hospital, a brain scan confirmed that my father had had a stroke. His speech was unimpaired and he had full control of his movements. It was just that he did not recognize any of us or have any idea where he was or what had happened. He was utterly confused, beached in a world that he did not understand, that made no sense. Of course, my family and I were distraught. What arrangements do you make for someone who is capable of maximum mobility, but who might easily walk across a busy road or burn down the house? The doctors shook their heads and showed me the scans: part of my father's brain resembled Swiss cheese. But then, a seeming miracle occurred. Within a week or so, the paternal world started to right itself. A few months later, he had made a full recovery and, within the year, he had even regained his driver's licence. Now, at the age of eighty-three, he has been considering a sponsored bungee jump for charity – an idea quite understandably vetoed by my mother.

In this way, I saw with my own eyes how someone I knew and loved well could vanish in an instant, but then gradually reappear. My father's brain could not replace the neurons he had lost, but gradually the ones that remained were able to take on the functions of their deceased colleagues. Even in old age, brain plasticity can occur (Ricklefs and Finch 1995). The brain, or, rather, its internal circuitry, is constantly restless.

Certain configurations of neuronal connections, then, imperceptibly personalize the brain and it is this personalized aspect of the physical brain that actually is the mind. This individual mind continues to respond and react by shifting neuron allegiances as we live out our lives. However, as we mature, the dialogue with the outside world will become less one-sided than when we were younger. Instead of processing brute lights and noises as independent happenings, certain consistent combinations of shape, colour, sound and smell that constitute one's mother, for example, will start to trigger connections that have already been stimulated and established by previous experience. The unique concatenation of sensory experience that was one's mother will now mean something as a complex but single entity corresponding to one's female parent. It is this preconceived concept that is so hard for most of us who are not artists to unpick into mere colours and shapes again, for relaying into a painting of what we literally see at the purely sensory level. For most of us, our carefully nurtured, preconceived notions intervene.

Within the brain, certain scientists such as the physicist Erich Harth (1993) and the physiologist Semir Zeki (1993) are starting to identify circuits that might underlie this interaction between the incoming sensory flood and pre-existing associations, that is, the established connections between groups of neurons. In both cases, it is now well established that visual signals are not just relayed passively into the deep recesses of the brain and up into the cortex. Instead, there are also other connections that intercept this incoming stream of information, projecting it back down in the opposite direction to modify the way the incoming signal is relayed and thus how the world is perceived. We see the world in terms of what we have seen already.

The more complex the brain, the greater the potential for variations in the neuronal connectivity that underlies its interpretations. The longer the childhood, the more the brain will be able to forge connections that mirror not just the demands of the species or the immediate habitat, but the particular and peculiar history of the individual concerned. As the brain becomes more sophisticated, particularly in primates, the part played by the environment becomes even more marked compared with the generic, genetic programming seen in, say, goldfish. Animals that interpret the world in a way that is beneficial and necessary to the stereotyped repertoire and lifestyle of the species rather than to that of an individual would not need to learn from experience, nor would they need a highly developed mind. They would be at the – literally mindless – dictates of their genes.

When we are born and our brain, at last unconstrained by the demands of a narrow birth canal, starts to swell through the establishment of connections, we humans start to learn and remember in earnest. During learning and memory, signalling from one neuron to the next becomes more efficient. This concept is referred to as 'synaptic strengthening' and it was first introduced by the visionary psychologist Donald Hebb almost half a century ago.[6] Only more recently, however, have the actual nuts and bolts of Hebb's idea become clearer.

Think of a warm-up comedy act. Once an audience had been primed to laugh, it will respond much more readily to a joke that might normally have left it cold. Similarly, following the kind of repeated stimulation that might occur during learning or exercise, neurons can be primed to respond more sensitively in the future. In the world of the neurons, *long-term potentiation*, as its name suggests, can last for many hours. Much is now known about how transmitters and receptors contribute to the effect,[7] but long-term potentiation is just the beginning. As the neuron is being primed, changes start to occur inside the cell itself. Eventually, these changes might alter the density of connections, or at least the manufacture of further molecular machinery for more effective communication, indefinitely (Rose 1995; Martin *et al.* 1996, 1997).

But, this local cross-talk from one tiny brain cell to another is not all there is to memory and, hence, to mind. Not every experience changes the contact between every neuron all over the brain, like a vast homogeneous soup in the bony bowl of the skull, slopping first one way and then the next. Instead, specialized brain regions will change for special situations. Here, then, is a very big difference between a brain and any artificial device. [Elsewhere, I have written that] computational methods might easily be able to cope with a model for synaptic strengthening, for learning, at the level of isolated contacts between the equivalent of one cell and the next. Unfortunately, such models fail to incorporate the additional, macro-level of complex brain regions and their respective diversity of function. And this further level of organization of specialized yet interconnected brain regions is critical to understanding brain function.

Although memory might seem like a single process in everyday life, the brain treats it as it treats vision[8] and language (Neville *et al.* 1992), for example, as a multitude of different operations,[9] and this is where it becomes important to distinguish different brain regions. One type of memory is known as 'procedural memory'. It is needed for skills such as playing the piano and driving. These labouriously acquired talents, as most of us know from tedious first-hand experience, require many repeated trials before the brain masters the required coordination between senses and movement for the eventual, seemingly effortless execution. Memory for this type of learned sequence of procedure is organized within the region dubbed the brain's 'autopilot', a cauliflower-shaped structure that sits seemingly in semi-autonomy at the back of the head. It is even referred to as though it were a separate entity, 'the little brain', or 'cerebellum'. Processes here have been successfully modelled in silicon.[10] They enable the brain to coordinate inputs and outputs and therefore lend themselves to the algorithmic processes of biasing connections that have been stimulated or exercised more than others.

However, the ability to ride a bicycle or drive a car, once learned, makes little intrusion into that special first-person, personal world of our consciousness. These memories for skills can therefore be left within the orderly interstices of cells that make up the cerebellum. Consider instead the other broad class of memory, the type that permeates most intimately our conscious, everyday thoughts and determines our view of the outside world.

Completely separate from implicit, procedural memory is 'declarative memory' (Squire 1998). Declarative memory is explicit, in that we are aware we are remembering something in the first place. But what we are remembering can be divided further. On the one hand, there is memory for facts, such as the French word for *table* or the habits of cockroaches. On the other hand, there is the memory of spending a day last summer at the seaside with Auntie Flo. Initially, these two types of memory are treated in the same way by the brain. Central to operations is the hippocampus, so named because of its supposed resemblance in shape to a seahorse. [...]

In some way, the role of the hippocampus appears to be like scaffolding on a building or training wheels on a 5-year-old's bicycle: an essential feature during the development/learning/building process but obsolete once the end point is established. The vastly longer timescale of months and even years, exceeding as it does more familiar events at the one-to-one cellular level, suggests that for the memory of a complex event, which presumably requires the participation of many banks of neurons, the net activity of those neurons collectively must be consistently in a state of flux for very long periods.

You do not need to practise many excursions to the seaside with Auntie Flo in order to recall a single day trip. The simple model, then, of an increased efficiency between individual neuronal contacts established through repeated stimulation is therefore not sufficient here. One way of explaining why the hippocampus might be needed for such a long time, to lay down a unique memory of a complex event, might be precisely because it is a unique memory. Perhaps the hippocampus is acting like some kind of internalized practice device, in turn stimulating and eventually strengthening many types of earlier associations, covertly linked to a day at the seaside: perhaps for large numbers of neurons to be pressed into retaining a well-established memory, the scale of operations is such that the net time taken is much longer than for the strengthening of a single connection between two neurons isolated by neuroscientists under highly contrived experimental conditions, where a thin sliver of brain slice is kept alive in a dish for a few hours.

Internal iterations between hosts of disparate neurons would take time. In any event, during this lengthy period of consolidation of a memory, there would be some kind of cross-talk between the hippocampus and the all-enveloping outer region, the cortex. [...] The cortex has long been associated with higher functions, not only because damage there causes an impairment of memory and language functions but because, the more sophisticated the animal, in the evolutionary scheme of things, then seemingly the greater the surface area of cortex that species possesses.

The constellations of associations. finally forged after lengthy activation by the hippocampus, would constitute a single memory. As time goes on, however, the connections might be strengthened by further associations, or weakened or distorted. Biological memories, unlike those of a computer, are highly dynamic and continuously subject to subsequent influences meddling after the event.[11] [...]

By the end of the first year, the immediate world is sufficiently familiar and there are enough pre-established associations to elicit fear when a new stimulus impinges. As children start to make voluntary utterances to name objects spontaneously, they could be exhibiting the first early signs of communication – a sign that we know from bone relics preceded the Neanderthals. It is now, as they approach two years of age, that human infants start to exercise the unique birthright of the species, that is, the use of language.

According to the archaeologist Steven Mithen,[12] as we hominids have evolved, so have we been able to accommodate an increasing number of functional compartments within our brains, each of which is responsible for a different aspect of survival. For example, in addition to a general intelligence that presumably would come into play for problem-solving, we, along with many other species, also have a social intelligence that enables us to live in a highly organized tribe and to communicate by grooming and a series of signals. In addition, animals such as chimpanzees have a natural history intelligence that enables them to interpret immediately the significance of a snake as danger. Mithen's idea is that these specialized intelligences can be distinguished from the type of general intelligence that we have already seen liberates us from stereotypical, predictable, genetically ordained behaviour. Nowhere is this idea more obvious than with language.

Of course, it is very unlikely that language evolved overnight. As one of the first scientific thinkers, Lucretius, pointed out in the century preceding the birth of Christ, '… it was practical convenience that gave a form to the names of objects … . To suppose that someone on some particular occasion allotted names to objects, and that by this means men learnt their first words, is stark madness' (Lucretius 1994).

Evidence dating as far back as the Neanderthals some 200,000 years ago indicates that we were already communicating with language. The angle of bones in the jaw can be used to indicate the position of a long-decomposed larynx (Lieberman 1991). A low-lying larynx, just above the windpipe, would suggest ability for speech. Our adult human larynx is positioned low so that we can make a fuller range of non-nasal sounds: the larynx acts as a complex valve for exhaled air to come out in puffs, thus providing the energy for speech shaped by the lips and tongue. In non-human primates, and indeed in all other non-human animals, the larynx is positioned high so that it seals off the windpipe when food and liquids are being ingested. This anatomy is also characteristic of the human infant, who can thus suckle and breathe without choking to death. By contrast, we humans, as Darwin pointed out, have evolved with the unique ability of choking to death. Bones from the Neanderthals indicate that they, too, had low larynxes: such a risky anatomical move would probably only have been worth it if there was a very great pay-off, such as the ability to make a wide range of non-nasal sounds.

The anthropological neuroscientist, Terrence Deacon,[13] argues that language is distinct from complex avian vocalizations, the often subtle, conditioned responses of intelligent mammals, or indeed from our own emotional sobbing and laughter. Rather, the quintessence of language is the manipulation of symbols in a whole variety of flexible and changeable ways. At the age of around two years, this specialized language module is activated in the young human brain. The human child will suddenly have a specific talent, as starkly obvious in comparison with the chimp counterpart as if I (who am tone-deaf) had grown up with Mozart.

From this very early stage, the difference in agenda is clear: very young children, unlike intensively trained chimps, volunteer information about passing planes, cats and distant cars, even when such observations are not needed for survival. However, both Mithen and the physiologist William Calvin (1996) suggest that this language talent could also bootstrap with it other new skills. For example, language might go hand-in-hand with tool making. Once one has a word for an entity, a way of focusing one's thoughts on an object that is not actually present, then one can design and build, say, an axe head.

Rather than a specialized language intelligence, Mithen suggests that the rudimentary proto-language seen in chimpanzees and small children is a result of a general intelligence stretched to its limit and doing its best. Even primates that have been taught very sophisticated proto-languages, including complex manipulation of symbols, are incapable of copying our ancient hominid ancestors and building such artefacts. The only tool so far that a primate has built is a stick for fishing termites. Mithen, however, points out that such a task is relatively straightforward, given that the leaves are mere fragile appendages and lend themselves readily to being stripped off. The construction of a stick for fishing termites requires very little imagination, compared with an axe head, where the lump of stone itself offers very little inspiration in envisaging the finished product.

Calvin goes along with the idea that we share a proto-language with many animals, namely, the use of symbols and of naming, but that this talent is very different from the seemingly unique human ability to construct meaningful sentences. This task is, of course, far more intellectually challenging than generating single words, but sentences act as a kind of cerebral Trojan horse, via which a host of other very powerful benefits are unleashed. From here it follows that once sentence construction is in place, one can pass from mere labels to whole stories and once one has access to stories, then one ceases merely to react to the immediate, purely sensory, world around one.

Now, liberated from the present moment, we are thus at a huge advantage over even those other animals that can assign rudimentary labels to objects around them, the proto-language of manipulating plastic letters or computer icons. Along with sentence construction, the argument runs, one can pass from mere labels to whole stories with complex narratives and once one has access to story lines, one can plan ahead.

The idea of sentence construction inspires Calvin to turn to a 'two-for-the-price-of-one' principle of evolution. If we were developing skills to structure and order words, then an analogous structuring and ordering of actions could also be bootstrapped on, or vice versa. Hence, increasingly skilled movements would go hand-in-evolutionary-hand with more elaborate verbal relations – what Calvin refers to for both skills and speech as a 'structured string'. The idea of such structured strings of mental activity makes it possible to generalize still further from words and movements to abstract ideas. […]

It is in early childhood that the imagination is most fertile for the majority of us. Young children start to see links between objects, albeit frequently superficial or idiosyncratic ones: because these associations will be the result of relatively few experiences, they may well be suppressed later because more frequent associations become dominant or because the original pairings turn out to be supernumerary. On the other hand, at this early stage, thanks to language, connections are agile enough to be formed in the absence of external sensory cues, yet sufficiently unconstrained by inner resources rigorously cross-checked against endless variants of reality. At this stage, a child has a robust enough mind to become engrossed in a comic, with its visual prompts, but not mature enough to conjure up pictures entirely from words alone, as in adult novels. His or her need for sensory stimulation is decreased sufficiently in urgency to listening to stories, where the narrator adds tones of voice and interacts, but not to read a story undistracted on his or her own. And before these censoring inner resources are so firmly established, how much easier it is for a large cardboard box to become a car or a house, or to believe that Teddy really is alive like you are. It is this ability to see something in terms of something else, to use one's imagination, that Mithen points to as the apotheosis of human achievement over that of the other primates.

But as we grow further, we stunt our imaginations. Gradually, one screens out the instinctive fear of the dark, the sensual joy of a sunset or the awesome impact of the sheer size of the sea. Whereas Mithen offers the final stage of human evolution as the stage at which we can actually use our imaginations, I would argue there is one more stage, where the attainment of an individual adult mind matches the true civilizing of our ancestors. Wisdom and understanding replace magic and superstition. [...]

Notes

1 The initial stage, in concept formation is the recognition of an object that can move as a connected whole; see Spelke *et al.* (1995). The second step is to view an object not as all or none, but as composed of a number of different variables (Baillargeon 1996). However, the abstraction of the overriding property that distinguishes, say, a cat from a dog, irrespective of variables such as size, remains largely a debate for philosophers and is referred to as the question of 'universals'.

2 The neuronal mechanisms underlying the formation of new associations are still a subject of intense investigation. However, the best-known process is that of long-term potentiation, whereby a priming stimulation of a neuronal connection makes that connection more sensitive to subsequent, incoming signals; see Bliss and Collingridge (1993). A further important process is the modification to sticky sugars (cell adhesion molecules) that will help determine the configuration of neuronal connections: see Rose (1995) and Bailey and Kandel (1995).

3 Descartes's original dichotomy, that mind and physical matter are two separate entities, is known as 'substance dualism'. The problem with this distinction is that the concept of the non-physical as it stands can conflate mind, a mortal property of an individual, from soul, an entity that is allegedly immortal. This blurring has been circumvented by double aspect, or property, dualism, which acknowledges that the non-physical aspect of a person, his or her mind, is an implicit feature of his or her physical body, yet one not reducible to the physical components; see Kripke (1980) and McGinn (1982).

4 The implications of Skinner's ideas were that humans possessed no inner life, will, or intentions at all – that we possess no mind; see Skinner (1971).

5 See Parnavelas (1998). This article, written in a style that is only a little technical is also a useful overview of the early development of the brain.

6 Donald Hebb was a pioneer in psychology. As far back as the 1940s he was already suggesting that synapses could be strengthened by experience (Hebb 1949), a phenomenon shown experimentally some thirty years later.

7 For an overview for the more general reader, see Bliss (1998).

8 For a brief overview for the general reader, see Greenfield (1997).

9 For a simplified overview for the general reader, see Greenfield (1997).

10 See the chapter on *Sensorimotor Integration* in Churchland and Sejnowski (1992: 331–411).

11   For an account of 'Orwellian' and 'Stalinist' brain processes, see Dennett (1992).
12   See Steven Mithen's *The Prehistory of the Mind* (1996), a highly readable account for
     the general reader of 'the search for the origins of art, religion and science'. This book is
     ambitious in scope but clearly illustrated with provocative ideas.
13   In his book *The Symbolic Species* (1997), Deacon attempts to explain the question
     posed by his small son, 'Why don't animals speak a simpler language?' The book is com-
     prehensible to the general reader on the whole but becomes rather drawn out as it pro-
     gresses. Perhaps too many unnecessary excursions into, for example, the nature of
     consciousness, distract the reader from the original question, but overall, it is a good
     and fascinating read.

References

Bailey, C. H. and Kandel, E. R. (1995) 'Molecular and structural mechanisms underlying
    long-term memory', in M. S. Gazzaniga (ed.) *The Cognitive Neurosciences* (pp. 19–36),
    Cambridge, MA: MIT Press.
Baillargeon, R. (1996) 'Physical reasoning in infancy', in M. S. Gazzaniga (ed.) *The Cognitive
    Neurosciences* (pp. 181–204), Cambridge, MA: MIT Press.
Bliss, T. V. P. (1998) 'The physiological basis of memory', in S. Rose (ed.) *From Brains to
    Consciousness?* (pp. 73–93), Princeton, NJ: Princeton University Press.
—— and Collingridge, G. L. (1993) 'A synaptic model of memory: long-term potentiation
    in the hippocampus', *Nature* 361: 31–9.
Calvin, W. H. (1996) *How Brains Think: Evolving Intelligence, Then and Now*, London:
    Weidenfeld and Nicolson.
Churchland, P. and Sejnowski, T. J. (1992) *The Computational Brain*, Cambridge, MA: MIT
    Press.
Deacon, T. (1997) *The Symbolic Species: The Co-evolution of Language and the Human Brain*,
    New York: W. W Norton and Co.
Dennett, D. (1991) *Consciousness Explained*, Boston: Little, Brown and Co.
—— (1992) 'Temporal anomalies of consciousness: implications of the uncentered brain', in
    Y. Christen and P. Churchland (eds) *Neurophilosophy and Alzheimer's Disease* (pp. 5–17),
    New York: Springer-Verlag.
—— (1998) *Brainchildren: Essays on Designing Minds*, New York: Penguin.
Devlin, B., Daniels, M. and Roeder, K. (1997) 'The heritability of IQ', *Nature* 388: 468–71.
Greenfield, S. A. (1997) *The Human Brain: A Guided Tour*, London: Weidenfeld and
    Nicolson.
Harth, E. (1993) *The Creative Loop: How the Brain Makes a Mind*, Reading, MA: Addison-
    Wesley.
Hebb, D. O. (1949) *The Organization of Behavior*, New York: John Wiley and Sons.
James, W. (1890, reprinted 1981) *The Principles of Psychology*, Vol I, New York: Cambridge
    University Press.
Kandel, E. R., Schwartz, J. H. and Jessell, T. M. (eds) (1991) *Principles of Neural Science*,
    3rd edn, New York: Elsevier.
Kolb, B. (1995) *Brain Plasticity and Behavior*, Mahwah, NJ: Lawrence Erlbaum Associates.
Kripke, S. (1980) *Naming and Necessity*, Cambridge, MA: Harvard University Press.
Lacoutere, L. J. (1995) *Results: A Multibiography*, Washington, DC: Counterpoint.
Levitan, I. B. and Kaczmarek, L. K. (1996) *The Neuron: Cell and Molecular Biology*, 2nd edn,
    New York: Oxford University Press.

Lieberman, P. (1991) *Uniquely Human: The Evolution of Speech, Thought and Selfless Behavior*, Cambridge, MA: Harvard University Press.

Lucretius (1994) *On the Nature of the Universe*, trans. R. E. Latham, revised and annotated J. Godwin, New York: Penguin.

Martin, K. C. and Kandel, E. R. (1996) 'Cell adhesion molecules, CREB, and the formation of new synaptic connections during development and learning, *Neuron* 17: 567–70.

——, Michael, D., Rose, J. C., *et al.* (1997) 'MAP kinase translocates into the nucleus of the presynaptic cell and is required for long term facilitation in Aplysia', *Neuron*, 18: 899–912.

McGinn, C. (1982) *The Character of Mind*, New York: Oxford University Press.

Mithen, S. (1996) *The Prehistory of the Mind: A Search for the Origins of Art, Religion and Science*, London: Thames and Hudson.

Neville, H., Mills, D. and Lawson, D. (1992) 'Fractionating language: different neural subsystems with different sensitive periods', *Cerebral Cortex* 2: 244–58.

Parnavelas, J. (1998) 'The human brain: 100 billion connected cells', in S. Rose (ed.) *From Brains to Consciousness?* (pp. 18–32), Princeton, NJ: Princeton University Press.

Purves, D. (1994) *Neural Activity and the Growth of the Brain*, New York: Cambridge University Press.

Ricklefs, R. E. and Finch, C. E. (1995) *Aging: A Natural History*, New York: Scientific American Library.

Rose, S. (1995) 'Cell adhesion molecules, glucocorticoids and long-term memory formation', *Trends in Neuroscience* 18: 502–6.

Skinner, B. F. (1971) *Beyond Freedom and Dignity*, New York: Knopf.

Spelke, E. S., Vishton, P. and von Hofsten, C. (1995) 'Object direction, object direction action and physical knowledge in infancy', in M. S. Gazzaniga (ed.) *The Cognitive Neurosciences*, Cambridge, MA: MIT Press.

Squire, L. R. (1998) 'Memory and brain systems', in S. Rose (ed.) *From Brain to Consciousness?* (pp. 53–72), Princeton, NJ: Princeton University Press.

Zeki, S. (1993) *A Vision of the Brain*, Oxford: Blackwell Scientific.

2.2 Constructing scientific knowledge in the classroom

Rosalind Driver, Hilary Asoko,
John Leach, Eduardo Mortimer
and Philip Scott

The core commitment of a constructivist position, that knowledge is not transmitted directly from one knower to another, but is actively built up by the learner, is shared by a wide range of different research traditions relating to science education. One tradition focuses on personal construction of meanings and the many informal theories that individuals develop about natural phenomena (Carey 1985; Carmichael *et al.* 1990; Pfundt and Duit 1985) as resulting from learners' personal interactions with physical events in their daily lives (Piaget 1970). Learning in classroom settings, from this perspective, is seen to require well-designed practical activities that challenge learners' prior conceptions, encouraging them to reorganize their personal theories. A different tradition portrays the knowledge-construction process as coming about through learners being encultured into scientific discourses (e.g. Edwards and Mercer 1987; Lemke 1990). Yet others see it as involving apprenticeship into scientific practices (Rogoff and Lave 1984). Our own work has focused on the study of ways in which school students' informal knowledge is drawn upon and interacts with the scientific ways of knowing introduced in the classroom (e.g. Johnston and Driver 1990; Scott 1993; Scott and Emberton 1994). Clearly there is a range of accounts of the processes by which knowledge construction takes place. Some clarification of these distinct perspectives and how they may interrelate appears to be needed.

A further issue that requires clarification among science educators is the relationship being proposed between constructivist views of learning and implications for pedagogy. Indeed, Millar (1989) has argued that particular views of learning do not necessarily entail specific pedagogical practices. Furthermore, the attempts that have been made to articulate 'constructivist' approaches to pedagogy in science (Driver and Oldham 1986; Fensham *et al.* 1994; Osborne and Freyberg 1985) have been criticized on the grounds that such pedagogical practices are founded on an empiricist view of the nature of science itself (Matthews 1992; Osborne 1993), an argument that is expanded later in this chapter.

In this chapter, we shall present our view of the interplay among the various factors of personal experience, language and socialization in the process of learning science in classrooms, and discuss the problematic relationships between scientific knowledge, the learning of science and pedagogy.

The nature of scientific knowledge

Any account of teaching and learning science needs to consider the nature of the knowledge to be taught. Although recent writings in the field of science studies emphasize that scientific practices cannot be characterized in a simplistic unitary way, that is, there is no single 'nature of science' (Millar *et al.* 1993), there are some core commitments associated with scientific practices and knowledge claims that have implications for science education. We argue that it is important in science education to appreciate that scientific knowledge is both symbolic in nature and also socially negotiated. The objects of science are not the phenomena of nature but constructs that are advanced by the scientific community to interpret nature. Hanson (1958) gives an eloquent illustration of the difference between the concepts of science and the phenomena of the world in his account of Galileo's intellectual struggles to explain free-fall motion. For several years, Galileo collected measurements of falling objects representing acceleration in terms of an object's change in velocity over a given distance, a formulation that led to complex and inelegant relationships. Once he began to think about acceleration in terms of change of velocity in a given time interval, then the constant acceleration of falling objects became apparent. The notion of acceleration did not emerge in a non-problematic way from observations but was imposed upon them. Scientific knowledge in many domains, whether explanations of the behaviour of electrical circuits, energy flow through ecosystems or rates of chemical reactions, consists of formally specified entities and the relationships posited as existing between them. The point is that, even in relatively simple domains of science, the concepts used to describe and model the domain are not revealed in an obvious way by reading the 'book of nature'. Rather, they are constructs that have been invented and imposed on phenomena in attempts to interpret and explain them, often as results of considerable intellectual struggles.

Once such knowledge has been constructed and agreed within the scientific community, it becomes part of the 'taken-for-granted' way of seeing things within that community. As a result, the symbolic world of science is now populated with entities such as atoms, electrons, ions, fields and fluxes, genes and chromosomes; it is organized by ideas such as evolution and encompasses procedures of measurement and experiment. These ontological entities, organizing concepts and associated epistemology and practices of science are unlikely to be discovered by individuals through their own observations of the natural world. Scientific knowledge, as public knowledge, is constructed and communicated through the culture and social institutions of science.

There are studies in the history and sociology of science that portray the knowledge that emerges as a result of activity within the scientific community as relativist and solely the result of social processes (Collins 1985; Latour and Woolgar 1979). Moreover, this relativist position argues that there is no way of knowing whether such knowledge is a 'true' reflection of the world and that the notion of scientific 'progress' is therefore problematic. This apparent 'irrationalism' and associated relativism of science is currently a matter of dispute in science studies and science education. However, a view of scientific knowledge as socially constructed does not logically imply relativism. In proposing a realist ontology, Harré (1986) suggests that scientific knowledge is constrained by how the world is and that scientific progress has an empirical basis, even though it is socially constructed and validated (a position that we find convincing).

Whether or not a relativist perspective is adopted, however, the view of scientific knowledge as socially constructed and validated has important implications for science education. It means that learning science involves being initiated into scientific ways of knowing. Scientific entities and ideas, which are constructed, validated and communicated through the cultural institutions of science, are unlikely to be discovered by individuals through their own empirical enquiry; learning science thus involves being initiated into the ideas and practices of the scientific community and making these ideas and practices meaningful at an individual level. The role of the science educator is to mediate scientific knowledge for learners, to help them make personal sense of the ways in which knowledge claims are generated and validated, rather than to organize individual sense-making about the natural world. This perspective on pedagogy, therefore, differs fundamentally from an empiricist perspective.

Learning science as an individual activity

Although Piaget did not refer to himself as a 'constructivist' until later in his life (Piaget 1970), the view that knowledge is constructed by the cognizing subject is central to his position. As his statement 'l'intelligence organise le monde en s'organisant elle-même' (intelligence organizes the world by organizing itself; 1937: 311) reflects Piaget's central concern was with the process by which humans construct their knowledge of the world. In broad terms, Piaget postulated the existence of cognitive schemes that are formed and developed through the coordination and internalization of a person's actions on objects in the world. These schemes evolve as a result of a process of adaptation to more complex experiences (through the process Piaget called equilibration). New schemes thus come into being by modifying old ones. In this way, intellectual development is seen as progressive adaptation of an individual's cognitive schemes to the physical environment. Piaget acknowledged that social interaction could play a part in promoting cognitive development through, for example, making different viewpoints available to children through discussion. For development to occur, however, equilibration at the individual level is seen as essential.

Although later in his life Piaget addressed the relationship between individual knowledge schemes and the history of science (Piaget and Garcia 1989) and, indeed, his underlying quest was essentially epistemological, the focus of much of his research programme was on how individuals make sense of the physical world through the development of content-independent logical structures and operations. By contrast, the research programme into children's scientific reasoning that has emerged over the past twenty years has focused on domain-specific knowledge schemes in the context of children's learning of science. Children's conceptions of physical phenomena have been documented in a wide range of science domains (Carmichael *et al.* 1990; Driver *et al.* 1985; Pfundt and Duit 1985; West and Pines 1985). Although this field of research focuses on domain-specific knowledge rather than general reasoning schemes, it shares a number of commonalities with a Piagetian perspective and can lead to similar perspectives on pedagogy. Both view meaning as being made by individuals and assert that meaning depends on the individual's current knowledge schemes. Learning comes about when those schemes change through the resolution of disequilibration. Such resolution requires internal mental activity and results in a previous knowledge scheme being modified. Learning is thus seen as involving a process of conceptual change. Teaching approaches in science based on this perspective focus on providing children with physical experiences that induce cognitive conflict and hence encourage learners to develop new knowledge schemes that are better adapted to experience. Practical activities supported by group discussions form the core of such pedagogical practices (see, for example, Nussbaum and Novick 1982; Rowell and Dawson 1984). From this personal perspective, classrooms are places where individuals are actively engaged with others in attempting to understand and interpret phenomena for themselves and where social interaction in groups is seen to provide the stimulus of differing perspectives on which individuals can reflect. The teacher's role is to provide the physical experiences and to encourage reflection. Children's meanings are listened to and respectfully questioned. In the following passage, Duckworth describes clearly the kinds of interventions that are helpful:

> What do you mean? How did you do that? Why do you say that? How does that fit in with what she just said? Could you give me an example? How did you figure that? In every case these questions are primarily a way for the interlocutor to try to understand what the other is understanding. Yet in every case, also, they engage the other's thoughts and take them a step further.
>
> (Duckworth 1987: 96–7)

The teacher's activities and interventions are thus portrayed as promoting thought and reflection on the part of the learner with requests for argument and evidence in support of assertions. There is, in our view, a significant omission from this perspective on knowledge construction. Developments in learners' cognitive structures are seen as coming about through the interaction of these structures with features of an external *physical* reality, with meaning-making being stimulated by peer interaction. What is not considered in a substantial way is the learners' interactions with *symbolic* realities, the cultural tools of science.

Furthermore, in viewing learning as involving the replacement of old knowledge schemes with new, the perspective ignores the possibility of individuals having plural conceptual schemes, each appropriate to specific social settings. (Scientists, after all, understand perfectly well what is meant when they are told 'Shut the door and keep the cold out' or 'Please feed the plants'.) Rather than successive equilibrations, it is argued that learning may be better characterized by parallel constructions relating to specific contexts (Solomon 1983). Bachelard's (1940/1968) notion of 'conceptual profile' can usefully be drawn on here. Instead of constructing a unique and powerful idea, individuals are portrayed as having different ways of thinking, that is, a conceptual profile, within specific domains. For example, in everyday life, a continuous view of matter is usually adequate in dealing with the properties and behaviour of solid substances. Different perspectives can, however, be drawn upon: a quantum view of matter is epistemologically and ontologically different from an atomistic view and both of these are different from a continuous model. These three perspectives might form an individual's conceptual profile for solids and each will be appropriate in different contexts. Thus, a chemist dealing with a synthesis reaction might find it more useful to consider atoms as material particles rather than as a set of mathematical singularities in fields of force (Mortimer 1993).

Learning science as the social construction of knowledge

Whereas the individual construction of knowledge perspective places primacy on physical experiences and their role in learning science, a social constructivist perspective recognizes that learning involves being introduced to a symbolic world. This is well expressed in Bruner's introduction to Vygotsky's work:

> The Vygotskian project [is] to find the manner in which aspirant members of a culture learn from their tutors, the vicars of their culture, how to understand the world. That world is a *symbolic world* in the sense that it consists of conceptually organized, rule bound belief systems about *what exists*, about how to get to goals, about what is to be valued. There is no way, none, in which a human being could possibly master that world without the aid and assistance of others for, in fact, that world *is* others.
>
> (Bruner 1985: 32)

From this perspective, knowledge and understandings, including scientific understandings, are constructed when individuals engage socially in talk and activity about shared problems or tasks. Making meaning is thus a dialogic process involving persons-in-conversation and learning is seen as the process by which individuals are introduced to a culture by more skilled members. As this happens they 'appropriate' the cultural tools through their involvement in the activities of this culture. A more experienced member of a culture can support a less experienced member by structuring tasks, making it possible for the less experienced person to perform them and to internalize the process, that is, to convert them into tools for conscious control.

There is an important point at issue here for science education. If knowledge construction is seen solely as an individual process, then this is similar to that which has traditionally been identified as discovery learning. If, however, learners are to be given access to the knowledge systems of science, the process of knowledge construction must go beyond personal empirical enquiry. Learners need to be given access not only to physical experiences but also to the concepts and models of conventional science. The challenge lies in helping learners to appropriate these models for themselves, to appreciate their domains of applicability and, within such domains, to be able to use them. If teaching is to lead students toward conventional science ideas, then the teacher's intervention is essential, both to provide appropriate experiential evidence and to make the cultural tools and conventions of the science community available to students. The challenge is one of how to achieve such a process of enculturation successfully in the round of normal classroom life. Furthermore, there are special challenges when the science view that the teacher is presenting is in conflict with learners' prior knowledge schemes.

Informal science ideas and common-sense knowledge

Young people have a range of knowledge schemes that are drawn on to interpret the phenomena they encounter in their daily lives. These are strongly supported by personal experience and socialization into a 'common sense' view. Research conducted worldwide has shown that children's informal science ideas are not completely idiosyncratic; within particular science domains, there are commonly occurring informal ways of modelling and interpreting phenomena that are found among children from different countries, languages and education systems. One of the areas that has been most thoroughly studied is informal reasoning about mechanics. Here there is a commonly held conception that a constant force is necessary to maintain an object in constant motion (Clement 1982; Gunstone and Watts 1985; Viennot 1979). This notion differs from that of Newtonian physics, which associates force with *change* in motion, that is, acceleration. It is not, however, difficult to understand how experiences such as pushing heavy objects across a floor or pedalling a bicycle can be seen to fit with a 'constant motion implies a constant force' notion. In another domain, that of reasoning about material substance, children see no problems in considering matter as appearing and disappearing. When a log fire burns down to a pile of ash, children state that matter is 'burnt away' (Andersson 1991). Older children may acknowledge that there are gaseous products from the fire. These, however, are not seen as substantive but as having different ethereal properties (Meheut *et al.* 1985). 'Gases, after all, cannot have mass or weight; otherwise, why don't they just fall down?' Indeed, for many young people, the idea that air or gas can have weight is most implausible. Many even postulate that they have negative weight in that they tend to make things go upwards (Brook *et al.* 1989; Stavy 1988). A similar form of reasoning is used about the role of gases in biological processes such as photosynthesis, respiration and decay.

These are just some examples of the types of informal ideas that are pervasive in the reasoning of young people and adults. In the domains such as those referred to here, we argue that there are commonalities in informal ways of reasoning, partly because members of a culture have shared ways of referring to and talking about particular phenomena. In addition, the ways in which individuals experience natural phenomena are also constrained by the way the world is.

As far as people's everyday experiences are concerned, the informal ideas are often perfectly adequate to interpret and guide action. Fires *do* burn down to result in a small pile of ash – a widely used way of getting rid of unwanted rubbish. If you want to keep a piano moving across the floor, you *do* need to keep up a constant push. It is not surprising that ideas that are used and found useful are then represented in everyday language. Phrases such as being 'as light as air' or something being 'completely burned up' both reflect and give further support to underlying informal ideas. We argue, therefore, that informal ideas are not simply personal views of the world but that they reflect a shared view represented by a shared language. This shared view constitutes a socially constructed 'common sense' way of describing and explaining the world.

During the years of childhood, children's ideas evolve as a result of experience and socialization into 'common sense' views. For very young children (aged 4–6), air only exists as a wind or a draught – young children do not conceptualize air as a material substance. The notion of air as *stuff* normally becomes part of children's models of the world by age seven or eight. This stuff is then conceptualized as occupying space but as being weightless or even having negative weight or *upness* (Brook *et al.* 1989). This example illustrates a much more general point: that the entities, such as air-as-stuff, that are taken as real by children, may be quite different at different ages. In other words, children's everyday ontological frameworks evolve with experience and language use within a culture. This change corresponds to that which others describe as radical restructuring of children's domain-specific conceptions (see Carey 1985; Vosniadou and Brewer 1992).

'Common-sense' ways of explaining phenomena, as pictured here, represent knowledge of the world portrayed within everyday culture. They differ from the knowledge of the scientific community in a number of ways. Most obviously, common sense and science differ in the ontological entities they contain: the entities that are taken as real within everyday discourse differ from those of the scientific community. Second, common-sense reasoning, although it can be complex, also tends to be tacit or without explicit rules. Scientific reasoning, by contrast, is characterized by the explicit formulation of theories that can then be communicated and inspected in the light of evidence. In science, this process involves many scientists in communication with one another. Although tacit knowledge undoubtedly has a place in science, the need for explicitness in the formulation of theories is central to the scientific endeavour. Third, everyday reasoning is characterized by pragmatism. Ideas are judged in terms of being useful for specific purposes or in specific situations and, as such, they guide people's actions. The scientific endeavour, on the other hand, has an additional purpose of constructing a general and coherent picture of the world. The scientific commitment, therefore, is not satisfied by situationally specific models, but strives for models with the greatest generality and scope.

Learning science as involving individual and social processes

We now consider what we see as the implications of the distinctions between common sense and scientific reasoning for the learning of science. We have argued that learning science is not a matter of simply extending young people's knowledge of phenomena – a practice perhaps more appropriately called nature study – nor of developing and organizing young people's common-sense reasoning. It requires more than challenging learners' prior ideas through discrepant events. Learning science involves young people entering into a different way of thinking about and explaining the natural world; becoming socialized to a greater or lesser extent into the practices of the scientific community with its particular purposes, ways of seeing and ways of supporting its knowledge claims. Before this can happen, however, individuals must engage in a process of personal construction and meaning-making. Characterized in this way, learning science involves both personal and social processes. On the social plane, the process involves being introduced to the concepts, symbols and conventions of the scientific community. Entering into this community of discourse is not something that students discover for themselves any more than they would discover by themselves how to speak Esperanto. [...]

A social perspective on learning in classrooms recognizes that an important way in which novices are introduced to a community of knowledge is through discourse in the context of relevant tasks. Science classrooms are now being recognized as forming communities that are characterized by distinct discursive practices (Lemke 1990). By being engaged in those practices, students are socialized into a particular community of knowledge, a process described as a cultural apprenticeship (Rogoff and Lave 1984; Seely Brown *et al.* 1989). The discursive practices in science classrooms differ substantially from the practices of scientific argument and enquiry that take place within various communities of professional scientists; this is hardly surprising when one considers the differences between schools and the various institutional settings of science in terms of purposes and power relationships. This disjunction has been recognized and some science education researchers are experimenting with ways of organizing classrooms so as to reflect particular forms of collaborative enquiry that can support students in gradually mastering some of the norms and practices that are deemed to be characteristic of scientific communities (Eichinger *et al.* 1991; Roseberry *et al.* 1992).

Learning in the science classroom

In this section, we identify some of the discursive practices that support the co-construction of scientific knowledge by teachers and students and that also reflect features of scientific argumentation. We present brief episodes of teaching and learning in science classrooms and draw upon both personal and social perspectives on learning to interpret what is happening in each case. The examples are taken from studies that we have conducted in science classrooms in the United Kingdom, in collaboration with teachers, in which explicit attention has been given to the differences between students' informal thinking about a particular topic and the science view (Scott *et al.* 1992).

The episodes are not intended to present exemplary instances of teaching and learning. Rather, they have been selected to illustrate the ways in which students develop personal meanings in the social context of the classroom, how scientific meanings are appropriated and how ontological and epistemological differences between informal and science views can create obstacles to personal understanding.

Light rays: negotiating 'new conceptual tools' – new ontological entities

A class of eight- to nine-year-old pupils was involved in an introductory series of lessons on light (see Asoko 1993). Children at this age tend to consider light as a source or an effect (Guesne 1985) and are less likely to conceptualize light as existing in space and travelling out from a source. The teacher, Michael, was interested in helping the class to develop the idea that light travels through space and that it travels in straight lines. Once he had established agreement that light travels in straight lines, he planned to introduce the conventional representation of light 'rays'.

Initially, Michael invited the class to consider the light in their classroom, which the children all agreed was sunlight. He then explored this notion with them further by asking where the sunlight comes from.

Pupil 1:   From the Sun.
Michael: You mean that the light that's coming through that window has come from the Sun? (several simultaneous replies).
Pupil 2:   It's from the heat – because it is so hot it makes a bright light.
Michael: So how does it get here? If the light is at the Sun, how come it is here as well? Martyn?
Pupil 3:   'Cause the Sun's shining on us.
Michael: But it is ninety-three million miles away – so how come the light from the Sun is here on the table?
Pupil 4:   Is it because of the ozone layer? (There then followed a short exchange in which several pupils contributed ideas about the hole in the ozone layer allowing more sunlight through, after which Michael re-posed the question.)
Michael: But how does the sunlight get here?
Pupil 5:   It travels here.
Michael: Coulton says, and his exact words are, that 'it travels here'. In other words, light moves from the Sun to here ...
Pupil 5:   Yes.
Michael: Ninety-three million miles. Is that right?
Pupils: Yes (chorus of many voices).

In this interchange, Michael indicated that the Sun 'shining' could be further elaborated and, with contributions from the class, focused on the idea of light as something that travels out from the source through space. His interaction with the class as this idea was explored gives an indication that the idea is generally accepted as plausible, an important feature in the co-construction of classroom knowledge.

The idea that light travels was further developed through a practical activity carried out in groups. Each group of three-to-four children had a set of equipment comprising a 12-volt bulb placed centrally under an octagonal cardboard box about 35 cm in diameter, placed on a large sheet of paper. A slit about 12 cm high and 0.5 cm wide was cut in each of the eight faces. The children were asked to think about what they would see when the bulb was switched on and to draw what they expected to see on the paper. Almost all the children drew lines at 90° to the faces extending from the slit to indicate the path of the light. The lines varied in length from 2–3 cm to about 30 cm. When all the children had made at least one prediction, all the lamps were switched on simultaneously in the darkened room. The spectacular effect caused some excitement and not a little surprise when children realized that instead of travelling only a short distance, the beams of light continued across the paper and could be seen, in a vertical plane, when they met a surface such as the wall or a child's body.

Michael called the class together to discuss their observations. He drew a plan view of the octagonal box on a flip chart. Drawing a line to represent the path of the light, he commented that everyone had made predictions about the position of the line that agreed with what they saw, but commented that many people in the class thought the light would stop.

Michael: Is that right?
Pupil 1:   No, it carries on.
Michael: It carries on. How long would it carry on?
Pupil 2:   Right to the end. Just keeps carrying on.
Pupil 3:   Just keeps carrying on, is that …
Pupil 4:   It can't stop. You can't stop light without turning it off.

In this sequence, the notion that light 'keeps carrying on' is again interpreted in part of a shared discourse. Michael then invited children to come up and draw more lines on his drawing to show where the light will go. After the children had done this, he began using the words *ray of light* to describe the path of light.

In this extended set of sequences, Michael was introducing the children, through discourse, to the scientific *way of seeing*, making it plausible to them in the context of a memorable experience. Once he had satisfied himself that the children had a mental representation for 'the path the light travels along', he introduced the convention or symbolic representation of the light ray, a cultural tool that would be used in subsequent lessons. Throughout the sequence, a coherent story evolved, a story that Michael, through feedback, checked was shared by the class. This process of developing shared meaning between teacher and students is at the heart of making what Edwards and Mercer (1987) call *common knowledge* in the classroom. This common knowledge or shared discourse then referred to a new ontological framework about light, a framework in which light travels and travels in straight lines (represented symbolically by 'light rays') over long distances.

Air pressure: scaffolding 'a new way of explaining' – conflict between common sense and scientific views

The process by which new ways of explaining are developed by students can involve dialogic interactions between the teacher and individuals, or small groups of students. In these interactions, the adult (or a more competent peer) provides what Bruner (1986) called 'scaffolding' for the students' learning as they construct new meanings for themselves.

In an instructional sequence on air pressure with 11- to 12-year-old students (Scott 1993), the teacher had developed, through demonstrations and discourse with the class, a new way of explaining a range of simple phenomena (such as why a plastic bottle collapses inward when air is withdrawn from it). This new way of explaining was based on differences in air pressure inside and outside the bottle and the class was then asked to work in groups to use the pressure difference idea to explain further phenomena, such as how suction cups hold on to surfaces and how a liquid can be drawn into a teat pipette.

In the following passages, we see examples of an adult 'expert' attempting to 'scaffold students' reasoning in terms of a pressure difference model. We also see the ways in which students' existing informal theories, such as 'vacuums suck', influence their personal sense-making.

Christa and Adele completed an activity with the suction cups and were surprised at the amount of force needed to pull them off a smooth surface. They considered their explanation for this:

Christa: It's a flat surface and there's no air in the cup there, so there's less air in than there is in the outside, so it'll stick down.
Adult: So what *does* this pushing … this sticking it down?
Christa: Air.
Adele: Suction.
Adult: What's suction?
Adele: It's something that pulls … it's something that pulls it down …
Adult: A minute or two ago, you said it was something to do with pushing the air out here.
Adele: Yeah.
Adult: And then you also said it was something to do with suction. Are these the same explanations, or are they different?
Adele: They're nearly … (Adele is not sure and comes to a halt.)

The adult then referred the two girls to the earlier demonstration of the collapsing plastic bottle that they explained in terms of the difference in air pressure inside and out. The girls then returned to consider the case of the suction cups.

Adult:	Now, where's the inside and the outside of this?
Adele:	Well … that's the inside (indicates the underside of the suction cup).
Adult:	Yes, … right.
Adele:	Yeah, and that's the outside.
Adult:	Uh huh –can you use the explanation like the one used for the bottle to explain what happens here? (The adult refers once again back to the collapsing plastic bottle.)
Adele:	Has it got anything to do with gravity?
Adult:	What makes you say that?
Adele:	Pulling it down.

After further exchanges, Adele and the adult agreed that you can have gravity acting even when there is no air, so they are really different things. They continued considering the suction cups:

Adele:	It's sticking to the bottom of there – it [air] all comes out of the sides.
Adult:	All right, and what about the air on the outside?
Christa:	And the air on the outside's pushing it *down.*
Adele:	So it's hard to pull up.

In this extract, the adult structured the course of the reasoning, first reminding the girls of the explanation the class constructed for the collapsing plastic bottle and then supporting the girls in making the link to the case of the suction cup by guiding them to consider the air inside and the air outside.

Shortly afterwards, Adele raised a further question.

Adele:	How is it when you put it down and then you pull a little corner up it slips up?
Adult:	That's a very good question. Do you want to think about that for a minute?
Adele:	It's, it's ….
Christa:	No, I'll show you what it is. It's the air, it can get back in, can't it?
Adele:	Yeah, it's getting back in it, so the air's pushing it upwards, isn't it?
Both:	Yeah!

Here, the adult withdrew support or scaffolding from the girls, except for being an interested audience, and the girls confidently used the pressure difference explanation by themselves. However, a final question from Christa suggests that problems may still exist:

Adult:	Now … (long pause) … do you have any questions about this?
Christa:	Why … why does air push it down … when air's come out of the side? Why does air push it down?

Christa's question suggests that although she had been successful (with the support of the adult) in constructing the pressure difference explanation in this case, it may still lack plausibility for her ('*Why* does air push it down?'). In fact, it is highly unlikely that any previous experience or talk about static air would support the idea that it creates such large pressures. The new way of explaining challenges the students' ideas about what air can and cannot do; it challenges their personal ontologies of air.

The examples presented here draw attention to the fundamental (but frequently overlooked) point that different domains of science involve different *kinds* of learning. In the first example, the young students appeared to experience little difficulty in understanding and believing that light travels and keeps on trav-elling unless blocked. They adopted the scientific discourse and used the ideas productively. The situation in the second example appears to be rather different. The teacher had carefully engaged students in activities and discourse to support them in constructing the science view and yet we see them experiencing real diffi-culties in making those science models meaningful and appropriating them for themselves. We suggest that these differences in student response can, in part, be accounted for by considering the ontological and epistemological demands of learning in the separate science domains in question. What is common to both cases, however, is the process whereby a teacher, familiar with the scientific way-of-seeing, makes the cultural tools of science available to learners and supports their (re)construction of the ideas through discourse about shared physical events.

Summary and final comments

The view that scientific knowledge is socially constructed, validated and commu-nicated is central to this chapter. We have presented a perspective on science learning as a process of enculturation rather than discovery, arguing that empirical study of the natural world will not reveal scientific knowledge because scientific knowledge is discursive in nature. We have shown that learners of science have everyday representations of the phenomena that science explains. These represen-tations are constructed, communicated and validated within everyday culture. They evolve as individuals live within a culture. We have shown that there are epistemological and ontological differences between everyday and scientific reasoning. Although learning science involves social interactions, in the sense that the cultural tools of science have to be introduced to learners, we have argued that individuals have to make personal sense of newly introduced ways of viewing the world. If everyday representations of particular natural phenomena are very different from scientific representations, learning may prove difficult. We have argued that the relationship between views of learning and pedagogy is problematic and that no simple rules for pedagogical practice emerge from a constructivist view of learning. There are, however, important features of the mediation process that can be identified. If students are to adopt scientific ways of knowing, then interven-tion and negotiation with an authority – usually the teacher, is essential. Here, the critical feature is the nature of the dialogic process. The role of the authority figure has two important components. The first is to introduce new ideas or cultural tools where necessary and to provide the support and guidance for students to make sense of these for themselves. The other is to listen and diagnose the ways in which the instructional activities are being interpreted to inform further action. Teaching from this perspective is thus also a learning process for the teacher. Learning science in the classroom involves children entering a new community of discourse, a new culture; the teacher is the often hard-pressed tour guide mediating between children's everyday world and the world of science.

What is presented here differs fundamentally from the positivist programme in education with its emphasis on technical rationality and a non-problematic portrayal of the knowledge to be acquired. By participating in the discursive activities of science lessons, learners are socialized into the ways of knowing and practices of school science. This presents a major challenge for educators: the challenge lies in fostering a critical perspective on scientific culture among students. To develop such a perspective, students will need to be aware of the varied purposes of scientific knowledge, its limitations and the bases on which its claims are made. A crucial challenge for classroom life is, therefore, to make these epistemological features an explicit focus of discourse and hence to socialize learners into a critical perspective on science as a way of knowing. [...]

References

Andersson, B. (1991) 'Pupils' conceptions of matter and its transformations (age 12–16)', *Studies in Science Education* 18: 53–85.

Asoko, H. (1993) 'First steps in the construction of a theoretical model of light: a case study from a primary school classroom', in *Proceedings of the Third International Seminar on Misconceptions in Science and Mathematics Education*, Ithaca, NY: Misconceptions Trust.

Bachelard, G. (1968) *The Philosophy of No*, trans. G. C. Waterston, New York: Orion Press (original work published 1940).

Brook, A., Driver, P. and Hind, D. (1989) *Progression in Science. The Development of Pupils' Understanding of Physical Characteristics of Air across the Age Range 5–16 Years*, Leeds: Centre for Studies in Science and Mathematics Education, University of Leeds.

Bruner, J. (1985) 'Vygotsky: a historical and conceptual perspective', in J. Wertsh (ed.) *Culture, Communication and Cognition: Vygotskian Perspective* (pp. 21–34), Cambridge: Cambridge University Press.

—— (1986) *Actual Minds, Possible Worlds*, Cambridge, MA: Harvard University Press.

Carey, S. (1985) *Conceptual Change in Childhood*, Cambridge, MA: MIT Press.

Carmichael, P., Driver, R., Holding, B., Phillips, I., Twigger, D. and Watts, M. (1990) *Research on Students' Conceptions in Science: A Bibliography*, Leeds: Centre for Studies in Science and Mathematics Education, University of Leeds.

Clement, J. (1982) 'Student preconceptions in introductory mechanics', *American Journal of Physics* 50(1): 66–71.

Collins, H. M. (1985) *Changing Order*, London: Sage Publications.

Driver, R., Guesne, E. and Tiberghien, A. (1985) *Children's Ideas in Science*, Milton Keynes: Open University Press.

Driver, R. and Oldham, V. (1986) 'A constructivist approach to curriculum development in science', *Studies in Science Education* 13: 105–22.

Duckworth, E. (1987) *'The Having of Wonderful Ideas' and other Essays on Teaching and Learning*, New York: Teachers' College Press.

Edwards, D. and Mercer, N. (1987) *Common Knowledge,* London: Methuen.

Eichinger, D., Anderson, C. W., Palincsar, A. S. and David, Y. (1991, April). 'An illustration of the roles of content knowledge, scientific argument, and social norms in collaborative problem solving', paper presented at the Annual Meeting of the American Educational Research Association, Chicago, IL.

Fensham, R., Gunstone, R. and White, F. (eds) (1994) *The Content of Science,* London: Falmer Press.

Guesne, E. (1985) 'Light', in P. Driver, E. Guesne and A. Tiberghien, *Children's Ideas in Science* (pp. 10–32). Milton Keynes: Open University Press.

Gunstone, R. and Watts, M. (1985) 'Children's understanding of force and motion', in R. Driver, E. Guesne and A. Tiberghien (eds) *Children's Ideas in Science* (pp. 85–104), Milton Keynes: Open University Press.

Hanson, N. F. (1958) *Patterns of Discovery,* Cambridge: Cambridge University Press.

Harré, R. (1986) *Varieties of Realism,* Oxford: Blackwell.

Johnston, K. and Driver, R. (1990) *A Constructivist Approach to the Teaching of the Particulate Theory of Matter: A Report on a Scheme in Action,* Leeds: Centre for Studies in Science and Mathematics Education, University of Leeds,

Latour, B. and Woolgar, S. (1979) *Laboratory Life. The Social Construction of Scientific Facts,* London: Sage.

Lemke, J. (1990) *Talking Science,* Norwood, NJ: Ablex.

Matthews, M. (1992) 'Constructivism and empiricism: an incomplete divorce', *Research in Science Education* 22: 299–307.

Meheut, M., Saltie, E. and Tiberghien, A. (1985) 'Pupils' (11–12-year-old) conceptions of combustion', *European Journal of Science Education* 7(l): 83–93.

Millar, R. (1989) 'Constructive criticisms', *International Journal of Science Education* 11(5): 587–96.

——, Driver, R., Leach, J. and Scott, P. (1993) 'Students' understanding of the nature of science: philosophical and sociological foundations to the study', Working Paper 2 from the project 'The development of understanding of the nature of science', Leeds: Centre for Studies in Science and Mathematics Education, The University of Leeds.

Mortimer, E. F. (1993) 'Studying conceptual evolution in the classroom as conceptual profile change', *Proceedings of the Third International Seminar on Misconceptions in Science and Mathematics Education,* Ithaca, NY: Misconceptions Trust.

Nussbaum, J. and Novick, S. (1982) 'Alternative frameworks, conceptual conflict and accommodation', *Instructional Science* 11: 183–208.

Osborne, J. (1993) 'Beyond constructivism', *Proceedings of the Third International Seminar on Misconceptions in Science and Mathematics Education,* Ithaca, NY: Misconceptions Trust.

Osborne, F. and Freyberg, P. (1985) *Learning in Science. The Implications of Children's Science,* Auckland: Heinemann.

Pfundt, H. and Duit, R. (1985) *Bibliography. Students' Alternative Frameworks and Science Education,* Kiel: IPN.

Piaget, J. (1937) *La Construction de Réel chez L'enfant,* Neuchâtel, France: Delachaux et Niestlé.

—— (1970) *Genetic Epistemology,* trans. E. Duckworth, New York: Columbia University Press.

—— and Garcia, R. (1989) *Psychogenesis and the History of Science,* New York: Columbia University Press.

Rogoff, B. and Lave, J. (1984) *Everyday Cognition: Its Development in Social Context,* Cambridge, MA: Harvard University Press.

Roseberry, A., Warren, B. and Conant, F. (1992) *Approaches to Scientific Discourse: Findings from Language Minority Classrooms*, Working Paper No. 192, Cambridge, MA: TERC.

Rowell, J. A. and Dawson, C. J. (1984) 'Equilibration, conflict and instruction: A new class-oriented perspective', *European Journal of Science Education* 7: 331–4.

Scott, P. (1993) 'Overtures and obstacles: teaching and learning about air pressure in a high school classroom', *Proceedings of the Third International Seminar on Misconceptions in Science and Mathematics Education*, Ithaca, NY: Misconceptions Trust.

——, Asoko, H. and Driver, P. (1992) 'Teaching for conceptual change: a review of strategies', in R. Duit, F. Goldberg and H. Neidderer (eds) *Research in Physics Learning: Theoretical Issues and Empirical Studies* (pp. 310–29), Keil, Germany: Schmidt and Klannig.

——, Asoko, H., Driver, P. and Emberton, J. (1994) 'Working from children's ideas: an analysis of constructivist teaching in the context of a chemistry topic', in P. Fensham, R. Gunstone and R. White (eds) *The Content of Science*, London: Falmer.

Seely Brown, J., Collins, A. and Duguid, P. (1989) 'Situated cognition and the culture of learning', *Educational Researcher* 18(l): 32–42.

Solomon, J. (1983) 'Learning about energy: how pupils think in two domains', *European Journal of Science Education* 5(l): 49–59.

Stavy, R. (1988) 'Children's conception of gas', *International Journal of Science Education* 10(5): 552–60.

Viennot, L. (1979) 'Spontaneous reasoning in elementary dynamics', *European Journal of Science Education* 1(2): 205–22.

Vosniadou, S. and Brewer, W. F. (1992) 'Mental models of the earth: a study of conceptual change in childhood', *Cognitive Psychology* 24: 535–85.

West, L. and Pines, A. (eds) (1985) *Cognitive Structure and Conceptual Change*, Orlando, FL: Academic Press.

2.3 Transforming schools into communities of thinking and learning about serious matters

Ann L. Brown

In this chapter, I describe a programme of research referred to as Fostering Communities of Learners (FCL) and how I came to develop it. The aim of the programme is to design an environment in urban classrooms where grade school children learn to think deeply about serious matters.

Jerry Bruner (1996), who visited these classrooms, singled out four crucial ideas underlying FCL: (a) agency, (b) reflection, (c) collaboration and (d) culture:

> *action*
>
> The first of these is the idea of agency: taking more control of your own mental activity. The second is reflection: not simply 'learning in the raw' but making what you learn make sense, understanding it. The third is collaboration: sharing the resources of the mix of human beings involved in teaching and learning. Mind is inside the head, but it is also with others. And the fourth is culture, the way of life and thought that we construct, negotiate, institutionalize and finally (after it's all settled) end up by calling 'reality' to comfort ourselves.
>
> (Bruner 1996: 87)

Unfortunately, I could not have said it better myself.

There are three main themes running through this chapter. First is the theoretical question of learning to learn, or deuterolearning, a topic with an honourable history in psychology and education. Psychologists have been interested in this form of agency because of well recognized stumbling blocks to lasting learning: inert knowledge and passive learning. Students acquire facts that they cannot access and use appropriately; their knowledge is said to be inert (Whitehead 1916) or welded (Brown 1974) to its original occasion of use. Furthermore, students experiencing learned helplessness (Dweck 1975) do not readily engage in intentional, self-directed action.

During my career, I have been concerned with methods for helping passive learners achieve agency and reflection by introducing them to learning strategies that lead to transfer, or the flexible, appropriate, and even creative, use of knowledge. Ideally, understanding leads to generative, inventive and experimental use of knowledge as well as the ability to reflect on one's own activity. This area of research is known as metacognition (Brown 1975). Historically, there has been a tendency to think of such processes as domain-independent. But one cannot learn in a vacuum – being an expert novice (Brown *et al.* 1983) can take one only so far. In more recent years, I have become increasingly interested in what it is that children are required to learn and where and how they are required to learn it. The *what* of learning is the content; the curriculum or the domain, if you will. The *where* and the *how* of learning are the situation, or, in the case of FCL, the collaborative culture.

A second leitmotiv of this chapter is the contribution of basic and applied research. The reason I wrote the chapter is because I received an award for the application of psychology, primarily for my work in classroom settings. This is interesting because for most of my career, I studied children's learning in laboratory settings. My change in focus was gradual. Even though the research setting, laboratory versus classroom, changed dramatically, my goals remained the same: to work toward a theoretical model of learning and instruction rooted in a firm empirical base. I regard the classroom work as just as basic as my laboratory endeavours, even though the situated nature of the classroom research lends itself more readily to practical application. In the classroom, just as in the laboratory, I am in the business of devising design experiments (Brown 1992; Collins 1992) based on theoretical concepts that delineate why they work and thus render them reliable and repeatable. [...]

The third thesis of this chapter is that a knowledge of developmental psychology is not just nice but necessary if one wants to study learning in children, in whatever setting one chooses. Even though the major overarching psychological learning theories had their impact on educational practice, for better or for worse, developmental theories rarely did. The one exception is Piagetian theory, which often has been used to emphasize what children cannot do rather than what they can achieve.

Ideally, as a designer of learning environments, I should be a primary consumer of information from developmental psychology, to use a biological metaphor. Many of the most talented developmental psychologists spend a great deal of time arguing about what's biological about young children's thought. I need that information to design environments that encourage the growth of biological knowledge. But, by the same token, developmental psychologists should be primary consumers of design experiments that show what it is that children are ready to learn easily and what is resistant to exquisitely designed instruction.

Received wisdom about child as learner

My own early research efforts were aimed at mapping *bandwidths of competence* (Brown and Reeve 1987) or, if you will, zones of proximal development, through which children can navigate at various times and various speeds (Vygotsky 1978). While not ignoring the fact that young children are often less adept learners than are older ones, I took part in the movement to show earlier competence than was supposed, to offset the relatively pessimistic view of the child as learner that existed when I began. At the very least, the glass half-full is a more positive metaphor through which to view children's learning than is the glass half-empty. However, when I began to study the child as learner, there were four major perceived impediments to children's learning.

Learning capacity

There was a widespread belief that children are fragile learners because they lack mental capacity per se. This theory dates back to the turn of the century and is still alive today. And when background knowledge is controlled, as when no one 'has' it, undoubtedly older students outperform younger learners. This is true in a wide variety of situations that require effortful learning,

Strategic intervention

A great deal of work in the 1970s, including my own (Brown 1978), provided evidence that children's problems in learning were not simply a matter of mental capacity; the main culprit was children's inability to make use of what capacity they had. Passive in the face of instructions to learn, children were not known to recruit classical strategies to help them. Trained to use a variety of strategies, such as classifying, organizing, summarizing and so forth, children dramatically improved their learning performance. But there was a catch: when left to their own devices, there was little evidence of continued use (maintenance) or flexible deployment (transfer) of these strategies.

Metacognition

Gradually, it became apparent that children's failure to make use of their strategic repertoire was a problem of understanding; they had little insight into their own ability to learn intentionally; they lacked reflection. Children do not use a whole variety of learning strategies because they do not know much about the art of learning; they fail to appreciate the constraints of limited human memory capacity. Nor do children know how to alleviate the problem by using clever tactics. Furthermore, they know little about monitoring their own activities; that is, they do not think to plan, orchestrate, oversee or revise their own learning efforts. These are complex problems of metacognition.

Yet, even in problematic domains that demand effort and ingenuity, young children's strategic and metacognitive limitations are overstated. When very young children are asked to perform meaningful activities in hospitable environments (remembering the location of a desired object, etc.), they are strategic and monitor their performance quite successfully. One of my favourite examples of young ingenuity is that of three-year-olds who were asked to remember under which of three cups a toy dog had been hidden. One child looked at the target cup and nodded 'yes' and then looked at the non-target cups and nodded 'no'. Another three-year-old sneakily marked the correct cup by resting, his hand on it;

another moved the correct cup to a salient position – yes, cheating. They didn't know the rules of the game, but they knew about remembering. They were anything but passive and non-strategic (Wellman *et al.* 1975). This example involves strategies and the dawning of metacognition, a combination apparent in children as young as 18 months under the right conditions (Brown and DeLoache 1978).

Universal novices

Historically, however, it was assumed that young children are less effective learners than their older counterparts. The fact that the first five years of life represent an enormous growth in linguistic and conceptual competence did not allay that opinion. It is true that, because of their general lack of knowledge and expertise, children have been referred to as 'universal novices' (Brown and DeLoache 1978), but it is important to make the distinction between *ignorance* (i.e. lack of knowledge within which to reason) and *stupidity* (i.e. the inability to reason within knowledge fields one does understand). Children are ignorant in many ways but certainly not stupid.

For example, consider the classical analogy task, A:B::C:D. Piaget *et al.* (1977) believed that the ability to solve problems of this type was part of formal operational thought and this task is still used to select graduate students (Miller Analogies Test 1994). However, estimates of this ability typically confound knowledge and reasoning. When children fully understand the basis of analogy (e.g. simple causality such as cutting, breaking or wetting) or that the relation involved is a thematic one (bird:nest::dog:dog house), even pre-school children can achieve success. Take, for example, a four-year-old child who just correctly solved a series of thematic analogies. The child looked at the A:B::C:? problem, *bird:bird nest::dog:?* Without even considering the choices, the child answered incorrectly, 'puppy'.

Child: Bird lays eggs in her nest. Dog … dogs lay babies – um – and the name of the baby is puppy.
Experimenter: Let's look at our pictures [choices].
Child: I don't have to look. The name of the baby is puppies.
Experimenter: Just one look.

The child looks and selects the correct picture, a dog house (even though a picture of a puppy is present as a choice), but refuses to justify the correct solution, which is *lives in*.

As the experimenter prepared the next problem, the child was heard muttering in the background, 'And the name of the baby *is* puppy' (Goswami and Brown 1990).

Predisposition to learn in privileged domains

Until now, I have concentrated on constraints on children's learning interpreted in a negative sense. Another branch of developmental psychology turned in the other direction, looking at young children's positive biases to learn certain privileged classes of information readily and early in life. We now know that young children attend selectively to certain sources of information rather than others. To give just one example, infants learn rapidly about what makes objects and people move. Young children show an early understanding that animate objects have the potential to move themselves because they are 'biological stuff' – they obey what Gelman (1990) called the 'innards principle of mechanism'. Inanimate objects, in contrast, obey the external–agent principle; they cannot move themselves but must be propelled into action by an external force. And that force must be adequate for the job, as even 18-month-olds know when playing with sticks and strings as means for pulling and pushing (Brown 1990).

Fundamental to learning, from this position, is a search for cause, for determinism and mechanism. Children implicitly assume that events are caused and it is their job to uncover potential mechanisms. Indeed, they overdetermine cause, sometimes blinding themselves to essential notions of randomness and chance – a big problem in learning biology. These initial biases constrain what is selected from the range of available perceptual inputs to form the basis of emergent categories. The early differentiation between the properties of natural and artificial kind provides the impetus for growing knowledge about biological and physical causality. I discuss the advantage of capitalizing on the importance of understanding children's natural precocity to learn about biological mechanisms when designing environments in which they must learn about biological phenomena.

The contents and culture of learning

I turn now to what children are required to learn and when they are required to learn it. During the 1970s, psychologists interested in learning gradually shifted from the study of how learners remember lists of words, pictures and paired associates to a concentration on how learners understand coherent content. They began to look at the acquisition of expertise within a domain – gained over long periods of time through concentrated and self-motivated learning (e.g. chess, cooking). Contemporary learning theorists concentrate on how learners come to understand disciplined bodies of knowledge characteristic of academic subject areas (mathematics, physics, history, biology, etc.). [...]

Fostering a community of learners (FCL)

In this section, I describe my attempts to turn urban grade-school classes into science learning communities. The FCL project involves corridors of classrooms, sometimes whole schools, including primarily six- to twelve-year-old minority students. Obviously, I cannot describe the programme in detail. Here, I concentrate on the main philosophy and the science 'curriculum' that is practised.

The means by which a metacognitive culture of learning is set up is summarized in Figure 2.3.1. At its simplest level, there are three key parts. Students engage in independent and group research on some subset of a topic of inquiry. Mastery of the entire topic is ultimately the responsibility of all members of the class. This requires that they share their expertise with their classmates so that all may have

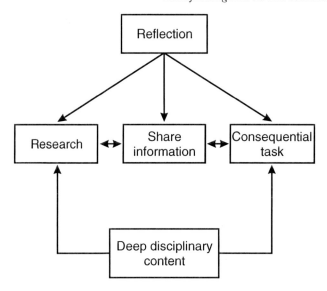

Figure 2.3.1 Schematic representation of the basic system of activities underlying FCL (Fostering Communities of Learners) practices

Source: Brown, A.L. and Campione, J.C. (1996), p. 273, reprinted with permission.

access to the entire topic. This sharing is further motivated by some consequential task or activity that demands that all students have learned about all aspects of the joint topic. This consequential task can be as traditional as a test or a quiz or some non-traditional activity such as designing a biopark to protect an endangered species. These three key activities – (a) research, (b) in order to share information, (c) in order to perform a consequential task – are overseen and coordinated by self-conscious reflection by all members of the community. In addition, the research–share–perform cycles of FCL cannot be carried out in a vacuum. The community relies on the fact that the participants are trying to understand deep disciplinary content. They are learning about something meaningful. As a concrete example of FCL, I discuss how children learn about environmental science.

Halfway through the year, the research process is well under way in a second-grade class. The big idea underlying the students' research is that of animal–habitat interdependence. Rarely do children choose to conduct research on a plant. Children do not identify with plants – after all, they are not alive: they just sit there (Gelman 1990). Six research groups are formed and begin working concurrently. Their chosen subtopics are (a) defence mechanisms, (b) predator–prey relations, (c) protection from the elements, (d) reproductive strategies, (e) communication and (f) food getting. There is, of course, overlap among the topics, but each group has a distinct agenda.

Each group has one piece of the puzzle it will need to perform the consequential task: to design an animal of the future that has evolved a solution to the six research groups' questions – reproductive strategies, protection from the elements, and so on. Opportunistically during the unit (of approximately 10 weeks), and always at the end of it, the students divide up into jigsaw (Aronson 1978) teaching groups. Each teaching group consists of one designated member of each of the research groups.

These designated members have the responsibility of teaching the remaining members of the group about their research topic in order to complete the consequential task, in this case to design an animal of the future. Thus, in each teaching group, the reciprocal teaching (RT) leader is an expert on the topic he or she leads. One child knows about predator–prey relations, someone can talk wisely on the strengths and weaknesses of possible methods of communication, and so forth. All pieces are needed to complete the puzzle, to design the 'complete animal'; hence jigsaw. Each jigsaw group designs an animal and presents it to the class and an array of visitors.

On the 'Design an Animal of the Future' task, I scored the proportion of biological solutions mentioned and the constraining links between solutions. By constraining links, I mean that if an animal were endowed with webbed feet to fit a swamp-like environment, other related design features would follow such as: has long legs and a beak, eats fish and waterborne insects, lays eggs, camouflages in reeds. In other words, a coherent picture akin to something like a marsh bird. Children could, however, include no links: that is, all of their six solutions could be independent. And that is indeed what happened in my first iteration when only one FCL unit was practised for three months. Although the children did provide five or six design solutions as required, those solutions were independent of each other.

To check whether this finding was typical developmentally, I then conducted a cross-sectional laboratory study where children not in FCL were asked to complete the same task after experience with only two similar tasks: design an animal to fit a specified habitat and design a habitat to fit a given, unfamiliar animal. These data, taken from children in grades 2, 4, 6 and 8, are shown in the left panel of Figure 2.3.2. These cross-sectional data confirmed my original microgenetic data: second-graders did not provide coherent, interrelated linkages in their design of animal survival mechanisms, whereas older children did so to a much greater extent.

But I did not stop there. I conducted a year-long intervention with second graders and found that they did manage some linkages, usually concerning the food chain and predator–prey relations. And, in the third replication, the class decided to design the habitats first and then the animal of the future to fit that habitat. This change resulted in a major improvement in the number of habitat-constrained linkages, with these second graders performing as well as sixth to eighth graders. These data are shown in the right panel of Figure 2.3.2.

Models of metacognition and expertise

On the importance of reflection and discussion

In Figure 2.3.1, I show that the research–share–consequential task scheme is subsumed under the overarching concept of reflection. The FCL programme, historically and intentionally, is a metacognitive environment. The classroom talk

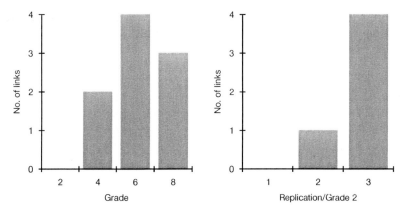

Figure 2.3.2 Cross-sectional (left) and microgenetic (right) data on the number of coherent connections between invented solutions in the design of an animal of the future

in FCL is largely metacognitive: 'Do I understand?' 'That doesn't make sense.' 'They [the audience] can't understand X without Y', and so forth.

Reflection and discussion are essential to the FCL classroom in which I explicitly aim to simulate the active exchange and reciprocity of a research seminar. FCL classrooms are intentionally designed to foster interpretive communities of discourse. FCL encourages newcomers to adopt the discourse structure, goals, values and belief systems of a community of research practices. The FCL community relies on the development of a discourse genre in which constructive discussion, questioning, querying and criticism are the mode rather than the exception. In time, these reflective activities become internalized as self-reflective practices and foster children's growing theories of learning (Brown *et al.* 1993).

How does one encourage this growth? Through adults, children and computers! Adults and visiting experts in FCL classrooms provide welcome sources of domain-area expertise but, most importantly, they also provide role models of thinking, planning and reflective processes.

Adults as role models

Visiting experts and classroom teachers bring the whole class together for benchmark lessons that serve several functions. First, they serve to *introduce the class to the big ideas and deep principles* at the beginning of a unit. Second, they occur when the class is ready to *progress toward higher levels of abstraction*. The experts lead the students to look for higher-order relations, encouraging students in the class to pool their knowledge in a novel conceptualization of the topic. For example, if the students have discovered the notion of energy and amount of food eaten, the experts might lead them toward the biological concept of metabolic rate. Third, the adults *model thinking and self-reflection* concerning how they would go about finding out about a topic or how they might reason with the information given or not given, as in the case of reasoning on the basis of incomplete information. Fourth, the adults continually ask students to *justify their opinions and support them with evidence*, to think of counter-examples to their rules, and so forth. Fifth, the adults ask the group to *summarize what is known and what still needs to be discovered*. Sixth, the adults lead the class in setting *new learning goals* to guide the next stage of inquiry.

Children teaching children

Children, as well as adults, enrich the system by contributing their particular expertise. Even after just one year in the programme (and more so after two or three years), FCL students have considerable expertise concerning both the domain itself and learning and teaching. Therefore, cross-age teaching becomes an important support for new learning. FCL uses cross-age teaching, both face-to-face and via electronic mail, and also provides older students as discussion leaders. Cross-age teaching not only increases the knowledge capital of the community but also provides students with invaluable opportunities to talk about learning. Cross-age teaching gives students responsibility and purpose and reinforces collaborative structures throughout the community (Bruner 1972).

On-line consultation

Face-to-face communication is not the only way of building community and expertise: FCL classrooms have the benefit of wider experience via electronic mail. Teachers' and students' expectations concerning excellence, or what it means to learn and understand, may be limited if the only standards are local. Experts coaching via electronic mail provides FCL with an essential resource: freeing teachers from the sole burden of being knowledge guardians and allowing the community to extend in ever-widening circles of expertise.

Face-to-face and on-line experts are not merely providers of much needed information, they act as role models of thinking, wondering, querying and making inferences on the basis of incomplete knowledge. Extending the learning community beyond the classroom walls to form virtual communities across time and space not only enriches the knowledge base available to students but also exposes them to models of reasoning and reflection about the learning process itself.

Deep disciplinary content at a developmentally appropriate level

Disciplinary content

Although initially designed as a thinking curriculum, FCL has always relied heavily on disciplinary content units of sufficient rigour to sustain in-depth research over substantial periods of time. One cannot expect students to invest intellectual curiosity and disciplined inquiry on trivia. There must be a challenge; there must be room to explore, to delve deeply, to understand at ever deepening levels of complexity. Here I discuss the development of the environmental science content about which the children are asked to reason and reflect.

FCL does not involve a curriculum in the usual sense because the students are partially responsible for designing their own. The curriculum teams, consisting of psychologists, teachers and domain-area experts, decide on central themes to be revisited over time. To support the 'discovery' of these themes, the classrooms are rich with human resources, such as visiting experts, older tutors and contacts via electronic mail. Ideally, classrooms are also provided with a selection of artefacts, hands-on experimental set-ups, books, videos, newspapers, periodicals and so forth that the students can use in the service of their research.

A main tenet is that an FCL unit should lead students to conduct research, read, write and think about a compelling deep theme at a developmentally appropriate level. It is precisely because the field knows something about the development of children's theories of biology that I initially selected the biological underpinnings of environmental science as a focus. The idea is to understand children's emergent theories about biology and lead them gradually toward deep principles of the discipline, such as interdependence, biodiversity, adaptation and evolution.

Although I believe it to be somewhat idealistic to think of young children entering the community of practice of adult academic disciplines, awareness of the deep principles of such disciplines enables the design teams to develop intellectual practices for young children that are stepping stones to mature understanding, or at least are not glaringly inconsistent with the end goal. For example, in the domain of ecology and environmental science, I realize that contemporary understanding of the underlying biology would necessitate a ready familiarity with biochemistry and genetics that is perhaps not within the grasp of young children. Instead of watering down such content to a strange mixture of the biological and the biochemical, as textbooks for young children often do, I invite young students into the world of nineteenth-century naturalists – scientists such as Darwin who also lacked modern knowledge of biochemistry and genetics. The idea is that by the time students are introduced to contemporary disciplinary knowledge, they have developed a thirst for that knowledge, as indeed has been the case historically.

Practically speaking, this means that as students across grades revisit, for example, the topic of endangered species, they gradually reach toward increasingly sophisticated disciplinary understanding. I rely on establishing a developmental corridor within a school. Children remain in this corridor for several years, during which time they delve more deeply into the underlying principles of a domain. Second-, fourth-, sixth-, and eighth-graders may be working on similar topics: extinction, endangered species, rebounding and assisted populations, selective breeding, and so forth. All will be guided by the basic disciplinary principles of interdependence and adaptation, but different levels of sophistication will be expected at each age, a spiralling curriculum (Bruner 1969), if you will. Topics are not just revisited willy-nilly at various ages at some unspecified level of sophistication, but each revisit is based on a deepening knowledge of that topic, critically dependent on past experience and on the developing knowledge base of the child. It matters what the underlying principles are at, say, kindergarten and grade 2; it matters that the sixth-grade students have experienced the fourth-grade curriculum.

As a primary consumer of information about children's biological understandings, I use this information to help develop an age-sensitive curriculum. Unfortunately, my suppliers are still uncertain about the age at which biology emerges as an intuitive theory. Carey (1996) claimed that biology does not emerge as an autonomous domain until the end of the first decade of life. Inagaki and Hatano (1993) and Keil (1992) argued that pre-school children have constructed an autonomous, intuitive biological theory. Wellman and Gelman (1992) are agnostic as to whether pre-school children have constructed biology as an intuitive theory. Whether or not one wants to call it theory, there is agreement that young children can reason at a primitive level about specific causal mechanisms: for example, maturational growth, inheritance of physical properties and disease transmission (Keil 1994, Wellman and Gelman 1992). And it seems safe, despite the controversy, to grant the six-year-old child with knowledge of causal agents (essences, innards, mechanical causality, etc.), in which case I can build on this reasoning, to develop an educational corridor.

A similar developmental guideline governs my approach to reasoning within the domain. For example, initially I capitalize on functional and teleological reasoning (Keil 1992) and an over-reliance on mechanistic causality in general, but then I press for an increasingly more sophisticated consideration of variability, uncertainty, probability and chance. Personification as analogy is a very powerful, if limited, reasoning strategy used by young children (and by adults, for that matter). It supports inductive reasoning and helps children distinguish between biological kinds and artefacts. I allow children to reason on this basis, putting off until later discussion of the limitations of this way of thinking.

Moving target

By deliberately aligning instruction to children's developing theories, I face a theoretical and practical issue about developmental sensitivity. Will ten-year-olds with prior experience in the programme be capable of acquiring and using domain knowledge of considerably greater complexity than ten-year-olds in the programme for the first time? To the degree that FCL is successful, I should be mapping a moving target. Of considerable theoretical interest to developmental psychologists are answers to the following question: 'Which forms of understanding are eminently teachable and which are immutable in the face of carefully tailored instruction?'

Developmental trajectories

Although FCL has made considerable headway at aligning an understanding of children's growing biological knowledge and the design of a biology curriculum for

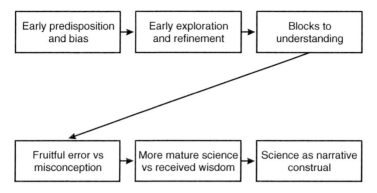

Figure 2.3.3 Idealized developmental corridor for the design of science instruction

grade school children, the field has far to go. Quite simply, a great deal more research is needed in both domains. Ideally, one needs to understand a developmental trajectory that grows in stepping stones toward mature thinking that would fill in the gaps of the schematic shown in Figure 2.3.3, beginning with knowledge of the early precocity of children as they enter pre-school. (In biology this would include form–function reasoning; differentiation between animate and inanimate, however shaky; a reasonable understanding of animal behaviour, particularly if the animal shares human characteristics, etc.) One can build on this early knowledge by extending and refining it and, at the same time, concentrating on suspected problems of interpretation, for example, the difference between dead in the biological sense and never alive in the sense of artefacts. Plants are alive too, a notion somewhat alien to first graders.

Implicit theories get one going and almost definitely form the basis of everyday concepts and plausible reasoning biases, such as those studied by Tversky and Kahneman (1974), and Bartlett (1958), for that matter. However, they can get in the way of formal reasoning that demands theory revision and radical conceptual change, which take time (Carey 1985). Schools came into existence to foster formal reasoning because *it is hard* and often involves abandoning naive theories for scientific ones. These are the blocks to learning shown in the schematic in Figure 2.3.3. Some consider that the concept of a rational number is such a block because it does not build on the early implicit theories of number. Statistical notions such as sample versus population and randomness and probability appear to be equally problematic for the development of biological thought. One needs to recognize children's conceptions that are fruitful errors – ones that are not mature understandings but, if carefully harnessed, will lead toward more mature understanding. Fruitful errors are distinct from misconceptions, which lead in the wrong direction and will impede the growth of scientific thinking unless they are replaced. Finally, the field needs to look at the hallmarks of the mature science as received wisdom undergoing change, to a relativist position that adds the essential notion of narrative invention (Bruner 1996; Medawar 1982) to a student's understanding of learning of science.

The field needs to understand such a trajectory in science *and* in the student's understanding of learning and reasoning about science; the child's epistemology, if you will. The field of developmental psychology is slowly but surely moving in that direction. This agenda will go a long way toward expanding on Vygotsky's (1978) notions of everyday versus scientific concepts and Piaget's (1978) conceptions of success and understanding and the epigenesis of formal operational thought. It will take thoughtful collaboration between domain-area specialists, science educators, psychologists, grade school teachers, and, yes, even students for us to reach these desired goals.

First principles of learning

Guiding the design of FCL is a set of learning principles that are addressed in detail elsewhere (Brown 1995; Brown and Campione 1994, 1996). Here I mention a subset that follows from Bruner's (1996) description quoted in the first paragraph of this chapter and the schematic summary of FCL shown in Figure 2.3.1.

Agency

FCL is intentionally designed to be an environment that emphasizes the active strategic nature of learning. Children consistently, routinely engage in a search for understanding and effort after meaning, as do teachers, students and researchers.

Reflection

Effective learners operate best when they have insight into their own strengths and weaknesses and access to their own repertoires of strategies for learning. For the past twenty years or so, this type of knowledge and control over thinking has been termed *metacognition*. Again, FCL is historically and intentionally a metacognitive environment with an atmosphere of wondering, querying and worrying about knowledge. All actors in the arena are engaged in reflective practices (most of the time or some of the time!). Initially, young learners are trapped into these thinking activities through such participant structures as RT and jigsaw, where everyone must think aloud, thus making the invisible visible (Brown 1980). However, over time, it becomes second nature to appreciate good questions and to critically evaluate answers that are themselves partially correct and in need of revision.

Collaboration

In FCL, collaboration is necessary for survival. Students must share, as each member is privy to only part of the puzzle. Expertise is deliberately distributed (Brown *et al.* 1993) but is also the natural result of students majoring in different arenas of knowledge. Learning and teaching depend heavily on creating, sustaining and expanding a community of research practice. Members of the community are critically dependent on each other. No one is an island; no one knows it all; collaborative learning is necessary for survival. This interdependence promotes an atmosphere of joint responsibility and mutual respect and a sense of personal and group identity.

Culture

A culture of learning, negotiating, sharing and producing work that is displayed to others is the backbone of FCL. It involves multiple ways into membership (Lave and Wenger 1991), shared mores of behaviour and ways of community building. Differences are legitimized and used for the common good. The culture of FCL fosters change by encouraging newcomers to adopt the discourse structure, goals, values and belief systems of the community. Ideas seeded in discussion migrate throughout the community via mutual appropriation and negotiated meaning. These classrooms are intentionally designed to foster interpretive communities that afford multiple roles and multiple voices (Bakhtin 1986) and the active exchange and reciprocity of a seminar.

Deep disciplinary content

It is axiomatic in FCL that one cannot think deeply about trivia; one cannot think in a vacuum. Therefore, FCL helps students to reason at the upper bounds of their capability about serious scientific issues. They must support their reasoning by research, by seeking advice from others more expert than themselves, and by presenting the fruits of their work in exhibitions modelled after the displays made by working scientists.

Developmental corridors

It is essential to the philosophy of FCL that students be engaged in research in an area of inquiry that is based on deep disciplinary understanding and that follows a developmental trajectory based on what is known about children's developing understanding within that domain. I argue that those who design learning environments for children should be primary consumers of research on children's learning in the domains they wish to foster. Only by so doing, can we capitalize on students' need-to-know about certain phenomena at critical times, surely the greatest motivator for deep and lasting learning about serious matters.

References

Aronson, E. (1978) *The Jigsaw Classroom*, Beverly Hills, CA: Sage.

Bakhtin, M. M. (1986) 'Speech genres and other late essays', in C. Emerson and M. Holquist (eds), trans. V. W. McGee, Austin: University of Texas Press.

Bartlett, F. C. (1958) *Thinking: An Experimental and Social Study*, New York: Basic Books.

Brown, A. L. (1974) 'The role of strategic behavior in retardate memory', in N. R. Ellis (ed.) *International Review of Research in Mental Retardation*, Vol. 7 (pp. 55–111), New York: Academic Press.

—— (1975) 'The development of memory: knowing, knowing about knowing, and knowing how to know', in H. W. Reese (ed.) *Advances in Child Development and Behavior*, Vol. 10 (pp. 103–52), New York: Academic Press.

—— (1978) 'Knowing when, where, and how to remember: a problem of metacognition', in R. Glaser (ed.) *Advances in Instructional Psychology*, Vol. 1. (pp. 77–165), Hillsdale, NJ: Erlbaum.

—— (1980) 'Metacognitive development and reading', in R. J. Spiro, B. Bruce and W. Brewer (eds) *Theoretical Issues in Reading Comprehension* (pp. 453–81), Hillsdale, NJ: Erlbaum.

—— (1990) 'Domain-specific principles affect learning and transfer in children', *Cognitive Science* 14: 107–33.

—— (1992) 'Design experiments: theoretical and methodological challenges in creating complex interventions in classroom settings', *Journal of the Learning Sciences* 2: 141–78.

—— (1995) 'The advancement of learning', *Educational Researcher* 23: 4–12.

——, Ash. D., Rutherford. M., Nakagawa, K., Gordon, A. and Campione, J. C. (1993) 'Distributed expertise in the classroom', in G. Salomon (ed.) *Distributed Cognitions: Psychological and Educational Considerations* (pp.188–228), New York: Cambridge University Press.

——, Bransford, J. D., Ferrara, R. A. and Campione, J. C. (1983) 'Learning, remembering and understanding', in J. H. Flavell and E. M. Markman (eds) *Handbook of Child Psychology* (4th edn), *Cognitive Development*, Vol. 3 (pp. 77–166), New York: Wiley.

—— and Campione, J. C. (1994) 'Guided discovery in a community of learners', in K. McGilly (ed.) *Classroom Lessons: Integrating Cognitive Theory and Classroom Practice* (pp. 229–70), Cambridge, MA: MIT Press/Bradford Books.

—— and —— (1996) 'Psychological learning theory and the design of innovative learning environments: on procedures principles, and systems', in L. Schauble and R. Glaser (eds) *Contributions of Instructional Innovation to Understanding Learning* (pp. 289–325), Hillsdale, NJ: Erlbaum.

—— and DeLoache, J. S. (1978) 'Skills, plans, and self-regulation', in R. S. Siegler (ed.) *Children's Thinking: What Develops?* (pp. 3–36), Hillsdale, NJ: Erlbaum.

—— and Reeve, R. A. (1987) 'Bandwidths of competence: the role of supportive contexts in learning and development', in L. S. Liben (ed.) *Development and Learning: Conflict or Congruence?* (pp. 173–223), Hillsdale, NJ: Erlbaum.

Bruner, J. S. (1969) *On Knowing: Essays for the Left Hand*, Cambridge, MA: Harvard University Press.

—— (1972) 'Immaturity M–: its uses, nature and management', *Times Educational Supplement*: 62–3.

—— (1996) *The Culture of Education*, Cambridge, MA: Harvard University Press.

Carey, S. (1985) *Conceptual Change in Childhood*, Cambridge, MA: Bradford Books and MIT Press.

—— (1996) 'On the origin of causal understanding', in D. Sperber, D. Premack and A. J. Premack (eds) *Causal Cognition: A Multidisciplinary Debate* (pp. 268–308), New York: Clarendon Press/Oxford University Press.

Collins, A. (1992) 'Toward a designed science of education', in E. Scanlon and T. O'Shea (eds) *New Directions in Educational Technology* (pp. 15–22), Berlin: Springer-Verlag.

Dweck. C. S. (1975) 'The role of expectations and attributions in the alleviation of learned helplessness', *Journal of Personality and Social Psychology* 31: 674–35.

Gelman, R. (1990) 'First principles organize attention to and learning about relevant data: number and the animate–inanimate distinction as examples', *Cognitive Science* 14: 79–106.

Goswami, U. and Brown, A. L. (1990) 'Higher-order structure and relational reasoning: contrasting analogical and thematic relations', *Cognition* 36: 207–26.

Inagaki, K. and Hatano, G. (1993) 'Young children's spontaneous personification as analogy', *Child Development* 58: 1013–20.

Keil, F. C. (1992) 'The origins of autonomous biology', in M. R. Gunnan and M. Maratsos (eds) *Minnesota Symposium on Child Psychology: Modularity and Constraints on Language and Cognition* (pp. 103–37), Hillsdale, NJ: Erlbaum.

—— (1994) 'The birth and nurturance of concepts by domains: the origins of concepts of living things', in L. A. Hirschfeld and S. A. Gelman (eds) *Mapping the Mind: Domain Specificity in Cognition and Culture* (pp. 234–54), Cambridge, MA: Cambridge University Press.

Lave, J. and Wenger, E. (1991) *Situated Learning: Legitimate Peripheral Participation*, New York: Cambridge University Press.

Medawar, P. (1982) *Pluto's Republic*, Oxford: Oxford University Press.

Miller, W. S. (1994) *Miller Analogies Test*, San Antonio, TX: The Psychological Corp. (original work published 1926).

Piaget, J. (1978) *Success and Understanding*, trans. A. Pomerans, Cambridge, MA: Harvard University Press.

——, Montanegero, J. and Billeter, J. (1977) 'Les correlats', in J. Piaget (ed.) *L'Abstraction Reflechissante*, Paris: Presses Universitaires de France.

Tversky, A. and Kahneman, D. (1974) 'Judgement under uncertainty: Heuristics and biases', *Science* 185: 1124–31.

Vygotsky, L. S. (1978) *Mind in Society: The Development of Higher Psychological Processes* (N. I. Cole, V. John-Steiner, S. Scribner and E. Souberman, eds and trans.), Cambridge, MA: Harvard University Press.

Wellman, H. M. and Gelman, S. A. (1992) 'Cognitive development: foundational theories of core domains', *Annual Review of Psychology* 43: 337–75.

——, Ritter, K. and Flavell, J. H. (1975) 'Deliberate memory behavior in the delayed reactions of very young children', *Developmental Psychology* 11: 780–7.

Whitehead, A. N. (1916, November) *The Aims of Education*, Address to the British Mathematical Society, Manchester, England.

2.4 Narratives of science

Jerome Bruner

My remarks in this chapter take their inspiration from Robert Karplus, who was a key figure in the curriculum reform movement of the late 1960s and 1970s. His ideas about how to teach science were not only elegant but came from the heart. He knew what it felt like 'not to know', what it was like to be a beginner. As a matter of temperament and principle, he knew that not knowing was the chronic condition not only of a student but of a real scientist. That is what made him a true teacher.

What he knew was that science is not something that exists out there in nature, but that it is a tool in the mind of the knower – teacher and student alike. Getting to know something is an adventure in how to account for a great many things that you encounter in as simple and elegant a way as possible. There are lots of different ways of getting to that point and you don't really ever get there unless you do it, as a learner, on your own terms. All one can do for a learner en route to he or she forming a view of his or her own is to aid and abet him or her on his or her own voyage. The means for aiding and abetting a learner is sometimes called a 'curriculum', and what we have learned is that there is no such thing as *the* curriculum. For, in effect, a curriculum is like an animated conversation on a topic that can never be fully defined, although one can set limits upon it. I call it an 'animated' conversation not only because it is always lively if it is honest, but also because one uses animation in the broader sense – props, pictures, texts, films and even 'demonstrations'. So the process includes conversation plus show-and-tell, plus brooding on it all on one's own.

Robert Karplus's film on the 'reversibility' of physical phenomena was a wonderful example of a prop. Rather than answering a question, it opens one – the great meta-question of whether you can describe something in nature without specifying the frame of reference or position from which you view it. 'Obvious' distinctions like up–down, right–left, moving–stationary suddenly become non-obvious – as they are in physics. Not only does the film make everybody think (which in itself is a glorious pedagogical outcome), but it also livens the conversation. Well, the two are not so very different: thinking comes very close to being an internal conversation and conversation can't be much good unless, in some degree, you are thinking aloud in the midst of it. That is what these days has come to be called, after Bakhtin, the 'dialogic imagination'. I shall have more to say about it presently.

I'd like to take a moment, before getting into my main topic, to contrast the spirit of the 'curriculum reform' movement in which Karplus was so deeply involved with the present wave of school reform – what for lack of a better expression I shall call 'assessment reform', or perhaps I should call it 'governors' reform'.

I have no objection in principle to creating better measuring instruments in order to find out how well our students are doing in science, in mathematics, in literature, in reading. For that matter, I don't even object in principle to assessments of how well our teachers are doing their jobs. If you think that the poor performance of our education establishment is due principally to a failure in teacher evaluation or in student assessment, then such a reform movement would be appropriate enough. Our state governors, in solemn conclave, proclaim that, by the turn of the century, we will 'turn things around' and be tops in the world in science and mathematics. And just what is it that is to be turned around? Assessment procedures and 'standards'? If only that, then we will succeed only in fuelling our internal indignation about how little geography our students know, how badly they read, how sorely lacking they are in mathematical skills, how deficient they are in understanding what science is about. Surely, that is a curiously indirect route to improving matters? – indirect in the sense that indignation just *might* conceivably lead us to do something further about how we conduct our schools and the process of education generally. It might even, conceivably, lead to a different message on public lips about financial support for schools and schooling.

Of course, we need standards and resources to make our schools work well in solving the myriad tasks they face. But resources and standards alone will not work. We need a surer sense of what to teach to whom and how to go about teaching it in such a way that it will make those taught more effective, less alienated and better human beings. The nation's teachers have been struggling to carry out this daunting task and, under the circumstances, have been doing it with courage and skill against enormous odds. We in the universities and in scientific and cultural institutions have been giving them precious little help. [...]

What we need is a school reform movement with a better sense of where we are going, with deeper convictions about what kind of people we want to be. Then we can mount the kind of community effort that can truly address the future of our educational process – an effort in which all of the resources of intellect and compassion that we can muster, whatever the price, are placed at the disposal of the schools. That is what Robert Karplus stood for in the domain of science – that human beings would be the richer for understanding the physical universe. He did his part by trying to help teachers do their task better. All the standards in the world will not, like a helping hand, achieve the goal of making our multicultural, our threatened society come alive again; not alive just as a competitor in the world's markets, but as a nation worth living in and living for.

Now let me turn to the main topic of this chapter – narrative as a mode of thinking, as a structure for organizing our knowledge and as a vehicle in the process of education, particularly in science education. In order to do so, I must take a step back to consider some fundamentals.

A long time ago, I proposed the concept of a 'spiral curriculum', the idea that, in teaching a subject, you begin with an 'intuitive' account that is well within the reach of a student and then circle back later to a more formal or highly structured account until, with however many more recyclings are necessary, the learner has mastered the topic or subject in its full generative power. In fact, this was a notion that grew out of a more fundamental, more obvious view of epistemology. I had stated this more basic view in the form, almost, of a philosophical proverb, to the effect that 'Any subject can be taught to any child at any age in some form that is honest'. Another way of saying the same thing might be to say, 'Readiness is not only born but made'. The general proposition rests on the still deeper truth that any domain of knowledge can be constructed at varying levels of abstractness or complexity. That is to say, domains of knowledge are *made,* not *found:* they can be constructed simply or complexly, abstractly or concretely. And it can easily be demonstrated within certain interesting limits that a so-called 'higher-level' way of characterizing a domain of knowledge encompasses, replaces and renders more powerful and precise a 'lower-level' characterization. For example, the intuitive statement 'the further out a weight is from the fulcrum of a lever, the more force it will exert' is contained, as it were, in the more powerful and precise Archimedean rules about how levers operate. And Archimedes, in turn, is replaced and contained by the rules of levers as described by quadratic equations. The child who understands the intuitive rule of the lever and applies it to the playground see-saw is well on his or her way to becoming Archimedean, just as Archimedes was on his way toward that Renaissance algebraist who recognized that expressions in the form $(x^2 + 4x + 4)$ could be equated to the multiplicative pair of the form $(x + 2)(x + 2)$. All of which could tell you some canny ways of placing weights on a beam so that they would balance. A ten-year-old once said to me, having discovered how all of this mathematical abstraction can guide one to making a beam balance, 'This gadget knows all about algebra'. I tried to dissuade him, to convince him that it was *he* who knew the algebra, not the balance beam, but I doubt whether I succeeded. That insight might come later up the curriculum spiral, perhaps in graduate school, or perhaps, with the luck of some good teaching, in the very next grade.

The research of the past three decades on the growth of reasoning in children has, in the main, confirmed the rightness of the spiral curriculum, although it has also provided us with some cautions. There are stages of development that constrain how fast and how far a child can leap ahead into abstraction. Piaget's views are always to be taken seriously in this regard, but they too must be regarded with caution. The child's mind does not move to higher levels of abstraction like the tide coming in. Development depends also, as Margaret Donaldson has so beautifully demonstrated (Donaldson *et al.* 1978), upon the child's practical grasp of the context or situation in which he or she has to reason. A good intuitive, practical grasp of a domain at one stage of development leads to better, earlier and deeper thinking in the next stage when the child meets challenging new problems in that domain. As a teacher, you do not wait for readiness to happen; you foster or 'scaffold' it by deepening the child's powers at the stage where you find him or her now (Wood *et al.* 1976).

I am fully aware that what I've been saying is old hat to working teachers. They have grasped all of this intuitively ever since Socrates, in the *Meno,* set forth the first version of the idea by illustrating how that slave boy could, starting from innocence, quickly grasp the main ideas of plane geometry. But it helps to push our understanding to another level. I still get a lot of mail from teachers; years back it used to average ten letters a week. Most of it was to cheer me on for going public with what every teacher already knew. But there was also a steady trickle of doubting Thomases who dared me to try to teach calculus or Mendeleev's periodic table in nursery school. Well, five-year-olds are delighted with the story of the tortoise and the hare. And you can go easily on from there to the joke-story that is embodied in Zeno's paradox – there's still halfway to go, wherever you are, so how do you ever get there? Invariably, given the superiority of intuition, young children think Zeno's paradox is 'silly'. But it bothers them. Have you ever heard a six-year-old tell a friend about Zeno's paradox? He does it like a shaggy dog story (which it is, of course). And that now brings me to the heart of the matter – narrative.

Let me say a little about stories and narratives generally, for it is very likely the case that the most natural and the earliest way in which we organize our experience and our knowledge is in terms of the narrative form. It may also be true that the beginnings, the transitions and the full grasp of ideas in a spiral curriculum depend upon embodying those ideas into a story or narrative form. So what is a narrative? Fortunately, we are aided by a decade of lively research on this problem from a variety of sources – linguistics, literary theory, psychology, philosophy, even mathematics.

I'll begin with some obvious points. A narrative involves a sequence of events. The sequence carries the meaning: contrast 'The stock market collapsed, the government resigned' with 'The government resigned, the stock market collapsed'. But not every sequence of events is worth recounting. Narrative is discourse and the prime rule of discourse is that there is a reason for it that distinguishes it from silence. Narrative is justified or warranted by virtue of the sequence of events it recounts being a violation of canonicity: it tells about something unexpected, or something that one's auditor has reason to doubt. The 'point' of the narrative is to resolve the unexpected, to settle the auditor's doubt, or in some manner to redress or explicate the 'imbalance' that prompted the telling of the story in the first place. A story, then, has two sides to it: a sequence of events and an implied evaluation of the events recounted.

What is particularly interesting about a story as a structure is the two-way street that it travels between its parts and the whole. The events recounted in a story take their meaning from the story as a whole. However, the story as a whole is something that is constructed from its parts. This part/whole tail-chasing bears the formidable name 'hermeneutic circle', and it is what causes stories to be subject to interpretation, not to explanation. You cannot explain a story; all you can do is give it variant interpretations. You can *explain* falling bodies by reference to a theory of gravity. But you can only *interpret* what might have happened to Sir Isaac Newton when the legendary apple fell on his head in the orchard. So we say that scientific theories or logical proofs are judged by means of verification or test – or more accurately, by their verifiability or testability – whereas stories are judged on the basis of their verisimilitude or 'lifelikeness'. Indeed, one of the reasons why it is so difficult to establish whether a story is 'true' or not is precisely because there is a sense in which a story can be true *to* life without being true *of* life. For those who have concerned themselves with such arcane matters as the theory of meaning, this means that stories can make sense but have no reference. It is much harder to construct 'fictional science' (not to be confused with science fiction) simply because it is immediately caught up in issues of verifiability with respect to a specifiable possible world. And that, after all, is what *real* science is about.

Science uses as its apparatus of exposition such means as logic or mathematics to help it achieve consistency, explicitness and testability. One of its favoured weapons is the hypothesis which, if well formed, will be 'frangible' – easily found to be false. However derivationally deep any scientific theory may be, its use should lead to the formulation of falsifiable hypotheses, as Karl Popper would say. But you can falsify an awful lot of hypotheses, historians of science make clear, without bringing down the theory from which they have been derived, and this has suggested to many in recent years that grand theories in science are perhaps more story-like than we had expected.

A few other points about stories are relevant here. Stories, notably, are about human agents rather than about the world of nature – unless the world of nature is conceived 'animistically' as human-like. What marks human agents is that their acts are not produced by such physical 'forces' as gravity, but by intentional states: desires, beliefs, knowledge, intentions, commitments. It is intrinsically difficult to 'explain' exactly why it is that human agents, impelled by intentional states, do as they do or react to each other as they do – particularly in the unexpected or non-canonical situations that constitute stories. This reinforces the requirement of interpretation in understanding stories, as does one other thing: stories are the product of narrators, and narrators have points of view, even if a narrator claims to be an 'eyewitness to the events'. Now this is also the case where science is concerned, although the language of science, cloaked in the rhetoric of objectivity, makes every effort to conceal that view except when it is concerned with the 'foundations' of its field. The famous 'paradigm shifts' that occur during scientific revolutions reflect this cover-up situation, since they betray the fact that the so-called data of science are constructed observations that are designed with a point of view in mind. Light is neither corpuscular nor wavelike; waves and corpuscles are in the theory, in the mind of the theory makers and holders. The observations they devise are designed to determine how well nature fits these pieces of 'fictional science'.

It has been a curious habit of Western thought since the Greeks to assume that the world is rational and that true knowledge about that world will always take the form of logical or scientific propositions that will be amenable to explanation. It was thought until quite recently that theories, made up of such propositions, would be found to be true or false by virtue of whether they corresponded to that world. Nowadays, we quite properly ask how it is that we can ever know what *the* world is actually like, save by the odd process of constructing theories and making observations once in a while to check how our theories are hanging together – not how the world is hanging together, but our theories. The more advanced a science becomes, the more dependent it is upon the speculative models it constructs and the more 'indirect' its measurements of the world become. My physicist friends are fond of the remark that physics is 95 per cent speculation and 5 per cent observation. And they are very attached to the expression 'physical intuition' as something that 'real' physicists have: they are not just tied to observation and measurement but know how to get around in the theory even without them.

Constructing 'speculative models' at the levels of science is, of course, highly constrained by the mathematical languages in which advanced theories are formulated. They are formulated in that way, of course, so that we may be as explicit as possible. Through explicitness, logical contradictions can be avoided. But the mathematics has another function: a well-formed mathematical statement is also a carefully derived logical system and it is the full derivational power of the mathematics that the scientist is out to exploit. After all, the object of a mathematized theory in physics is not just description, but generativeness. So, for example, if the algebra of quadratic functions describes what might be happening in the domain of levers and balance beams, then the application of such general algebraic rules as the associative, distributive and commutative laws should (with luck) lead to previously unimagined predictions about levers, fulcrums, balance beams and so forth. When that happens, it is science heaven and a time for prizes.

But as every historian of science in the last 100 years has pointed out, scientists use all sorts of aids and intuitions, stories and metaphors to help them in the quest of getting their speculative model to fit 'nature' (or getting 'nature' to fit their model by redefining what counts as 'nature'). They will use any metaphor or any suggestive figure or fable or foible that may luckily come to hand. Niels Bohr once confessed the story of how he had arrived at the idea of complementarity in physics – illustrated, for example, by the principle that you cannot specify both the position and the velocity of a particle simultaneously and therefore you cannot include both in the same set of equations. The general idea had first struck him as a moral dilemma. His son had stolen a trinket from the local haberdashery shop, but some days later, stricken with guilt, he had confessed the theft to his father. As Bohr put it, although he was greatly touched by this moral act of contrition, he was also mindful of his son's wrongdoing: 'But I was struck by the fact that I could not think of my son at the same moment both in the light of love and in the light of justice', (personal communication). This led him to think that certain states of mind were like the two aspects of one of those trick Gestalt figure–ground pictures where you can see either the duck or the rabbit, the vase or the profiles, but not both at the same time. Then some days later, as if the idea were blossoming, it occurred to him that you could not consider the position of a particle as stationary in a particular position and at the same time as moving with a velocity in no particular position at all. The mathematics was easy to fix. It was grasping the right narrative that took the hard work.

To come directly to the point, let me propose that we characteristically convert our efforts at scientific understanding into the form of narratives or, say, 'narrative heuristics'. 'We' includes both scientists and the pupils who occupy the classrooms in which we teach. This would consist of turning the events we are exploring into narrative form, better to highlight what is canonical and expected in our way of looking at them, so that we could more easily discern what is 'fishy' and off-base and what, therefore, needs to be explicated. Here are a couple of examples, one from the frontier, one from the classroom. A physics colleague lamented to me some years ago that what was wrong with contemporary physical theory was that it conceived of most events as entirely in the extremely short-term nanosecond range, which made no sense since the physical world went on forever. So, he asked, what kind of 'story' could you tell about an enduring universe? I jokingly suggested to him that he should invent a kind of hypothetical physical glue, a substance that went on and on in time, and call it, say, glueterium. 'Brilliant, brilliant', he said, for reasons still unclear to me. Several years later he told me that the idea of glueterium had been a turning point in his thinking. My second example comes from a classroom discussion. The topic was 'atomicity', the smallest unit of which other things might be made, which is as old a topic as you can get. The discussion became lively when it reached the point of 'cutting up' matter into smaller and smaller pieces until, as one of the children put it, 'they've got to be invisible'. 'Why invisible?' somebody asked. 'Because the air is made of atoms' – which produced a general pause. A child took advantage of the pause to ask, 'Does everything have to be made of the same atoms?' 'Well, so how could the same atoms make stones and water both?' 'Let's have different kinds of atoms then – hard ones and soft ones and wet ones.' 'No, that's crazy: let's have them all the same and they can make up into different shapes like Lego or something.' 'And what happens when you split an atom?' 'Then the whole thing goes Boom!' Echoes of the early Greek philosophers: not Thales but Empedocles prevailed.

What happens when the discussion takes that turn? Well, to put it as bluntly as possible, the focus of attention shifts from an exclusive concern with 'nature-as-out-there' to a concern with the *search* for nature – how we construct our model of nature. It is that shift that turns the discussion from dead science to live science-*making*. And once we do that, we are able to invoke criteria like conceivability, verisimilitude and the other fundamentals of good stories. Gerald Holton, the distinguished historian of science and a keen observer of the scientific *process*, comments that scientists from earliest times have relied on just such narrativizing to help them, using metaphors, myths and fables along the way – snakes that swallow their own tails, how to lift the world, how to leave traces that can be followed back, and so on.

Let me put it in a somewhat different language. The process of science-making is narrative. It consists of spinning hypotheses about nature, testing them, correcting the hypotheses and getting one's head straight. En route to producing testable hypotheses, we play with ideas, try to create anomalies, try to find neat puzzle forms that we can apply to intractable troubles so that they can be turned into soluble problems, figure out tricks for getting around morasses. The history of science, as James Bryant Conant tried to show us (1957), can be dramatically recounted as a set of almost heroic narratives in problem-solving. His critics liked to point out that the case histories that he and his colleagues had prepared, while very interesting, were not science but the history of science, and I am not proposing that we should now substitute the history of science for science itself. What I am proposing, rather, is that our instruction in science from the start to the finish should be mindful of the lively processes of science-making, rather than being an account only of 'finished science' as represented in the textbook, in the handbook and in the standard and often deadly 'demonstration experiment'. [...] I'll conclude with a few suggestions and perhaps a princilpe or two.

The first suggestion might even qualify as one of those principles. It says: 'The art of raising challenging questions is easily as important as the art of giving clear answers'. And I would have to add, 'The art of cultivating such questions, of keeping good questions alive, is as important as either of those'. Good questions are ones that pose dilemmas, subvert obvious or canonical 'truths', force incongruities upon our attention. In fact, much of the best support material produced by the science projects of the curriculum reform movement of the 1960s was of this order. Let me mention a couple of them, both of them produced by the Physical Science Study Committee. One was a 'frictionless puck', a squat can of dried ice with a hole in its bottom, such that thawed carbon dioxide seeped through, causing the puck to float frictionlessly atop its cushion of gas on a pane of window glass. On that surface, under those conditions, bodies set in motion seemed virtually to stay in motion just as counter-intuitively as required by Newtonian laws of motion. It is only a neat little hardware store trick, but it leads to endless questions about the 'ideal conditions' required by general physical laws, how you figure out ideal conditions, what you might mean by such things as 'perfect vacuums' and 'frictionless planes' and so on. [...]

The other demonstration was a ceiling-hung pendulum with a large can of finely ground sand at its terminus, with a tiny hole in the middle of the bottom of the can and wrapping paper spread on the floor beneath it. The notable thing about this gadget is that it leaves a trail of its movements – trajectory length, damping effects, Lissajous figures for its eccentric excursions, the lot. Now, the objective in making any scientific instrument (whether for research or teaching) is to enable the scientist/learner to observe or describe or measure events in nature that previously were too small or weak, too big and ubiquitous, too fleeting or not fleeting enough, to observe or describe. I think the idea of the 'tin can pendulum' had originally been hit upon by Frank Oppenheimer at the Exploratorium in San Francisco. It is perfect for exploring an otherwise inaccessible world of forces and symmetries: you can dream up and do experiments at the rate of a dozen an hour. I have seen a group of 12-year-olds at summer session in Cambridge learn more fundamentals in an afternoon through such experiments than many children learn in a term from a standard text.

The recording pendulum has a lesson that goes with it, which runs something like this: 'If one picture is worth a thousand words then one well-wrought guess is worth a thousand pictures'. A well-wrought guess, of course, is usually and rather grandly called 'a hypothesis'. What is important about a hypothesis (or a well-wrought guess) is that it derives from something you already know, something generic that allows you to go beyond what you already know. That 'something generic' is what I used to call the 'structure' of a subject, the knowledge that permitted you to go beyond the particulars you had already encountered. The structure is, so to speak, in the head. Being able to 'go beyond the information' given [and] to 'figure things out' is one of the few untarnishable joys of life. One of the great triumphs of learning (and of teaching) is to get things organized in your head in a way that permits you to know more than you 'ought' to. And this takes reflection, brooding about what it is that you know. The enemy of reflection is the breakneck pace – the thousand pictures.

In some deep sense, just as Mies van der Rohe said of architecture, we can say of learning, and in particular science learning, that 'less is more'. That again has a narrative tang to it. The story is how you can get the most out of the least. The denouement is learning to think with what you've already grasped. I believe that this truism lies at the heart of every good curriculum, every good lesson plan, every learning-and-teaching encounter. So, when it becomes time for the bureaucrats to set their standards and to make up their tests for monitoring how we are doing, they ought to adopt this one as their primary standard. They will have to construct better tests than the ones we have now. And when the time has come again for us to help each other in devising or constructing curricula in science, I hope this ideal will shine over the effort.

References

Bryant Conant, J. (1957) *Harvard Case Histories in Experimental Science,* 2 vols, Cambridge, MA: Harvard University Press.

Donaldson, M. C. (1978) *Children's Minds,* New York: Norton.

Wood, D., Bruner, J. S. and Ross, G. (1976) 'The role of tutoring in problem solving', *Journal of Child Psychology and Psychiatry* 17: 89–100.

2.5 Preparing students for competent scientific practice

Implications of recent research in science and technology studies

Michelle K. McGinn and
Wolff-Michael Roth

An often cited goal for science education reform is to increase the 'scientific literacy' of graduates (American Association for the Advancement of Science [AAAS] 1993; National Research Council [NRC] 1994; National Science Teachers Association [NSTA] 1992, 1995; Rutherford and Ahlgren 1990), yet massive amounts of money, time and effort associated with these reforms have effected little overall change in scientific literacy (Eisenhart *et al.* 1996; Shamos 1995). One possible reason for these shortcomings relates to the predominance of narrow and conventional interpretations of scientific literacy. To achieve increased scientific literacy, classrooms have been organized around activities intended to help students develop and practise scientific process skills (i.e. the 'scientific method') and accepted scientific knowledge and curricular materials have been developed with the intention for students to engage in hands-on activities and discover the natural world for themselves. These changes are predicated on the belief that students best learn scientific concepts through engaging in the practices of 'real scientists' (Eisenhart *et al.* 1996). However, the visions of 'real scientists' and 'real science' that underlie these curricular reforms tend to be based on the myth that scientists are a special class of people who are particularly endowed with superior mental abilities, exceptional problem-solving competence, and well-tuned scientific process skills that they use in an impartial pursuit of truth.

Over the past two decades, the mythical views of scientists and science have been challenged by research following the traditions of sociology, anthropology and ethnomethodology (e.g. Bijker *et al.* 1987; Button 1993; Jasanoff *et al.* 1995; Pickering 1992). This research, which we label science and technology studies, has seen researchers follow scientists around in their daily work in laboratories, field sites, offices, meeting rooms, conference centres and wherever else scientists do their work (e.g. Latour 1987; Traweek 1988). When viewed 'up close', traditional descriptions of scientists, scientific activities and scientific intellect are no longer tenable. As we will argue, this research amply documents the situated actions and contingent decisions that comprise scientific work (e.g. Knorr-Cetina 1981; Latour and Woolgar 1986). Within this field, scientific knowledge is seen as emerging from disciplined ways of organizing and making sense of the natural world through particular discourses (e.g. Barnes *et al.* 1996; Gooding 1992; Lynch 1985) and visual representations (e.g. Henderson 1991; Lynch and Woolgar 1990; Star 1989).

If descriptions of science and scientists that emerge from science and technology studies are legitimate, there are considerable implications for educational aims guiding science instruction, learning experiences directed toward those educational aims, and resources that support those learning experiences and educational aims. These implications are important for at least two reasons. First, considered in the context of educational reforms calling for more 'authentic' scientific practices in schools (Brown *et al.* 1989), these new understandings about science invite a reformulation of what can be considered 'authentic science'. Second, many reports from science and technology studies show that people from every walk of life, even without scientific training, can become important forces in shaping the way science, scientific facts and technological products are constituted in various arenas of public life (Clarke and Montini 1993; Epstein 1995, 1997; Solomon and Hackett 1996). This requires a vision of scientific literacy as preparation for competent participation in scientific laboratories, product development firms, activist movements, the judicial system or other locations/communities where science is created and used. As we argue, this participation could be conceptualized as a trajectory of legitimate peripheral participation (Lave and Wenger 1991) in science-related discourses and practices (including visual representation practices). This perspective therefore allows us to consider science education as more than training for would-be laboratory scientists.

Our intent in this chapter is to introduce some of the diversity of scholarship within science and technology studies and to point to some of the potential implications for classroom practice. We do not provide a complete review of the field of science and technology studies nor of educational programmes building on science and technology studies; rather we provide an introduction for educators to the field of science and technology studies. We focus our discussion around three key topics in science and technology studies: the nature of science and scientific inquiry, science as discourse and the use of visual representations. For each topic, we briefly review understandings gleaned from science and technology studies and discuss associated curricular implications in terms of educational aims, learning experiences and resources. We hope that this work can provide a starting point for educators to consider understandings from this rich area of research and scholarship, and that these understandings may provide guidance for curricular decision-making.

Nature of science and scientific inquiry

An increasing number of investigators with ethnographic orientations have negotiated access to and studied scientists and technicians in their everyday work in scientific domains. [...] These ethnographies generally support the claim that the 'scientific method' is largely a myth and does not describe what scientists actually do. Scientific research and its products are now recognized as situationally contingent achievements involving scientists, technicians, granting agencies, politicians, tools and instruments, local cultures and so on. That is, scientific knowledge emerges from a nexus of interacting people, agencies, materials, instruments, individual and collective goals/interests and the histories of all these factors. Ethnographic studies of engineers and technological innovations indicate a similar situation in engineering design and technology (Bucciarelli 1994; Frickel 1996; Sørenson and Levold 1992).

In scientific laboratories, scientists' reasoning is influenced by the overall research context and the specific research situation (Knorr-Cetina 1981). Local idiosyncrasies, know-how, interpretations, physical and social resources (equipment, materials, co-workers, etc.) affect each accomplishment within a laboratory. Projects take particular turns because certain apparatus is available, new uses are discovered for equipment developed for other projects, or scientists happen to come across a specific paper or individual. For example, Knorr-Cetina (1981) described a biochemist's innovative use of a centrifuge. This instrument had been designed and originally purchased for use in separating various substances in the laboratory but the biochemist discovered that it could also be used to measure densities of substances. This innovative use of the equipment constituted a new scientific technique for the biochemist, making subsequent experiments possible. Scientists – even in their own descriptions (cf. Suzuki 1989) – are 'tinkerers' (Knorr-Cetina 1981) or 'bricoleurs' (Turkle and Papert 1991) who improvise to make the most out of each situation as they pursue their interests and goals; they construct local theories by arranging and rearranging, negotiating and renegotiating with materials; and they draw on a variety of social, cultural, material, political and economic resources to proceed.

The personal interests and life experiences of scientists influence the ways their research evolves. For example, Boyle (1996) recounts the interesting case of a universal, newborn screening programme implemented in the 1950s to detect a rare form of mental retardation known as phenylketonuria (PKU). The decision to screen all newborns for this condition (a medical rarity that most physicians would never encounter in a lifetime of practice) arose because one physician-researcher began some exploratory research after discovering that both his son and niece suffered from the condition.

Current research also highlights the larger contexts in which scientists and their laboratories work without which scientists could not construct new knowledge. Scientific discovery is embedded in webs of social relationships in which scientific actors reason and act (Law 1994). Funding agencies, political pressures and lobbyists all contribute to what, where, when and how science is conducted and, therefore, to making scientific knowledge. Research monies become available for research that is deemed interesting and useful by a funding agency. Results that match some desired outcome are more widely advertised and disseminated. Social and political commitments influence which research is made public and given priority in policy decisions.

For example, opposition to the Norwegian government's 1992 decision to resume commercial hunting for minke whales rested predominantly on commitments to animal rights rather than data about whale stocks or the impact a continuing ban could have on fish stocks (Roll-Hansen 1994).

These descriptions of the situated ways scientists and engineers work, think and act converge with descriptions of the ways 'just-plain-folks' do mathematics as they shop for groceries in local supermarkets, put together their daily diet allowances or cook their meals (Lave 1988). All of this suggests that scientific knowledge and technological artefacts cannot be understood as the outgrowth of a special scientific and technological rationality. Further, scientific practice and scientific knowledge are not relegated solely to scientific laboratories or science classrooms and their production is not limited to scientists and scientific bodies (Knorr-Cetina 1992). Science, scientific validity and approaches to science are influenced by judges, activists, consumers, engineers, scientists and a whole host of others engaged across a broad range of sites including legislatures, courts of law, sites of activism, the press and the marketplace (e.g. Clarke and Montini 1993; Epstein 1995, 1997; Roll-Hansen 1994; Rosen 1993; Solomon and Hackett 1996).

As an example, Epstein (1995) documents the ways that AIDS activists who have little formal training in science or medicine have constructed themselves as credible actors and genuine participants in the design, conduct and interpretation of clinical trials used to test the safety and efficacy of AIDS drugs. First, activist groups have presented themselves as the legitimate, organized voice of people with AIDS/HIV, thereby establishing themselves as the 'obligatory passage point' (Latour 1987) between researchers and potential subject populations for clinical trials. A second important strategy for many activists was to learn to communicate scientifically. By attending conferences, scrutinizing research protocols and learning from sympathetic professionals, activists appropriated the scientific discourses of journal articles and conference centres. Once their arguments were couched in the language of medical science and biostatistics, researchers' norms of discourse and behaviour demanded that they consider the merits of the activists' arguments. Third, activists have used their newly acquired discourses to construct powerful arguments, drawing together epistemological, methodological, political and ethical claims. These arguments emphasized individuals' rights to assume risks inherent in testing therapies and to insist that populations in clinical trials should be more formally representative of different social groups affected by AIDS/HIV (haemophiliacs, injection drug users, women and men, whites and minorities, homosexuals and heterosexuals). Finally, activists have shifted the focus of clinical trials from tests of 'ivory tower theoretical questions' (Epstein 1995: 423) to information that can be used by patients and doctors to make meaningful decisions when confronted with treatment dilemmas in the context of day-to-day clinical practice. This has prompted a shift from scientists' interest in maintaining scientific standards to produce solid, trustworthy results toward the interests of people with life-threatening illnesses (and the medical practitioners who support them), who use whatever knowledge is available to make the best treatment decisions possible. Activist engagements in science have led to changes in therapeutic care techniques and modifications to clinical trial design including broader entry criteria, more diverse subject populations and access to concomitant medication during clinical trials. [...]

AIDS activists have also influenced science by serving as 'role models' for other health-related activists such as the support groups for Lyme disease patients who successfully pressured the organizers of an international conference on Lyme disease to reinstate conference papers that initially had been rejected, or the chronic fatigue patients who launched a lawsuit against a drug manufacturing company that violated its promise to continue to supply an experimental drug after the clinical trial ended (Epstein 1995). As these cases show, activists and others who lack scientific training have entered domains traditionally limited to scientists and have influenced validity claims, experimental designs and treatment protocols.

Activists are not the only ones who have had impact on the construction and interpretation of scientific or technological knowledge. [...] Clarke and Montini (1993) described the ways that understandings about and decisions regarding the controversial abortifacient RU486 have been influenced by representatives of reproductive and other scientific groups; family planning, population control and abortion provider organizations; pharmaceutical companies; medical groups; anti-abortion groups; feminist pro-choice groups; women's health movement groups; politicians; and women users and consumers of RU486. Solomon and Hackett (1996) studied the precedent-setting case of *Daubert v. Merrell Dow Pharmaceuticals, Inc.* in which the plaintiffs charged that their birth defects were caused by maternal use of a drug intended to alleviate morning sickness. The Supreme Court's ruling in this case called upon judges to evaluate scientific evidence and expert testimony, despite their lack of scientific training, thereby placing judges in the roles of gatekeepers for scientific knowledge and boundary-workers to negotiate scientific validity. A fuller discussion of interactions between science and the courts is presented in Jasanoff (1995). Some of her conclusions include the point that courts 'defer to the working rules of science only when they do not interfere with the rules or goals of the legal process' (p. 112). Courts analyse the validity of scientific procedures or findings only when alerted to the issue by a litigant and provided with guidance from the scientific community. Consider as a further example the widely publicized O. J. Simpson trial, where a decision about the defendant's guilt appeared to be critically dependent on DNA analyses that require polymerase chain reaction (PCR) assays. It is widely known among molecular biologists that it takes extraordinary skill to effectively use PCR assays (Jordan and Lynch 1993), yet there was virtually no reference to this difficulty during the trial. Better (public) understandings of science and scientists' work are necessary to evaluate scientific authority in criminal cases and other public venues and to provide appropriate contexts for considering scientific knowledge.

Given that science is created and used by heterogeneous groups of people across diverse settings, some form of scientific literacy is required for a much wider range of occupations and interests than has previously been thought. This scientific literacy can empower people to engage in the discourses and practices associated with scientific laboratories and conferences, as well as a broad spectrum of other domains.

Implications for educational practice

Science and technology studies reveal that scientific knowledge is far more complex and tenuous than implied by myths of the scientific method and heroic scientists. In light of these findings, traditional descriptions of scientists, scientific activities and scientific intellect are no longer tenable. If educators wish to follow the recommendations from professional associations to engage students in 'authentic science' activities (see AAAS 1993; NRC 1994; NSTA 1992, 1995), then those activities should not be modelled after mythic visions of science and scientists. Instead science education needs to look toward new educational aims that reflect the situated, contingent and contextual nature of science, while also acknowledging the diverse range of communities and locations where science is created and used. We believe that these aims can be best realized through learning experiences and resources that differ markedly from those prevalent in traditional science classrooms.

Educational aims

At the moment, society confers on scientists special authorities, both in positive and negative senses. Many advertising campaigns choose images of scientists to support their claims (e.g. 'Four out of five dentists recommend [Brand X] for their patients who chew gum'). Scientists appear in courts of law and legislatures as authorities who act as resources to various parties who make ethical and legal decisions. Scientific authority is also reflected in everyday sayings, for example, situations are considered evident when they do not require 'a rocket scientist' or 'an Einstein' to arrive at a particular assessment. At the same time, critical perspectives are frequently lacking,

   To circumvent these shortcomings, educators might look for guidance from the field of science and technology studies. Educational aims informed by science and technology studies emphasize the provision of the necessary conditions to help students become members in a scientifically literate society that understands and appreciates science as one of its many endeavours. That is, science education could occur within learning environments that support students' development toward competent participation in a science-and-technology-infused world, not just as laboratory scientists, but as judges and lawyers, health professionals, environmental consultants, engineers and citizens. The new scientific literacy requires increasing ability and willingness to reflect on the positive and negative sides of science, the fallible and contingent character of science and scientists and the heterogeneity of science and its products. Such reflections allow a scientifically literate citizen to critically evaluate science and scientific authority.

Learning experiences

There are already small projects in place all over the world that show that participation in the collection and interpretation of data can be a lifelong endeavour (e.g.

Greenall Gough 1992; Helms 1996). This endeavour includes, for example, elementary students who participate in seeding a new green corridor with butterfly pupae, high school students who monitor pollution levels in a nearby inlet, hikers who sample biodiversity before logging companies enter an area, lighthouse keepers and their families who record meteorological data, amateur astronomers who search the night sky and nature enthusiasts who actively engage in counting bird populations. These projects share a commitment to involving students and citizens in science, rather than assuming that science is the exclusive domain of trained scientists. Of course, trained scientists could (and often do) gather such data with greater reliability, accuracy and efficiency than students or untrained citizens. [...]

In classrooms modelled after science as practised, students pursue investigations of their own interests, negotiate with their collaborators as to problem and solution frames and debate the merits of different processes for seeking solutions. 'Authentic science' requires that students pursue their activities under the constraint that they make their actions and products accountable to themselves, their peers and their teachers; that is, classrooms are organized as knowledge-producing communities in which rhetorical dimensions similar to those in science are enacted. In such classroom environments, small-group work related to students' own investigations is punctuated by interactions with other groups at the small-group and whole-class levels, allowing information to diffuse and new discursive and material (or tool-related) practices to develop (McGinn *et al.* 1995). But even without the formal institution of interactions beyond collaborating peer groups, interactions between students occur frequently, allowing the transfer of information, materials and practices, and therefore an evolution of the community and its available knowledge resources (Roth and McGinn 1996). Studies have already shown that classrooms organized according to the principles of open investigation, accountability of activities and rhetorical aspects of scientific knowledge construction lead to qualitative and quantitative advances in students' knowledge (Johnson and Stewart 1990; Rosebery *et al.* 1992; Roth and Bowen 1995; Scardamalia and Bereiter 1992).

By reading, discussing and even role-playing scientific controversies, students see situated, contingent and contextual features of scientific knowledge (Costa *et al.* 1997). By designing and building models, students see and experience the situated nature of science and technology (Harel 1991; Roth 1996). Experiences like these provide the foundation for students to learn to understand and appreciate science as one of society's many endeavours, not as the crowning achievement of civilization as implied by traditional myths.

Resources

Curricula that allow students to experience scientific fact-making cannot specify every concept to be covered by all students at a given time. Rather, such curricula need to allow students to pursue investigations of their own interests, though they may be under the umbrella of particular types of phenomena. In this way, grade 11 physics students learned principles of general motion by investigating models of boats and cars, yo-yos and plasticine objects submerged in various liquids (Roth, 1994); grade 8 students learned about relationships between biological and physical variables by designing their own investigations in small ecozones (Roth and Bowen 1995); and elementary students learned about material properties, forces and engineering design principles by designing and building their own architectural structures (Roth 1996). In all of these examples, students learned significantly more science than prescribed by the existing curriculum documents, despite the self-directed nature of their work. With respect to curricular materials, the single normative textbook was replaced by a wide range of resources including tools, materials, computers, software for statistical and mathematical modelling, instruments, books about science content and methods of inquiry, and encyclopedias.

Curricula that allow students to learn about the nature of science, scientific knowledge and everyday scientific work cannot be based on textbooks that are the most currently available. First, even reflective high school students recognize that textbooks present scientific knowledge as unshakable truths (Roth and Lucas 1997). Second, textbooks do a poor job introducing students to science-related discourses and practices (Roth *et al.* 1997). Instead, a wide range of original and secondary sources (texts, films, etc.) can provide opportunities for students to reflect on the nature of science, scientific knowledge and scientists' work. These resources for reflecting on scientific work (and the associated organization of activities) are particularly important so that students can also reflect on the processes of fact construction in their own investigations.

In particular, the Internet is becoming increasingly important as a resource for students to support their investigations through access to external data and expertise and as a venue for disseminating their findings. Through networked connections, students can participate in a 'knowledge society' (Scardamalia and Bereiter 1996) where their products can provide direct and indirect value to government, industry and the wider community (cf. Radinsky and Gomez 1998). However, participation in a knowledge society requires communication among members of that society.

Science as discourse

Scientific communities, like all communities of practice, are characterized by their specific forms of talk. These are variously referred to as discourses, registers or language games; they allow scientists to accomplish their everyday activities and to reflect on their practice. Scientists planning investigations, framing observations and interpreting outcomes, adopt and adapt discourse specific to their communities (Barnes *et al.* 1996). In addition, within their laboratories, discourse is central to scientists' sense-making and negotiations within their research groups. Discourse changes as scientists attempt to obtain better fits between descriptions and experience and this leads to concomitant changes in their understandings (Gooding 1992). At some stage in their work, scientists communicate 'findings' to a wider audience. In the process, initially tentative propositions go through a process of 'hardening' as the scientific community at large accepts the new discourse and accompanying interpretations (Latour and Woolgar 1986).

The most common means of communicating scientific findings is through scientific papers (Costa *et al.* 1997). In the process of writing these papers, scientists 'clean up' or 'sanitize' their originally tentative hypotheses and fuzzy methodological steps. Analyses of scientific publications show that these publications are rhetorical events (Bastide 1990; Latour 1987, Sinding 1996). Each element in an article, including the design of the study, data collection and presentation, visual representations and interpretations, are 'constructed like some military strategy, an ambush without an escape route. Each time that a reading of the results different from that of the authors could possibly be made, the departure is barred by an adequate argument' (Bastide 1990: 208). Scientific authors rally other human and non-human actors – well-known researchers, published reports, common sense, established theories and accepted experimental procedures – to construct their research questions, experimental designs and interpretations as reasonable (Latour 1987). Similarly, journalists rally their own list of allies in presenting science in more public forums. However, in constructing their arguments, scientists and journalists focus on different issues and reference different actors (Roll-Hansen 1994). The differential conventions of academe and journalism determine acceptable literary genres and influence the way knowledge claims can be made. When scientists present their work, they emphasize research methods, findings and discrepancies with other research. In contrast, journalists are constrained by economic competition to concentrate instead on deadlines, time limits, space constraints in a particular issue, audience preferences, pressures from advertisers and dramatic impact (Roll-Hansen 1994). Even within science writing, different literary genres emerge depending on the particular publication venue and its audience. For example, Sinding (1996) analysed the literary strategies adopted by a biologist as he wrote experimental and review papers, and found that review and conference papers afford better opportunities for new knowledge claims than experimental papers because the latter have more routinely standardized structures and less flexibility in literary style.

Sinding's (1996) research also showed the way this biologist supported his main knowledge claim by first framing his work in the language of endocrinology rather than his own disciplinary language, thereby gaining support from members of this other scientific community. Other analyses have shown that appropriating scientific discourse and culture has allowed activists to construct their own credibility as participants in science (Brown 1992; Epstein 1995, 1997). As Epstein (1995) argued, once AIDS activists presented their arguments in the language of medical science and biostatistics, researchers were compelled to pay attention. The common language shared among activists and researchers has since contributed to changes in therapeutic care techniques, clinical trial design and clinical trial access. Evidence of changes in activists' discourse practices can also be seen in activist publications such as *AIDS Treatment News* and *Treatment Issues,* which provide forums to assist patients and practitioners in evaluating clinical research and finding out about clinical trials.

Other interesting cases of adopting and adapting the language of science can be seen in publications such as *The New Our Bodies, Ourselves* (Boston Women's Health Book Collective 1992), which have arisen from feminist health movements. Bell (1994) describes her own contributions to this popular text: 'As an author of "Birth Control" in *The New Our Bodies, Ourselves*, I am a translator of science to women, but I am not a biologist, endocrinologist or demographer. I am an outsider to the discourses which I have interpreted' (p. 10). As a translator of science, she (a) simplified technical terms and complex formulae using ordinary language; (b) revealed the uncertainties and limitations of scientific knowledge (but not so stringently as to introduce confusion and paralysis); (c) provided a feminist critique of scientific knowledge; and (d) represented multiple positions by including the voices of scientists, doctors, women's activists, women who use birth control and potential readers of the text. Through these efforts, Bell bridged the discourses of science, medicine, feminism and everyday life. Such bridging allows communication across discourse communities as members of those communities come together under a new shared discourse. Sharing discourse about science-related topics is a means to, and evidence of, the kind of scientific literacy that we envision as a goal for science education. Such literacy enables wide ranges of people to understand and communicate about scientific issues, which is itself a form of participation in scientific practice.

Implications for educational practice

Viewing scientific knowledge as competence in scientific discourses rather than as bodies of facts and theories has important implications. As in learning any language, competence is acquired through participation in ongoing practice (Lave and Wenger 1991). Without engaging in ongoing practice, students learn only decontextualized vocabularies that lead to brittle understandings (Brown *et al.* 1989); in contrast, participation in ongoing practice fosters the development of robust understandings and discourse.

Educational aims

The aim of science education informed by science and technology studies would not be to impart a few scientific facts, but for students to begin their participation in ongoing science discourses. Some students (traditionally a small number) will traverse trajectories that lead to full participation in scientific laboratories; others may begin trajectories that lead to participation in activist movements, environmental agencies, the health system, product development teams, policy think tanks, educational organizations or the judicial system. Regardless of the choice of trajectory, science education needs to prepare students to engage in science-based discourses relevant to the associated communities of practice. All graduates would be expected to increase their participation in public science-related discourses and science education could be conceptualized as a trajectory of legitimate peripheral participation (Lave and Wenger 1991) in science-related discourses.

Activist movements are examples of the power and influence that can be gained through competent participation in public science-related discourses. Such competency involves formulating arguments that use the resources of the community to increase the rhetorical strengths of a particular position. Even school-age students can, with the results of their research made available to politicians and media, influence environmental policy and decision-making and thereby already engage in the public production of science (e.g. Greenall Gough 1992; Helms 1996). The aim of science education, as informed by science and technology studies, would therefore be to prepare graduates to engage in science-related discourses in their chosen field, whether in a traditional scientific domain such as biology or physics, or in any of the other communities where science discourse is used. [...]

Learning experiences

Science and technology studies conceptualize scientific knowledge in terms of discourse that members of communities use to accomplish their goals through situated action. Following this lead, classrooms cannot be viewed as places where students receive knowledge as they listen to teachers talk. The notion of scientific knowledge as discourse implies that students learn through active participation (Lemke 1990; Orsolini and Pontecorvo 1992; Théberge Rafal 1996). When students come to science, this participation begins on the basis of everyday language that they bring to instruction. Past research shows that this discourse shares only small amounts with accepted scientific discourses. However, through increasing competence and participation, this discourse increasingly comes to resemble the discourse adopted by working scientists (McGinn *et al.* 1995; Théberge Rafal 1996).

It is evident that, in large science classes, the number of students who can participate is limited, as is the length of their contributions. At the same time, students who work on their own in small groups may draw little benefit from the discursive competence of their peers and teacher. Learning scientific discourse therefore implies a flexible organization between whole-class conversations and small-group activities that are open to interaction between various groups (Roth and McGinn 1996). Court cases in which scientific knowledge plays an important role, scientific conferences in which individuals and groups present and defend their research, or legislative debates, may be fruitful images and models for organizing whole-class science conversations that involve a maximum number of students. In each of these scenarios, students could initially work in small groups – with consultation from other students, teachers and resource materials – to prepare a 'case' that would then be presented and defended before the whole class. [...]

Given the extent of scientific topics, it may not be reasonable to give every student the opportunity to talk about all details of atomic theory, cell division or entropy phase changes. Some traditional science topics may fall by the wayside, only to be picked up when they are relevant in the context of particular student projects. Roth (1994) found that when grade 11 and grade 12 physics students were given the opportunity to decide which phenomena to investigate and research questions to answer, they were little interested in verifying motion equations and other standard high school physics investigations. In contrast, because of their varied interests and enhanced motivations, their investigations often went beyond the subject matter specified by the prescribed curriculum, in physics as well as mathematics.

The centrality of written papers as scientific discourse (Costa *et al.* 1997; Latour 1987; Latour and Woolgar 1986) suggests that, in addition to talking about science, science writing should also be central to science education (see AAAS 1993; NRC 1994; NSTA 1992, 1995). Costa *et al.* (1997) propose two distinct forms of science writing that students could produce based on their investigations: (a) traditional, standardized laboratory reports with standard sections detailing the procedure, results and conclusions and (b) informal notebooks that describe the 'faults and foibles' of scientific processes. By comparing these two accounts, students could begin to understand the rhetorical nature of scientific arguments and the implications of 'sanitized' accounts of research. Similar understandings could emerge from comparing such writing with journalistic, narrative or even poetic accounts of research.

Resources

Science curricula that focus on debate, argumentation and rhetoric invite different conceptions of content, which in turn necessitate different curricular materials and resources. Consistent with the science-related activism in today's society, it makes a great deal of sense to teach science through current issues. Science education in schools would then constitute a natural precursor to greater engagement in science during later life and the beginning of a trajectory characterized by increasing participation in science-related discourses and practices. As the media continuously report various controversies that involve science and scientists (e.g. the ethics of aborting one of two foetuses, preservation of natural habitats in the Pacific Northwest, drug testing procedures in the search for AIDS treatments), currently relevant topics are continuously available. Some choice of which topics to pursue together with access to case materials, information via the Internet, libraries and various media are necessary prerequisites for such a focus in science education.

But even if the curriculum is organized along more traditional models, learning about linear motion, for example, could include re-enacting the debates between Galileo and his adversaries. Galileo's writings lend themselves ideally to historical case studies and re-enactments because Galileo framed his work in direct opposition to that of Aristotle. Throughout 'De motu', Galileo (1960) used text and chapter titles (e.g. 'In opposition to Aristotle, it is proved that' or 'In opposition and the general view, it is shown that') to contrast his world view with prevailing common-sense understandings. Students need access to historical case materials in order to reconsider the central arguments that led to changes in scientific understandings/discourse. More recent scientific debates could also become focal discussion topics by providing a series of current journal articles presenting opposing arguments about some topic. Using journal articles would have the added benefit of introducing students to this primary mode of communication within scientific communities, a mode of communication that combines text and graphics (cf. Roth *et al.* 1997).

Visual representations

[…] For scientists and engineers, visual representations are central to communication and interaction within and across communities; representations enlist the participation of others in their creation and provide shared interactional spaces to talk over and about them. In this way, visual representations serve at least three functions in the work of scientists and engineers: as inscriptions, conscription devices and boundary objects (Henderson 1991; Star 1989). First, they are *inscriptions* that constitute the phenomena of interest. Visual representations provide pictorial or graphical inscriptions of important aspects of the phenomena under investigation. These inscriptions are then readable, presentable, moveable and combinable to create other inscriptions (Latour 1987). Second, these inscriptions serve as *conscription devices* that provide attentional and conversational foci. Scientists' and engineers' conversations are often about these inscriptions and are conducted in their presence. Third, inscriptions act as *boundary objects* that coordinate work across groups, time and space. For example, a single set of engineering design drawings of an aeroplane is used at various sites throughout a manufacturing plant by design engineers, structural (statics) engineers, welders, business managers, advertising agents and inventory clerks who all have different goals and engage in widely different discursive and material practices (Henderson 1991). The drawings give rise to particular, coherent sets of practices in each group, but different practices across groups and sites. That is, the drawings allow multiple and divergent interpretations and meanings (Star 1989). […]

Implications for educational practice

Learning experiences

Science and technology studies emphasize that representations are only meaningful in relation to the situated practices that produce and use them, so that curricular implementations need to emphasize representational practices rather than 'representations'. Classroom environments organized to allow students to collaboratively construct visual representations to serve as means of communication within the classroom community would fulfil this objective (see Gordin and Pea 1995; Meira 1995; Roschelle 1992; Roth and Roychoudhury 1992). Within these environments, students would be expected to use visual representations as integral aspects of arguments and to adapt and transform their representations to make more convincing arguments. For example, students might be expected to produce a graph of data from a physics investigation to help defend their findings before their classmates, or obtain class approval for their design diagrams before proceeding with construction during a civil engineering unit.

All three functions of visual representations – as inscriptions, conscription devices and boundary objects – are relevant to science and science learning. For example, students could be asked to work in small groups to construct models or concept maps of phenomena under investigation. The evolving inscriptions would serve as conscription devices, providing a common focus and topical cohesion for student conversations and a basis for establishing common discourse. Students would be expected to reach a group consensus about how to represent phenomena and then could be asked to present and defend their representations before the whole class or some other (wider) audience. Students' representations would then serve as boundary objects to mediate across groups and discourse communities. The focus of all such conversations would be to ascertain the viability of particular visual representations (made by students, peers or texts) and whether they provide convincing arguments. Research shows that such interactions provide opportunities for students to engage in sustained scientific discourse, where they learn its form and content (Gordin and Pea 1995; Roschelle 1992; Roth and Roychoudhury 1992).

Resources

Curricular materials and tools to support these goals include devices to record data, cameras, graphing calculators, computers, the World Wide Web and other resources that would allow students to create, transform and display visual representations. Students would also need access to multiple and varied forms of visual representations as models for their own work and as representations to evaluate. These representations may come from the work of their peers or a multitude of scientific resources. The sorts of visual representations that serve as resources and conversational foci in classrooms enable possibilities for student participation. For example, Roth and McGinn (1996) found that visual representations in the form of teacher transparencies or student worksheets and design notebooks were important resources in that they served as scenarios for action, as backdrops for ongoing conversations and as referents that allowed situated, efficient language in a grade 6/7 science classroom.

Textbooks can also provide an important means of access to visual representations in classrooms. However, Roth et al. (1997) provide evidence that current textbooks use visual representations in ways that bear little resemblance to those in scientific journal articles. In comparison with high school biology textbooks, scientific journal articles provide different types of visual representations, more informative descriptions of those representations in the main text and captions, and provide more resources to facilitate interpretation of the representations. Based on these findings, Roth et al. provide specific guidelines for improving the readability and interpretability of graphs in textbooks and these guidelines could be extended to other visual representations in texts. Until such revisions are commonplace, students could use textbooks as case studies for analysing the suitability and rhetorical strength of visual representations in formulating arguments.

There are now computer-based tools that, although not professional tools, allow students to model relationships conceptually and thereby engage in scientific inscription practices. For example, several existing software packages allow students to model (a) ecological phenomena by establishing linear structural relations (Jackson *et al.* 1996); (b) global weather phenomena by relating actual weather data (Gordin and Pea 1995); or (c) architectural design and building maintenance costs by changing design specifications (Hall and Stevens 1995). These software packages allow students to construct inscriptions and implement assumptions; the results are represented in other sets of inscriptions. That is, inscriptions as conceptual modelling tools allow students to configure, argue and test many models in short periods of time.

Concluding remarks

We have outlined how science and technology studies can be used as a resource for understanding science, scientists and scientific inquiry and therefore for deciding what and how we want to teach. Through analyses of scientists' work practices, activist movements and the judicial system, science and technology studies can help educators establish educational aims that go beyond 'imparting content knowledge.' These broad aims are consistent with a vision of scientific literacy as preparation for participating in scientific laboratories, activist movements, the judicial system or other locations/communities where science is created and used. The multiple purposes and sites for scientific knowledge recognized by science and technology studies also reflect a new vision of what can be considered 'authentic science.'

Because science and technology studies are concerned with science in everyday life (scientists, activists, just-plain-folks), they provide a natural complement to science education research that is concerned with knowing and learning science during formal years of schooling. By forging stronger links between science in everyday life and science in schools, students can be supported to move along trajectories leading from classrooms to participation in various non-school communities. The implications we outline, if practised, lead to a critically engaged citizenship that views science and scientists in a new light, which should provide a foundation for competent participation in a number of communities where science is created and used.

However, changes as we propose them may not come easily because they undermine the unquestioned authority scientists (and science teachers) have so far enjoyed. Standard textbooks, cookbook laboratory assignments and lectures by teachers provide insufficient opportunities for students to develop competencies that will lead to competent participation and civic responsibility in a society infused with science and technology. Further, these changes suggest that some traditional science topics may fall by the wayside, only to be picked up when they are relevant in the context of particular student projects. However, such changes are paramount to increased scientific literacy.

References

American Association for the Advancement of Science (1993) *Benchmarks for Scientific Literacy*, New York: Oxford University Press.

Barnes, B., Bloor, D. and Henry, J. (1996) *Scientific Knowledge: A Sociological Analysis*, Chicago, IL: University of Chicago Press.

Bastide, F. (1990) 'The iconography of scientific texts: principles of analysis', trans. G. Myers, in M. Lynch and S. Woolgar (eds) *Representation in Scientific Practice* (pp. 187–229), Cambridge, MA: MIT Press.

Bell, S. E. (1994) 'Translating science to the people. Updating *The New Our Bodies, Ourselves*', *Women's Studies International Forum* 17: 9–18.

Bijker, W. E., Hughes, T. P. and Pinch, T. J. (eds) (1987) *The Social Construction of Technological Systems: New Directions in The Sociology and History of Technology*, Cambridge, MA: MIT Press.

Boston Women's Health Book Collective (1992) *The New Our Bodies, Ourselves*, New York: Touchstone.

Boyle, P. (1996) 'Genetic services, social context, and public priorities', in S. Aronowitz, B. Martinsons and M. Menser (eds) *Technoscience and Cyberculture* (pp. 205–11), New York: Routledge.

Brown, J. S., Collins, A. and Duguid, P. (1989) 'Situated cognition and the culture of learning', *Educational Researcher* 18(1): 32–42.

Brown, P. (1992) 'Popular epidemiology and toxic waste contamination: lay and professional ways of knowing', *Journal of Health and Social Behavior* 33: 267–81.

Bucciarelli, L. L. (1994) *Designing Engineers*, Cambridge, MA: MIT.

Button, C. (ed.) (1993) *Technology in Working Order: Studies of Work, Interaction, and Technology*, London and New York: Routledge.

Clarke, A. and Montini, T. (1993) 'The many faces of RU486: tales of situated knowledges and technological contestations', *Science, Technology, and Human Values* 18: 42–78.

Costa, S., Hughes, T. and Pinch, T. (1997, October) 'Bringing it all back home: some implications of recent science and technology studies for the classroom science teacher', paper presented at the Society for Social Studies of Science annual meeting, Tucson, AZ.

Eisenhart, M., Finkel, E. and Marion, S. F. (1996) 'Creating the conditions for scientific literacy: a re-examination', *American Educational Research Journal* 33: 261–95.

Epstein, S. (1995) 'The construction of lay expertise: AIDS activism and the forging of credibility in the reform of clinical trials', *Science, Technology, and Human Values* 20: 408–37.

—— (1997) 'Activism, drug regulation and the politics of therapeutic evaluation in the AIDS era: a case study of ddC and the "surrogate markers" debate', *Social Studies of Science* 27: 691–726.

Frickel, S. (1996) 'Engineering heterogeneous accounts: the case of submarine thermal reactor Mark–1', *Science, Technology, and Human Values* 21: 28–53.

Galileo, G. (1960) *On Motion and on Mechanics*, Madison, WI: University of Wisconsin Press.

Gooding, D. (1992) 'Putting agency back into experiment', in A. Pickering (ed.) *Science as Practice and Culture* (pp. 65–112), Chicago, IL: The University of Chicago Press.

Gordin, D. N. and Pea, R. D. (1995) 'Prospects for scientific visualization as an educational technology', *The Journal of the Learning Sciences* 4: 249–79.

Greenall Gough, A. (1992, April) 'Environmental education as a challenge to science education in schools', paper presented at the annual meeting of the American Educational Research Association, San Francisco, CA.

Hall, R. and Stevens, R. (1995) 'Making space: a comparison of mathematical work in school and professional design practices', in S. L. Star (ed.) *The Cultures of Computing* (pp. 118–45), Oxford, England: Blackwell.

Harel, I. (1991) *Children Designers: Interdisciplinary Constructions for Learning and Knowing Mathematics in a Computer-rich School*, Norwood, NJ: Ablex.

Helms, J. V. (1996, April) 'Science in action, action with science: studying wetlands restoration', paper presented at the National Association for Research in Science Teaching annual conference, St Louis, MO.

Henderson, K. (1991) 'Flexible sketches and inflexible data bases: visual communication, conscription devices, and boundary objects in design engineering', *Science, Technology, and Human Values* 16: 448–73.

Jackson, S., Stratford, S. J., Krajcik, J. S. and Soloway, E. (1996) 'Making system dynamics modeling accessible to pre-college science students', *Interactive Learning Environments* 4: 233–57.

Jasanoff, S. (1995) *Science at the Bar*, Cambridge, MA: Harvard University Press.

——, Markle, G., Petersen, J. and Pinch, T. (eds) (1995) *Handbook of Science and Technology Studies*, Thousand Oaks, CA: Sage.

Johnson, S. K. and Stewart, J. (1990) 'Using philosophy of science in curriculum development: an example from high school genetics', *International Journal of Science Education* 12: 297–307.

Jordan, K. and Lynch, M. (1993) 'The mainstreaming of a molecular biological tool: a case study of a new technique', in G. Button (ed.) *Technology in Working Order: Studies of Work, Interaction, and Technology* (pp. 162–78), London and New York: Routledge.

Knorr-Cetina, K. D. (1981) The *Manufacture of Knowledge: An Essay on the Constructivist and Contextual Nature of Science*, Oxford: Pergamon Press.

—— (1992) 'The couch, the cathedral and the laboratory: on the relationship between experiment and laboratory in science', in A. Pickering (ed.) *Science as Practice and Culture* (pp. 113–38), Chicago, IL: University of Chicago Press.

Latour, B. (1987) *Science in Action; How to follow Scientists and Engineers through Society*, Milton Keynes: Open University Press.

—— and Woolgar, S. (1986) *Laboratory Life: The Social Construction of Scientific Facts*, Princeton, NJ: Princeton University Press.

Lave, J. (1988) *Cognition in Practice: Mind, Mathematics and Culture in Everyday Life*, Cambridge: Cambridge University Press.

—— and Wenger, E. (1991) *Situated Learning: Legitimate Peripheral Participation*, Cambridge: Cambridge University Press.

Law, J. (1994) *Organizing Modernity*, Oxford: Blackwell.

Lemke, J. L. (1990) *Talking Science: Language, Learning and Values*, Norwood, NJ: Ablex Publishing.

Lynch, M. (1985) *Art and Artifact in Laboratory Science: A Study of Shop Work and Shop Talk in a Laboratory*, London: Routledge and Kegan Paul.

—— and Woolgar, S. (eds) (1990) *Representation in Scientific Practice*, Cambridge, MA: MIT Press.

McGinn, M. K., Roth, W.-M., Boutonné, S. and Woszczyna, C. (1995) 'The transformation of individual and collective knowledge in elementary science classrooms that are organized as knowledge-building communities', *Research in Science Education* 25: 163–89.

Meira, L. (1995) 'The microevolution of mathematical representations in children's activity', *Cognition and Instruction* 13: 269–313.

National Research Council (1994) *National Science Education Standards: Draft*, Washington, DC: National Academy Press.

National Science Teachers Association (1992) *Scope, Sequence, and Coordination of Secondary School Science*, Vol. I, Washington, DC: NSTA.

—— (1995) *Scope, Sequence, and Coordination of Secondary School Science*, Vol. II, Washington, DC: NSTA.

Nelkin, D. (1996) 'Perspectives on the evolution of science studies', in S. Aronowitz, B. Martinsons, M. Menser and J. Rich (eds) *Technoscience and Cyberculture* (pp. 31–6), New York, NY: Routledge.

Orsolini, M. and Pontecorvo, C. (1992) 'Children's talk in classroom discussions', *Cognition and Instruction* 9: 113–36.

Pickering, A. (ed.) (1992) *Science as Practice and Culture*, Chicago, IL: University of Chicago Press.

Radinsky, J. and Gomez, L. M. (1998, April) 'Goals of participants – high stakes projects beyond the classroom', in L. M. Gomez *A Framework for Authenticity: Mutual Benefits Partnerships*, symposium presented at the American Educational Research Association annual meeting, San Diego, CA.

Roll-Hansen, N. (1994) 'Science, politics, and the mass media: on biased communication of environmental issues', *Science, Technology, and Human Values* 19: 324–41.

Roschelle, J. (1992) 'Learning by collaborating: convergent conceptual change', *Journal of the Learning Sciences* 2: 235–76.

Rosebery, A. S., Warren, B. and Conant, F. R. (1992) 'Appropriating science discourse: findings from language minority classrooms', *Journal of the Learning Sciences* 2: 61–94.

Rosen, P. (1993) 'The social construction of mountain bikes: technology and postmodernity in the cycle industry', *Social Studies of Science* 23: 479–513.

Roth, W.-M. (1994) 'Experimenting in a constructivist high school physics laboratory', *Journal of Research in Science Teaching* 31, 197–223.

—— (1996) 'Art and artifact of children's designing: a situated cognition perspective', *Journal of the Learning Sciences* 5: 129–66.

—— and Bowen, G. M. (1995) 'Knowing and interacting: a study of culture, practices, and resources in a grade 8 open-inquiry science classroom guided by a cognitive apprenticeship metaphor', *Cognition and Instruction* 13: 73–128.

—— and Lucas, K. B. (1997) 'From "truth" to "invented reality": a discourse analysis of high school physics students' talk about scientific knowledge', *Journal of Research in Science Teaching* 34: 145–79.

—— and McGinn, M. K. (1996) 'Differential participation during science conversations: the interaction of display artifacts, social configuration, and physical arrangements', in D. C. Edelson and E. A. Domeshek (eds) *Proceedings of ICLS 96* (pp. 300–7), Charlottesville, VA: Association for the Advancement of Computing in Education.

——, McGinn, M. K. and Bowen, G. M. (1997, March) 'Towards an anthropology of graphing', poster presented at the American Educational Research Association annual conference, Chicago, IL.

—— and Roychoudhury, A. (1992) 'The social construction of scientific concepts or the concept map as conscription device and tool for social thinking in high school science', *Science Education* 76: 531–57.

Rutherford, J. and Ahlgren, A. (1990) *Science for all Americans*, New York: Oxford University Press.

Scardamalia, M. and Bereiter, C. (1992) 'Text-based and knowledge-based questioning by children', *Cognition and Instruction* 9: 177–99.

—— and —— (1996) 'Engaging students in a knowledge society', *Educational Leadership* 54(3): 5–10.

Shamos, M. H. (1995) *The Myth of Scientific Literacy*, New Brunswick, NJ: Rutgers University Press.

Sinding, C. (1996) 'Literary genres and the construction of knowledge in biology: semantic shifts and scientific change', *Social Studies of Science* 26: 43–70.

Solomon, S. M. and Hackett, E. J. (1996) 'Setting boundaries between science and law! Lessons from Daubert *v.* Merrell Dow Pharmaceuticals, Inc.', *Science, Technology, and Human Values* 21: 131–56.

Sørenson, K. H. and Levold, N. (1992) 'Tacit networks, heterogeneous engineers, and embodied technology', *Science, Technology, and Human Values* 17: 13–35.

Star, S. L. (1989) 'The structure of ill-structured solutions: boundary objects and heterogeneous distributed problem solving', in L. Gasser and M. N. Huhns (eds) *Distributed Artificial Intelligence*, Vol. 2 (pp. 37–54), London: Pitman.

Suzuki, D. (1989) *Inventing the Future: Reflections on Science, Technology, and Nature*, Toronto: Stoddart.

Théberge Rafal, C. L. (1996) 'From co-construction to takeovers: science talk in a group of four girls', *Journal of the Learning Sciences* 5: 279–93.

Traweek, S. (1988) *Beamtimes and Lifetimes. The World of High Energy Physicists*, Cambridge, MA: MIT Press.

Turkle, S. and Papert, S. (1991) 'Epistemological pluralism and the revaluation of the concrete', in I. Harel and S. Papert (eds) *Constructionism: Research Reports and Essays, 1985–1990* (pp. 161–91), Norwood, NJ: Ablex.

2.6 Where's the science?

Understanding the form and function of workplace science

Peter Chin, Hugh Munby, Nancy Hutchinson, Jenny Taylor and Fiona Clark

This chapter reports the findings of a study that focused on the extent to which high school co-operative (co-op) education students recognized the science found in science-rich workplaces such as a medical laboratory, a veterinary clinic and a dental office. It also explores how these high school co-op students conceptualized the science of the workplace (i.e. workplace science) and its relationship to the science they learned in school (i.e. school science). As shown later, the co-op students were able to assume successfully many of the duties associated with the role of a laboratory technician, veterinary technician and dental assistant, but they saw few relationships between workplace science and school science. Some researchers might see this as a failure of a major objective of work-based programmes. In contrast, a significant outcome from our in-depth analysis of the data from case studies in each of the aforementioned settings has been the development of a theoretical framework aimed at understanding the form and function of workplace science and how it is different from school science. Just as importantly, our theoretical framework is suggestive of the kinds of instructional interventions that can enhance students' understandings of the form and function of workplace science and its relationship to school science.

This chapter begins by describing the significance of co-op education programmes, and continues with a presentation of salient research literature from which our theoretical framework has been developed. The research methods and findings are then presented within the context of our theoretical framework and we conclude with some instructional suggestions for helping co-op students recognize the relationships between school science and workplace science.

Significance of co-op education

Co-op education is a valued part of secondary education in both Canada and the United States. For example, in Canada, several provinces are moving towards making co-op education programmes available in all schools and, in the United States, a major provision of the 1994 School-to-Work Opportunities Act was to make work-based learning a significant part of the education of America's youth. In Canada, these programmes are available as credit courses with an in-school and workplace component and extend over one or two semesters. The in-school component is a small part of a co-op education course, so students can spend up to four half-days per week in the workplace component, which is unpaid and is typically during school hours. Co-op education is extensive and growing in the United States and in Canada. For example, at any given time about 10 per cent of Canada's grade 11 and 12 high school students enrol in co-op education (Munby *et al.* 1998). In the United States, Hershey, Silverberg and Haimson (1999) reported that more than 25 per cent of 1998 high school seniors surveyed in eight states participated in school-sponsored paid or unpaid work positions.

For Berryman (1993), studies of informal learning are 'critical to the current enthusiasm for work-based apprenticeships, [but they] are so few as to preclude a review of any length' (p. 235). Remarkably, little is known about curriculum and learning in co-op education settings despite its scope (Stasz 1997). Even with an increased emphasis placed on out-of-school learning contexts, research shows that there are varying accounts of the purposes and significance of co-op education within the curriculum (e.g. Chin *et al.* 2000). Hamilton and Hamilton (1997) identified acquisition of occupation/technical or workplace readiness skills, career exploration and planning, psychosocial development and preparation, and reinforcement of academic learning through contextual or situated learning as the main benefits of work-based learning.

In recent years, attention has moved to the role of work-based programmes in reinforcing academic learning (e.g. Moore 1986; Stasz and Brewer 1998). Research in this area has focused on the generally held assumption that classroom learning and workplace learning are related in two ways: (a) students apply academic knowledge to workplace activities and (b) learning in the workplace somehow reinforces school-based knowledge. In Canada, the academic reinforcement claim serves as the basis for granting subject area credits for co-op placements because the intended learning in the workplace is seen as a 'mode of delivery' of subject matter in a particular course. Thus, for example, it is customary to grant a co-op biology credit to a student who is placed in a veterinary clinic. That being said, the student can only receive this credit if he or she is enrolled in (or has completed) the regular school-based biology course.

Although co-op education is a valued part of secondary school education, the link between work-based learning and school-based learning is not clear. In a study of twenty-five student interns placed in a variety of workplaces (including health-care related), Hughes *et al.* (1999) concluded that they were hard pressed to locate clear instances of academic knowledge being reinforced through practical experience. '[Students] do not predictably transfer school knowledge to everyday practice. They do not predictably transfer sound everyday practices to school endeavours, even when the former seems clearly relevant to the latter' (p. 6). This raises questions about the gap between what students know and what work demands (e.g. Smith 1999).

Theoretical underpinnings

In contrast to the approach of Smith (1999) and others, we conceptualize school science and workplace science as different forms of the discipline. Our argument depends on making some distinctions about science. These distinctions are driven by our commitment to developing instruction that will help students learn in the workplace. Part of this commitment is played out in recognizing that the instruction needs to be metacognitive, that is, focused on the reasons for the actions as well as the actions, and that it should strive to make the implicit explicit (Munby *et al.* 2002). Accordingly, when we ask about the implicit character of science in the workplace, we are compelled to explore differences among the science of the workplace, the science of school, and theoretical and experimental science.

To match our instructional interests, we find it useful to draw out the features of versions of science on three dimensions: purpose, accountability and substance. The idea of 'versions of science' echoes *Versions of English* (Barnes and Barnes 1984), an exhaustive study of high school English curricula, and some of the following discussion originates in Layton's (1991) work. We may begin, for example, with Layton's view that the separation of science from technology resulted in a disjunction between knowing and doing (p. 53) and that scientific knowledge, as encountered in formal educational settings, 'needs to be reworked and integrated with other kinds of knowledge if it is to be functional for practical action' (p. 66). For present purposes, it is not productive to ask questions about the nature of science knowledge. Rather, the 'substance' of the versions of science is of interest to us. By 'substance', we mean the body of scientific information, laws, theories and principles that have been made available to us over the centuries. Presently, those who contribute in a major way to this 'substance' work in theoretical or experimental science, or *bench science,* which is our first version of science. The purpose of bench science is to develop new scientific information and its accountability lies in its attention to the validity of the information it generates. Of course, the substance of bench science is constructions of scientific information, laws, theories and principles that are germane to its purpose.

Our next version of science is *school science,* a term used in a previous study (Munby *et al.* 2000). Again, because we do not think it serves our argument, we do not want to get embroiled in debates about the purpose of science education. To make clear the implicit distinction between bench science and school science, we can say that the purpose of the latter is scientific literacy; that the accountability of school science lies in assessment; and that the substance of school science is constructions of scientific information, laws, theories and principles that meet its purpose.

Our third version of science is *workplace science.* In an earlier discussion about the curriculum differences between classroom learning and workplace learning, we showed how the purposes were different because the settings were different. Even though a veterinary clinic is a co-op placement, its primary purpose is the health and well-being of its patients and not the learning of the students, which is the primary purpose of the classroom (Munby *et al.* 2003). So the purpose of workplace

Table 2.6.1 The three versions of science

	Bench science	*School science*	*Workplace science*
Purpose	Generate new science	Promote scientific literacy	Support the goals of the workplace
Accountability	Validity	Assessment	Aptness and correct application
Substance	Constructions of scientific information, laws, theories and principles that meet the purpose	Constructions of scientific information, laws, theories and principles that meet the purpose	Constructions of scientific information, laws, theories and principles that meet the purpose

science is to support the goals of the workplace, and the accountability lies in ensuring that the science invoked is current and is used appropriately. The substance of workplace science is constructions of scientific information, laws, theories and principles that meet its particular purpose. A summary of the three versions of science is presented in Table 2.6.1.

By depicting the different forms of science in terms of their purposes, attention to accountability and substance, we have taken the first step in articulating how science learning in the formal context of schools is different from the science found in the informal context of a science-rich workplace. Hughes *et al.* (1999) and Hennessy (1993) concluded that understanding the connection between the knowledge gained in an academic setting and the knowledge needed to solve real-world problems is critical. Our depiction helps one to understand why a student who is successfully participating in a science-rich workplace does not necessarily see a direct relationship between workplace science and school science. That is because, within our theoretical framework, a direct relationship does not exist. In the case of the veterinary clinic, the form (i.e. its breadth and depth) of the 'substance' is dictated primarily by the purpose of the workplace – namely, patient health and recovery. That is, the scope of the necessary 'substance' of science is exclusively limited by the purpose of the particular context. This stance is consistent with McCain and Segal's (1969) claim that the use of science in the workplace does not necessarily depend on the worker thinking about general scientific theories or principles in his or her everyday tasks. Researchers within the context of mathematics have reported similar findings (e.g. Bishop 1988; Fitzsimons 2001; Nicol 2000).

Understanding the workplace as a context for learning highlights the importance of theoretical perspectives that recognize learning as inherently situated, and where novices are gradually introduced to their roles and responsibilities within the workplace (e.g. Lave and Wenger 1991). We find it particularly helpful to think of situated cognition as consisting of social engagement and cognitive engagement. Social engagement refers to the components of a social theory of learning that Wenger (1998) called community and identity. He used community to refer to 'the social configurations in which our enterprises are defined as worth pursuing and our participation is recognizable as competence' (p. 5). By identity he referred to how learning changes who we are and creates personal histories within communities. Cognitive engagement refers to the components that Wenger called meaning and practice. By meaning, he referred to 'our changing ability – individually and collectively – to experience our life and the world as meaningful' (p. 5). By practice, he referred to shared historical and social resources as well as perspectives that can sustain mutual engagement in action.

Wenger (1998) used participant observation to show these components in action in the claims processing department of a health insurance company. While the claims processors enjoyed their participation in a community that celebrated birthdays and acknowledged identity, Wenger described the 'C, F and J thing' (pp. 35–8) as an example of the way in which the processors were denied cognitive engagement. Their 'understanding' of the worksheet that they call the 'C, F and J thing' was not conducive to cognitive engagement, either meaning or practice. The procedures were clear; however, 'the very technique by which computational steps were made transparent also rendered invisible the reasons that the calculation was the way it was' (p. 40). These reasons included institutional systems, legal contracts, insurance concepts and economic issues, none of which were ever explained to the processors. Wenger described these employees as learning how not to learn and how to live with the lack of cognitive engagement. To a large extent, he described how they use social engagement to 'find little joys' and a 'liveable identity' (p. 41).

Our interest in researching high school co-op students in workplace settings is to better understand their learning in the workplace, especially in those where science is a predominant focus. Our approach to understanding co-op education is based on the position that it is a curriculum (like English or biology) and, thus, its curriculum should have the same features as curricula found in other subject areas (Hutchinson *et al.* 1997). More important, a curriculum perspective focuses our attention on the learning that takes place within the workplace. Wenger's (1998) distinction between social engagement and cognitive engagement is quite helpful to us. Our curriculum focus places our interests predominantly within the area of cognitive engagement. We do acknowledge the importance of social engagement, but our real interest, especially when we want to understand the relationship between school science and workplace science, lies in cognitive engagement. Our hope is to improve the co-op education experience of students by improving the ways in which they learn *at* work (i.e. practice and meaning) rather than the ways they learn *about* work (i.e. identity and community).

We believe that the quality of cognitive engagement is initially dependent on the quality of access the co-op student has to opportunities for learning within the workplace setting. This improved access is more likely to occur when the student adopts a progression of self-regulated forms of activity, apprenticeship and appropriation (Hung 1999). This access is also dependent upon the willingness of the workplace to create such opportunities for co-participation (Billett 2001). Increased access to learning opportunities increases the potential breadth of cognitive engagement, but does little to enhance its depth. Deeper learning occurs when the student utilizes a reflective stance to better understand his or her role within the community of practice, and to better understand the reasons behind his or her particular duties. In this way, the student is encouraged to synthesize the knowledge underlying the actions. Thus, in addition to access, we contend that cognitive engagement is comprised of two more parts: procedural knowledge (knowing how) and declarative knowledge (knowing that). These can be seen as being similar to practice and meaning. Learning at the workplace is enhanced when students can carry out specific actions and when they also understand the knowledge underlying those actions. We believe that workplace science becomes apparent at the level of declarative knowledge and the co-op student needs to understand the form and function of the workplace science before he or she can see its relationship to school science. Thus, we see the importance of creating instructional strategies so that co-op students can increase their access to learning, can perform proper practices and understand the knowledge underlying those actions.

The meshing of our understanding of the different versions of science with our understanding of cognitive engagement (with its access, procedural and declarative components) results in the creation of our theoretical framework that allows us to understand workplace learning from an instructional perspective. In this way, it provides researchers with possibilities for designing instruction that can enhance the quality of students' co-op experiences, and of their understanding of the relationships between school science and workplace science. Figure 2.6.1 illustrates the conceptual relationships depicted within our theoretical framework, which will now be used to illustrate varying degrees of students' understandings of workplace science within the case studies. In summary, our theoretical framework provides us with a way of understanding the complexities of learning within the workplace and of understanding why students have difficulty seeing the school science within workplace science.

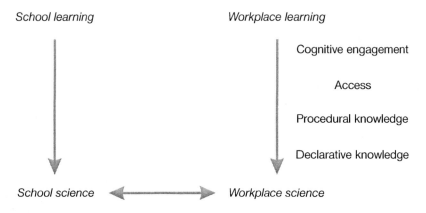

Figure 2.6.1 A depiction of the theoretical framework

Method and analysis

The data are drawn from three case studies of students participating in co-op education in a mid-sized city in Canada. The first case involved Kathy, a grade 11 student who was placed in a medical laboratory. The data for this case was a set of separate interviews with Kathy, her school co-op teacher, her father and the work-place supervisor. The other two case studies focused on the co-op students' learning throughout the semester. One case involved Denise, a student in her final year of high school, who was placed in a dental clinic, and the other involved Ruth, a grade 12 student, who was placed at a veterinary clinic. Both of these studies involved more than 60 hours of ethnographic observations of the co-op student in the workplace, supplemented by informal interviews to clarify specific observations that had just been made. In addition, we formally interviewed the co-op students and their respective workplace supervisors (i.e. the dentist and the dental assistant, the vet and the veterinary technician). Interviews focused on the co-op students' learning, with particular attention to their understanding of the science present in the workplace and its relationship to the science that they learned in school. All data were audio taped and transcribed. Data were subjected to techniques of pattern and thematic analyses typical of qualitative research (McMillan and Schumacher 2001).

Examining access

Turning our attention to cognitive engagement and, more specifically, to the access to opportunities for learning, it is quite evident that Ruth and Denise were quite successful in achieving this. In both settings, the co-op students entered the workplace with little knowledge or familiarity with it, yet by the end of the place-ment, they were performing many of the roles of the veterinary technician or the dental assistant. The following excerpt, written from research field notes, illus-trates the level of participation that Denise, the co-op student in the dental office, had achieved.

> On 15 November (eight weeks since the start of the placement), I am watching Denise assisting Dr Peters [the dentist] alone. That is, without one of the dental assistants present. Denise is attired in her track pants and a dental smock similar to those worn by the other dental assistants. She is also wearing a surgical mask, rubber gloves and safety glasses. Dr Peters begins by explaining the procedure to the young patient and then uses a Q-tip to administer a topical anaesthetic. Denise receives the Q-tip from Dr Peters, proceeds to retrieve the suction with one hand, and then leans and places her arm over the patient's body while the doctor administers the needle. (Later, I find out that this is done in order to pre-vent the patient from suddenly reacting with his/her arms as the needle is being administered.) All of Denise's actions have occurred without verbal requests from Dr Peters. He then asks for the explorer and Denise retrieves it for him, and then she returns to her preparation of the amalgam. Before using it, Dr

Peters asks Kayla [the dental assistant] to check Denise's amalgam to make sure it is of the proper consistency. It is fine. Dr Peters then asks for the explorer and some suction and Denise reacts accordingly. The procedure ends and Denise begins the process of 'turning over' the room before the next patient arrives.

(Field note, 15 November)

An excerpt written from research field notes at the veterinary clinic illustrates similar levels of student involvement. In our research at this clinic there were typically two co-op students at the placement, although our attention focused mainly on Ruth.

The tasks that the co-op students were expected to learn included some very simple daily tasks that were built into their daily routines. On the first day of the placement, the students were told about the job list that they were to work their way through once they arrived at the clinic. This included feeding animals in the kennels, cleaning cages, filling water bowls, and taking the dogs out for walks. The students were given these responsibilities early on and they were expected to do them without overt supervision. Assuming such responsibilities had the two-fold effect of: (a) making the co-op students immediately feel as contributing clinic team members by doing tasks that needed to be done as part of a functioning clinic, and (b) motivating the co-op students to complete these tasks proficiently so that they could later be available to observe and eventually participate in the more interesting aspects of a clinic – namely, the treatment of animals.

Expected tasks were introduced early on, and were followed by numerous exposures to these tasks to reinforce them through repetition. In the example of learning the task of preparing spay packs, the co-op students were introduced to the required cleaning techniques for surgical equipment and the need for maintaining sterile fields. Within the learning associated with preparing a spay pack, a series of gradual steps are used implicitly. These include: (a) showing the students the location of the soap and instructing them which brushes to use (and which ones not to use), (b) showing the students how to remove scalpel blades during the cleaning technique, (c) instructing the students on which surgical tools (including the names and functions of these tools) go into a spay pack, and which ones are put in a 'cold' sterile pan, (d) instructing the students how to clean and fold surgical gowns, and (e) showing the students how to properly fold the sterile pack and prepare it for autoclaving. The co-op students were not allowed to perform the autoclaving themselves because the clinic's autoclave was somewhat old and had to be operated in 'just the right way' to prevent the spay pack from catching fire.

(Field note, 18 September)

Attention needs to be drawn to two important issues raised by these excerpts. First, although social engagement is not our focus, elements of community and identity are evident. Second, the co-op students' development into these roles involves their active participation and that of the workplace supervisors. More specifically, Billett

(2001) refers to the importance of co-participation where the students actively aim to broaden their exposure to elements of the workplace and the workplace supervisors actively work at encouraging and accommodating these possibilities. This is reinforced from an interview with the dentist where he stated that students 'are there to learn' so 'why not try to teach them' (Interview, 27 November). Further, he indicated that employers should 'love to teach' if they accept co-op students (Interview, 27 November). Also, the veterinary technician believed that 'you see people who really want to get into it and learn about it. Those people you obviously take more time with' (Interview, 26 March). She added that:

> When someone looks like they've 'got' a job, and they know how to do it, and it's down pat now, and it's taking them half as long as it used to, you know that they're ready to do something else. If I see that, then we go on. If I don't see that, we stay at that level for a little while. I usually take it from what I see of them.
> (Interview, 26 March)

At both the dental and veterinary clinics, the co-op students were required to learn and demonstrate the mastery of the skills, knowledge and attitudes that are deemed relevant to that particular workplace. The assessment of the co-op students' workplace performance by the supervising staff members directly influenced their access to new responsibilities and opportunities for learning. In these settings, greater opportunities for learning and increasing responsibilities for co-op students were dependent on positive workplace performance assessment by the respective clinic personnel. For these students, the assessment of their apparent keenness by the clinic personnel was directly related to being assessed positively and subsequently being offered greater responsibilities.

In contrast, Kathy's experiences were not as successful at the medical laboratory. Kathy described how she had learned procedures to conduct the tests on samples in the lab, found it repetitive and 'was starting to get bored about half-way through'. She worked with 'few people' and wished she could 'see patients' (Interview, 2 February). Kathy's experiences were limited because, as the workplace supervisor stated, 'they really can't get their hands into a lot of different areas because we're talking real-life patients, real-life tests and so there are some things that we cannot give them to do. They can't take the responsibility of it'. (Interview, 23 March). The absence of co-participation is evident. The workplace supervisor perceived that she could not expose the co-op student to many of the roles within the medical laboratory and thus Kathy's role was quite specific. Kathy also got to the point where she was 'sick of having to ask questions' because she felt like she 'was more of a burden' (Interview, 2 February). Taken together, these factors limited the degree to which there was access to opportunities for learning. Fitzsimons's (2001) research demonstrated that workers who were hired to perform a specific role benefited from gaining a 'big picture' understanding 'of the site and the interconnections between all work roles' (p. 381). The perceived barriers of the 'real lives' associated with the medical laboratory tests prevented Kathy from seeing the 'big picture' and, thus, made her co-op experience less meaningful.

The concept of access to opportunities for learning was a critical component in the eventual quality of co-op students' workplace experiences. Simply put, limiting their access limited the breadth of the potential learning that can occur. As well, interview data with the dental and veterinary supervisors suggested that, in these particular settings, access to opportunities for learning were increased as the co-op student was seen to be achieving procedural competence, and that when such evidence was not present, the access was not increased.

Examining procedural knowledge

The co-op students in the dental clinic and veterinary clinic gained high access to opportunities for learning. As mentioned before, in both settings, access to new opportunities for learning were granted once it was apparent to the workplace supervisors that the students demonstrated they were able to perform the actions associated with assigned tasks. It is not surprising then, that these students gained the appropriate procedural knowledge as evidenced by the following depictions.

In the dental clinic, we observed that there were many routines to learn and considerable knowledge about tools and their functions to assimilate before the novice could begin constructive activity. Denise spent many hours learning the names of the tools and how dental procedures are coded, based on the tooth and the surface in question. This knowledge was necessary for her to prepare dental trays for each of the scheduled procedures. For example, as she explained to a researcher, that a 2-5 MOD refers to the fifth tooth on a person's upper left and 'mesial is the front surface, occlusal is the biting surface, and D is the back, the distal [surface]' (Observation, 2 October). Denise indicated that she understood the process of learning routines in the dental office, learning 'by memory, and by always doing the same thing every day, you get like used to turns and how to do stuff' (Observation, 2 October).

However, by the end of our observations, Denise was anticipating the doctor's needs while assisting him, without coaching. Even before the end of our observations, Denise demonstrated that she could visualize the steps in a dental procedure (an example of reconstructing an event) while preparing a tray of instruments for that procedure. She recounted the steps saying, Dr Peters first looks at the tooth, 'then he injects the freezing, and then the etching'. 'Then he washes that off, and he puts the Mylar strip in the wedge ... then it's cured with the light' and 'after all of them, you put the fortifier on' (Observation, 18 October).

Ruth also exhibited this ability to anticipate the doctor's needs. The following excerpt, written from a research field note, captures this.

> Ruth brings the clippers to the vet on cue. The vet takes the clippers, shaves a patch of fur in the hind leg and administers the Valium/ketamine mixture. The vet hands the clippers back to Ruth and he prepares the anaesthetic while she returns the clippers to their holders. She begins to collect the necessary equipment that the vet will need for the neuter. The vet turns to Ruth and asks, 'Got a blade for me?' to which she responds 'Yeh, it's right under there.' The

procedure continues in silence. Towards the end of the procedure, Ruth disengages the cat from the anaesthetic machine.

(Field note, 1 May)

Examining declarative knowledge

In contrast to the co-op students' competent capabilities in carrying out appropriate actions within the dental clinic and veterinary clinic, which is indicative of the acquisition of procedural knowledge, it was much more difficult to find instances where they displayed declarative knowledge. That is, in many cases, the students could not provide the science-based reasons behind certain actions. In those instances in which they did provide an explanation, it operated at a superficial level as illustrated in the following examples.

In the veterinary clinic, Ruth was setting up the anaesthetic machine for the next procedure and was organizing the bags on the machine. The following exchange occurs between the researcher, Ruth, and the vet technician.

Ruth:　　　　I have the right bag on now.
Researcher:　　How do you determine which bag goes on?
Ruth:　　　　You have to have the right size bag for …
Vet technician: There's a certain calculation that you go through if I want to be really technical but basically what we do is say that it's the cat bag size 1. You're looking about basically the size of their lung capacity. You're not going to throw a 3 litre on there, you'd drown the cat.
Researcher:　　So the bag is more or less the capacity of the lung?
Vet technician: It's supposed to be like total volume and everything but we don't do that here. We just say 1 is a cat bag, 2 is a small dog bag, and 3 is a large dog bag. It makes it a lot easier.
Researcher:　　Sometimes there is a dispute over what is a large cat and what is a small dog then?
Vet technician: Yes. Sometimes I'll put something on and he'll [the vet] rip it off and put something else on.

(Observation, 8 May)

Although this exchange began with an interaction between the researcher and the co-op student, it ended up being a conversation between the researcher and the veterinary technician. What is important to note here is the form and function of the science being conveyed. Although the veterinary technician mentioned that there are calculations, and that they are related to concepts such as lung capacity and total volume, this is all simplified into three categories based on the size of the cat or dog.

In a different exchange, Ruth discussed the importance of sterilization tablets that are placed in the autoclave. Basically, if 'all these go green like up to three then it is sterile. It reached the proper temperature, but if it's a little before green then it is overcooked but still sterile' (Observation, 29 May). As in the previous case with the veterinary technician, Ruth's explanation of the sterilization tablets was given in terms of the pragmatics of clinic procedure. Attention to the differences between the purposes of schools and workplaces is helpful in understanding this lack of cognitive engagement within the declarative knowledge component of the co-op students' workplace learning. Science learning in schools is quite obvious, because the purpose of school is such learning, whereas workplace science always serves the purpose of the workplace, which, in our two case studies, was patient health and recovery. Thus, because student learning of the science in the workplace was not central to the purposes of the workplace, the science was less apparent in the workplace, which in turn made it less accessible to the co-op students. This is also consistent with our earlier work (i.e. Hutchinson *et al.* 1997), where we argued that school learning is focused predominantly on declarative knowledge while workplace learning is focused predominantly on procedural knowledge.

Even in instances where science knowledge was accessed, the workplace science was different from the school science. The form of the workplace science is related to its function (i.e. patient health and recovery), which is different from the form of school science in relation to its function (i.e. scientific literacy). Thus the workplace science for understanding which bag to use on animals undergoing anaesthesia was limited to making sure that the animals can breathe correctly. It did not delve into the school science related to this topic with its reliance on calculations of total volume, tidal volume or residual volume, nor did it explore the mechanisms that control breathing. Within workplace science, declarative knowledge about sterilization was limited to knowing that the sterilization tablets changed to the appropriate colour to ensure that the surgical tools were sterile. The same concept within school science would focus on the different kinds of bacteria, the structures that some bacteria have (i.e. endospore capsules) that make them resistant to heat and the required conditions necessary to kill such bacteria. Just as important, the examples illustrate that the required science of the workplace was embedded within the workplace procedures themselves.

The co-op students in the workplace were quite aware they were learning a great deal within their placements, and they recognized that learning in the workplace was quite different from learning in schools. As Denise articulated 'this is better … in a way it's school … but it's a different kind of schooling … it's easier to learn more here because you're interacting, you're doing it, actually doing it' (Observation, 31 October). She went on to say that if she did not understand something in school, she 'just memorize[s] what's down on paper' whereas in the dental clinic 'I ask them' (Observation, 31 October). Ruth reiterated this in her comparison of school learning and workplace learning in the following quote.

It's very planned out [at school], it's on the blackboards. You look at it, you write it, you remember it, you put it down. And a lot of the stuff you forget about it, but actual learning at the clinic, it's doing it over and over again. It's a system of a repeated pattern and it gets ingrained. It's a lot of things you don't even have to think about, you just do it.

(Interview, 10 April)

Both Denise and Ruth recognized the different kind of learning that takes place in the workplace, where there is little note-taking or exam writing. But they also recognized that assessment of their workplace learning was always taking place. When asked about how she knew how well she was doing, Ruth responded:

> Pretty much any time you do anything right ... and you get complimented on it. You know, that there was a test and you passed it, or if you're criticized ... you know you made a mistake. You'll learn how to do it for next time.
>
> (Interview, 10 April)

She later added that 'you know it's for your own good and for everyone else's good that you learn it properly'. Denise stated that in 'a test at school you feel you're getting graded, and [here] ... in a way you're getting graded, but kinda not. It's for your own benefit that you know these things' (Observation, 31 October).

When cast within the context of our depiction of the purpose and accountability of school science and workplace science, these statements by Denise and Ruth appear to be consistent. Specifically, both of the students recognized that they were being assessed in the workplace but that the assessment focused on what they needed to do in order to be contributing members working towards patient health and recovery. They also recognized that their workplace learning centred around the hands-on learning of procedures that were part of the daily routines of the workplace. Unlike school learning where learning is focused on what they knew (for an exam), their workplace learning was focused on what they could do (as a contributing member of the workplace team). Thus, the science found in the workplace was in a form that met the purpose and accountability of the workplace and, as such, it differed significantly from the science learned in schools.

Even though Ruth and Denise had excellent access to the workplace, and demonstrated competence in the procedural knowledge of the workplace, it is not surprising that the co-op students saw little of their understanding of school science present within the context of their science-rich workplace contexts. When Denise was asked about ways in which the co-op placement made her think of something she may have learned in a science class, she responded 'There's a couple of things. I can't remember them now, but I remember thinking I had learned that in biology. Oh, there was a couple of times, I can't remember them now'. However, she did add that the placement was helping her with the anatomy of the head for the short physiology unit in gym class. When asked the same question, Ruth responded 'not really, we did genetics and that kind of stuff but we don't do anything like that in the clinic' (Interview, 10 April). She added that in 'grade 11 biology you did all the organs ... that kind of stuff, but with [senior] biology it's more getting down to the nitty-gritty ... the atoms and that stuff'.

An added factor that limits the access to the science within the workplace is that the technological machinery of the workplace hides the science. In fact, the more complex the machinery, the more hidden the science. We highlight one visit to the veterinary clinic where the technician was using a set of handwritten directions in order to prepare a blood sample for a red blood cell count using a microscope and slide. She commented that they are currently in the process of hooking up the new machine (since the old one had just been replaced) and that she could hardly wait. She added that she hadn't done actual red blood cell counts for several years because the machines took care of that. Kathy's experiences in the medical laboratory illustrated this all too well.

> I would watch the lab tech and she'd tell me things that were going on but they did so little testing there and a lot of it was on a machine and so they weren't actually doing the test. So it was like, there is a machine and they put the blood or whatever in the machine and the machine did the work and then they just got the results.
>
> (Interview, 2 February)

Our analysis of the lack of cognitive engagement in the declarative knowledge component highlights the need to find ways to help co-op students understand the nature of workplace science and how it is different from school science in terms of its purpose, accountability and substance. The students already understand that the learning is different and the assessment is different, but they need ways to examine and understand how the science is different. More specifically, the science present in the workplace is constituted within the context of doing rather than within the context of knowing. Understanding the situated character of knowledge-use is one of the potential benefits of work-based learning programmes, and helping students know what is appropriate in school and what is appropriate at work makes them more globally competent (Moore and Hughes 2000). Instructional strategies that meet this challenge can only enhance co-op students' understanding of how the form and function of science is different in the world of work.

Discussion

This study focused on high school co-op students in science-rich workplaces with the intent of understanding the degree to which these students recognized the science in the workplace, and how that science was related to the science they learn in school. Our in-depth case studies clearly revealed that, as the semester progressed, the co-op students in the dental and veterinary clinics took on the roles of dental and veterinary technicians, respectively. Interviews with the students suggested that they saw little relationship between the science-rich workplace and the science they learned at school. Our own understanding of school science and our newly gained appreciation for the science in the workplace led us to believe that we needed to develop a theoretical framework that could account for this apparent contradiction.

As such, our theoretical framework offers a helpful way of understanding how co-op experiences can be more fruitful in achieving results more consistent with the academic reinforcement objective of work-based programmes. The instructional implications for bridging the science found in school and in the workplace are situated in three specific areas within the framework. Attention to these three areas will increase the focus on the co-op students' learning in the workplace.

Figure 2.6.2 identifies the three areas in which instructional strategies must be developed. In area 1, instructional strategies can be developed for co-op students, co-op teachers, and workplace supervisors who overtly attend to the issue of co-participation so students can maximize their access to opportunities for learning. For example, students can be taught about the importance of asking questions of the workplace personnel about what they need to learn in the workplace. In area 2, instructional strategies for co-op students and workplace supervisors can be developed to help students understand the meta-cognitive function of routines (practices) and to identify and understand the declarative knowledge (meaning) that is embedded within typical workplace routines and within the 'machinery' of the workplace. For example, workplace personnel can receive instruction on how to 'think aloud' when performing tasks or making decisions so that the co-op students can see the reasoning behind actions. This will enhance their access to the declarative knowledge in the workplace. In area 3, instructional strategies for co-op students, workplace supervisors and co-op teachers can be developed to help students recognize the differences between the form and function of workplace science and school science. For example, students could receive instruction that emphasizes how they can see they are being successful within the accountability of the workplace. They need to be encouraged to understand the science behind their procedural knowledge and to recognize that the scope of the workplace science underlying those procedures is limited solely to the purpose of the workplace in question. These three areas in which instructional strategies must be developed are the focus of our current research on co-op education. We believe that the instructional strategies will enhance the quality of co-op experience for all students, including those with exceptionalities.

For researchers with experience in studying teacher education and the process of learning to teach, the depiction above seems all too familiar. Specifically, pre-service teachers see little connection between the university component (i.e. school learning) and the practicum component (i.e. practice teaching). As a parallel to our

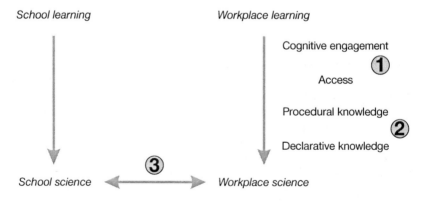

Figure 2.6.2 Areas for the development of instructional strategies

figure, instructional strategies within teacher education focus on improving communication among the members of the triad (i.e. the student teacher, the associate teacher and the faculty associate) to enhance the practicum experience. Additional reflective strategies are available to help pre-service teachers improve their classroom practice and enrich their understanding of this and, in some universities, field-based courses are in place to help pre-service teachers recognize the relationship between the theory from the university and the practice found in the classroom. We highlight the similarity between co-op education and teacher education to make an important point. Specifically, instructional strategies need to be available for use by all participants so that we can ensure a successful teacher education experience.

Our case studies of science-rich workplaces highlight the distinct form that science takes in the workplace and the service functions of that science in meeting the central purposes of the workplace. If we want high school co-op education students to better understand the relationship between school science and workplace science, science teachers and workplace supervisors need to help them recognize and understand the situated form and function of workplace science, and this can only occur when the access, procedural and declarative components of cognitive engagement are present. This must also be a reflexive process such that school science needs to be modified in light of our understandings of how science is used in the workplace (e.g. Resnick 1987). Otherwise, one of the key espoused rationales for work-based learning will be unrealized and, sadly, the idea that school science has little to do with science-rich workplaces will only be reinforced. Without such instructional strategies, we leave the success or failure of the experience in the hands of the participant who is least prepared to make sense of it.

References

Barnes, D. L. and Barnes, D. F. (1984) *Versions of English*, London: Heinemann.

Berryman, S. (1993) 'Learning for the workplace', *Review of Research in Education* 19: 343–401.

Billett, S. (2001) *Learning in the Workplace: Strategies for Effective Practice*, St. Leonards NSW, Australia: Allen and Unwin.

Bishop, A. J. (1988) *Mathematical Enculturation*, Dordrecht, The Netherlands: Kluwer Academic.

Chin, P., Munby, H., Hutchinson, N. L. and Steiner-Bell, K. (2000) 'Post-secondary students' intentions for participating in high school co-operative education programs: a descriptive study', *Journal of Vocational Education Research* 25: 126–54.

Fitzsimons, G. E. (2001) 'Integrating mathematics, statistics, and technology in vocational and workplace education', *International Journal of Mathematical Education in Science and Technology* 32: 375–83.

Hamilton, M. and Hamilton, S. (1997) *Learning Well at Work – Choices for Quality*, Ithaca, NY: Cornell University Press.

Hennessy, S. (1993) 'Situated cognition and cognitive apprenticeship: implications for classroom learning', *Studies in Science Education* 22: 1–41.

Hershey, A., Silverberg, M. and Haimson, J. (1999) 'Expanding options for students: report to Congress on the national evaluation of school-to-work implementation', Princeton: Mathematical Policy Research.

Hughes, K. L., Moore, D. T. and Bailey, T. R. (1999, April) *Work-based Learning and Academic Skills,* paper presented at the annual meeting of the American Educational Research Association, New Orleans, LA, Institute on Education and the Economy (IEE) Working Paper No. 15, New York: Columbia University.

Hung, D. (1999) 'Activity, apprenticeship, and epistemological appropriation: Implications from the writings of Michael Polanyi'. *Educational Psychologist* 34(4): 193–205.

Hutchinson, N., Munby, H. and Chin, P. (1997) *Guidance and Career Education Curriculum Background Research,* Toronto, ON: Ministry of Education and Training for the Province of Ontario.

Lave, J. and Wenger, E. (1991) *Situated Learning: Legitimate Peripheral Participation,* Cambridge: Cambridge University Press.

Layton, D. (1991) 'Science education and praxis: the relationship of school science to practical action', *Studies in Science Education* 19: 43–79.

McCain, G. and Segal, E. M. (1969) *The Game of Science,* Belmont, CA: Brooks/Cole.

McMillan, J. and Schumacher, S. (2001) *Research in Education: A Conceptual Introduction,* 5th edn, New York: Addison Wesley Longman.

Moore, D. (1986) 'Knowledge at work: An approach to learning by interns', in K. Borman and J. Reisman (eds) *Becoming a Worker* (pp. 116–39), Norwood, NJ: Ablex.

—— and Hughes, K. (2000) 'Developing work-based learning pedagogies', paper presented at the School-to-Work: Origins and Destinations Conference, Temple University Center for Research in Human Development and Education, Philadelphia, PA.

Munby, H., Chin, P. and Hutchinson, N. L. (2003) 'Co-operative education, the curriculum, and working knowledge', in D. Trueit, W. Doll, H. Wang and W. Pinar, (eds) *The Internationalization of Curriculum* (pp. 205–18), New York: Peter Lang.

——, Cunningham, M. and Chin, P. (1998, May) 'Co-operative education: the functions of experience in workplace learning', paper presented at the annual meeting of the Canadian Society for the Study of Education, Ottawa, Ontario.

——, Cunningham, M., Chin, P. and Lock, C. (2000) 'School science culture: a case study of barriers to developing professional knowledge', *Science Education* 84: 193–211.

——, Versnel, J., Hutchinson, N. L., Chin, P. and Berg, D. H. (2002) 'Workplace learning and the metacognitive functions of routines', paper presented at the annual meeting of the American Educational Research Association, New Orleans, LA.

Nicol, C. (2000, May) 'Where's the math: prospective teachers visit the workplace', paper presented at the annual meeting of the Canadian Society for the Study of Education, Edmonton, AB.

Resnick, L. (1987) 'Learning in school and out', *Educational Researcher* 16(9): 13–20.

Smith, J. (1999) 'Tracking the mathematics of automobile production: are schools failing to prepare students for work?', *American Educational Research Journal* 26: 835–78.

Stasz, C. (1997) 'Do employers need the skills they want? Evidence from technical work', *Journal of Education and Work* 10: 205–23.

—— and Brewer, D. (1998) 'Work-based learning: students' perspectives on quality and links to school', *Educational Evaluation and Policy Analysis* 20(1): 31–46.

Wenger, E. (1998) *Communities of Practice: Learning, Meaning, and Identity,* New York: Cambridge University Press.

2.7 Laboratories

John Wallace and William Louden,
with contributions by Bevan McGuiness,
Wolff-Michael Roth and Penny J. Gilmer

Introduction

The laboratory is a commonplace of science and school science. For more than a century, it has been uniquely associated with the pursuit of school science. The science curriculum is infused with images of students conducting rigorous laboratory-based experiments, mimicking the behaviour of real scientists in real scientific laboratories. 'Hands-on' has become a catch cry for science education, particularly over the past forty years, driving curriculum development (and facilities management) in the developed and developing worlds. And yet, notwithstanding the central place of the laboratory in school science, there is a growing corpus of research which calls into question both its value and effectiveness, and its connection to the enterprise of science (Hegarty-Hazel 1990; Hodson 1993; Lazarowitz and Tamir 1994; Milne and Taylor 1998; Tobin 1990).

Two major critiques of school science laboratories have emerged in recent times. The first critique draws attention to the mismatch between the high ideals of laboratory-based inquiry and the reality of most 'cookbook' style practical work, with its emphasis on skill development and confirmation of predetermined conclusions (Hodson 1993). The presumption that the school science laboratory is a place for genuine inquiry is largely a myth (Hodson 1990; Milne and Taylor 1998). Much of what goes on under the guise of experimentation is routinised and more concerned with technique and data than discourse. Assessments typically reflect an image of laboratory work as a closed rather than an open-ended enterprise. Genuine experimentation is rare, often confined to extra-curricular science activity such as science fairs. Given this state of affairs, many commentators are now calling for more 'authentic' forms of laboratory work and assessment, emphasising intellectual and problem-solving skills, a much reduced emphasis on technical skill-based bench work (Arzi 1998) and an expanded definition of the term 'laboratory' to incorporate recent advances in information technology and data collection and processing.

A second and related critique of laboratory work centres on the assumption that students can mimic in some way what happens in 'real' science laboratories. Many scholars have observed that science in 'real' laboratories is conducted within a social milieu of interpretation, justification and argumentation. Scientific positions are 'constituted by the researchers' paradigmatic affinities which contribute to frame a phenomenon, to define the operating conditions under which its observation is carried out' (Désautels and Larochelle 1998: 118) and to determine how data are to be treated (Woolgar 1990). These positions are socially derived and argued within particular communities of scholars, in accordance with sets of beliefs, rules and assumptions. By contrast, school students typically act from an individualistic perspective, believing that objects or phenomena offer up observations to the observer, that data speak for themselves, and that observations and data form the basis for theory building or modification (Désautels and Larochelle 1998). Indeed, in the absence of an interpretative frame, students appear ill-equipped to mimic the mature and complex patterns of social behaviour of 'real' scientists.

Taken together, these two critiques – about the mismatch between goals and realities and about the difference between school science and 'real' science – provide a complex set of issues for teachers and others who wish to reform the school science laboratory. These issues include how to imagine a form of laboratory work which is 'authentic' in a world where students lack the social and cognitive resources to mimic the scientific endeavour, how to move the emphasis from an individualistic view of science towards science as a social practice, and how to shift from a culture of right answers to a culture of interpretation, negotiation and justification. These issues form the backdrop to the story that follows. In *Titrations, titrations*, Bevan McGuiness recounts his experience in teaching the technique of titration to a group of grade 11 senior chemistry students. In doing so, he raises questions about the relevance of the activity and the type of learning taking place. The story is followed by his own commentary on the activity and commentaries by Wolff-Michael Roth and Penny Gilmer.

Titrations, titrations

Bevan McGuiness

Teaching senior chemistry can be a mixed blessing sometimes. There are times when you just have to slog through lengthy theoretical sections, such as atomic theory and electron configurations, where there simply aren't any easily performed experiments available. And then there are times when there is a whole series of intricate and demanding experiments. Such a time is titration time. It comes along every year at the same stage of the course, when we dust off the burettes, find the volumetric flasks and introduce the students to the joys of titres, aliquots and equivalence-points.

I remember one year, I had an excellent class. They were motivated, quick to grasp concepts and eager to excel. So naturally, when it became time for the titration section, I was keenly anticipating the way in which they would approach their work. In preparation, I found some of my laboratory notebooks from my university days and made sure of the intricacies. If any class I had was likely ever to stretch my understanding of a technique, it would be this one. So, I practised, I spoke to the laboratory technicians and asked them to check that all the burettes they provided were of the new type with the Teflon taps that would not fall out unexpectedly and generally made a nuisance of myself around the laboratory workshop.

In class, I prepared the students by directing them to the appropriate sections in their textbooks so that when they came to class they would be well prepared for the experiment. We talked in advance about the idea of experimental uncertainty and how it could be reduced by the use of precise apparatus, and we discussed the difference between accuracy and precision. In all, I thought I had them well prepared for the, what I considered, fun ahead.

At last the day arrived. I remember it clearly. It was warm and sunny, the students came in just after lunchtime and they were all a bit hot and sweaty. Immediately they came in, I called their attention to the demonstration titration I had set up. Carefully, I went through the steps. I demonstrated the technique that my teacher had shown me when I had been in high school.

First of all, I went through the use of the pipette, showing the manipulation of the two different types of pipette fillers and discussing the reasons for not pipetting by mouth. Then I put the conical flask under the burette and, with my right hand swirling the flask, I put my left hand around the burette and carefully opened the tap to allow the low concentration acid to dribble out into the swirling flask. It was at this stage that I remembered that I had not put in any indicator, so I played my favourite game of 'spot the deliberate mistake' and challenged the students to identify what I had forgotten. It was gratifying to have several students volunteer the correct answer. Carefully, I added the appropriate indicator, demonstrating the technique of introducing it to the aliquot of alkali.

It was great. I did three titrations and got them to within 0.5 ml of each other. At the third, the students even gave me a little round of applause. We then discussed the use of error analysis to correctly record the results. This last exercise slowed down the interest of the class as the realities of the complexities of percentage errors dawned upon them. By the time all of this had been covered, the period came to an end. I bade farewell to my class with cheerful cries of 'See you tomorrow' and reflected on a very successful demonstration lesson.

The next day, when the students started their own titrations, I had second thoughts about the success of the demonstration. At the outset, the students made basic errors in their pipetting techniques. Then they insisted on making the actual titration a two-student job, with one swirling the conical flask and the other operating the tap. I watched in disbelief as I walked around the room. Finally, I could take it no more and called them all to stop what they were doing and pay attention to the front of the room. Once again, I went through the whole procedure, demonstrating and explaining as I carried out another titration and, once again, I sent them back to their desks to try the technique. This time they performed a bit better, but still there were errors. Oh, well, there is always tomorrow.

Tomorrow came and the students tried once more to master the technique of titrating. It is worth pointing out at this stage that we were working through a series of experiments. The first was to prepare a standard solution, then to use that to standardise another solution. This standardised solution was then to be used to calculate the concentrations of two or three commercial products. Naturally, a certain amount of time had been allocated to this set of practical work, an amount that is, on paper, quite generous. Of course, it was becoming apparent that this class would run over time but, as always, I chose to ignore that in preference to finishing the work.

The work continued on the following day, the one following that, and on for several days. During that time, the students' skills improved and their titrations became more and more accurate and more precise. Once this had occurred, it was time to discuss error analysis. Typically, this elicited groans of complaint, indeed disbelief when the complexities involved became apparent. This class was no exception and there came the predictable 'Oh, no' and 'You're kidding' and even a few 'I don't get this at all' remarks. But, being good students, they buckled down and made the effort to learn the mathematical manipulations necessary to deal with percentage errors and experimental uncertainties.

However, after all these difficulties, we struggled on through together. I say 'together' seriously as it felt that I became a part of the class, joining in with their struggle with this long and demanding period of their studies. We had worked hard and we had come to the stage where the titration technique had been successfully tackled and, dare I say it, mastered.

Finally, the time came when we faced the last hurdle, the end-of-unit test. Somewhat nervously, I collected the test papers from my colleague who had written it. Walking to the class, I read through it and felt comfortable. As tests went, this was a fair, if predictable, one. There were three nice titration calculations and even a few multiple-choice questions based on titration technique. That pleased me, considering how much work we had put in on the technical side of the course.

However, when I marked the tests, I was shattered. Apart from the predictable few students who would succeed at anything, the marks were very poor. Indeed they were appalling. I couldn't believe it. Hadn't we spent more time than normal? Hadn't I personally spent literally hours going over and over again the whole titration system?

The answer, when it came, should not have been a surprise. I asked one of the mid-range ability students (you know the type; he averaged a C, but on a good day pushed it up to a B, a good lad who tried hard and gave his best) what had happened.

'What happened, Bill? We spent heaps of time on titrations and you all bombed badly on the test. What's the story?' I asked him.

'Yeah, but we spent all the time on the skills, the experiments. The test was all on calculations about titrations. We all studied up on the techniques, you know, all the stuff you taught us. We didn't think too much about the calculations,' he said, a little bitterly.

'But I told you all that the whole thing was about the calculations at the end. I said that', I protested.

'Oh yeah, you did. But we spent all that time on the pracs. So we thought that was the big thing.'

As he walked away, carrying his test paper with the 29 per cent grade in red on the front page, I was forced to reflect that maybe I did indeed have to think, perhaps rethink, my priorities in teaching chemistry.

Teacher commentary

Bevan McGuiness

Whenever we teach students we take on a wide range of tasks and problems. The task of teaching chemistry is no different in that it has its own peculiar brand of problems. One of the major problem areas that is highlighted in this everyday story of a commonplace event is that of assessment. When we assess students, what exactly are we assessing? And, even more significantly in this story, do our ideas of assessment always coincide with those of our students?

In this story, I had spent a noticeably long time with this particular class going over the practice of the titration analysis technique. While this was, of itself, not unusual, it is a difficult section, involving as it does new techniques as well as new concepts, and we spent more time than normal discussing the theory behind the practical considerations. As a consequence of this, the students assumed that the upcoming test would reflect this time allocation which is, in all fairness, a reasonable assumption. Something which I didn't mention in the story was that, at the beginning of the course, I gave the students a full assessment outline which detailed not only the allocation of marks but also relative weightings of each assessment item. They should have known, therefore, that the test was going to be primarily calculation-based, rather than practically based. But they did not make that step and were thus disappointed with the test when it came.

Another point about the testing of titrations, and indeed any practical work, is the question of how best to assess it. Clearly in the test I gave, the work was assessed on a theoretical basis, with most emphasis on the calculation side of the work. There were some questions, simple ones to be sure, on the technique of titration but the bulk of the test was about the work that follows from a successfully completed experiment. When we assess a practical section of a course such as chemistry, what are we actually assessing? If we test them with a pen-and-paper test, are we assessing the student's practical ability or their literacy? Can a student pass a pen-and-paper test on an experimental technique without having done the experiment? In my experience this is possible.

There are at least two different ways of assessing practical work, both of which I have used since. One method is to use a specifically designed written test based explicitly on the actual processes of the experiment. Such a test is a useful tool for discerning if a student can remember the steps involved in carrying out a titration and then completing the calculations associated with such a procedure. It does not, however, give any information as to whether the student has the skills personally to carry out the equipment manipulations necessary.

Another assessment tool that can be used is the practical test where a student is given a set of equipment, or access to a wide range of equipment, and a problem to solve. Such a test gives the student the opportunity to use the equipment to solve the given problem. This test will enable the teacher to watch students carry out an experiment and then check their calculations based on their results.

As is usual with a senior teaching programme, the major problem with an assessment tool like this is the perennial one of time. It takes time to set up a test, time to set up the equipment and solutions necessary and time to carry out the test. Unlike a normal test, the time constraint issue comes up for comment. If the test is to be testing the student's practical ability, then why must there be a limited time? In industry, while there are certainly rigorous time constraints, they are unlikely to be as short as a standard high school period. Similarly, would we be testing their actual ability or just how much they can do in a short period of time?

Clearly, the assessment tool I used was inappropriate for the work we had done, but how to assess something as complex as titration is not an easy area to address. Another issue which I raise as a possibly peripheral point is that the other class who sat the same test as my class performed much better. The time my class had spent on the practical work had been spent by the other class on solving problems, and they had been given a couple of demonstration titrations. As a consequence of the time they spent on activity, the students in my class were disadvantaged in their final grade.

When I thought about this story, considering writing this commentary, it occurred to me to ring some chemical analysis companies. I asked the chemists working at eight such companies whether they actually used titrations in the course of their normal duties. The responses were mixed, with five companies saying that titrations were a normal, regular part of their analysis, two saying they were never used at all, and the last company saying that titrations could be used on irregular occasions, if nothing else would do the job. The general impression I gained from talking to these chemists in the workplace was that the titration technique would never totally disappear, but it was gradually being replaced by new techniques. One chemist said that they use the ideas and techniques of titrations, but not with 'burettes and stuff'; they use dosimeters. Also, there was a distinct feeling that titrations belonged to 'classical chemistry', to be replaced as soon as another technique could be developed to do the same job.

However, at present, titrations are an important part of chemical analysis in the industry. This is an aspect that I have since incorporated in my own teaching of this part of the course. Now, whenever I introduce this topic, I emphasise the overall importance of the technique in industry. Using part of the information I gained from some of the companies I contacted, I can describe actual analyses done in industry so as to put the experiments into a real-life context.

Phenomenology, knowledgeability and authentic science

Wolff-Michael Roth

Titrations, titrations raises a large number of serious questions that many teachers and science educators fail to address adequately. Why do we ask students to engage in laboratory activities? What is the relationship between moving some equipment around and the canonical discursive practices students develop? What is the purpose of the activities in which students engage? What is the relationship between these activities and the activities of scientists? What is the relationship between the activities in which students engage in class and those they engage in during tests? In other words, to what extent do tests assess what students have learned? I begin with a reflection on the phenomenology of knowing and learning and continue to a description of authentic scientific practices.

Learning from laboratories (and demonstrations)

The most fundamental question to ask is what students are expected to learn when they engage in laboratory activities or watch demonstrations. Science education ideology and common lore holds that 'hands on' (or, more recently, 'hands-on, minds-on') helps students to learn the canonical theoretical discourses and practices of science. However, there is virtually no research that shows how and in which ways manipulating some equipment or apparatus should change someone's understanding of theoretical frameworks of science. What evidence do we have that doing a titration (even 'correctly') helps students to learn any chemistry? It has been argued that the claims about the value of traditional laboratory activities are largely unexamined and constitute a 'powerful, myth-making rhetoric' (Hodson 1990: 34); school laboratory activities are largely ill-conceived, confused and unproductive in that many students learn little of or about science and do not engage in doing science. To understand why this may be so, we need to take a learner's point of view on curricular activities; that is, we need to view science laboratory activities (labs or demos) from the perspective of someone who does not yet know the science these activities are intended to teach. Let us take a look at a phenomenological view on cognition.

We live in a world that we take for granted without continuously expressing how the world looks to us (Heidegger 1977). The world is a background to our daily activities. However, when asked, we begin to focus to individuate objects and events, that is, we make some of the vague background more salient and therefore 'foreground' some aspects. However, what we foreground depends on the situation and the horizon of past experiences which we bring to the situation. What we know strongly influences what and how we make salient and therefore what the structural properties are that we attend to. Given the great differences between the experiences of teachers and students – or even more pronounced, between students and scientists – it is therefore not surprising that when students look at the world, they structure it differently (Roth 1995, 1996). My research showed that physics students ordered their laboratory experiences and constructed regularities in ways that were not compatible with the theory that the teacher wanted to teach (Roth *et al.* 1997a); and during demonstrations, students made salient aspects that were irrelevant, and even contradictory, to the laws which the teacher wanted to explain by drawing on the demonstrations as resources (Roth *et al.* 1997b).

These comments make it quite clear that it is, therefore, unreasonable to expect students to construct the same laws and theories that it took scientists 2,000 years to construct. That is, 'discovery' is largely a myth. Furthermore, students cannot just be shown some demonstration and told some structure in order for them to understand the theoretical framework of the science. The view I sketched here also provides a different frame for understanding how we might want to look at 'knowledge' and 'knowing' and, therefore, at teaching and learning. From a phenomenological perspective, we are always already in a world shot through with meaning. From birth onwards, we participate in activities which constitute the way things are for the community (Heidegger 1977). The social and material worlds we experience are sensible because of the way we co-participate, acting in and interacting with these worlds. Such co-participation in ongoing, situated and structured activity produces knowledgeability which is 'routinely in a state of change rather than stasis, in the medium of socially, culturally and historically ongoing systems of activity, involving people who are related in multiple and heterogeneous ways' (Lave 1993: 17). Lave further points out that social locations, interests, reasons and subjective possibilities of co-participants are different, and co-participants therefore engage in contingent improvisation to negotiate particular situation definitions. The production of failure is as much a part of such routine collective activity as the production of average, ordinary knowledgeability.

This is a very activity-centred view of knowing and learning. As we change our participation, we learn. But as we change our participation, the world we experience also changes. Learning is therefore constituted by changing participation in a changing world. This therefore also changes how we might look at teaching. Teaching no longer is the transfer of information but has to be conceptualised in terms of the opportunities we can set up that afford students possibilities to change their participation in a changing world (Lave 1996). Because we participate with others, intelligibility of discourse and action are first and foremost social. Our activities, and in fact the world as we see it, make sense because we already share it within a community. That is, the consensual nature of scientists' practices arises from co-participation in accountably doing science.'[1]

When we use this phenomenological perspective to reflect on the titration episode we begin to ask how students' activities are part of a larger whole that contextualizes what they are doing. We also ask how students' changing participation in shaking the flasks and opening and closing the tap may change their participation in calculation activities. If there is little in common between participating in titration activities and doing paper-and-pencil tests, one needs to question, 'What is the value of doing titrations?' Once we decide that we want students to participate in titrating, our evaluations of their competence should be during the practice of undertaking titrations. Why isolate learners from the resources they have in normal activity to test them in artificial contexts and ways that give little information about competence in normal activity? Finally, … students are asked to get the titration activities right – although they may have never co-participated in the authentic practices of titration – not to make their titrations accountable to others. […]

The kind of laboratory work that students undertook in the titration story is predictable from the very beginning. Here, we do not deal with 'discovery' work but with the nitty-gritty of technicians' work, which, although exacting, reveals little of the exhilarating experience of the discovery sciences and the ways and means by which scientists construct the knowledge that we later come to accept as 'truths'. Students learn little about scientists' purposes for using precision in titration, about making their actions accountable to research co-participants and to the research community at large. Given these stories about 'real' science, how can anyone expect students to get it right on the first occasion? How could they be able to separate signal from noise? How should they know which is the signal that is relevant to the phenomenon at hand?

As a community, science educators and science teachers need to change their thinking about teaching and learning. At the moment, students and teachers focus on grades. What we need to do is change teaching practices to make them compatible with the learning perspective espoused in these reflections. As a community, we need to bring about co-participation in sensible and plausible activity and the production of ordinary knowledgeability in chemistry (and other sciences); we need to bring about contexts with a primary purpose of learning rather than grading; and we need to bring about contexts in which producing reasonable accounts guides students' laboratory activity rather than getting some purported 'right' answer.

Assessment and students' interest: connecting to learning

Penny J. Gilmer

Considering forms of assessment

Bevan McGuiness listened to his student respond to his question about why the students did so poorly on the unit examination on titrations, 'Oh yeah, you did [emphasise the calculations at the end]. But we spent all that time on the pracs. So we thought that was the big thing.'

As teachers, we must remember that both the method we choose to assess our students and what we emphasise during class time drive the students' learning. Bevan chose to assess his students' learning by an end-of-the-unit examination on titrations that emphasised the ends (i.e. the final calculations and error analysis) but not the means to the learning (the practicalities of preparing a standard buffer, titrating the base and using that standardised base to determine the concentrations of unknown commercial acids). Bevan's students spent many class periods learning the process skills of conducting titrations but only the final day of the unit calculating the concentrations of some commercial acids and performing the error analysis.

Capturing our students' interest

A teacher needs to capture the students' interest for them to learn the complexities of titrations including, as Bevan wants, the 'joys of titres, aliquots and equivalence-points' and of the error analysis. For instance, Bevan's students might be interested to know that there are natural indicators in certain plants called anthocyanin dyes that give geraniums, raspberries, strawberries and blackberries their red colour. Poppies get their red colour from a cyanidin dye that is red when in acidic conditions but blue under basic conditions. It is actually the sap of the plant that controls the pH of the flower, so poppies' sap is acidic leading to red flowers and cornflowers' sap is basic, giving blue flowers. These natural dyes are used sometimes in foods, as people discovered that some of the artificial red dyes caused cancer in laboratory animals (Oxtoby *et al.* 1994). Ideas like this might enable Bevan's students to see the relevance of chemistry and why it interests people. The power of chemistry is that it can explain so much of the world.

Sharing personal experiences in chemistry

I always try to give some practical experience from my life as a chemist on how the topic under study has been important in my career. For example, with titrations, when working on my doctorate in biochemistry at the University of California, Berkeley, my research contributed towards an understanding of the mechanism of action of a particular transaminase enzyme as it formed a covalent bond with one of two substrates. The person who had studied this enzyme previously had reported that there were *two* active sites per tetrameric protein (i.e. two binding sites for the substrate to this enzyme with four identical protein chains per intact unit). Not intending to observe anything different from that which had been reported previously, I titrated the enzyme with the substrate, quantitating it by using a visible colour change that occurred on binding. From my very first experiment, I found that my data indicated that there were four binding sites per tetramer (Gilmer *et al.* 1977) and it took me a year's worth of experiments to convince my directing professor that the literature was wrong. This story always impresses students that science is an incremental process of understanding and that it is rigorous. However, I also share with my students how good I felt when my major professor did a titration himself of the same enzyme but with another substrate that he was studying, and he confirmed my report of *four* binding sites per tetramer.

Using the Internet

Another thing that might have helped Bevan's students to see the importance and practicality of determining the concentrations of the commercial acid products would have been to encourage his students to look on the Internet for practical applications of undertaking titrations. His students might have even selected a commercial product that they wanted to titrate.

Alternately, his students might have become interested to determine the amount of acid in acidic rainfall isolated from different locales within their country. The students would become motivated to do a standard titration first to develop their methods, so that they could test unknowns that could be more meaningful to them. When testing the samples of acid rain, instead of having a fully outlined procedure, students would have to think about how to conduct the experiment, making the results meaningful and reproducible. Bevan's students would come to know science as it is done, with its frustrations and rewards. They could take ownership of their own data. They could also interact with students around the world who are conducting similar studies through Project GLOBE on the Internet at <http://www.globe.gov>.

For a chapter on acids and bases in a biochemistry course that I taught recently at university level, students became interested in the practical applications of buffers through searches on the Internet. My students found that buffers are used in electrophoresis of DNA, to determine gene sequences, and in feed for cattle, to increase the mass of beef.

Using portfolios in assessing students' learning

Bevan might have included within his assessment not only his traditional end-of-the-unit written test, but also alternative assessment such as his students' learning of their Internet project. Since many students still do not know how to use search engines on the Internet, he would have had to teach them how to do that. When students are given freedom to explore, they will innovate and find all sorts of things that the teacher did not realise beforehand. This means that the teacher must be a learner too, be open to learning from his or her own students, but at the same time also be critical and questioning of what the students proclaim.

I find in my own class activities that if I have the students working in collaborative groups, it helps them learn, as they must use the language of the discipline when they try to explain to each other what it is that they know, as they teach each other. Students all come to the classroom with their own prior knowledge and experiences (Glasersfeld 1989). Each student can share understandings with peers in the classroom. Students can learn from each other as well as from the teacher.

For Bevan's assessment of what his students contributed and learned, each student could write an entry into a portfolio which contains evidence of the student's learning (Collins 1992). I have found it helpful to guide the students in their writing by having them follow a written rubric of what should be included. For instance, my most recent five-point rubric (which is always evolving) for individual students' electronic portfolios included:

- *sharing accurate understanding of the science content* (helping both the student to utilise the discourse of science and the teacher to realise students' misconceptions)
- *using good grammar and spelling to communicate learning* (helping the student to communicate more clearly)

- *reflecting on prior learning and current learning* (helping the student link what he/she had learned already to new learning; students also realise through reflection what helps and inhibits their learning)
- *referencing where the student learned additional material* (from a website, book or newspaper article that the student has found that facilitated learning)
- *asking a good question that the student still has in his/her mind at the end of the student's research* (giving the teacher a window into the student's mind to see how far each student is in his/her learning).

It takes time for the teacher to read what the students have written and to respond individually. However, doing this allows the beginning of a connection to his/her students' learning, to find out what the students know and don't know while still teaching the unit. As the teacher does this and reflects on his/her teaching, the feedback received influences the teaching later in the week. Instead of finding out at the end of the unit what the students do not know, the teacher finds out while there still is an opportunity to change emphases, clear up misconceptions and enhance learning in the classroom. This is the first step towards conducting action research in your own classroom. Action research in elementary (Spiegel *et al.* 1995), middle (McDonald and Gilmer 1997) and high school (Yerrick 1998) settings can provide teachers at all levels with visions of how to improve science teaching and learning in their own classrooms.

Synthesis

Perhaps more than most laboratory activity, titration technique in school chemistry has been raised to the status of high art (or science). In some parts of the world, serious state and national competitions are held for school students to demonstrate their titration skills. This emphasis on perfecting the technique appears as the overriding focus of the lesson described in *Titrations, titrations* (the word 'technique' appears eighteen times in McGuiness's story and commentary). The zeal with which this teacher pursues titration technique will, no doubt, be familiar to those who have taught senior chemistry. However, given the critiques of laboratory work offered at the beginning of the chapter, we are left to wonder how this kind of activity might rate as 'authentic' science. Several angles on this issue are provided by the commentators.

The first angle is that the science laboratory needs to proceed in an atmosphere of accountability rather than rightness. As Roth suggests, 'we need to bring about contexts in which producing reasonable accounts guides students' laboratory activity rather than getting some purported 'right' answer'. This is a complex business, as Roth points out, as knowledgeability develops from a culture of co-participation in 'ongoing, situated and structured activity'. He draws parallels with images of scientists at work. His observations of the complex social milieu of conducting science are confirmed by Gilmer's account of her doctoral research in biochemistry. Apart from doing endless titrations, one of Gilmer's major tasks was to convince her directing professor that the literature was wrong. Authentic school science, according to these commentators, develops within a context of persuasion, negotiation and argumentation.

Second, the titration activity needs to be considered in relation to its scientific, problem-solving context. The importance of capturing student interest is raised by Gilmer in her discussion of the value of studying plant dyes, commercial acid products and acid rain. However, capturing interest is a tricky business as her own experience can testify. Her own research on the properties of a particular transaminase enzyme clearly captured her interest at the time, but would probably have been of little interest to more than a few others. Clearly, though, authenticity contains important elements of relevance and interest to the individuals concerned.

A third angle considered by our commentators is that the activity needs to tap into 'real-world' resources and techniques. As McGuiness observes, while burettes may still be used in some chemistry laboratories, they are rapidly being replaced by more modern tools. Gilmer canvasses some of the possibilities of using the Internet to explore a number of the practical applications of titration chemistry. Other possibilities include the use of computer simulations. As the respondents to McGuiness's straw poll indicated, it is not the ideas behind titrations that are being superseded but the equipment and the particular skills for using that equipment. Authenticity, it would appear, involves approaching scientific problems using a range of resources and techniques.

The final angle concerns the relationship of the activity to the assessment practices. All three commentators draw attention to the mismatch between the activity in the story (with its emphasis on process) and the assessment (with its emphasis on calculations). While McGuiness offers several possibilities for rectifying this situation, including a practical test where students are given 'access to a wide range of equipment and a problem to solve', he still hints at the need to check the students' answers. Roth proposes that assessment should be conducted in normal rather than artificial contexts, based on the notion of explaining to others rather than getting right answers. In Gilmer's commentary, she suggests that assessment be based around the means to learning (such as the practicalities of preparing a standard buffer) rather than the ends (the final calculations). She also explores some of the possibilities for using portfolios (including electronic portfolios) to tap into students' understandings. Authentic laboratory work, it would seem, needs to be matched by authentic assessments.

These four angles on authenticity – about social context, relevance, resources and assessment – provide some ways of interpreting the events in the story, *Titrations, titrations*, and a number of ideas about how to move forward. It would appear that it is not necessarily titrations (or even technique) which are the issue in this story but the social, intellectual and cognitive milieu within which this laboratory activity is located. It is entirely possible that titrations (and technique) can be part of authentic scientific practice, as Gilmer's own research experience can attest. However, her experience was part of a scientific, rather than a school science, endeavour, with different norms of conduct. The challenge for McGuiness and his fellow science teachers is to find ways of assisting students to develop parallel norms of behaviour, to marshal the social and cognitive resources to conduct authentic laboratory work.

Note

1   Etymologically, words such as communicate, community, consensual and collaborate derive their first syllable from the Latin *cum*, meaning 'with'. Communication and community therefore always and already presume our being with others, allowing us to share, have something in *common*, *consent* and *collaborate*.

References

Arzi, H. J. (1998) 'Enhancing science education through laboratory environments: more than walls, benches and widgets', in B. J. Fraser and K. G. Tobin (eds), *International Handbook of Science Education* (pp. 595–608), Dordrecht, The Netherlands: Kluwer.

Collins, A. (1992) 'Portfolios for science education: issues in purpose, structure and authenticity', *Science Education* 76: 451–63.

Désautels, J. and Larochelle, M. (1998) 'The epistemology of students: the "thingified" nature of scientific knowledge', in B. J. Fraser and K. G. Tobin (eds), *International Handbook of Science Education* (pp. 115–26), Dordrecht, The Netherlands: Kluwer.

Gilmer, P. J., McIntire, W. S. and Kirsch, J. E. (1977) 'Pyridoxamine-pyruvate transaminase: 1. Determination of the active site stoichiometry and the pH dependence of the dissociation constant for 5-deoxypyridoxal, *Biochemistry* 16: 5,241–6.

Glasersfeld, E. von (1989) 'Cognition, construction of knowledge, and teaching', *Synthèse* 80: 121–40.

Hegarty-Hazel, E. (ed.) (1990) *The Student Laboratory and the Science Curriculum*, London: Routledge.

Heidegger, M. (1977) *Sein und Zeit* [Being and time], Tübingen, Germany: Max Niemeyer.

Hodson, D. (1990) 'A critical look at practical work in school science', *School Science Review* 70: 33–40,

—— (1993) 'Re-thinking old ways: towards a more critical approach to practical work in school science', *Studies in Science Education* 22: 85–142.

Lave, J. (1993) 'The practice of learning', in S. Chaiklin and J. Lave (eds) *Understanding Practice: Perspectives on Activity and Context* (pp. 3–32), Cambridge: Cambridge University Press.

—— (1996) 'Teaching, as learning, in practice', *Mind, Culture, and Activity* 3: 149–64.

Lazarowitz, R. and Tamir, P. (1994) 'Research on using laboratory instruction in science', in D. L. Gabel (ed.) *Handbook of Research on Science Teaching and Learning* (pp. 94–128), New York: Macmillan.

McDonald, J. B. and Gilmer, P. J. (eds) (1997) *Science in the Elementary School Classroom: Portraits of Action Research* [Monograph], Tallahassee, FL: SouthEastern Regional Vision for Education; available on-line: <http://www.serve.org/Eisenhower/publications/FEAT.html>.

Milne, C. and Taylor, P. C. (1998) 'Between a myth and a hard place: situating school science in a climate of critical cultural reform', in W. W. Cobern (ed.) *Socio-cultural Perspectives on Science Education: An International Dialogue* (pp. 25–48), Dordrecht, The Netherlands: Kluwer.

Oxtoby, D. W., Nachtrieb, N. H. and Freeman, W. A. (1994) *Chemistry: Science of Change*, Philadelphia, PA: Saunders College Publishing.

Roth, W.-M. (1995) 'Affordances of computers in teacher–student interactions: the case of Interactive Physics™, *Journal of Research in Science Teaching* 32: 329–47.

—— (1996) 'Art and artifact of children's designing: a situated cognition perspective', *Journal of the Learning Sciences* 5: 129–66.

——, McRobbie, C., Lucas, K. B. and Boutonné, S. (1997a) 'The local production of order in traditional science laboratories: a phenomenological analysis,. *Learning and Instruction* 7: 107–36.

——, McRobbie, C., Lucas, K. B. and Boutonné, S. (1997b) 'Why do students fail to learn from demonstrations? A social practice perspective on learning in physics', *Journal of Research in Science Teaching* 34: 509–33.

Spiegel, S. A., Collins, A. and Lappert, J. (eds) (1995) *Action Research: Perspectives from Teachers' Classrooms* [Monograph], Tallahassee, FL: SouthEastern Regional Vision for Education.

Tobin, K. (1990) 'Research on science laboratory activities: in pursuit of better questions and answers to improve learning', *School Science and Mathematics* 90, 403–18.

Woolgar, S. (1990) 'Time and documents in researcher interaction: some ways of making out what is happening in experimental science', in M. Lynch and S. Woolgar (eds) *Representation in Scientific Practice* (pp. 123–52), Cambridge, MA: MIT Press.

Yerrick, R. (1998) 'Reconstructing classroom facts: transforming lower track science classrooms', *Journal of Science Teacher Education* 9: 241–70.

Part 3

Opportunities for developing inclusive science learning

Elizabeth Whitelegg

The four chapters in this part of the book are concerned with developing science learning opportunities for all students, opportunities that motivate students from different cultural backgrounds, ethnicities and genders.

In the first chapter, Jegede and Aikenhead offer a challenging perspective by outlining the difficulties a traditional science curriculum has for students who are trying to relate science learning to their everyday lives outside the classroom. Rather than blaming the students and expecting them to change, the authors offer their perspectives on how science curricula and the role of teachers should adapt to help the majority of students become successful science learners in their own terms. The article introduces new ways of thinking about science curricula from a cultural perspective.

Next, Tobin continues this theme using physics classrooms as examples and demonstrates the importance of relating science learning to students' everyday lives within and outside the classroom. He foregrounds issues associated with culture, language and power distribution in science classes and emphasizes the importance of this for students in multicultural classrooms, by particularly considering issues concerned with learning science in English when this is not your first language.

Cobern and Loving expand on this theme by examining the definition of what counts as science within multicultural classrooms, and particularly the place of indigenous knowledge within science classrooms. They argue that the domination of Western science knowledge would result in the sublimation of indigenous science in the classroom if it was incorporated as science, so it is better placed outside the canon of scientific knowledge where it can be valued in its own right.

Finally, Hughes critically examines a science curriculum that practises a science–technology–society approach. She takes the example of the Salters' chemistry course for post-16 students and describes how it was put into practice in some UK schools. She particularly focuses on the gendered aspects of this approach and examines whether its implementation had beneficial outcomes for girls' engagement with chemistry.

3.1 Transcending cultural borders

Implications for science teaching

Olugbemiro J. Jegede and
Glen S. Aikenhead

Perhaps spurred on by reform efforts such as the National Curriculum in the UK, the National Research Council's *Standards* (NRC 1996) and the American Association for the Advancement of Science's (AAAS 1989) *Project 2061* in the USA, or UNESCO's *Project 2000+* (1994), science educators have reopened a global discussion about new directions in science education (Korean Educational Development Institute [KEDI] 1997). Many nations are currently rethinking their needs and priorities for school science in terms of 'Science for All'. Some reformers have targeted conceptual change as a focus for education change. However, the limited success of the conceptual change movement, according to McTaggart (1991), is due to its narrow superficiality grounded on psychological constructs. Others suggest that contemporary work on conceptual change instruction should be grounded on a social constructivist pedagogy (Werstch and Toma 1992).

Social constructivism characterizes the nature of knowledge to include the following:

1   knowledge is not a passive commodity to be transferred from a teacher to learners;
2   pupils cannot and should not be made to absorb knowledge in a spongy fashion;
3   knowledge cannot exist separate from the knower;
4   learning is a social process mediated by the learner's environment;
5   the prior or indigenous knowledge of the learner is of significance in accomplishing the construction of meaning in a new situation.

All learning is mediated by culture and takes place in a social context. The role of the social context is to scaffold the learner and provide hints and help that foster co-construction of knowledge while interacting with other members of the society (Linn and Burbulies 1993). Contemporary literature has shown that recognizing the social context of learning, as well as the effect of the learner's sociocultural background in the teaching and learning of science, is of primary importance if a strong basic foundation is to be established for successful pupil achievement and affect outcomes (Driver 1979; Ogawa 1986; Ogunniyi 1988; Cobern 1994; Jegede 1995). Indeed, the call appears now to be for culture-sensitive science education which probes what actually occurs in the minds and hearts of learners when they are being taught science (Solomon 1987; Hewson 1988). This is particularly relevant in the present circumstance in which the science education community seems to be travelling towards two destinations: understanding concept learning and developing Science-for-All programmes.

In this chapter, we argue that these two destinations can be achieved simultaneously by giving attention to (1) the cross-cultural experiences of most pupils when they attempt to construct scientific knowledge; and (2) a cognitive explanation (collateral learning theory) of that experience. These two ideas are presented and then synthesized in the context of teaching science. Implications for teaching will describe new teaching roles, strategies and curricula.

A multicultural perspective

As we negotiate through the maze of daily interactions, we come across a mesh of different cultures or subcultures (Cobern 1993; Jegede 1995; Medvitz 1996). For instance, a pupil encounters the culture of home, the culture of peers, the culture of school, the culture of the science classroom and the overarching culture determined by the community in which the pupil lives. The concept of 'culture' is a shared way of living which includes knowing, valuing, interacting with others, feeling, etc. (Geertz 1973). These characteristics of culture help explain the differences between a pupil's home culture and the culture of school science. The characteristics also differentiate between the various social groupings within the community: subcultures of the dominant genres of cultures. Whenever pupils enter the world of school science, it soon becomes evident that science, too, is another culture with which he or she has to interact, bringing with him or her the other baggage of cultures he or she already carries. It does not take too long for the pupil to recognize that the science being taught at school has been influenced by the culture of the scientific community itself.

In an anthropological study, Traweek (1992) described the culture of a high-energy physics community:

> A community is a group of people with a shared past, with ways of recognizing and displaying their differences from other groups, and expectations for a shared future. Their culture is the *ways*, the strategies they recognize and use and invent for making sense, from common sense to disputes, from teaching to learning, it is also their ways of making things and making use of them ...
>
> (Traweek 1992: 437–8, original emphasis)

Traweek uncovered some coping behaviours by Japanese physicists as they negotiated transitions between the subculture of their Japanese national physics community and the subculture of the international physics community. She found that risks, power and subjectivity were all intermingled in ways that encouraged conformity with the national physics community and therefore made crossing the border into the international community difficult for the Japanese physicists.

Consistent with both Geertz's (1973) and Traweek's (1992) ideas of culture, Phelan *et al.* (1991: 228) suggested that culture be conceptualized as the 'norms, values, beliefs, expectations and conventional actions' of a group. This cogent definition will guide our exploration of cultural border crossing and collateral learning in science education. (For an overview of other definitions of culture used in science education, see Aikenhead 1996: 8).

From the viewpoint of cultural anthropology, to learn science is to acquire the culture of science (Maddock 1981; Wolcott 1991; Pickering 1992). To acquire the culture of science, pupils must travel from their everyday life-world to the world of science found in their science classroom. More often than not, and more pervasive within local cultures in less industrialized or non-Western regions of the world, the imported science curriculum or, indeed, the Western science taught at school, is often shown to be superior to knowledge within the local culture. According to Taylor and Cobern (1998)

> … local cultures are in danger of suffering erosion and loss of integrity as a powerful culture-insensitive science education, operating through the agency of local schools, delegitimates and rapidly displaces traditional ways of knowing, being and valuing.

Needless to say, this exerts a significant effect on achievement in schoolwork (Jegede 1988; Jegede and Okebukola 1989; Okebukola and Jegede 1990), and in other cognitive activities (Glaser 1991). Ogbu (1992) states that school learning and performance are influenced by complex social, economic, historical and cultural factors. As a result, the less-than-friendly clash of cultures within the science classroom might lead to the loss of meaningful learning of science necessary for useful application in understanding nature outside of the school. The learning of what is, therefore, central to science education is inevitably lost within a system which legitimizes the so-called superiority of the imported culture over the life-world experiences of the learner.

Different cultural processes are involved in the acquisition of science culture. When the culture of science generally harmonizes with a pupil's life-world culture, science instruction will tend to support the pupil's view of the world, and the process of *enculturation* tends to occur (Hawkins and Pea 1987; Contreras and Lee 1990; Wolcott 1991). This process is characterized by smooth border crossings into school science.

However, when the culture of science is generally at odds with a pupil's life-world, science instruction will tend to disrupt the pupil's world view by trying to force that pupil to abandon or marginalize his or her life-world concepts and reconstruct in their place new (scientific) ways of conceptualizing. This process is *assimilation*. Assimilation can alienate pupils from their indigenous life-world culture, thereby causing various social disruptions (Maddock 1981; Baker and Taylor 1995); or alternatively, attempts at assimilation can alienate pupils from science, thereby causing them to develop clever ways (school games) to pass their science courses without learning the content in a meaningful way assumed by the school and community.

The game can have explicit rules, which Larson (1995) discovered as 'Fatima's rules', named after an articulate pupil in a high school chemistry class. For example, one rule advises us not to read the textbook but to memorize the bold faced words and phrases. Fatima's rules can include such coping or passive resistance mechanisms as 'silence, accommodation, ingratiation, evasiveness and manipulation' (Atwater 1996: 823). The result is not meaningful learning but merely 'communicative competence' (Kelly and Green 1998) or 'an accoutrement to specific rituals and practices of the science classroom' (Medvitz 1996: 5). Loughran and Derry (1997) investigated pupils' reactions to a science teacher's concerted effort to teach for meaningful learning ('deep understanding'). The researchers found a reason for Fatima's rules that helps explain the avoidance of assimilation for some pupils, a reason related to the culture of public schools.

> The need to develop a deep understanding of the subject may not have been viewed by them [the pupils] as being particularly important as progression through the schooling system could be achieved without it. In this case, such a view appears to have been very well reinforced by Year 9. This is not to suggest that these students were poor learners, but rather that they had learnt how to learn sufficiently well to succeed in school without expending excessive time or effort.
>
> (Loughran and Derry 1997: 935)

Their teacher lamented, 'No matter how well I think I teach a topic, the students only seem to learn what they need to pass the test, then, after the test, they forget it all anyway' (p. 925). On the other hand, Tobin and McRobbie (1997: 366) documented a teacher's complicity in Fatima's rules: 'There was a close fit between the goals of Mr Jacobs and those of the students and satisfaction with the emphasis on memorisation of facts and procedures to obtain the correct answers needed for success on tests and examinations.' When playing Fatima's rules, pupils (and some teachers) go through the motions to make it appear as if meaningful learning has occurred but, at best, rote memorization of key terms and processes is only achieved temporarily.

For a large majority of pupils, science teaching is experienced as an attempt to assimilate them (Costa 1995; Ogawa 1995). A vast range of science education research into pupils' construction of scientific concepts concludes that most pupils exhibit creativity and intransigence in their quest to circumvent the construction of scientific concepts (Loughran and Derry 1997; West and Pines 1985; Driver *et al.* 1994; Pfundt and Duit 1994), that is, to circumvent assimilation and at the same time avoid expending unnecessary effort.

When pupils learn science within a multicultural environment ([including when] science [is] being treated as a subculture of the Western environment) they need to move between their everyday life-world and the world of school science. For a small proportion of pupils, crossing these cultural borders does not present problems serious enough to affect their learning of science. But many do experience serious problems and must deal with cognitive conflicts between those two worlds. According to Aikenhead and Jegede (1999), this conflict is played out daily in science classrooms around the world where science pupils are expected to construct scientific concepts meaningfully; for example, in Africa, where pupils' traditional cosmologies (Jegede and Okebukola 1991) conflict with the norms, values, beliefs, expectations and conventional actions of the Western science community; in Canada, where the indigenous culture of First Nations pupils tends to be at odds with the culture of Western science (Aikenhead 1997a); and in the USA where mainstream Euro-American pupils with aesthetic or religious orientations towards nature reject the world view of Western science and choose not to learn it in any meaningful way (Cobern 1996).

These cultural clashes between pupils' life-worlds and the world of Western science can create hazards for many of them which they must deal with to learn science effectively and meaningfully. In response to such hazards, pupils understandably invent ways to avoid constructing scientific ('foreign') knowledge, or pupils conveniently store the constructed scientific knowledge in their minds out of harm's way from interfering with their life-world experiences. The cultural clashes between pupils' life-worlds and the world of Western science present a challenge to science educators. These clashes create a major obstacle to many reform movements around the world that have taken on a Science-for-All ideology. Specifically, it makes science teaching a Herculean task and the meaningful learning of science an ordeal for many pupils. The ideas of cultural border crossing and collateral learning can inform this worldwide discussion by offering new insights into the resolution of familiar problems related to the teaching and learning of science.

Cultural border crossings

[...] In the context of teaching science for all, Aikenhead and Jegede (1999) described the act of cultural border crossing into school science and its cognitive explanation (collateral learning). They drew upon cultural anthropology, which regards the learning of science as the acquisition of the culture of science. They opine that to acquire the culture of science, pupils must travel from their everyday life-world to the world of science found in their science classroom. A brief summary of this border crossing is presented here.

The capacity to think differently in diverse cultures (everyday and science cultures, for instance), and the capacity to resolve conflicting beliefs between those cultures, are familiar human traits. However, these capacities are not equally shared among all people, as anthropologists Phelan *et al.* (1991) discovered when they investigated pupils' movement between the worlds (subcultures) of families, peer groups, school and classrooms:

> Many adolescents are left to navigate transitions without direct assistance from persons in any of their contexts, most notably the school. Further, young people's success in managing these transitions varies widely.
>
> (Phelan *et al.* 1991: 224)

Costa (1995) studied pupils' varied success at moving between the subculture of their family and the subculture of their science classroom. She confirmed Phelan *et al.*'s findings and proposed a categorization scheme that described pupils in terms of their ease of navigating the cultural border into school science. The four categories of pupils are:

1   *Potential scientists* whose transitions are *smooth* because the cultures of family and science are congruent;
2   *Other smart kids* whose transitions are *manageable* because the two cultures are somewhat different;
3   '*I don't know*' students whose transitions tend to be *hazardous* when the two cultures are diverse;
4   *Outsiders* whose transitions are virtually *impossible* because the cultures are highly discordant.

This categorization scheme will be used extensively throughout this article (see Table 3.1.1).

One overwhelming conclusion emerges from educational research in cultural anthropology (Aikenhead and Jegede 1999): success in science courses depends on: (1) the degree of cultural difference that pupils perceive between their life-world and their science classroom; (2) how effectively pupils move between their life-world culture and the culture of science or school science; and (3) the assistance pupils receive in making those transitions easier.

A concept that describes the high risk of failure during cultural border crossing is 'cultural violence', the explicit version of Bourdieu's (1992) tacit 'symbolic violence'. When language or conventional actions of a group have little or no meaning to a person who happens to be immersed in that group and who needs to accomplish some action, the person can experience cultural violence. [...]

In the context of pupils learning science, O'Loughlin (1992), Tobin (1996) and Lee (1997a) argue that the language and conventional actions of many Euro-American teachers in science classrooms may be experienced as cultural violence by pupils belonging to a culture different from that of the teacher. In non-Western countries, the science curriculum itself may be experienced as cultural violence by pupils who strongly believe in their community's indigenous belief system, whether it be anthropomorphic Africa (Jegede 1995) or Solomon Island magic (Lowe 1995). Science education worldwide aims to eradicate cultural violence and to nurture equitable opportunities for success for all pupils (UNESCO 1994). Because success at science depends, in large measure on how effectively pupils can move between their life-world culture and the culture of science, it is imperative to understand how these border crossings take place in order to plan and develop effective and sensitive instruction.

Collateral learning

Effective cultural border crossing is indeed a complex event. The *cognitive* experience of border crossing is captured by the theory of collateral learning (Jegede

Table 3.1.1 An overview of a cultural approach to science education

Border crossings	Student categories	Cultural processes of instruction/learning; alternatives to assimilation or playing Fatima's rules	Role of teacher	Collateral learning
Smooth	Potential scientists	Enculturation	Coaching apprentices	None, parallel or secured
Managed	Other smart kids	'Anthropological'	Travel-agent culture broker	Parallel, simultaneous or secured
Hazardous	'I don't know' students	Autonomous acculturation	Tour-guide culture broker	Dependent or simultaneous
Impossible	Outsiders	Autonomous acculturation	Tour-guide culture broker	Possibly dependent if at all

1995). The phenomenon to which collateral learning refers is universal and well known worldwide, and the theory was proposed to explain why many pupils, non-Western and Western, experienced culturally related cognitive dissonance in their science classes (Jegede 1995).

Collateral learning generally involves two or more conflicting schemata held simultaneously in long-term memory. Jegede (1995, 1996, 1997) recognized variations in the degree to which the conflicting ideas interact with each other and the degree to which conflicts are resolved. Collateral learning theory postulates a spectrum of cognitive experiences (parallel, simultaneous, dependent and secured collateral learning) to explain cultural border crossings. These four types of collateral learning are not separate categories but points along a spectrum depicting degrees of interaction/resolution.

At one extreme of collateral learning, the conflicting schemata do not interact at all. This is *parallel* collateral learning, the compartmentalization technique. Pupils will access one schema or the other, depending upon the context. For example, pupils will use a scientific concept of energy only in school, never in their everyday world where common-sense concepts of energy prevail (Solomon 1983). This segregation of school science content within the minds of pupils was called 'cognitive apartheid' by Cobern (1996).

At the opposite extreme of collateral learning, conflicting schemata consciously interact and the conflict is resolved in some manner. This is *secured* collateral learning. The person will have developed a satisfactory reason for holding on to both schemata even though they may appear to conflict, or else the person will have achieved a convergence towards commonality by one schema reinforcing the other, resulting in a new conception in long-term memory. Various ways to resolve conflicts and to achieve secured collateral learning are described in the next section.

Between these two extremes of parallel and secured collateral learning, we find varying degrees and types of interaction between conflicting schemata and we detect various forms of conflict resolution. In this context, it will be convenient to designate points in between the two extremes, one of which is called *dependent* collateral learning. For many pupils, learning science in order to imbibe its culture meaningfully often involves cognitive conflicts of some kind. Therefore, meaningful learning often results in parallel, dependent or secured collateral learning. For a learner who needs to move into the culture of science, he or she requires an effective use of collateral learning with a heavy reliance on successful cultural border crossings into school science.

Cross-cultural science education

In many different cultural settings, educators have anguished over teaching Western science without assimilating pupils at the expense of diminishing their cultural identities (Philips 1972; Ogbu 1992; O'Loughlin 1992; Hodson 1993; Pomeroy 1994, 1997; Baker and Taylor 1995; Jegede 1995; Kawagley 1995; Lowe 1995; MacIvor 1995; Nelson-Barber and Estrin 1995; Lee 1997b). Kaunda (1966) in Africa, for example, voiced the dilemma in terms of preserving what is good in pupils' personal cultural tradition while at the same time allowing them to benefit from Western science and technology. His position occupies the middle ground between two extremes: the total assimilation into Western science and the rejection of Western science.

Science educators have developed innovative programmes, new curricula and creative instruction to help pupils. By engendering a feeling of ease in the culture of science, educators have tried to encourage pupils to cross cultural borders into school science. Pomeroy (1994) reviewed this literature and found nine different (and overlapping) research agendas. Her work frames several decades of research and development in multicultural and cross-cultural science education. The nine agendas are listed here along with some major research findings.

1   Systems or programmes to support under-represented groups: role models are less effective than mentors. A critical mass of 'minority' scientists is highly effective, but how to best achieve a critical mass remains debatable. No long-term or exemplary programmes have been identified.
2   Situate the science curriculum in the context of pupils' lives: research is only beginning to focus on local autonomy for curriculum development and pupil assessment. Examples of a relevant localized context for science instruction can be cited, but their impact has not been systematically studied.
3   Culturally sensitive instruction strategies: research has focused on identifying the problems that exist (discrepancies between pupils and their science classes in terms of interpersonal mores, conventions and expectations, such as eye contact, questioning, authoritarianism, etc.) and focused on theoretical frameworks that should address the problem. Teachers' high expectations of pupils appear to improve achievement.
4   Inclusion of scientific contributions made historically by non-Western scholars: Western science has appropriated knowledge of nature from other

cultures, thus giving the impression that other cultures have not helped in the historical development of Western science. Systematic studies have not yet assessed this initiative.

5   Demystifying stereotype images of science: stereotype images of science (e.g. science is purely objective and value-free) inhibit many pupils from wanting to learn science. The 'nature of science' literature is extensive with systematic studies offering an array of implications for teaching science.

6   Science for language minority pupils: learning science in a language that is not one's mother tongue creates major problems for one's achievement. Mother tongue instruction is the best solution.

7   Indigenous knowledge and technologies for science to explain: by addressing pupils' cultural heritage as objects of scientific inquiry or explanation, pupils' attitudes towards science tends to improve. For instance, by simply acknowledging omens and taboos in science classrooms (without discussing them in terms of scientific principles), pupils tend to transcend cultural barriers (to cross borders) between their indigenous culture and the culture of science. The instructional outcome is likely to be dependent collateral learning.

8   Compare and bridge the world view of science and the world views of pupils: pupils' scientific preconceptions (the object of constructivist teachings) can be perfectly logical when considered in terms of a pupil's world view and, therefore, efforts to modify the preconception will be ineffective. Effective teaching tends to use science activities that do not conflict with pupils' beliefs or, alternatively, activities that attend to those beliefs but provide bridges between them and the scientific content. The instructional outcome is likely to be parallel or simultaneous collateral learning.

9   Explore the content and epistemology of both scientific and indigenous knowledge systems: the exploration encourages pupils to identify any conflicts between the two systems and to feel secure with those conflicts. The impact on pupils has not yet been studied extensively. The instructional outcome will usually be secured collateral learning.

Agendas 1–6 tend to assimilate pupils into Western science, whereas agendas 7–9 challenge us to conceive of alternatives to assimilation (and to Fatima's rules); a challenge clarified by the concepts of cultural bordering crossing and collateral learning.

Implications for science teaching

Cultural differences between a pupil and school science inspired a cross-culture pedagogical paradigm for teaching science – a conceptual eco-cultural paradigm: 'a state in which the growth and development of an individual's perception of knowledge is drawn from the sociocultural environment in which the learner lives and operates' (Jegede 1995: 124). This approach to teaching science was recommended by Jegede primarily for Africans, by Arseculeratne (1997) for Sri Lankans, by Nelson-Barber and Estrin (1995) for Native Americans, by Pomeroy (1992) for

Native Alaskans, by Ogawa (1995) for Japanese pupils, by George and Glasgow (1988) for Caribbeans, by Solomon (1992) for all pupils and by Aikenhead (1996) for Western pupils who are not potential scientists (using Costa's [1995] category scheme). Teaching science within an eco-cultural paradigm aims to empower pupils to feel at ease (in the Lugones [1987] sense of ease) in each culture: for instance, the culture of science and the pupil's indigenous life-world cultures. According to Jegede (1995), a conceptual eco-cultural paradigm consists of the following features:

1   generating information about the pupil's everyday environment to explain natural phenomena;
2   identifying and using the indigenous scientific and technological principles, theories and concepts within the pupil's community;
3   teaching the typical values of the indigenous community in relation to, and in the practice of, science and technology as human enterprises.

Because all three features relate to Lugones' (1987) criteria for feeling at ease in a 'foreign' culture, the features should help pupils negotiate their cultural borders into school science. In short, the eco-cultural paradigm acknowledges cultural differences, provides emotional support for pupils, and sets the stage for cross-cultural instruction.

Because success in science courses depends on how effectively pupils move between their life-world culture and the culture of science, other implications for teaching science (complementary to, and overlapping with, Jegede's eco-cultural paradigm) have been proposed (Aikenhead 1997b, 1996; Cobern and Aikenhead 1998):

1   make border crossings explicit for pupils;
2   facilitate these border crossings;
3   promote discourse so pupils are: (a) talking in their own cultural interpretive framework as well as in the framework of Western science without cultural violence; (b) immersed in either the pupils' indigenous life-world culture or the culture of science; and (c) cognizant about which culture they are talking in at any given time;
4   substantiate and build on the validity of pupils' personally and culturally constructed ways of knowing;
5   teach the canonical content of Western science and technology *in the context of* science's societal roles, for instance, science's social, political, military, colonial and economic roles.

These implications strengthen agenda item 9 in Pomeroy's (1994) cross-culture research agendas, but they may not be comfortable for pupils with a holistic outlook on knowledge (described in Aikenhead and Jegede 1999), and they may seem foreign to many potential scientists who desire enculturation into science. [...]

Teacher as culture broker

Success in science courses depends on teachers helping pupils mediate or negotiate cultural borders and engage in some form of collateral learning. The metaphor 'teacher as culture broker' was used by Stairs (1995) to analyse a teacher's role in resolving cultural conflicts that arise in cross-cultural education. A science teacher who is a culture broker will guide pupils between their life-world culture and the culture of science and help them resolve any conflicts. Atwater (1996) described this role as a coordinator, facilitator and resource person in multicultural education, while in a sociological paradigm, Kelly and Green (1998) talked about a 'social mediator'.

For pupils who require a high degree of guidance when border crossing, just like *tourists* in a foreign country on a guided bus tour, teachers will be *tour-guide* culture brokers. Drawing upon Costa's (1995) scheme, we would describe their pupils as predominantly 'I don't know' students and, perhaps outsiders who are amenable to becoming 'I don't know' students within a supportive eco-cultural paradigm and with an effective culture-broker teacher. A tour-guide culture broker takes pupils to some of the principal sites in the culture of science (its significant phenomena, knowledge, skills and values) and coaches pupils on what to look for and how to use it in their everyday lives outside of school. A tour guide helps smooth the otherwise hazardous or impossible border crossings that pupils face. A tour-guide teacher often expects that a science course will develop an appreciation of science, not unlike a music appreciation course that aims to guide pupils through the world of music and its critique, without requiring them to compose music or exhibit virtuosity with an instrument. The role of the tour guide does not imply didactic teaching methods; a much wider repertoire of methods is needed (Aikenhead 1996).

For pupils who require much less guidance when border crossing, just like world *travellers* in a foreign country making their own way around, teachers will be *travel-agent* culture brokers. Their pupils will be predominantly other smart kids, also learning within an eco-cultural paradigm. A travel-agent teacher provides incentives for pupils, such as topics, issues, activities or events that create the need to know the culture of science. The need to know establishes an academic bridge between pupils' life-worlds and the culture of science. These academic bridges represent less guidance than most 'I don't know' students need. Academic bridges help other smart kids manage their border crossings into the culture of science. The bridges assist pupils in constructing key scientific abstractions (e.g. DNA) and assist them to be articulate in analysing or critiquing the culture of science itself. Pupils will likely perceive the subculture of science as interacting with other subcultures that form a fairly coherent unity in their lives. The teacher's travel agent role is one of co-learner facilitating issue-directed learning (Ritchie 1994).

A detailed comparison between tour guide and travel agent roles for culture-broker science teachers is illustrated in Aikenhead (1996). The difference between the two roles is a matter of *degrees* of guidance and pupil intellectual maturity, rather than different kinds of guidance or different types of intellectual maturity. The two roles are not dichotomous. In either role, a teacher makes the culture of science accessible to pupils by methods predicated on cross-cultural instruction (Atwater 1996; Pomeroy 1994) and guided by Lugones's (1987) flexibility, playfulness and feelings of ease.

Ogawa's (1995) 'multiscience' instruction supports a culture-broker role, as does Nelson-Barber and Estrin's (1995: 24) view of science education for Native American pupils: 'The task for teachers ... becomes one of helping students mediate between their personal meanings, their own culture-based systems, and the systems of school.' The culture broker is a fairly new idea, but one that can make intuitive sense to teachers. We can all imagine how we would introduce a foreigner into our own culture, under the constraints of formal schooling. The idea of a culture broker has potential for helping teachers hone their existing teaching strategies, or reformulate and develop additional strategies, to harmonize with their classroom subculture and personal practical knowledge.

Interactive teaching strategies

Many specific teaching strategies for culture brokers have yet to be identified, developed, or investigated (Pomeroy 1994; Battiste and Barman 1995; Lee *et al.* 1995; Snively 1995; Atwater 1996; Jegede 1997; Lee 1997b). However, some research has been undertaken by people exploring the consequences of introducing interactive teaching strategies that relate school content with the pupils' everyday world. (Interactivity among pupils and content relevancy for pupils' lives are two criteria that seem to make the biggest difference to pupils' meaningful achievement in science [Aikenhead 1994].) [...]

An example of a strategy for culture broking in a science classroom comes from Canada, where border crossing was made concrete for pupils by a line that divided a notebook page in half, forming two columns: 'my ideas' and 'culture of science ideas' (Aikenhead 1996). After exploring phenomena or discussing explanations, pupils made personal notes by writing either in the 'my ideas' column or in the 'culture of science ideas' column, or both. Entries in the science column signified a pupil's understanding of the content, not necessarily a pupil's *belief* that the content is universally true (Cobern 1996; Ogunniyi 1988). The dichotomized notebook page served as a type of journal which helped guide pupils' thinking and their use of language, just as a culture tour guide or travel agent would. It was up to the teacher to assess the quality of the pupils' entries in both columns; both had a place in the assessment.

When moving back and forth over the line dividing the notebook page, a pupil consciously moves back and forth between the everyday world (the pupil's cultural identity) and the science world (the culture of science): switching terminology explicitly, switching language frameworks and conventions explicitly, switching conceptualizations explicitly, switching ontological assumptions explicitly, switching epistemologies explicitly and switching values explicitly. This is the essence of thinking differently in two different cultures. This notebook technique, by itself, will not ensure smoother border crossings for pupils, but it may help a teacher develop his or her own repertoire of cross-cultural teaching strategies.

Solomon's (1992) success with some pupils learning energy concepts is encouraging. She described how teachers explicitly coached pupils to move between their life-world and the science world, accentuating flexibility, playfulness and feelings of ease. Snively (1995) delineated fifteen specific instructional strategies and considerations for culture brokers to use when teaching Western science to First Nations pupils. These are summarized here:

1   Use a variety of materials and resources, and ensure that racially stereotyped material is either eliminated or addressed in an anti-racist fashion.
2   'The oral narratives and heritage of the Native community should become part of the school science experience' (p. 65). These should not be demeaned as being merely myth and legend.
3   'The similarities and differences and the strengths and limitations of the two traditions should be articulated and explored during instruction' (p. 66).
4   Teachers should give attention to the language of science and help pupils who are accustomed to an oral tradition or who have language difficulties.
5   'Cultural imperialism should be acknowledged' (p. 66).
6   Integrate discussions about science with history, morality, justice, equality, freedom and spirituality.
7   Where possible, direct comparisons should be made between classification schemes in both traditions.
8   Show pupils how concepts such as heat, snow and life cycles are culture-laden in both traditions.
9   Instruction should provide sensory experiences and experiential pupil-centred learning.
10   'Instruction should identify local approaches for achieving sustainability' (p. 66).
11   The pupil's world should be related to science instruction.
12   Teachers should provide a 'multicultural view' of science and technology by drawing upon a variety of cultures when teaching science.
13   'Activities should be designed to help students recognize the likelihood of continual change, conflict, ambiguity and increasing interdependence' (p. 66).
14   Interactivity among pupils should encourage them to identify their own ideas and beliefs.
15   'Teaching strategies should emphasize solving science and technology problems, environmental problems, resource management and sustainable societies' problems' (p. 67). Pupil empowerment is the goal.

Snively's ideas, grounded in research and experience, offer practical advice and extend our vision of a new pedagogy for cross-culture science teaching.

We have already recognized the negative consequences of attempts by conventional science instruction to enculturate and/or assimilate pupils into science. We subscribe to the belief that enculturation for potential scientists (a very small proportion of the pupil population) is desirable in many cases. Our 'no assimilation' rule would not preclude us from capturing pupil interest or curiosity in science and then doing a good job at a rite-of-passage enculturation into the culture of science (Costa 1993; Hawkins and Pea 1987). Because the process of enculturation – producing scientists and engineers – has preoccupied the science education community (Hawkins and Pea 1987; Contreras and Lee 1990; Costa 1993; Driver *et al.* 1994; Pomeroy 1994; Aikenhead 1996), the process of enculturation is given low priority in this chapter, except in our exploration of collateral learning. Instead, we privilege other smart kids, 'I don't know' students, and outsiders, in all cultures; pupils who conventionally have been the target of assimilation processes because their border crossings into school science have not been smooth. Attempts to assimilate may work for potential scientists, but the attempts lead most other pupils to Fatima's rules. What are the alternatives to enculturation and assimilation?

Two alternatives exist. The first one is acculturation, a process of intercultural borrowing or adaptation in which a person incorporates attractive content or aspects of another culture into the person's own culture (Spindler 1987). To emphasize the empowerment of pupils and the usefulness of the incorporated content, Aikenhead (1997b) used the term 'autonomous acculturation' in which:

> … a pupil borrows or adapts (incorporates) some content from Western science and technology because the content appears useful to him/her, thereby replacing some former indigenous views. Everyday thinking is an integrated combination of common-sense thinking and some science/technology thinking.
>
> (Aikenhead 1997b: 230)

Autonomous acculturation, associated with dependent collateral learning is demonstrated in a case study of Luke, an Aboriginal [Native Canadian] boy in grade 6 (11–12 years old), studying the seashore (Snively 1990). Luke's teacher explicitly supported the culture of his First Nation and she helped all her pupils negotiate impossible or hazardous borders into school science. As a successful culture broker, she was able to transform some outsiders into 'I don't know' students, or even into other smart kids. Other examples of autonomous acculturation are detailed in Aikenhead (1996). One feature of acculturation's dependent collateral learning (for teachers to keep in mind) is the modification or replacement of pupil's pre-existing schemata, a modification motivated by how relevant the new schemata are to a pupil's cultural identity and life-world.

Autonomous acculturation is not the only alternative to enculturation and assimilation. Pupils need not modify or relinquish pre-existing schemata before they understand science. In other words, pupils do not need to modify their cultural identity to understand and participate in some of the cultural ways of science (Ogunniyi 1988). Instead, pupils might engage in parallel collateral learning by *adding* a science schema (one that conflicts with pre-existing schemata) to their long-term memory and by compartmentalizing the science schema so no conflict is experienced (Cobern's cognitive apartheid mentioned previously). These pupils probably learn the content of science in a way similar to an anthropologist learning a foreign culture (Medvitz 1996, 1985). The culture of science is understood by pupils (just as anthropologists understand another culture), but scientific thinking does not guide their everyday thinking; yet these pupils can do either type of thinking, depending on the context. Thus, a different cultural process can be identified to guide science teaching strategies, a process Aikenhead (1996: 34) called '"*anthropological*" instruction of science'. Pupils are placed in a position similar to that of an anthropologist. 'Anthropological' instruction/learning recognizes that many preconceptions are highly useful to pupils in certain contexts (Hills 1989; Kwon 1997). Hence, when pupils learn scientific explanations, they learn to contextualize those explanations as belonging to a 'tribe' of scientists and, at the same time, pupils are invited to use their preconceptions in appropriate everyday contexts (but not science contexts). In other words, pupils are invited to use the 'my ideas' column or the 'culture of science ideas' column in their notebook, depending on the situation. This amounts to concept proliferation, rather than concept modification or replacement (Solomon 1987) and has been the object of research in the situated cognition paradigm (Hennessy 1993).

'Anthropological' instruction may seem too academic or too removed from the everyday world to nurture feelings of ease for 'I don't know' students and outsiders. It may appeal only to other smart kids, and perhaps to some potential scientists. 'Anthropological' instruction addresses the needs of pupils who find border crossings to be manageable or smooth. The culture of science is treated as an intellectual game.

However, the culture of science can also be treated as 'a repository to be raided for what it can contribute to the achievement of practical ends' (Layton *et al.* 1993). For instance, the technological success of Japan in the twentieth century was explained by Ogunniyi *et al.* (1995: 822): 'The Japanese never lost their cultural identity when introducing Western science and technology, because they introduced only the practical products of Western science and technology, never its epistemology or world views'.

For many pupils worldwide, conventional school science seems highly disconnected from practical ends. 'Science learned in schools is learned as science in school, not as science on the farm or in the health clinic or garage' (Medvitz 1985: 15). This criticism is addressed by cross-cultural science instruction that promotes parallel, simultaneous, dependent, or secured collateral learning, which may be achieved through enculturation, 'anthropological' instruction/learning, or autonomous acculturation. These cultural processes rely on the effectiveness of culture brokers, such as Luke's science teacher, who make Western science accessible to all pupils in their everyday worlds by assisting them to negotiate cultural borders into school science. These pedagogical culture workers need to be brought into the research programmes of cross-cultural science education. They have much to offer.

In summary, some relationships among cultural border crossing, collateral learning and implications for science teaching are summarized in Table 3.1.1. The anthropological research conducted by Phelan *et al.* (1991) established four types of border crossings that pupils experience when attending school (column 1 in

Table 3.1.1). Costa (1995) confirmed these results specifically for science pupils and suggested at least four categories of pupils (column 2). The next two columns depict a cultural perspective on science education associated with Costa's categories by identifying three cultural processes endemic to meaningful and non-coercive learning (column 3) and three concomitant roles for science teachers to play (column 4). Collateral learning theory postulates a spectrum of cognitive experiences (parallel, simultaneous, dependent and secured collateral learning) that helps explain cultural border crossings (column 5).

Curriculum and assessment

Culture-broker science teachers will need a cross-cultural curriculum, a curriculum sensitive to the cultural identity of pupils (Ogunniyi 1988; Jegede 1996) and characterized by agenda items 7, 8 and 9 in Pomeroy's (1994) review of multicultural and cross-cultural science education. Instead of bringing pupils into Western science and insisting they assume a scientist's perspective on nature and technology (the conventional enculturation or assimilation into science), a cross-cultural science curriculum appropriates knowledge, skills and values from Western science and places them into a perspective that has scope and force (relevance) for pupils, that is, science for all. For instance, a unit of study or lesson could be introduced by recognizing a community's indigenous knowledge or world view in a way that creates a *need-to-know* Western science (Pomeroy's seventh agenda).

Alternatively, a unit of study or lesson might include indigenous content along with Western science content to explore certain phenomena in depth (Pomeroy's eighth agenda). For example, First Nations traditional ecological knowledge (TEK) can be combined with various fields of Western science (ecology, botany, biology, medicine and horticulture, to name a few) to give pupils an enriched understanding of nature in line with sustainable development (Corsiglia and Snively 1995). Snively (1995) outlines a five-step process for producing a TEK unit in cross-cultural science teaching. For Western pupils who fit Costa's (1995) categories of other smart kids and 'I don't know' students, Aikenhead (1996) provided details for critically analysing both the students' indigenous common-sense knowledge and canonical content of Western science. Curriculum topics included mixtures, concentration, the logic of inference and the manipulation of scientific data.

Exemplifying Pomeroy's ninth agenda, cross-cultural Science, Technology and Society (STS) curricula that combined indigenous common-sense knowledge, indigenous and Western technology, and indigenous and Western knowledge of nature (science) were proposed for First Nation pupils by Aikenhead (1997b), Cajete (1994), Kawagley (1995), MacIvor (1995) and Nelson-Barber and Esterin (1995) and for African pupils by Jegede (1997). Their 'multiscience' approaches (Ogawa 1995) included a reflection on the epistemology and ontological assumptions of indigenous and Western science knowledge systems. These types of curriculum proposals should help teachers create an appropriate eco-cultural paradigm for instruction. A TEK Western science curriculum could also be developed along these lines, as described by Corsiglia and Snively (1995). Curriculum development in cross-cultural science education is only in its infancy stage. Consequently, of the examples that exist, all come from local initiatives only. For example, Lines and Circles is a grade 7–9 science curriculum for First Nations pupils in Ontario, Canada (Henderson 1996; Ahkwesahsne Mohawk Board of Education 1994).

The assessment of pupil achievement within the cross-cultural science curricula mentioned above has been mapped out by Nelson-Barber *et al.* (1996). They offer guidance and specific recommendations for developing a culturally responsive assessment system, beginning with 'treat linguistic and cultural diversity as strengths' (p. 8). An example from the Navajo Nation demonstrated the fruitfulness of 'portfolio assessment'. Portfolios were shown to promote pupil autonomy and reflected the context of learning, not just the process and product of learning.

Summary

Several years ago, it would have been difficult, if not impossible, to dwell so much on the cultural aspects of science education as we have done in this chapter. Many who perhaps claim to be gatekeepers of Western science would have rationalized their objection with arguments ranging from the rationality and objectivity of science (the so-called marked differences between the realm of science and the realm of culture) to the universality of science (a controversial issue in itself; Stanley and Brickhouse 1995). Contemporary changes in science education, however, have given high priority to the goal 'Science for All', for reasons which include equity, equality and economic, political, and cultural realities of the modern world (UNESCO 1994). For example, we live in a world of globalization which requires the demystification of science and the elimination of science's exclusive preserve as a place for an elite select few (Fensham 1992). The multicultural realities of many of the world's classrooms dictate that if any nation ignores the development of a Science-for-All curriculum, it does so at its own peril (KEDI 1997).

Whether in Africa, the South Pacific, Asia and South America, where indigenous pupils form part of the predominant culture, or in other parts of the world, such as Canada, the USA, Australia and Europe, where the minority indigenous populations are made to function within the dominant Western culture, science education is neither culturally appropriate nor culturally inclusive (Jegede 1996). Even for pupils who come from the dominant Western culture, studying science can pose major cultural problems (Costa 1995; Aikenhead 1996). Worldwide, pupils are reacting to inappropriate and exclusive school science by voting with their feet. The exodus from science classes stares science teachers in their face everyday (KEDI 1997).

It is evident from the literature that pupils experience at least two types of culture when they study science in a formal Western-type educational setting: the culture of school science and the culture of their life-world, To make meaning out of their experiences in science classrooms, pupils need to negotiate a cultural transition from their life-world into the world of school science. The ease or difficulty with which pupils make the transition (that is, the ease or difficulty with which they cross cultural borders) will determine their understanding of the subject. The absence of psychological pain leads to a smooth border crossing. At the opposite extreme, the experience of unbearable psychological pain necessitates avoidance and leads to an impossible border crossing.

As emphasized throughout this chapter, cultural border crossing relates to pupils from both indigenous and Western cultures. Life-world cultural knowledge (Shutz and Luckmann 1973) acts as reliable prior information and as a framework through which further learning takes place. Life-world cultural knowledge affects the case of cultural border crossing. When science culture is in harmony with a learner's life-world knowledge, learning science concepts reinforces the pupils' world-view suppositions. This, in turn, leads to enculturation (Contreras and Lee 1990). Even for the pupils who cross cultural borders smoothly into science, however, certain factors (such as a lack of motivation, lack of interest, ineffective instructional strategies, inability to relate what is learned to the world of work) might make border crossing problematic and at odds with school science, as Champagne et al. (1980) found in their study of pupils in Western societies.

Pupils in non-Western societies confront additional complications to the factors which engender low interest in Western societies. At home, non-Western pupils function within a life-world knowledge system diametrically opposed to the knowledge, skills, attitudes, values, language, etc. taught in school science – content that bears characteristics of a Western orientation (Rashed 1997). The eco-cultural environment of non-Western learners (Jegede 1995, 1989) determines their social and cultural imprints of how knowledge is acquired and how it is used. At school, the science concepts taught as symbolic knowledge (Shutz and Luckmann 1973) can become a source of 'cultural violence' (the explicit form of Bourdieu's [1992] 'symbolic violence') and non-empowerment (O'Loughlin 1992), resulting in serious conflict between what pupils bring into the science classroom and what they are expected to take away from it. As a result, a large majority of pupils in non-Western societies cannot cross cultural borders smoothly into school science and, therefore, they do not learn science in the meaningful way expected of them. Instead they play some form of Fatima's rules (Larson 1995).

We recognize that some pupils (and they are in a very small minority) are able to negotiate smoothly the transition from their non-Western culture to the culture of science. According to Medvitz (1985), these pupils felt comfortable in each world but found themselves thinking differently in each setting. In relation to our thesis of cultural border crossing and collateral learning theory, where smooth and effortless transitions should result in a good fit between one cultural idea and the other, one can still question the acceptability of what these people experience as smooth cultural border crossings. It may well be that the attainment of secured collateral learning is being stunted.

Science education must be culture-sensitive for it to serve the emerging global community, the norm in the next millennium. Taylor and Cobern (1998) have proposed a new perspective for science education reform called 'critical enculturation', which takes a dynamic view of culture, involves a dialectical view of the process of cultural adaptation, and which must recognize the need for reciprocal accommodation of the beliefs, values and practices of modern science and the host culture. It is only through this process of mutual respect of cultures within a multi-cultural environment that education for scientific culture can flourish. In this article we have provided a modest start towards identifying the teaching and learning of science from this new perspective, in which learners attempt to transcend the borders of the culture of science and the culture of the learner's environment. Curriculum and instruction must make science more accessible to all pupils, no matter what differences there are with their immediate culture. Indeed, these differences, as demonstrated in this chapter, could be harnessed to provide rich, robust and holistic experiences for the learner in a multi-faceted world.

References

AAAS (1989) *Project 2061: Science for All Americans*, Washington, DC: American Association for the Advancement of Science.

Ahkwesahsne Mohawk Board of Education (1994) *Lines and Circles*, Cornwall, Ontario: Ahkwesahsne Mohawk Board of Education.

Aikenhead, G. S. (1994) 'Consequences to learning science through STS: a research perspective', in J. Solomon and G. Aikenhead (eds) *STS Education: International Perspectives on Reform* (pp. 169–86), New York: Teachers' College Press.

—— (1996) 'Science education: border crossing into the subculture of science', *Studies in Science Education* 27: 1–52.

—— (1997a) 'Teachers, teaching strategies, and culture', in *Globalization of Science Education*, pre-conference proceedings for the International Conference on Science Education (pp. 133–6), Seoul: Korean Educational Development Institute.

—— (1997b) Toward a First Nations cross-cultural science and technology curriculum', *Science Education* 81: 217–38.

—— and Jegede, O. J. (1999) 'Cross-cultural science education: a cognitive explanation of a cultural phenomenon', *Journal of Research in Science Teaching* 36(3): 269–87.

Arseculeratne, S. N. (1997) 'Science and technology education and scientific literacy in Sri Lanka: concepts and problems', in E. W. Jenkins (ed.) *Innovations in Science and Technology Education*, Vol. VI (pp. 251–70), Paris: UNESCO.

Atwater, M. M. (1996) 'Social constructivism: infusion into the multicultural science education research agenda', *Journal of Research in Science Teaching* 33: 821–37.

Baker, D. and Taylor, P. C. S. (1995) 'The effect of culture on the learning of science in non-Western countries: the results of an integrated research review', *International Journal of Science Education* 17: 695–704.

Battiste, M. and Barman, J. (eds) (1995) *First Nations Education in Canada: The Circle Unfolds*, Vancouver: University of British Columbia Press.

Bourdieu, P. (1992) *Language and Symbolic Power*, Cambridge, MA: Harvard University Press.

Cajete, G. (1994) *Look to the Mountain*, Durango, CO: Kivaki Press.

Champagne, A. B., Klopfer, L. E. and Anderson, J. (1980) 'Factors influencing the learning of classical mechanics', *American Journal of Physics* 48: 1074–9.

Cobern, W. W. (1993) 'Contextual constructivism: the impact of culture on the learning and teaching of science', in K. Tobin (ed.) *The Practice of Constructivism in Science Education* (pp. 51–69), Washington, DC: American Association for the Advancement of Science.

—— (1994) 'Thinking about alternative constructions of science and science education', a plenary presentation for the Second Annual Southern African Association for

Mathematics and Science Education Research Conference, University of Durban, Westville, Durban, South Africa.

—— (1996) 'Worldview theory and conceptual change in science education', *Science Education* 80: 579–610.

—— and Aikenhead, G. S. (1998) 'Cultural aspects of learning science', in B. J. Fraser and K. G. Tobin (eds) *International Handbook of Science Education*, Dordrecht: Kluwer.

Contreras, A. and Lee, O. (1990) 'Differential treatment of students by middle school science teachers: unintended cultural bias', *Science Education* 74: 433–44.

Corsiglia, J. and Snively, G. (1995) 'Global lessons from the traditional science of long-resident peoples', in G. Snively and A. Mackinnon (eds) *Thinking Globally about Mathematics and Science Education* (pp. 25–51), Vancouver: University of British Columbia, Centre for Study of Curriculum and Instruction.

Costa, V. B. (1993) 'School science as a rite of passage: a new frame for familiar problems', *Journal of Research in Science Teaching* (pp. 25–51), Vancouver: University of British Columbia, Centre for the Study of Curriculum and Instruction.

—— (1995) 'When science is "another world": relationships between worlds of family, friends, school, and science', *Science Education* 79: 313–33.

Driver, R. (1979) 'Cultural diversity and the teaching of science', in H. Trueba and C. Barnett-Mizrahi (eds) *Bilingual Multicultural Education and the Classroom Teacher: From Theory to Practice*, Rowley, MA: Newberry.

——, Asoko, H., Leach, J., Mortimer, E. and Scott, P. (1994) 'Constructing scientific knowledge in the classroom', *Educational Researcher* 23: 5–12.

Fensham, P. J. (1992) 'Science and technology' in P. W. Jackson (ed.) *Handbook of Research on Curriculum* (pp. 789–829), New York: Macmillan.

Geertz, C. (1973) *The Interpretation of Culture*, New York: Basic Books.

George, J. and Glasgow, J. (1988) 'Street science and conventional science in the West Indies', *Studies in Science Education* 15: 109–18.

Glaser, R. (1991) 'The maturing of the relationship between the science of learning and cognition and educational practice', *Learning and Instruction* 1: 129–44.

Hawkins, J. and Pea, R. D. (1987) 'Tools for bridging the cultures of everyday and scientific thinking', *Journal of Research in Science Teaching* 24: 291–307.

Henderson, M. (1996) 'Ahkwesahsne math and science pilot project', *Canadian Aboriginal Science and Technology Society's 4th Annual Conference Proceedings*, Vancouver: First Nations House of Learning, University of British Columbia.

Hennessy, S. (1993) 'Situated cognition and cognitive apprenticeship: implications for classroom learning', *Studies in Science Education* 22: 1–41.

Hewson, M. G. (1988) 'The ecological context of knowledge: implications for learning science in developing countries', *Journal of Curriculum Studies* 20: 317–26.

Hills, G. L. C. (1989) 'Students' "untutored" beliefs about natural phenomena: primitive science or common sense?', *Science Education* 73: 155–86.

Hodson, D. (1993) 'In search of a rationale for multicultural science education', *Science Education* 77: 685–711.

Jegede, O. J. (1988) 'The development of the science, technology and society curricula in Nigeria', *International Journal of Science Education* 10(4): 399–408.

—— (1989) 'Toward a philosophical basis for science education of the 1990s: an African view-point', in D. E. Herget (ed.) *The History and Philosophy of Science in Science Teaching* (pp. 185–98), Tallahassee, FL: Florida State University.

—— (1995) 'Collateral learning and the eco-cultural paradigm in science and mathematics education in Africa', *Studies in Science Education* 25: 97–137.

—— (1996) 'Whose education, whose worldview, and whose framework?: an indigenous perspective on learning', a paper presented at the conference on *Pathways: Indigenous Education: Past, Present, Future*, Toowoomba, Australia: University of Southern Queensland.

—— (1997) 'School science and the development of scientific culture: a review of contemporary science education in Africa', *International Journal of Science Education* 19: 1–20.

—— and Okebukola, P. A. (1991) 'The effect of instruction on socio-cultural belief hindering the learning of science', *Journal of Research in Science Teaching* 28: 275–85.

—— and Okebukola, P. A. O. (1989) 'Some socio-cultural factors militating against drift towards science and technology in secondary schools', *Research in Science and Technological Education* 7: 141–51.

Kaunda, K. (1966) *Humanism in Zambia*, Lusaka: Zambian IS.

Kawagley, O. (1990) 'Yup'ik ways of knowing', *Canadian Journal of Native Education* 17: 5–17.

—— (1995) *A Yupiaq Worldview*, Prospect Heights, IL: Waveland Press.

KEDI (1997) *Globalization of Science Education*, pre-conference proceedings for the International Conference on Science Education, Seoul, Korea.

Kelly, G. J. and Green, J. (1998) 'The social nature of knowing: toward a sociocultural perspective on conceptual change and knowledge construction' in B. Guzzetti and C. Hynd (eds) *Perspectives on Conceptual Change* (pp. 145–81), Mahwah, NJ: Lawrence Erlbaum.

Kwon, J. S. (1997) 'The necessity of cognitive conflict strategy in science teaching', in *KEDI, Globalization of Science Education*, pre-conference proceedings for the International Conference on Science Education, Seoul: Korean Educational Development Institute.

Larson, J. O. (1995) 'Fatima's rules and other elements of an unintended chemistry curriculum', paper presented at the American Educational Research Association annual meeting, San Francisco.

Layton, D., Jenkins, E., MacGill, S. and Davey, A. (1993) *Inarticulate Science?*, Driffield, East Yorkshire: Studies in Education.

Lee, O. (1997a) 'Diversity and equity for Asian American students in science education', *Science Education* 81: 107–22.

—— (1997b) 'Scientific literacy for all: what is it, and how can we achieve it?', *Journal of Research in Science Teaching* 34: 219–22.

——, Fradd, S. H. and Sutman, F. X. (1995) 'Science knowledge and cognitive strategy use among culturally and linguistically diverse students', *Journal of Research in Science Teaching* 32: 797–816.

Linn, M. C. and Burbules, N. (1993) 'Construction of knowledge and group learning', in K. Tobin (ed.) *The Practice of Constructivism in Science Education*, Washington, DC: American Association for the Advancement of Science Press.

Loughran, J. and Derry, N. (1997) 'Researching teaching for understanding: the students' perspective', *International Journal of Science Education* 19: 925–38.

Lowe, J. A. (1995) 'The impact of school science on the world-view of Solomon Island students', *Prospects* 15: 653–67.

Lugones, M. (1987) 'Playfulness, "world" travelling, and loving perception', *Hypatia* 2(2): 3–10.

MacIvor, M. (1995) 'Redefining science education for Aboriginal students', in M. Battiste and J. Barman (eds) *First Nations Education in Canada: The Circle Unfolds* (pp. 73–98), Vancouver: University of British Columbia Press.

McTaggart, R. (1991) 'Western institutional impediments to Australian aboriginal education', *Journal of Curriculum Studies*, 23: 297–235.

Maddock, M. N. (1981) 'Science education: an anthropological viewpoint', *Studies in Science Education* 8: 1–26.

Medvitz, A. G. (1985) *Problems in the Application of Science Education to National Development*, paper presented at the Institute of Development Studies, University of Nairobi, Kenya.

—— (1996) *Science, Schools and Culture: The Complexity of Reform in Science Education*, a paper presented to the eighth symposium of the International Organization for Science and Technology Education (IOSTE), Edmonton, Canada.

National Research Council (1996) *National Science Education Standards*, Washington, DC: National Academy Press.

Nelson-Barber, S. and Estrin, E. T. (1995) *Culturally Responsive Mathematics and Science Education for Native Students*, San Francisco: Far West Laboratory for Education Research and Development.

——, Estrin, E. T. and Shaw, J. M. (1996) 'Sociocultural competency in mathematics and science pedagogy: a focus on assessment', a paper presented to the eighth symposium of the International Organization for Science and Technology Education (IOSTE), Edmonton, Canada.

Ogawa, M. (1986) 'Toward a new rationale of science education in a non-Western society', *European Journal of Science Education* 8: 113–9.

—— (1995) 'Science education in a multi-science perspective', *Science Education* 79: 583–93.

Ogbu, J. U. (1992) 'Understanding cultural diversity and learning', *Educational Researcher* 21(8): 5–14, 24.

Ogunniyi, M. B. (1988) 'Adapting western science to traditional African culture', *International Journal of Science Education* 10: 1–9.

——, Jegede, O,. Ogawa, M., Yandila, C. D. and Oladele, F. K. (1995) 'Nature of worldview presuppositions among science teachers in Botswana, Indonesia, Japan, Nigeria and the Philippines', *Journal of Research in Science Teaching* 27: 817–31.

Okebukola, P. A. O. and Jegede, O. J. (1990) 'Eco-cultural influences upon students' concept attainment in science', *Journal of Research in Science Teaching* 27: 661–9.

O'Loughlin, M. (1992) 'Rethinking science education: beyond Piagetian constructivism toward a sociocultural model of teaching and learning', *Journal of Research in Science Teaching* 19: 791–820.

Pfundt, H. and Duit, R. (1994) *Students' Alternative Frameworks and Science Education*, 4th edn, Kiel: Institute for Science Education.

Phelan, P., Davidson, A. and Cao, H. (1991) 'Students' multiple worlds: negotiating the boundaries of family, peer, and school cultures', *Anthropology and Education Quarterly* 22: 224–50.

Philips, S. U. (1972) 'Participant structures and communicative competence: Warm Springs children in community and classroom', in C. B. Cazden, V. P. John and D. Hymes (eds) *Functions of Language in the Classroom* (pp. 370–94), New York: Teachers' College Press.

Pickering, A. (ed.) (1992) *Science as Practice and Culture*, Chicago: University of Chicago Press.

Pomeroy, D. (1992) 'Science across cultures: building bridges between traditional Western and Alaskan Native sciences', in G. L. C. Hills (ed.) *History and Philosophy of Science in Science Education*, Vol II (pp. 257–68), Kingston, Ontario: Faculty of Education, Queen's University.

—— (1994) 'Science education and cultural diversity: mapping the field', *Studies in Science Education* 24: 49–73.

—— (1997) 'STL in a culturally diverse world', in E. W. Jenkins (ed.) *Innovations in Science and Technology Education*, Vol VI (pp. 59–76), Paris: UNESCO.

Rashed, R. (1997) 'Science as a western phenomenon', in H. Selin (ed.) *Encyclopaedia of the History of Science, Technology, and Medicine in Non-Western Cultures* (pp. 884–90), Dordrecht: Kluwer.

Ritchie, S. M. (1994) 'Metaphor as a tool for constructivist science teaching', *International Journal of Science Education* 16: 293–303.

Shutz, A. and Luckmann, T. 1973) *Structure of the Life World*, London: Heinemann.

Snively, G. (1990) 'Traditional Native Indian beliefs, cultural values, and science instruction', *Canadian Journal of Native Education* 17: 44–59.

—— (1995) 'Bridging traditional science and Western science in the multicultural classroom', in G. Snively and A. MacKinnon (eds) *Thinking Globally about Mathematics and Science Education* (pp. 53–75), Vancouver: Centre for the Study of Curriculum and Instruction, University of British Columbia.

Solomon, J. (1983) 'Learning about energy: how pupils think in two domains', *European Journal of Science Education* 5: 49–59.

—— (1987) 'Social influences on the construction of pupil's understanding of science', *Studies in Science Education* 14: 63–82.

—— (1992) *Getting to Know about Energy*, London: Falmer Press.

Spindler, G. (1987) *Education and Cultural Process: Anthropological Approaches*, 2nd edn, Prospect Heights, IL: Waveland Press.

Stairs, A. (1995) 'Learning processes and teaching roles in Native education: cultural base and cultural brokerage', in M. Battiste and J. Barman (eds) *First Nations Education in Canada: The Circle Unfolds* (pp. 139–53), Vancouver: University of British Columbia Press.

Stanley, W. B. and Brickhouse, N. W. (1995) 'Science education without foundations: a response to Loving', *Science Education* 79: 349–54.

Taylor, P. C. and Cobern, W. W. (1998) 'Towards a critical science education', in M. Ogawa (ed.) *Cultural Perspectives on Science Education*, Dordrecht: Kluwer Academic Press.

Tobin, K. (1996) 'Cultural perspectives on the teaching and learning of science', in M. Ogawa (ed.) *Traditional Culture, Science and Technology, and Development: Toward a New Literacy for Science and Technology* (pp. 75–99), Tokyo: Research Project STS, Tokyo Institute of Technology.

—— and McRobbie, C. (1997) 'Beliefs about the nature of science and the enacted science curriculum', *Science and Education* 6: 355–71.

Traweek, S. (1992) 'Border crossings: narrative strategies in science studies and among physicists in Tsukuba science city, Japan', in A. Pickering (ed.) *Science as Practice and Culture* (pp. 429–65), Chicago: University of Chicago Press.

UNESCO (1994) *The Project 2000+ Declaration: The Way Forward*, Paris: UNESCO.

Wertsch, J. V. and Toma, C. (1992) 'Discourse and learning in the classroom: a sociocultural approach', in L. Steffe (ed.) *Constructivism in Education*, Hillsdale, NJ: Lawrence Erlbaum Associates.

West, L. H. and Pines, A. L. (eds) (1985) *Cognitive Structure and Conceptual Change*, New York: Academic Press.

Wolcott, H. F. (1991) 'Proprospect and the acquisition of culture', *Anthropology and Education Quarterly* 22: 251–73.

3.2 Cultural perspectives on the teaching and learning of science

Kenneth Tobin

The enduring problems in science education recently have been cast in terms of new theoretical frames. In the past decade, constructivism has been mentioned increasingly in the definitions of problems and their solutions (Tobin 1993). In many contexts (e.g. requests for proposals issued by funding agencies) constructivism, which is a way of thinking about knowledge and coming to know, was prescribed as a mandatory way of thinking about teaching and learning science. There was a tendency to equate constructivism with particular activities rather than a way of thinking about knowing and coming to know. Teachers were exhorted to employ constructivist ways of teaching by arranging students in small groups and providing them with greater autonomy. Trends such as these not only diminish the power of constructivism as a way of thinking but also take the focus off critical dimensions of teaching and learning. Instead of examining any activity and asking how it might be improved by thinking about learning from a constructivist perspective, there has been a tendency, for example, to advocate small-group activities over whole-class activities and student-focused activities over teacher-focused activities.

Science is regarded as a form of discourse that has evolved as a relatively recent activity of humankind. The goal of science is to make sense of a universe of phenomena in terms of knowledge that is viable. To be accepted as scientific, knowledge must meet several tests. First, it must be coherent with other viable knowledge claims. Second, it must be accepted by members of the scientific academy through a process of peer review. Third, it must withstand conceptual and empirical challenges in repeated attempts to refute its viability. Sceptical acceptance of scientific knowledge claims is a part of what is considered to act scientifically. Thus, even at the earliest of stages, an idea is carefully scrutinized in relation to what else is known and efforts are made to refute claims associated with the knowledge. In the event that knowledge withstands those tests, the activity of gaining acceptance becomes increasingly social as attempts are made to convince others of the acceptability of what is claimed. When viewed in this way, it is apparent that science can be regarded as a form of argument during which ideas are formulated and then argued out in a social forum in which efforts are made to persuade peers to a particular point of view. The process necessarily involves the production of evidence and discussions about the extent to which the evidence fits the knowledge claim.

If science is viewed as a form of discourse then learning science can be considered as learning a new way to make sense of experience. Discourse, as it is used here, refers to a 'social activity of making meanings with language and other symbolic systems in some particular kind of situation or setting' (Lemke 1995: 8). Lemke also noted that:

> Instead of talking about meaning making as something that is done by minds, I prefer to talk about it as a social practice in a community. It is a kind of doing that is done in ways that are characteristic of a community, and its occurrence is part of what binds the community together and helps to constitute it as a community. In this sense we can speak of a community, not as a collection of interacting individuals, but as a system of doings, rather than a system of doers.
>
> (Lemke 1995: 9)

In a school science community, one might expect to see students engage in ways such that, over a period of time, the discourse of a class would become more science-like. If the essence of science is to examine the coherence of evidence and knowledge claims then one might expect a form of discourse in science classrooms that involves students routinely in arguments over the efficacy of the warrants for knowledge claims. As has been advocated by Kuhn (1993), science could be regarded as a form of argument in which emerging conceptual understandings are related to evidence and the extent of the fit with canonical science.

If students are to learn science as a form of discourse it seems imperative that they are able to adapt their language resources as they practise science in a setting in which others who know science assist them to learn by engaging activities in which co-participation occurs (Schön 1985). As it is used here, co-participation implies the presence of a shared language that can be accessed by all participants to communicate with one another such that meaningful learning occurs. The shared language must be negotiated and would enable all participants in a community to engage the activities of the community. Students receive opportunities to practise and observe others practice such that, at any time, a person might be both a teacher and a learner with respect to others in the community. Co-participation that implies a concern for facilitating one another's learning and peer teaching is a critical constituent of such an environment. During interactions among participants, respect would be shown for the knowledge of others and efforts would be made to find out why particular claims were regarded as viable. There would be concern for knowing in a way that is scientific, and the knowledge that is learned within the community would be consistent with canonical science. Within this evolving knowledge community, concern would be shown for what is known by learners at any given time and how they can represent what they know.

Power, which is constituted in the discourse, would be equitably distributed among the teacher and students such that knowledge claims that made no sense would be clarified and discussion would occur, until such time that a learner was satisfied that he or she now understood. In a setting in which co-participation was occurring, students would have the autonomy to ask when they did not understand and the focus would always be on what students know and how they can represent what they know. Students would not feel that they could not understand and that their only recourse was to accept what was being said as an article of truth, based on faith that other authoritative sources understand the warrants for the viability of a claim. Thus, co-participation would involve discussions in which participants tested one another's understandings and were sensitive to their roles as both teachers and learners.

Understanding science

From the perspective of constructivism, learning is a social process of making sense of experience in terms of what is already known. In that process, learners create perturbations that arise from attempts to give meaning to particular experiences, through the imaginative use of existing knowledge. The resolution of these perturbations leads to an equilibrium state whereby new knowledge has been constructed to cohere with a particular experience and prior knowledge. An often misunderstood aspect of constructivism is that the theory incorporates a value position that any construction is as viable as another. Such a position ignores the social component of knowledge, that is, that knowledge must be viable not only personally, but also in the social contexts in which actions occur. Viability is thereby determined with respect to the actions of an individual and the extent to which those actions facilitate the attainment of goals in particular social contexts. Accordingly, teachers should be on the lookout for naive theories or incorrect knowledge held by students. The teacher, representing society, has an obligation to educate students, to assist them to learn what is currently regarded by society as viable knowledge. Accordingly, if a teacher perceives the constructions of any individual to be inviable, it is the teacher's duty to structure learning environments to facilitate the process of learning what society regards as appropriate at that particular time.

To understand can be thought of in at least three senses. First, and in the most trivial meaning of the term, one can know in a limited way, in which case links with other science knowledge are not extensive. Examples of limited understanding would include knowing the names of things, facts and definitions. Linkages between what is known might not be solely within a domain of science. For example, a link might be from something scientific to something non-scientific as occurs when students remember the colours of the spectrum associated with sunlight by remembering the first initial and order of the constituent colours in terms of a boy's name, Roy G. Biv. As well as memorizing the name, a learner must remember a one-to-one correspondence between the name and the first letter of a colour. If these links are recalled, an individual is able to reconstruct the order of colours when white light is dispersed.

Some individuals will stop at this point in their quest for understanding and others will go beyond it. Having reconstructed the colours to describe a spectrum, this knowledge can be related to dispersion, diffraction and refraction to form a semantic web that can then be expanded to include properties of electromagnetic radiation such as wavelength, frequency and velocity. New knowledge can be connected into the semantic web as a learner postulates a connection and then examines the extent to which the new knowledge coheres with existing knowledge. With some conceptual reorganization, learners can develop relational understandings by constructing webs of relationships for given scientific subject matter. Relational and limited understanding are ends of a continuum that differ in the number and quality of the linkages formed within a domain of knowledge.

At some stage in the process of learning, an individual might have a goal of linking scientific knowledge to his or her actions in the world outside of the classroom. Thus, knowledge of science is used to create patterns of understanding from everyday life experiences. We refer to this process as developing transformational understanding, in that scientific knowledge is transformed in such a way as to cohere with the beliefs of an individual's life-world, and is used as a basis for actions that extend beyond what might be regarded as science-related. [...]

The Galilean plane

What is involved in the process of making sense of science in terms of what is already known? As a student experiences phenomena, he or she does so by imposing patterns on what is already known and familiar. Consider, for example, a Galilean inclined plane that was used in an experiment/demonstration in a course for prospective and practising science teachers. A metal ball, presumably made from iron, was held in place by an electromagnet and released to roll down an incline. The incline was at a fixed angle and flashing lights were spaced along the incline such that, as the lights flashed in unison at intervals of one second, the ball was level with one of the lights. The ball completed its journey down the incline by dropping into a waste paper basket.

A physics professor demonstrated the motion of the ball on the plane as seventeen students gathered around the apparatus. There were many things to observe about the large and obviously old piece of apparatus. The lights were flashing together and a switch was thrown to release the ball which then began to accelerate down the incline. The ball was rolling fast as it reached the end of the incline and the students showed signs of doubt and interest as to whether or not the waste paper basket would capture the ball and withstand its impact. The relationship between factors was to be observed also, such as switching the electromagnet off, the ball beginning to accelerate, the lights being off or on, the time intervals for which the lights were on and off, that the ball reached each light just as they all flashed, and the significance of the distance between the lights.

To notice all of those events and to perceive their significance requires a certain way of looking at what was happening. The students observed the apparatus in a variety of ways. 'What's it called?' 'Do all the lights flash together?' 'What would happen if the ball was lighter?' The students asked many questions. I watched with interest as an elementary teacher positioned the waste basket in precisely the right spot to catch the speeding ball. She obviously knew some physics because she predicted exactly the place where the ball would land. 'The path was curved', she announced, relating her observation to what she learned about parabolic trajectories in a previous lesson. 'The ball did not fall straight down, nor did it continue in a straight line.' After a short discussion with her on parabolic motion, I asked 'How far is it between the lights?' A technical assistant interjected to re-phrase the question in terms of the distance travelled (i.e. displacement) at each time interval. One, four, nine, sixteen. Someone was counting. 'Aha!' exclaimed another. The technician returned carrying a wooden ball that had a piece of tape wrapped around it. The professor then asked whether the wooden ball would roll down the incline at the same rate as the iron ball. He demonstrated how to release the ball so that its movement would be synchronized with the flashing lights.

'It went slower.' 'It was the same speed.' 'The tape is slowing it down.' Many comments suggested that the students were interested in seeing what would happen. Some justified their predictions in terms of heavier objects falling faster than lighter objects. The technical assistant appeared again with a long thick glass tube containing a ball and a feather. He demonstrated that the ball did drop faster than the feather. Then he evacuated the tube using a vacuum pump to draw the air out and closed a metal tap to prevent air from re-entering the tube. The technician then handed the glass tube to the students to allow them to observe more closely and try out their hunches. Again there was much to see. The feather dropped at what appeared to be an astonishing rate but, occasionally, static electricity attracted it to the sides of the container. However, repeated manipulations enabled the students to see that the two dropped at about the same rate.

How did this relate to the balls on the inclined plane? The goal of the professor (or the technician who produced the additional demonstration) may have been for the students to see that the acceleration due to gravity was independent of the mass of the falling object. It is not clear how many students did relate those two activities to one another. The contexts were very different. Both were technically sophisticated in that they were configured to produce a microworld that was beyond the everyday experience of students. How similar were the two microworlds? What connected the two? They did not look the same and what connected them was the strategic appearance of the evacuated glass cylinder at the moment that a student raised questions about friction and the presence of tape on the wooden ball. Just how many students would see the feather and the cylinder falling at the same rate as being relevant to the problem of whether or not the wooden and iron balls rolled down the incline at the same rate?

In one instance the objects were falling and in the other instance they were rolling. And what were students to learn from the observations that the gap between the lights increased by two each time? Or that the total distance travelled by the ball at each unit of time was 1^2, 2^2, 3^2 and 4^2, respectively? Would students conclude that, for both balls, the displacement was proportional to the time squared?

The demonstration appears to have been set up to show that displacement is proportional to the square of time. However, to see that relationship requires a certain way of thinking about experience, a variety of knowledge about science and mathematics, and an awareness of what is and is not relevant. If an observer knows that, in the context of uniform acceleration, displacement is proportional to the square of the time, then the Galilean plane can readily be figured out and one might even marvel that an algebraic function can be used to place the lights and work out the angle of the incline. However absent that awareness, it is by no means certain that the distances will even be seen to have any sort of regularity. Furthermore, without others to point it out, it is possible that some students might not have noticed that the ball passed the lights just as they were flashing. There is a great deal to observe and wonder about with the Galilean plane demonstration and relationships are not revealed by a demonstration, but provide a context in which they might be constructed or applied.

Providing students ample time to manipulate the apparatus certainly provided opportunities for them to have direct and varied experiences. It also allowed them to answer some of their questions by manipulating the apparatus in a variety of ways. The students certainly enjoyed the hands-on experience and many rich conversations occurred throughout the room. But what was the nature of those conversations? There was interest in whether light and heavy things fell at the same or different rates. There was interest in where to place the waste basket and that the feather sometimes adhered to the glass walls of the container. Also, there was interest in a question that seemed to be related to the total time taken to get to the bottom of the inclined plane. Absent from the conversations I witnessed were discussions about the relationship between displacement and time. In fact, displacement at a given time interval was not identified by anyone I heard as a relevant variable, even though the technician asked a direct question about that. Neither was it evident that students noticed that a uniform increase in distance occurred in each unit of time. Even though the professor directed attention toward the regular increase of distance covered with time, I witnessed no discussion of that trend among the students. Furthermore, when one student added the distances covered to obtain measures of displacement, another student noticed the sequence of squares but there was no discussion that related those squared numbers to the time taken for the ball to travel that distance. There was no visible effort to search for a relationship between displacement and time. Nor was there an obvious need to invent acceleration and force. My conclusion is, despite the efforts of the teachers to set up a demonstration in which a functional relationship would be visible, and irrespective of the high quality hands-on activity and freedom to pursue their own interests, students did not construct the knowledge intended by those who designed the apparatus. This interpretation is associated with an assertion that it is necessary to know about the displacement–time-squared function, or almost know about it, in order to look for and observe it.

It might be inferred that this analysis is critical of the professor and the students. That is far from the situation. The students were highly motivated and the professor was extremely innovative in setting up what is a highly engaging and interesting set of physics experiences for prospective teachers. In addition, what was happening in the class could be described as good physics. Without being lectured to, students were making sense of demonstrations, talking about them and endeavouring to be scientific in their actions. I am not arguing that the students wasted their time or that the professor failed in his efforts to implement reform. I am trying to learn what I can from this experience. For it seems to me, a person with a background of doing physics and teaching it for many years, that the physics involved in this demonstration is typically taught to students in grades 9 or 10 (13–15 years old). Yet this college class, consisting of graduate and undergraduate students, practising and prospective teachers, did not learn what the demonstration was set up to show. Instead, they learned how to manipulate equipment, observe patterns that enabled them to predict, and how to pose questions that were potentially productive. They also learned how to adjust variables in order to test trends they thought they observed. In that regard, they improvized by using the demonstrations in ways that were not typical. The autonomy provided to students in this classroom enabled them to get whatever equipment they requested and to try investigations that were planned in their discussions with peers and others in the room. In terms of discourse, they also learned that there are right answers that might prove to be elusive, even for the best thinkers. The professor demonstrated on several occasions that he had to think issues through in order to construct explanations to fit the experience of a demonstration.

Throughout the lesson, the conversations were informal and students were able to bring forward their prior knowledge to make sense of what they were doing. The considerable range of prior knowledge was catered for by allowing students to form their own groups and work together. Those who understood the physics were able to explain to those who did not and there was evidence throughout the classroom that peer teaching was occurring and that at many stages, all students had chances to co-participate in the learning activities. In addition to the seventeen students, there was a professor, a technician and two observers who participated in the activities, listening and observing, and communicating with students in a language that was shared. The opportunity therefore exists for students to link their experiences and conversations to the discourse of science as they engage in other parts of the course, such as discussions of the problems in the textbook. Thus, a stage is set for students to become more like scientists as they engage in classroom activities and as they make sense of everyday phenomena.

Science as argument

Learning science is much like learning to speak a new language. To begin with, there is a precise vocabulary that must be used to communicate meaning and this is embedded within a set of conventions that apply to the goals of science and the ways that scientists practise their subject. Deanna Kuhn (1993) described the usefulness of the metaphor of science as argument in thinking about science. What she means by this is that a person who is doing science needs to be able to co-relate the knowledge claims of science with the evidence that supports and/or refutes those claims. In thinking of science as a form of argument, one is reminded to consider more than just the knowledge claims and to ask extra questions about the evidence that speaks to the viability of those claims. The argument also raises the possibility of choices being made between alternative claims. The evidence takes the form of an argument for one claim over another and might consist of an analysis of the coherence of what is claimed with other knowledge claims and the results of empirical tests of the knowledge.

In a classroom, there are numerous sites for the arguments that comprise science. The first of these sites would be in the minds of the learners as they consider what they are learning. Others would be the conversations among groups of students in a class, interactions between the teacher and students, and the written texts prepared by students. If science in classrooms is to be consistent with the argument metaphor then the organization of classroom activities should take into account the sites for argument. However, more than that is required. If students are to engage in a form of argument, it will be necessary for them to know they are required to argue, to know how to argue and to have sufficient knowledge of the conventions and subject matter knowledge to enable such arguments to occur. In addition, they must be willing to engage in argument and to see this form of engagement as being not only worthwhile for them but as being feasible and desirable. A specific example might allow me to build a better understanding of what is involved in science as argument. In this case, the analysis will focus on a group activity in which essential arguments were missing.

The viability of data

Last night in a physics class, four groups wrote their results from an investigation on the blackboard. The results were gained from a study that the group had undertaken in the previous lesson (2.5 hours in duration). The investigation involved the use of a mass falling under gravity to accelerate a trolley through a distance of less than a metre. Time was measured with a ticker timer. The students had amassed a variety of data that allowed them to explore the relationships between distance, displacement, velocity, acceleration and time. For homework, they had been asked to construct several graphs and, from them, to calculate the acceleration due to gravity. Then, for 2.5 hours of class time, they worked in groups of four to five and entered their data into a computer that was programmed to produce a velocity–time graph and calculate the acceleration due to gravity from the slope of the graph. The calculation took into account kinetic friction and errors of measurement. One group entered the following data from experiments for the acceleration due to gravity.

Mass of cart (g)	Own calculation (cm/sec²)	Computer calculation (cm/sec²)
300	513.3	530.54
500	887.5	804.99
1000	514.7	810.51

The anomalous nature of the above data was immediately evident to me as I observed the classroom. The anomalies were even more striking because of their discrepancies from the results of other groups. As I perused the data on the blackboard, I also observed the students from the group that had entered the data given above. They were working on two homework problems from the textbook. I approached the group and asked them what they thought about their results. They responded to me in terms of their satisfaction in being finished with a task that had been demanding. They were the last group to finish the task and were conscious of that fact. 'Does it concern you that some of your results are about 60 per cent of others on the board?' I asked. The group look startled at my question. 'Why are these results so much less than the others?' I asked. At that moment, various members of the group began to focus on the discrepant data.

I raise this issue because it is an illustration of the absence of an important component of a science learning environment. The argument over viability of the data was not present in this group. In other groups, I saw evidence of students engaged in arguments over the viability of their results, but not in this particular group. There are two points here. First, argument over the viability of data was not evident in some groups and it was evident in others. Second, the quality of the arguments is also an important factor. This is not just a case of arguments occurring or not occurring. Arguments need to be productive in the sense that, in this example, an examination of the discrepant data would lead to insights into the data themselves in terms of the constructs they represent (distance, displacement, time, constant velocity, acceleration, etc.), and an understanding that the data support the claim that the value for the acceleration due to gravity is constant at the site of the experiment. To arrive at that conclusion would require students to look at their results in a particular way.

Conventions are involved and these are not all that obvious to those who do not belong to the scientific community. One convention is to acknowledge that data are 'the same' when, in fact, they are different. The convention of tolerable measurement error is an accepted part of science that this group did not appear to understand. Yet, to conclude anything from the above data, one has to know whether it is permissible to claim anything between 800 and 900 as being the same. What if the value is less than 600? Not only did the group not think to discuss the conventions, they also did not seem to be aware that they might get about the same value for the acceleration due to gravity in each of their calculations. Thus, the acceptance of the table of data is a sign that there was no argument over the claims they were making about these data. Further, the group was making no claims about the data, at least not in an explicit way. That they did not do so seems to reflect three issues. First, they did not know the conventions for measurement error and how that would pertain to declarations associated with comparisons of values obtained for the acceleration due to gravity. Second, they did not know that they should examine the data for patterns and endeavour to represent those patterns as texts or mathematical functions. Third, they did not know that from this study of the acceleration of a cart and kinetic friction, they would be able to conclude that the acceleration due to gravity is constant at the site of the activity. For the students in this group, the semantic network associated with kinematics appeared to be limited to the extent that they could not think through the links to connect what was done in the investigation to conclusions about the acceleration due to gravity. Alternatively, because they did not belong to the scientific community, they may have had those links, but it might not have occurred to them that they should make the connections that would lead them to a value for the acceleration due to gravity. Thus, a component of the learning environment that is of significance has to do with the goals of the students and the extent to which they perceive their knowledge as relevant to the tasks they are to engage.

Refusal to engage

The discussions that occurred during the activity were revealing of what the students did and did not know about kinematics. For example, terms such as displacement were not a part of their vocabulary and the concept was not one they felt they knew about. My purpose in selecting this as a point for discussion is to illustrate that there were many occasions when the students perceived that they knew virtually nothing that was pertinent to the solution of a problem and they refused to engage. Refusal to engage appeared to be part of a learned helplessness that induced a frame of mind that they could not do this; that they did not know enough to make sense of what they were doing. This seems to be part of a larger issue of whether or not students feel they fit in a particular community. In this instance, all of the participants were either practising or prospective science teachers. Even so, there was evidence that several of them felt they did not belong and they exhibited various signs of alienation in the culture. As I write this, there are various issues floating around in my mind. The first is that the terminology of science constitutes a form of symbolic violence for some students. That is, the terms are used and students do not understand what they mean, or the meaning within the science community is obscure to them and different from the meaning of the same term in everyday life. Perhaps repeated symbolic violence of this form leads to a feeling of helplessness that is associated with a refusal to engage.

Power is associated here with the extent to which an individual can or cannot engage in a discourse that is appropriate for the community. Elsewhere, I have adopted Schön's (1985) concept of co-participation as a referent for judging whether or not a learning environment is ideal. What I mean by co-participation is the extent to which a student can make sense of a discourse and use that discourse to participate in the activities of a community. An essential requisite for co-participation is that, within a community, there is a shared language that fosters appropriate interactions.[1] There is also an implied suggestion that an individual wants to participate and feels comfortable in so doing. Thus, the issue of the extent to which an individual feels that he or she fits within a community is an important component of co-participation. In the physics class I discussed earlier in this chapter, it is evident that some of the students do not feel comfortable in engaging the activities of the community. Their feeling of not fitting is based largely on their histories as learners who have avoided physics and in some cases a view that they are 'only' elementary teachers (and hence to be implied they have a weak background in and a fear of studying physics). These students who do not fit are constantly identifying themselves with comments about their lack of belonging, self-effacing remarks about their ability to make sense of what is going on, their selection of tasks in group-oriented activities and, on occasions, their refusal to engage with tasks that they regard as beyond them.

Students can look busy and, in fact, be busy in the sense that they write and complete tasks, yet be disengaged in ways that would promote an understanding of the subject matter. As I walked around the class yesterday, I stopped to ask students about the graphs they had drawn or that had been computer-generated. My interest was to see if they had any idea of the functional relationship between velocity and time. Straight line graphs were distributed throughout the class and hence it may be inferred that most of the students had accomplished a technical level of understanding of how to organize the data into tables, plot the points and obtain a line of best fit. What is the slope of the graph? What meaning can you give to the slope of the graph? How do you calculate the slope of the graph? How would you calculate the acceleration from this graph? Questions such as these led me to an understanding that, despite the prevalence of graphs showing a linear relationship, there were few students in the class who could provide an oral text of what the graph meant in terms of velocity, time, the functional relationship between the two, and how acceleration is associated with a velocity–time graph. Furthermore, even though some could express a linear relationship in symbolic form as an equation, few could explain the meaning of the components of the equation in terms of what they had on their graphs. [...]

Symbolic violence

Symbolic violence is unintentional in that an individual, who feels misplaced within a community, feels a sense of devaluation for his or her cultural artefacts. In science classrooms, it often is the case that students do not feel comfortable asking for clarification when they do not understand, because they find their language limited in extent and do not want to risk ridicule by asking a question that is regarded as stupid, or perhaps that will require then to give clarification, something they feel they could not do. When there is no co-participation, there is always a risk that an individual will feel a sense of violence and will not learn as well as might otherwise be the case. What is often worse, is the feeling of not belonging that accompanies symbolic violence. It is the feeling of difference and marginalization that initiates symbolic violence and it is likely that those who experience it will feel sufficiently alienated as to opt out of science as soon as they have the chance. This can lead to science being regarded as a hostile community that favours certain cultural types, such as white males. Accordingly, teachers and policy makers should be on the lookout for examples of symbolic violence and should do what they can to create multicultural communities within the classroom, in the sense that diversity is catered for and that all participants are aware of the need to effectively communicate with all others and to do so through the agency of a shared and negotiated language. If all participants view themselves both as learners and teachers with respect to others, then there is less of a chance that individuals will experience symbolic violence.

As is the case with language and having limited proficiency in the language of instruction, there is more to symbolic violence than being unable to use the terminology and understand the concepts. There is also at issue a problem with the dominant modes of reasoning that characterize science. For example, if the dominant mode within a community involves a search for causal links and reductionist approaches to control and isolation of variables, then it is little wonder that an individual who searches for recursive relationships and holistic solutions might feel that his or her approach is devalued and that he or she does not belong.

Autobiography of a physics learner

My history as a learner of physics extends over a long period. One clear image I have is of a professor, covered in chalk dust, writing board after board of equations, shouting out what he was writing as he wrote it. My role as a learner was to copy what he wrote for hour after hour until my fingers became so sore that I could write no more. At one moment, he paused and, in a half apologetic voice, he explained to the twenty students in the class that we should not expect to understand it for a few weeks yet. A second related image was set two years later as I spoke to a peer in a graduate physics class in which we were dealing with quantum physics. He had reached his limit, I concluded. He could make no sense of what we were doing and he had opted out in a cognitive sense. In contrast, I had not understood either, but I knew that in order to understand I had to consult additional texts and sort through a semantic web in a process that would take many hours of moving forward, backtracking and taking excursions. I knew that learning was not a linear process, that it required enormous commitment of out-of-class resources and that the responsibility for making sense was my own. Unlike my peer who was lamenting the poor teaching, I was thinking of when I could get to the library to do what I knew had to be done. His goal in coming to class was to have his misunderstandings clarified whereas mine was to get a road map of where my learning needed to go. In essence, I came with a high tolerance of ambiguity whereas he came with a need to satisfy remaining doubts. It was a sad but predictable moment when he dropped out of physics because our cohort that began with approximately twenty white males had been reduced to just three. Another image that pertains to this issue is set in the library. This is the site where I spent several hours after many physics lectures. Here I searched for relevant texts that went over the subject we had covered in class. I found the relevant parts and opened them all up. I did not read in any linear way but scoured the pages in search of meaning. The reading of multiple texts on given topics exposed me to a wider community and enabled me to re-write those notes that were hastily put together in class. I must say here that my tendency to access this wide array of texts was not typical of others in my classes but, for me, it was the crux of becoming a successful learner. Whereas most of my colleagues focused only on learning from a single text, I was determined to learn from multiple texts and sources. A final image of myself as a learner is set at a blackboard in a lecture room, just prior to class. Here I am at the board, surrounded by three of my peers, as I demonstrate to them the subtleties of the relationship between a mathematical expression and a physical principle. No doubt they were learning from my expository style but the point here is that I was learning by teaching them. Thus, I maintain that peer-teaching is a resource for the learning of all, but especially for those selected to teach.

Language

Changing demographics in the USA create challenging circumstances for students for whom English is not a native language and for those teachers who seek to assist them to learn. In science classes, students with limited proficiency in the use of English face a challenge of making sense of instruction while, at the same time, building understandings of science.

Science can be regarded as a form of discourse that incorporates a language characterized by concepts and facts, ways of determining whether or not knowledge claims are viable and therefore acceptable, and ways of communicating what is known among participants in a community. Thus, all learners in a science classroom should have opportunities to observe those who can practise science and accept opportunities to engage in science-like ways and receive feedback on the adequacy of their performances. The notion of how students can learn from their observations of others and co-participation in a community has been documented at elementary and high school levels in a series of studies by Michael Roth (1995). His interpretive studies have shown in thick detail how knowledge is co-constructed in learning communities, how students can observe the practices of others and appropriate what they see in the contexts of their personal practices, and how artefacts within a given community can be used creatively as participants endeavour to meet their goals through the use of a characteristic discourse to engage the tasks of the community. An important feature of learning communities is the negotiation of a shared language that facilitates participants communicating, collaborating, teaching one another and learning from others. Verbal interaction between individuals can involve such characteristics as explaining, clarifying, elaborating, justifying, querying and evaluating. If a language is shared, participants are able to make sense of the texts of that community and create their own texts. Because students possess a shared language they have the option of choosing whether or not to engage. In this situation, empowerment comes from being able to use the language to make sense of written and oral texts and use verbal moves such as those listed above. Although this is not the only sense in which power is important in communities of practice, it is an important source of empowerment if learners are to employ written and oral texts as sources for their own learning.

The issue of language and learning is of great importance. As has been discussed previously, college students wanting to learn science encounter significant problems because of the different languages that pertain to the everyday worlds in which they live their lives and the world of science. Even when English is the native language of the teacher and students and the language of instruction, I have observed students who are disempowered and develop a learned helplessness, in part because they are unable to understand enough of what is going on even to formulate questions to clarify what they do not know. One might anticipate that this problem will be an order of magnitude more pronounced when the instruction is in English and the learners have limited English proficiency. In this instance, the gap between the language resources of students and the required language of science is at its greatest. In between are situations in which non-standard English is used by the students and the instruction requires standard English set in the context of the discourse of science. In each of these instances, the learning problems are predictable because of the difficulty of the teacher and learners negotiating and using a shared language. Yet, without the shared language, it seems that little can be done in class, as far as fostering meaningful learning is concerned, beyond staking out the territory of what is to be learned. If students are to build relational and transformational understandings of science, it will be necessary, at some stage, for them to construct and use a language that will facilitate their induction into the community of science. If opportunities are not provided at school then out-of-school learning resources must be accessed to facilitate learning.

Once a student has made sense of what is to be learned, say a segment of oral text, then it is necessary to reconstruct knowledge regarded by the learner as relevant to what is to be learned. Novak and other science educators have referred to this as relevant prior knowledge, meaning that the knowledge has been previously learned and is recognized by the learner as being relevant to a given learning situation. When the knowledge is reconstructed then it is 'used' by the learner to assign meaning to the oral texts of the classroom, and cognitive actions can connect the new experience and its associated meanings to previously existing semantic webs. In situations in which co-participation is occurring, the reconstruction and connection processes can happen as a matter of routine. If it is not clear what is happening then a learner can ask, and if texts are not comprehensible then the learner has the language to ask for elaboration or clarification. Situations in which a learner lacks the confidence to ask a question for fear of looking stupid should be rare. Furthermore, within a community, non-verbal signs such as head nods should occur to indicate to participants that a learner is making sense of what is happening. In terms of interactions, there should be evidence that students and teachers are in tune with the extent to which sense is being made of verbal interactions. For example, seeing a nod of the head, a teacher might stop an explanation, leaving the student to complete the text. Thus, evidence of co-participation might involve participants completing one another's sentences and incomplete sentences (Schön 1985).

Because of the distribution of power among the participants in the community, there should be a balance in the amount of talk and the types of talk in which the teacher and students engage. There are many ways in which teachers and students might strive to attain co-participatory environments, but one way that holds considerable promise in many situations is for teachers and students to provide one another with time to think and respond during verbal exchanges (Tobin 1987).

When the participants have limited English proficiency (LEP), they have additional interactions to undertake. They must make sense of the oral text using their personal language resources (first and second language), reconstruct relevant science knowledge, make the connections of the oral text to the relevant prior knowledge and, if necessary, frame questions to explicate the meanings of what is to be learned. If a decision is made to present a question orally, then the student is faced with the added difficulty of using English in such a way that what he or she wants to ask is communicated as he or she intends and in such a way that the teacher understands the question.

LEP learners have significant cultural capital that can enhance their learning and the learning of others, but for the most part the emphasis is on their lack of English and associated deficits in learning. Their pathways to learning might involve multiple translations as they use their native language to make sense of science and reconstruct their relevant prior knowledge. Having done so, they can translate their knowledge of science into English. For the most part, LEP students have difficulty in learning science because they are required to follow a path that requires knowledge of English (sense-making might not occur quickly because of the difficulties of translating from English to the native language), identify what they know that might be relevant in their native language and then make the necessary connections. Because of the difficulties of making translations in real time, students might resort to coping strategies whereby they copy key words and any inscriptions in English. These coping strategies allow students to reconstruct the events of the classroom at a later time, usually after school time, when they can assemble the necessary resources to make sense of what they are learning. In these circumstances, the learning environment for LEP students is not co-participatory and the extent to which they can build meaningful understandings of science (i.e. relational and transformational) depends on the nature of the resources they can access in out-of-school settings, or through the use of in-school resources such as peers and library books.

In the event that the additional resources needed to support the learning of LEP students are not available, a problem can arise in that such students might lose self-confidence and a lower self-esteem might result. In this instance, failure to negotiate a shared language is clearly a handicap to the student being able to make a satisfactory transition to the discourse community of science learners. [...]

The situation in Miami, Florida (Dade County), is that the socio-economic history of most learners is such that their opportunities to learn are not as great as they might be if their home conditions would guarantee them sufficient food, good health, sleep, comfort and resources to support learning. In addition to unfavourable economic factors, these students are often from homes where they have only one parent and receive little supervision of their activities. The challenges to teaching, and learning, science in these schools are increased for both the teachers and learners by diverse ethnic, linguistic and cultural factors associated with the students. Populations considered minorities in the United States as a whole are clearly majorities in many Dade County schools and the profile of linguistic and ethnic diversity often differs dramatically from one school to another. [...]

Culture

Some of the critical factors that relate to the learning of science concern culture, access to economic resources, educational background of parents, language and living with only one parent. Just how will students go about the task of learning science? Obviously, there are ways in which this can be done, but in the United States, the reform documents have for many years now recognized the central role of the learner in making sense of what is to be learned. It is recommended that the teacher adopts a mediational role in maintaining a learning environment that is conducive to the learning of all students. However, research that I have undertaken with my colleagues suggests that most teachers have not implemented the recommendations for reform but have, instead, maintained a traditional approach to the teaching and learning of science based on a transmission–absorption model of teaching and learning.

The discourse of the home is also a factor that can either foster or inhibit the learning of science. If discussions in the home involve negotiation and consensus-building, the generation of alternatives and selection from among them, and critical examination of all verbal assertions, then it is likely that persons from such a home would be well equipped to interact in a scientific community where similar patterns are customary. Similarly, the learning of science might be enhanced if students are encouraged to voice their opinion and provide evidence to support their points of view. Alternatively, students would not be well prepared for the learning of science if the discourse of the home required them to accept the voice of authority and use rules as the referent for interacting in the home. The point I am making here is that, even though the conversations do not involve science directly, they take a form that is science-like and thereby are strategic resources to support the learning of science.

The level of income and the residual that is available to provide experiences for children to learn at home is obviously important. Thus, having the income to have computers, books, manipulatives, tools and other learning support resources is an issue. So, too, is the safety of having a home that is free of violence and abuse. If students are to use the home effectively to support their learning, it is important that they have a place to work and think and engage home activities to support this. Having someone with whom to interact can also be beneficial, as can having someone to provide transport to museums, libraries and other places that can support the learning of science. This goes beyond having the economic means to support learning to include the availability of others whose primary goal is to enhance the quality of life of an individual and make it possible for them to access the resources they seek to promote their learning.

The home is also a source of learning cultural knowledge, which includes knowledge and values about such matters as respect for authority, religion, the purpose and role of education in life and potential careers. Students who learn these things might bring their knowledge with them to the classroom and use it to make sense of what is happening in science lessons. This knowledge can facilitate or inhibit the learning of science and it is often advantageous for a teacher to be aware of the potential impact, positive or negative, of cultural knowledge on the learning of science. When students come to the classroom, they bring their cultural knowledge with them and it can constrain the way they interact with others and engage the activities designed to promote learning.

The manner in which the curriculum is enacted is associated with the cultural capital that students bring with them to class. This relates to many factors, such as the cultural histories of learners, some of which are evident in the following comments from elementary teachers from Miami.

- The cultural and ethnic make-up of our school does play a role in how education is viewed by the parents and thereby the children of our school. Gender also has a role in that our Hispanic parents don't believe that science is important to their girls … they want their daughters to do well in reading and language arts.
- The values parents hold toward education affect participation. If they're not educated they don't know how to motivate their children.
- Economics plays an important part in the learning equation. When expendable money is in short supply it is not spent on educational materials for children at home. Until a parent understands how important education is and what it can mean to a child's future livelihood, there is no money for books, newspapers, magazines, let alone a computer. We are becoming a nation more economically divided than ever before, the 'filthy' and the 'filthy rich'.
- Of my twenty students, four live in homes with their own fathers and mothers. The majority of students live in single-parent homes without any other relatives in the household. Eighteen students are on free or reduced lunch. Two pay for lunch.
- Some students never talk. Although I call them and ask them about science they respond – I do not want to talk. They do not feel comfortable speaking English because they do not speak it properly. I understand these students because I have the same problem.

Factors such as those mentioned by the teachers need to be considered when teachers plan and implement a curriculum. It is not the case that there is any one approach to the teaching and learning of science that would advantage all learners. Instead there are some guidelines that suggest that any approach to learning ought to focus on the learning resources that can be accessed by each individual and then to consider what activities might be devised to enable all learners to succeed in meeting their goals. Such an approach necessitates a thorough investigation of the extant knowledge that learners can use to learn science. Once this has been done, it seems imperative that activities be devised so that all learners can fully employ the resources they have to support their learning. Thus, the teacher's role with respect to any learner will depend on what the learner knows and what goals are most appropriate for that learner.

Returning to the college physics class for a moment, it is certainly the case that the physics professor has goals and, in accordance with those goals, he has set up an approach to learning and teaching. However, the students in the class are not aware of his goals and have not experienced a class like this one. They do not know what they are expected to do as learners. Until they understand and can enact new roles in this classroom, it might be expected that some of them will flounder and express their dissatisfaction with the professor's approach. They understand transmission/absorption approaches to teaching and learning, but the hands-on, figure-it-out-for-yourself approach to learning is novel to them. They tend to judge the appropriateness of their own roles and those of the teacher in traditional terms and are seemingly unaware of their responsibilities to learn from peers, textbooks, the library and the professor. Thus, their transition into the community of physics is inhibited by a lack of understanding of the goals and the associated roles of learners and teachers. A discussion of roles and goals would most likely lead to a change in what is happening in the classroom as such discussions became a part of the discourse of the classroom community.

If students are to improve their learning it seems imperative that they are able to be critically reflective on their roles as learners. Yet most learners do not have a language to discuss their learning. [...] If students have alternative roles that they can enact when they get stuck in a process of solving problems then the exhortation to try harder might result in them undertaking an analysis of what they know that might be pertinent to this problem, an analysis of problems like ones that were worked in class, a review of problems worked in the textbook, a call to a peer to discuss the approach to the problem, and visiting the library to review additional texts on the topic of titrations [might also help them to progress].

Conclusions

The approach adopted in this chapter was to bring into the foreground issues associated with culture, language and power distribution in classes where the learning of science is a goal. The frame of co-participation offers the potential of improving the quality of science teaching and learning by considering a new set of roles for teachers and students. In addition, it focuses on the significance of negotiating a shared language and using that language as a tool for learning science. Providing students with autonomy to access resources to support their own learning in and out of class and acknowledging the significance of out-of-class learning activities are also important components of a plan to improve the quality of learning. However, language is at the core of any effort to improve learning. Once a shared language exists, efforts must be made to use that language to describe what is known and to reflect critically on what is known, what is to be learned, and the roles to be adopted in the process of learning. Through the agency of the shared language, learners can voice their needs to support learning. In this process, it needs to be acknowledged that teachers can make a difference, especially in terms of coping with the diversity that exists in any classroom. Rather than viewing cultural diversity as a challenge based on deficit ways of thinking about teaching and learning, teachers can consider the diversity a resource to support a variety of new roles as students co-participate within an evolving community that becomes more science-like over time.

Note

1   As I write that last sentence, I almost wrote action but did not do so because it would have not carried the sense of context that interaction does. Individuals can only exist and act in social settings and, in a classroom, the focus always ought to bring interaction to the foreground. An individual might be interacting with other individuals, objects or social artefacts, such as occurs when individuals think about concepts, terminology and conventions. In a more obvious sense, in a classroom any individual only acts in a context of the presence of others and a complex maze of perceptions, expectations, etc.

References

Kuhn, D. (1993) 'Science as argument: implications for teaching and learning scientific thinking', *Science Education* 77(3): 319–37.

Lemke, J. L. (1995) *Textual Politics: Discourse and Social Dynamics,* London: Taylor and Francis.

Roth, W.-M. (1995) *Authentic School Science: Knowing and Learning in Open-inquiry Science Laboratories,* Dordrecht: Kluwer Academic Publishers.

Schön, D. (1985) *The Design Studio,* London: RIBA Publications Ltd.

Tobin, K. (1987) 'The role of wait time in higher cognitive level learning', *Review of Educational Research* 57(1): 69–95.

—— (ed.) (1993) *The Practice of Constructivism in Science Education,* Ellsdale, NJ: Lawrence Erlbaum and Associates.

3.3 Defining 'science' in a multicultural world

Implications for science education

William W. Cobern and
Cathleen C. Loving

Is science universal? Only recently has this question been given any serious consideration at all. In the tradition of science as practised in the West for the past 300 years, and in the tradition of school science, the answer has been, 'Of course science is universal'. As Richard Dawkins likes to put it, there are no epistemological relativists at 30,000 feet. But today some will say, 'Not so fast!' Dawkins offers a brute definition of universality completely devoid of any nuance of understanding and equally devoid of relevance to the question at hand. No one disputes that without an aeroplane of fairly conventional description, a person at 30,000 feet is in serious trouble. The question of universality does not arise over the phenomenon of falling. The question of universality arises over the fashion of the propositions given to account for the phenomenon of falling, the fashion of the discourse through which we communicate our thoughts about the phenomenon and the values we attach to the phenomenon itself and the various ways we have of understanding and accounting for the phenomenon – including the account offered by a standard scientific description.

In today's schools, there are often competing accounts of natural phenomena, especially when schools are located in multicultural communities. There are also competing claims about what counts as science. […] The purpose of our chapter is to examine the definition of science put forward from multicultural perspectives in contrast to a universalist perspective on science, that is, the Standard Account. We will argue that good science explanations will always be universal even if we do incorporate indigenous knowledge as scientific and broaden what is taught as science. What works best is still of interest to most and, although we hate to use the word hegemony, Western science would co-opt and dominate indigenous knowledge if it were incorporated as science. Therefore, indigenous knowledge is better off as a different kind of knowledge that can be valued for its own merits, play a vital role in science education and maintain a position of independence from which it can critique the practices of science and the Standard Account.

Multicultural perspectives on science

If there are different ways of accounting for a phenomenon of nature then it is possible that some people will reject some of these accounts – including the account offered by Western science – and accept others. A. Gibson (1996, personal communication) tells of a time when she was working at a rainforest scientific station on a South Pacific island and a conversation she had with an indigenous islander. The islander commented that Westerners only think they know why the ocean rises and falls on a regular basis. They think it has to do with the moon. They are wrong. The ocean rises and falls as the great sea turtles leave and return to their homes in the sand. The ocean falls as the water rushes into the empty nest. The ocean rises as the water is forced out by the returning turtles. Is this islander scientific because he has accurate knowledge of the ocean tides that affect his island? Is he unscientific because his explanation for tidal action is scientifically inappropriate? Is science universal because the standard scientific account for tidal action applies to all local occurrences of tidal phenomena? Or, does one grant the obvious brute factuality of actual phenomenon but reject universalist claims for standard scientific accounts of actual phenomenon? Matthews states well the universalist perspective of the Standard Account:

> Just as volcanic eruptions are indifferent to the race or sex of those in the vicinity, and lava kills whites, blacks, men, women, believers, non-believers, equally, so also the science of lava flows will be the same for all. For the universalist, our science of volcanoes is assuredly a human construction with negotiated rules of evidence and justification, but it is the behavior of volcanoes that finally judges the adequacy of our vulcanology, not the reverse.
>
> (Matthews 1994: 182)

The undeterred critic, however, will still ask: Though the phenomenon are experientially universal, can't one argue that scientific accounts are not universal since such accounts are not universally accepted?

The resolution of such questions hinges on the definition of science, including the concept of universality, and this resolution is of considerable importance for both educators and the public at large. When a discipline earns the title 'science' it 'acquires the authority to promulgate truthful and reliable knowledge, control over education and credentials, access to money and manpower, and the kind of political clout that comes from possessing knowledge that is essential yet esoteric' (Fuller 1991: 177). In science education, the definition of science is a de facto gatekeeping device for what can be included in a school science curriculum and what cannot. A very large amount of money, for example, has been spent in the United States on litigating the question of whether or not 'creation science' can be properly included as an aspect of school science (Nelkin 1983; Overton 1983). Moreover, if science is deemed universal, it not only displaces scientific pretenders such as creation science, it also displaces any local knowledge that conflicts with it. Kawagley *et al.* (1998: 134) argue that 'such a narrow view of science not only diminishes the legitimacy of knowledge derived through generations of naturalistic observation and insight, it simultaneously devalues those cultures which traditionally rely heavily on naturalistic observation and insight'. The record is fairly clear. Around the globe where science is taught, it is taught at the expense of indigenous knowledge. [...]

People feel passionately about these issues. The passions in the academy have run so high that the controversies have been dubbed the 'Science Wars' (Anonymous 1997). At school levels, the struggle is over multicultural approaches to science and science education within multicultural situations. Actions taken are at times extreme. In 1987, the Portland Oregon School District published the *African-American Baseline Essays*, a set of six revisionist essays providing resource materials and references for teachers on the knowledge and contributions of Africans and African-Americans. The science baseline essay, written by Hunter Havelin Adams (1990), has serious problems, but it is widely distributed because of the current pressure on school districts to incorporate multicultural material into the classroom, coupled with the dearth of this kind of material. Hundreds of copies of the *Baseline Essays* have been sent to school districts across the country and have been adopted or are being seriously considered by school districts as diverse as Fort Lauderdale, Detroit, Milwaukee, Atlanta, Chicago, Prince Georges County, MD, and Washington, DC. Even more widely distributed is its predecessor, *Blacks in Science: Ancient and Modern*, edited by Ivan Van Sertima (1984). Vine DeLoria, who is involved with Indian science education through the American Indian Science and Engineering Society (AISES) has recently published a book entitled *Red Earth, White Lies: Native Americans and the Myth of Scientific Facts* (DeLoria 1995). These supplements on multicultural science, expressly intended to 'raise the self-esteem' of students, adopt a triumphalist approach to the material. That is, they present the achievements and the beliefs of the group described as superior and anticipatory to the achievements and beliefs of modern *Western* science. Thus, the Dogon of Mali supposedly studied Sirius B, which is invisible to the naked eye, hundreds of years ago. The Egyptians foreshadowed the Theory of Evolution thousands of years ago; they also anticipated many of the philosophical aspects of quantum theory (Adams 1990: 21), and they knew the particle/wave nature of light (p. 26).

The *Baseline Essays*, and similar publications, represent a radical revisionist historiography of science and culture. There are other examples of multicultural materials for science education that are far less controversial. Books such as Robertta Barba's (1995) *Science in the Multicultural Classroom: A Guide to Teaching and Learning* and the Addison-Wesley (Alcoze *et al.* 1993) teacher's guide, *Multiculturalism in Mathematics, Science, and Technology: Readings and Activities*, bring culture into the science classroom for pedagogical purposes without rewriting history. The nature of science implicit in these books, however, represents a subtle change from standard accounts. Looking elsewhere, the question of how *science* is to be defined is brought into clear relief (e.g. Kawagley and Barnhardt 1998; Kawagley *et al.* 1998; Snively and Corsiglia 2001). With specific reference to First Nations people in Canada and the Yupiaq people of Alaska, one finds that indigenous knowledge is reclassified as science – but not *science* according to the Standard Account, and therein lies the controversy.

Multiple culture-based sciences?

The Standard Account of science can be called '*Western*' given its historic origins in Ancient Greek and European culture. Speculative thought about nature, natural philosophy, and later what became known simply as '*science*' always engaged Western culture. The Western experience with science has been a long one and, in a sense, Western culture and science have matured in consort, but not without trials. 'There has been, on the one hand, a disintegrating effect on traditional values and forms of representation, and, on the other hand, a progressive integration into the dominant culture ... of the scientific mentality – the values, content of knowledge and patterns of action which underlie scientific practice and are formed by it' (Ladrière 1977: 12). This disintegrating effect appears to have been recognized by Charles Darwin who, late in life, lamented:

> I have said that in one respect my mind has changed during the last twenty or thirty years. Up to the age of thirty, or beyond it, poetry of many kinds ... gave me great pleasure, and even as a schoolboy I took intense delight in Shakespeare ... I have also said that formerly pictures gave me considerable, and music very great, delight. But now for many years I cannot endure to read a line of poetry: I have tried to read Shakespeare, and found it so intolerably dull that it nauseated me. I have also almost lost my taste for pictures or music ... I retain some taste for fine scenery, but it does not cause me the exquisite delight which it formerly did ... My mind seems to have become a kind of machine for grinding general laws out of large collections of facts ...
>
> (quoted in Owens 1983: 38)

And, of course, the European Romantic poets echoed this lament (see Barber 1963).

Moreover, Europe was an expansionist culture, and European exploration, conquest and colonization of lands beyond Europe brought Western science to those lands and their inhabitants. In these parts of the world where Western science is experienced as a relatively new phenomenon, the interaction of science 'with culture has taken a more violent form and the disintegrating effects have been much more sharply experienced' (Ladrière 1977: 14). Indeed, colonial education designed for indigenous peoples used science as the tool of choice to modernize and supplant indigenous culture. In the words of one colonialist: 'A literate nation is provided with the means for substituting scientific explanations of everyday events – such as death, disease, and disaster – for the supernatural, nonscientific explanations which prevail in developing societies ...' (Lord 1958: 340). A more reflective colonial teacher remarked, 'In common with so many others, I used to think that we could get rid of Bantu "stupidities" by suitable talks on natural science, hygiene, etc., as if the natural sciences could subvert their traditional lore or their philosophy' (Tempels 1959: 29). The point is, the West judged the rest of the world by its own measures of choice, Western science and Western technology, and used education to enforce change on those societies found deficient. According to Adas (1989: 4) European 'perceptions of the mate-rial superiority of their own cultures, particularly as manifested in scientific thought and technological innovation, shaped their attitudes toward and interac-tion with peoples they encountered overseas'. Why? Because:

> In the late eighteenth and nineteenth centuries, most European thinkers concluded that the unprecedented control over nature made possible by Western science and technology proved that European modes of thought and social organization corresponded much more closely to the underlying realities of the universe than did those of any other people or society, past or present.
>
> (Adas 1989: 7)

Western scientists did have scientific interests in the rest of the world. Many areas of the globe became field sites for the practice of Western science by Western scientists (Basalla 1967). Darwin's voyage on the Beagle is surely the best known example of Western scientific development derived from non-European field work. When scientists occasionally took note of indigenous knowledge of nature, that knowledge was distinctively labelled *ethnoscience* (e.g. Behrens 1989; Berlin 1972; Boster and Johnson 1989) – never simply *science*. This is not to say that such indigenous knowledge was regarded as without value. There is a long tradition of Western science finding value in indigenous knowledge, especially as an aid to pharmaceutical discovery (Linden 1991). But, finding value in indigenous knowl-edge is not the same as conferring the title '*science*' and admitting indigenous knowledge of nature to the Standard Account.

In the 1990s, non-Western peoples and some scholars within the West began to formally and overtly resist this imperial Western attitude toward indigenous knowledge of nature. This movement was abetted by the programme for the social study of science, founded in the 1970s at Edinburgh (Bloor and Barnes 1996), which argued that all science is socially contingent and culturally embedded. New epistemological perspectives such as multiculturalism (Stanley and Brickhouse 1994), post-colonialism (McKinley 1997) and postmodernism (Lyotard 1995) rose to challenge the conventional Western wisdom on the relationship between science and culture and the Standard Account itself. In education, Hodson (1993: 686) maintained that science curricula often 'portray science as located within, and exclusively derived from, a western cultural context. The implicit curriculum message is that the only science is western science …' Dr Thom Alcoze is Native American and a forestry professor at Northern Arizona University. In a taped interview for a science teacher development project (Smithsonian Institution 1996b) he poignantly presented a different perspective on science:

> Science is often thought of [pause] America has science. Mainstream America has science. And if you are a minority culture in this country you don't have

science. We started looking for Indian science where science is expressed in Indian tradition. And found it with plants, starting off. Medicines. And of course the stereotype is, well – Indian medicine is just superstition and mumbo-jumbo, sleight of hand, and basically it's a witch doctor kind of thing [pause] a stereotype. A lot of strange noises and dancin' and singin' and a lot of shakin' but that's all it is [pause] superstitious. It's not real. What we found out when we looked for facts, we found that even today in modern America there are over 200 medicines in the pharmacopoeia that we use that have direct origins in Native American medical practice. Yes, in fact Indian people did have science. They were using science all the time. They weren't using scientific terminology. They did not publish in scientific journals [pause] that's kind of facetious at that time. But the issue of science then started to be redefined in my definition of what science is all about when we started to see that science is just another word for nature.

Dr Alcoze's last sentence is of critical importance. He says, 'science is just another word for nature' and, therefore, American Indians being greatly knowledgeable about nature, had scientific knowledge of their own. This idea is further developed in Kawagley *et al.* (1998: 134): 'We contend that no single origin for science exists; that science has a plurality of origins and a plurality of practices.' They contend 'that there is no one way to do or think about science' (p. 139). As their case in point, they contend that Yupiaq culture in south-western Alaska holds 'a body of scientific knowledge and epistemology that differs from that of Western science' (p. 133):

> Much of Yupiaq scientific knowledge is manifested most clearly in their technology. One may argue that technology is not science. However, technology does not spring from a void. To invent technological devices, scientific observations and experimentation must be conducted. Yupiaq inventions, which include the kayak, river fish traps … represent technology that could not have been developed without extensive scientific study of the flow of currents in rivers, the ebb and flow of tides in bays, and the feeding, resting, and migratory habits of fish, mammals, and birds.
>
> (Kawagley *et al.* 1998: 136)

'*Science*' from this perspective refers to descriptive knowledge of nature developed through experience with nature. The definition of science used here is consistent with Ogawa (1995: 588), who refers to science simply as 'a *rational* perceiving of reality'. From this definition, Ogawa (1995) argues for the existence of many different legitimate sciences.

The knowledge described is from a domain of knowledge that Snively and Corsiglia (2001) call traditional ecological knowledge (TEK). It is the descriptive ecological knowledge about nature that First Nations peoples in Canada and Native Americans in the United States have acquired through long years of experience with their natural environment, and which has been vital to their survival.

Snively and Corsiglia (2001) show that this knowledge can be quite insightful and has much to offer Western science. For example, they tell the story of a Nisga'a fisherman in British Columbia who noticed that the Dungeness crabs he typically harvested were exhibiting strange behaviour patterns. The crabs were 'marching past the dock at the mouth of the Nass River, rather than staying in the deep water of Alice Arm' (Snively and Corsiglia 2001: 19). He grew concerned about possible industrial pollution of the Alice Arm waters from a nearby molybdenum mine and later his concerns were shown to be well-founded. Given the life and practice of the Nisga'a, this intuition should come as no surprise:

> Among the Nisga'a, and among other aboriginal peoples, formal observa-
> tion, recollection, and consideration of extraordinary natural events is taken
> seriously. Every spring members of some Nisga'a families still walk their
> salmon stream to ensure spawning channels are clear of debris and that
> salmon are not obstructed in their ascent to spawning grounds. In the course
> of such inspection trips, Nisga'a observers traditionally use all of their senses
> and pay attention to important variables: what plants are in bloom, what
> birds are active, when specific animals are migrating and where, and so forth.
> In this way, traditional communities have a highly developed capacity for
> building up a collective data base. Any deviations from past patterns are
> important and noted.
>
> (Corsiglia and Snively 2001: 19)

Similar accounts were obtained for people living traditional lives in many other regions of the world from Australia to Africa (see Warren 1991, 1997).

Multicultural science in the classroom

The reasons for including such examples of knowledge as part of the Standard Account, or the reasons for expanding the definition of science under the Standard Account, have to do with education. Proponents of a multiplicity view of science argue that this will better serve the needs of students coming from diverse cultural backgrounds and will help to change the culturally corrosive effect that Western science has had on non-Western cultures. 'The Harvard-Smithsonian Video Case Studies in Science Education' (Smithsonian Institution 1997a, 1997b) project on classroom science provides a glimpse of how this multicultural perspective on science can play out in a science classroom. The project produced videotape case studies of teachers. Each tape shows vignettes of a teacher teaching science, inter- spersed with interview segments with the teacher and a science education expert. One of the case studies was carried out at an elementary school in Flagstaff, Arizona, where the students come from American Indian and non-Indian families. Donna is a fifth-grade teacher and she has been teaching a unit on ecology. She also has drawn in her Native American students by collecting information on Indian culture. This information is publicly displayed on a large poster board in the classroom (see Figure 3.3.1).

- Nature is viewed as sacred

- Humans are part of the web of life

- Humans should live in harmony with nature

- The entire world is viewed as being alive

- Technology should be low impact

Figure 3.3.1 Native American views about nature

Source: Smithsonian Institution 1996b

Pointing to the poster board, the teacher speaks to her students.

Donna: We were talking earlier in here about looking at different cultures and finding ideas from cultures that might help us understand science better. Now, some of the traditional Native American views about nature are on this chart. Can you find one [Native American view] that helps us to understand this cycle of decompositions?

(Smithsonian Institution 1996b)

At this point a number of students raise their hands. The teacher calls on them to speak and she asks each student to explain the relationship of the Native American viewpoint to decomposition. Later, Donna is asked in an interview about the purpose of such activities.

Donna: My goal would be that all children would feel that they have a very important heritage. No matter what heritage they come from. And to be a scientist doesn't mean that you have to be any particular race or any particular gender or from any particular culture but that all people have contributed to the body of knowledge which we call science.

(Smithsonian Institution 1996b)

In this vignette, Donna has set a very nice stage with her Native American poster about views of nature. From here, she can go on to get her class to study what science has learned about ecological cycles, balances of nature, decomposition, etc. Loving (1998) and Cobern (1995b) offer similar views on using local culture to promote science learning.

One would only hope that, along the way, reference might be made back to the poster to see if science supports, ignores or rejects ideas from one's culture and what evidence there is to support that. In Donna's case, the controversial questions are about her meaning for the word 'science' and if she will lead her students to understand that there are different legitimate ways of thinking about nature. 'Nature is viewed as sacred' is one such legitimate way, but it is not the way of science. Thus, we would want to know if Donna intends to help her students cognitively construct two different, though complementary, explanations for the same phenomena. Or, will the students learn the multiplicity view that all of this simply represents different forms of science?

The universality of science

As much as we support science teaching that is both informed by culture and sensitive to culture, the issues raised by TEK and multicultural perspectives on science must not be accepted uncritically. We say this not in defence of science and the Standard Account, but because we think that science has shown itself sufficiently useful and remarkable to humanity so that there will be no withdrawal of science from modern life. And, it is arguable that science would suffer little harm if, for the purposes of curriculum, TEK and similar domains of knowledge were declared *scientific* tomorrow. In contrast, such an action would actually be counterproductive with respect to the concerns people have about indigenous knowledge being shut out of science by the Standard Account. Before developing that thought, however, we clarify our meaning of the Standard Account and the case for universality.

Defining the Standard Account

Loving's (1991) *Scientific Theory Profile* gives a good indication of the breadth of philosophical views on the nature of science. Philosophers of science run the gamut from rationalist to naturalist, anti-realist to realist, and the many combinations within these ranges. Within the philosophy of science and scholarship on the nature of science resides the important question of demarcation. How can science be distinguished from other intellectual domains? How does science differ from (say) historiography or theology or philosophy? According to Gieryn *et al.* (1985: 392) the goals of demarcation are the '(1) differentiation of a valued commodity uniquely provided by science, and (2) exclusion of pseudoscientists ...' and these goals 'are important for scientists' establishment of a professional monopoly over the market for knowledge about nature' (also see Gieryn 1983; Smith and Scharmann 1999). The demarcation of science from other disciplines, however, is not easily accomplished. Laudan (1983: 8–9) argues that:

> Philosophers have been regarded as the gatekeepers to the scientific estate. They are the ones who are supposed to be able to tell the difference between real science and pseudoscience. ... Nonetheless, it seems pretty clear to many of us ... that philosophy has largely failed to deliver the relevant goods. Whatever the specific strengths and deficiencies of certain well-known efforts at demarcation ... it can be said fairly uncontroversially that there is no demarcation line

between science and non-science, or between science and pseudo-science, which would win assent from a majority of philosophers.

Though we do not wish to minimize the philosophical complexity of the issue to which Laudan refers, nor are we immune to the ideological influences upon the Standard Account (Hesse 1980), there is a pragmatic view to science that is broadly acceptable in the scientific community and described in accounts by scientists themselves, such as biologist Frederick Grinnell (1987) and physicist A. F. Chalmers (1982). In addition, science educators (Driver *et al.* 1996) who thoughtfully examined the range of philosophical, historical and sociological views of science, were able to arrive at critical areas of consensus and were helpful in our Standard Account. The following is what we understand that definition of the Standard Account of science to be. In providing this definition, we have kept in mind Laudan's (1996: 24) point that what 'we need to provide is a way of distinguishing reliable knowledge claims from unreliable ones'.

1.0 *Science is a naturalistic, material explanatory system used to account for natural phenomena that ideally must be objectively and empirically testable.*
1.1 Science is about *natural phenomena.*

It is not about the things that humans construct, such as economic systems, nor is it about spiritual phenomena. Here we concur that TEK is about natural phenomena.

1.2 The explanations that science offers are *naturalistic* and *material.*

It follows from point 1.1 that scientific explanations are not about the spiritual, emotional, economic, aesthetic and social aspects of human experience. Snively and Corsiglia (2001) recognize that, with respect to TEK, this aspect of the Standard Account poses a problem, even though TEK is about natural phenomena. They note that many scientists refuse to recognize TEK as science 'because of its spiritual base, which they regard as superstitious and fatalistic' (p. 23). In response, they argue that 'spiritual explanations often incorporate important ecology, conservation, and sustainable development strategies' (p. 30); but nevertheless, they still assert that 'the spiritual acquisition and explanation of TEK is a fundamental component and must be promoted if the knowledge system is to survive' (Johnson 1992 quoted in Snively and Corsiglia 2001: 23).

1.3 Science explanations are *empirically testable* (at least in principle) against natural phenomena (the test for empirical consistency) or against other scientific explanations of natural phenomena (the test for theoretical consistency).

Science involves collecting data (i.e. evidence) and a scientific explanation must be able to account for this data. Alternatively, science involves the testing of proposed explanations against data (Driver *et al.* 1996: 43). This concept is nicely captured by Duschl in an interview where he is commenting on the activities of some first-graders. The first-grade class is experimenting with sound. The children have some ideas about sound and they test some of these ideas using rubber bands stretched over geoboard pegs. About this episode, Duschl remarks:

> When kids are given the same phenomena to observe, they see very different things. Their personal interpretations of the ideas are very different. And when we listen to the children in a circle you can hear this and see it. This is an opportunity to get this consensus that we want, to get some discussion because the scientific ideas just aren't any ideas. They are ideas grounded in evidence.
>
> (Smithsonian Institution 1996a)

Duschl tells us that 'the scientific ideas just aren't any ideas'. They are tested ideas. They are tested either in the *physical* world following from point 1.2, or they are tested for theoretical consistency with other scientific explanations, which in turn were tested in the physical world.

Moreover, scientific testing strives to be *objective*. In recent years this value in science has been derided as 'objectivism … a universal, value-free process' (Stanley and Brickhouse 1994: 389; also see Guba and Lincoln 1989). Perhaps some people have over-extended the concept of objectivity. In our view of the Standard Account, objectivity refers to the goal that experimental outcomes be not prejudged nor unreasonably constrained by prior belief, that data is collected fairly and accurately, and that research methods are executed with fidelity.

Is it possible that TEK is *tested* knowledge? Borrowing a phrase from Sagan (1996: 25 1), Kawagley *et al.* (1998: 137) maintain that 'Yupiaq traditional knowledge reflects an understanding of the natural world based on a "massive set of scientific experiments continuing over generations"'. No one would doubt that the Yupiaq, along with every other group of people that ever lived, have and continue to engage in 'trial and error' experimentation. People try different shampoos until they find the one they like best, but few would consider such 'experimentation' scientific. It is not scientific, but it is an effective and valuable process. Similarly, the building up of traditional knowledge through trial and error interactions with nature has produced important knowledge. But, it lacks the formal, controlled features of scientific experimentation.

1.4 Science is an explanatory *system* – it is more than a descriptive ad hoc accounting of natural phenomena.

Science seeks to parsimoniously explain how things work, invoking only natural causes, and these explanations are woven into a system of *theoretical* thought. Theories, however, are typically underdetermined; that is, they go beyond the available data and are therefore conjectural. Scientists choose between competing theories based on criteria such as accuracy of prediction, internal consistency and data consistency, breadth of scope (the more encompassing the theory, the more it is valued), simplicity and fruitfulness – all based, however, on human judgment

(Driver *et al.* 1996). To this aspect of the Standard Account, the sociology of science adds that human judgment does not exist in a vacuum. It exists and is exercised within the context of social and cultural life. There is an inherently social aspect to all knowledge construction. Thus, for example, to understand how Darwin came to his formulation of evolution, it is not sufficient to know about the voyage of the Beagle, his various observations, his knowledge of domestic breeding practices, and the like. One must also take into account the cultural environment in which Darwin lived (Cobern 1995a, 2000; Desmond and Moore 1991).

Moreover, it must be noted that scientific explanation (point 1.2) and scientific theory (point 1.4) represent two complementary levels of scientific knowledge (alternatively, the difference between what students think of as 'description' and 'explanation' in the theoretical scientific sense – see Horwood 1988; Matthews 1994). The first level is strongly related to direct human experience. Thus, for example, the location of salmon at any one time of the year can be explained in terms of the salmon's life cycle, where evidence relating to locality and life cycle are both directly observable. This explanation has considerable credibility regardless of cultural variation. In contrast, credibility at the second level is much more culturally dependent. At the second level, scientific theory would further explain that 'life cycle' can be viewed as an idealized pattern of sequenced events that is applicable across a great many organisms. Here, credibility depends on how accustomed a people is to abstract scientific theorizing. In a different culture, people would find it more plausible to explain 'life cycle' as the purposeful course of life uniquely belonging to each creature. Horton (1994) has demonstrated that much of traditional African thought at the lower level does not differ substantially from scientific explanation. The significant differences are at the secondary level with the 'webs of significance' (Geertz 1973) that give meaning to those first-level explanations. Similarly, here is the fundamental problem with taking TEK as science – TEK is embedded in a spiritual system of meaning that cannot easily be ignored, and should not be ignored.

2.0 *The Standard Account of science is grounded in metaphysical commitments about the way the world 'really is'* (e.g. see Burtt 1967; Cobern 1991, 1995b).

These commitments take the form of necessary (or first order) presuppositions. They are not descriptive of what science is, but what science presupposes about nature. By themselves, these necessary presuppositions are probably not sufficient motivation for any individual to be involved with science, hence any individual scientist or science teacher is likely to have augmented these necessary presuppositions with other (secondary) presuppositions that are necessary personally. Our focus, however, is on the metaphysical minimum for science.

2.1 Science presupposes the possibility of knowledge about nature.

Realists view this as actual knowledge – human thinking holds the potential for recognizing and understanding the actual order and causality inherent in the phenomena of nature. Idealists view this as instrumental knowledge – human thinking holds the potential for constructing viable understanding about the instrumental order and causality in the experience of natural phenomena. Roger Penrose and Stephen Hawking, respectively, are exemplars of the two positions (Hawking and Penrose 1996). Closely linked to the possibility of knowledge are the presuppositions of order and causality.

2.2 Science presupposes that there is *order* in nature.

The fact that the orbit of the Earth can be represented as a mathematical equation or that tidal action can be estimated within predictable limits of accuracy is evidence of order. Realists view this order as actual order – there is order in nature. Idealists view this as instrumental order – human experience with nature is amenable to ordered thinking about experience with nature. Historically, presupposed order in nature was profoundly important to the development of science in Europe. Gernet (1993–1994), following the pioneering work of Needham (1969), notes the crippling effect the lack of this presupposition had on the development of Chinese science.

2.3 Science presupposes *causation* in nature (Collingwood 1940).

For example, rain is linked causally with factors such as air temperature and humidity. Given enough water vapour in the atmosphere and the right air temperature, it is going to rain. Realists view this causation as actual causation – cause and effect are inherent attributes of nature. Idealists view this as instrumental causation – causal thinking is compatible with the human experience with nature.

3.0 *Nevertheless, what ultimately qualifies as science is determined by consensus within the scientific community.*

Thus, simply offering an idea which fits all these parameters will still not be science until judged so by the community of science. As we noted above, the problem is that there is no perfect account of science that clearly represents all of science, past and present, and just as clearly eliminates all endeavours that scientists do not consider to be science. In the final analysis, a human judgment must be made. However, the community of scientists is a community that requires that scientific knowledge be made public and withstand public scrutiny and testing. Thus, any conspiracy to include or exclude any domain of thought is unlikely to succeed in the long run.

The universality of science

Much of the multicultural literature on science seems to be saying that the problem with the Standard Account is that it is taken to be the only account of science – it is an exclusive and universally appropriate account. But we wonder if this really is the bone of contention among multiculturalists? Is it the alleged *universality* of science or is it the intellectual exclusiveness of science according to the Standard Account? We ask this because the post-colonialist arguments rejecting the universality of science seem to be arguments more about the exclusivity of science. It seems to us that, even if the definition of science were broadened to include what is now excluded, one would still have a 'universal' science. Indeed, if there is no universal concept of science then how can anything be either included or excluded as science?

It can be instructive to consider a different type of example altogether. Around the globe, 'football' is a widely recognized sporting game. We in America have a game called 'football', but it is significantly different from what the rest of the world calls football. In fact, the rest of the world, for the sake of clarity, refers to the American game as 'American football' to distinguish it from REAL football. With enough political agitation and economic clout, those of us Americans who resent this form of marginalization could possibly get the rest of the world to broaden its definition of 'football'. The term 'football' still is universal (we now all agree that the game of football includes the varieties played in the United States and elsewhere), but it now has a new meaning that is general enough to include what many previously took to be two rather distinct games. Undoubtedly, there are other games played with a ball and the feet. If the proponents of these games agitate as successfully as did the American footballers, where will the process end? In our opinion, this is anti-reductionism made absurd and the end result is that everyone loses. Diversity is lost. Meaning is lost. Communication is lost.

We thus conclude that the real difficulty multiculturalists have with the Standard Account is not its claim to universality, but its exclusiveness. Though technically difficult to accomplish, conceptually, the Standard Account could be broadened by simply getting a consensus in the science community for the rewriting of the definition of science in a more inclusive form. Then one could have 'Maori science' or 'First Nations science', (or for that matter, 'Christian science', 'Islamic science', etc.), just as 'football' could be broadened to include 'American' football. We could be even more inclusive by simply taking science to be knowledge of nature – but one needs to reconsider why would anyone want to do any of these things? Early in this article we quoted from Kawagley *et al.* (1998: 134) on the relationship between the Standard Account and indigenous knowledge:

> Such a narrow view of science not only diminishes the legitimacy of knowledge derived through generations of naturalistic observation and insight, it simultaneously devalues those cultures which traditionally rely heavily on naturalistic observation and insight.

We see in this statement that some people are troubled about the dominant intellectual position that modern Western science has come to hold in the public arena. It is a position of dominance that tends to disenfranchise competitors. One way for competitors to regain that franchise is to oust Western science. Another way to regain access to the public square – and this is the approach many multiculturalists

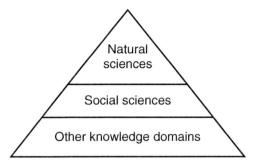

Figure 3.3.2 Epistemological pyramid

appear to be taking – is to get one's ideas included in the definition of the dominant player, in this case Western science or the Standard Account.

If such a thing were ever to happen, it would be a pyrrhic victory for indigenous knowledge. The new additions to science (TEK or any other form of indigenous knowledge) would soon face serious negative consequences. They would first lose their distinctiveness as a form of thought as they became absorbed by the dominant discourse of science, that is, the Standard Account. They would lose because the new additions would inevitably be taken as mere 'tokens' of cultural inclusiveness rather than as serious participants in the discourse of science. This tokenism would be reinforced by the inability of the new additions to compete where Western science is strongest – technical precision control, creative genius and explanatory power. Also, the new additions would lose by being co-opted into the cultural chauvinism scientism now holds in much of modern life. Snively and Corsiglia (2001) rightfully question where is the wisdom in science? As an incorporated part of science, that critique and challenge would be much more difficult to make.

The problem of scientism

The problem facing TEK and other forms of indigenous knowledge, as well as other domains of knowledge such as the arts and literature and religion, is the problem of scientism – the cultural hegemony science. The problem is not that science dominates at what it does best: the production of highly efficacious naturalistic understanding of natural phenomena. The problem is that too often science is used to dominate the public arena as if all other discourses were of lesser value. This is a hierarchic view of knowledge with science placed at the epistemological pinnacle (see Figure 3.3.2).

For example, the National Academy of Science, out of fear over religious incursions in school science, issued this statement:

> In a nation whose people depend on scientific progress for their health, economic gains, and national security, it is of utmost importance that our students understand science as a system of study, so that by building on past

achievements they can maintain the pace of scientific progress and ensure the continued emergence of results that can benefit mankind.

(National Academy of Sciences 1984: 6)

More recently, the International Council of Scientific Unions (ICSU) endorsed a similar perspective in the 'Proposed ICSU Programme on Capacity Building in Science' (ICSU 1996). The document epigram equates 'the global gap of well-being' with 'the global imbalance of science and technology development'. The ICSU intends to:

> demonstrate to the world that having the capacity to understand and use science is economically, socially, and culturally profitable. Indeed, the very habitability of the planet will depend on global popular consensus. As such, the spread of scientific culture, of scientific ways of thinking, and of knowledge is tied to the fate of humanity.

(ICSU 1996: 1)

About these statements we can say, of course, that few people question the productive role that science has played in the development of modern life, including medicine and contributions to good health. Nor will any deny the economic gains due to technical innovations grounded in science. But the relationship between science and technology is not nearly so straightforward as these statements from the science community suggest. These claims by the NAS and the ICSU, however, are vastly overstated and singularly one-sided. Good health, economic well-being and national security all depend on many things, only one of which is science. Moreover, as important as science surely is, it does not have an uncontested claim to be the most important of these many factors. Curiously, though the NAS and the ICSU appear eager to accept credit for good technological innovations, there is no parallel acceptance of technological disasters. If the science community wants credit for developing high-yield grains that ease food shortages, how can the same community refuse credit for DDT's adverse consequences? Something is wrong with this portrayal of science (we might even say *betrayal* of science). Garrard and Wegierski (1991: 611) suggest an explanation:

> It can be argued that technology and scientific positivism constitute the dominant ideology of Western civilization today. Technology has indeed become, as Heidegger noted, the metaphysics of our age, a totalistic form of secular religion ultimately incompatible with the existence of rival, non-technological assumptions, beliefs, or thought systems.

The problem for TEK – as well as for so many other domains of knowledge – is not the exclusivity of science as per the Standard Account, but the transmogrification of science as scientism in the public arena. [...]

Conclusion

Our position in this chapter is that science can be defined with sufficient clarity so as to maintain a coherent boundary for the practical purposes of school science curriculum development. That boundary excludes most forms of indigenous knowledge, if not all, just as it excludes art, history, economics, religion and many other domains of knowledge.

Being exclusive, however, does not confer science with any privilege vis-à-vis other domains. Science is properly privileged only within its own domain, for that is where its strength lies. When TEK and other forms of indigenous knowledge are devalued, it is not because of the exclusive nature of the Standard Account of science. It is because someone is involved in the scientistic practice of extending scientific privilege from its proper domain in science and technology into other domains. The solution is to resist this scientistic practice by emphasizing throughout schooling the concept of epistemological pluralism, bearing in mind that pluralism:

> is not relativism. … Pluralism is the civil engagement of our differences and disagreements about what is most importantly true. Against the monism that denies the variety of truth, against the relativism that denies the importance of truth, and against the nihilism that denies the existence of truth, we intend to nurture a pluralism that revives and sustains the conversation about what really matters, which is the truth.
>
> (Anonymous 1995: 12)

Bearing in mind *also* that truth is never under the sole proprietorship of any single domain of knowledge – not even science.

References

Adams, H. H. I. (1990) *African and African-American Contributions to Science and Technology,* Portland, OR: Multnomah School District, Portland Public Schools.

Adas, M. (1989) *Machines as the Measure of Man: Science, Technology, and Ideologies of Western Dominance,* Ithaca, NY: Cornell University Press.

Alcoze, T. and Barrios-Chacon, M. (1993) *Multiculturalism in Mathematics, Science, and Technology: Readings and Activities,* New York: Addison-Wesley.

Anonymous (1995) 'Putting first things first' (editorial), *First Things* 51: 11–13 <http://www.firstthings.com/ftissues/ft9503/opinion/editorial.html>.

Anonymous (1997) 'Science wars and the need for respect and rigour', *Nature* 385(6615): 373.

Barba, R. H. (1995) *Science in the Multicultural Classroom: A Guide to Teaching and Learning,* Needham Heights, MA: Allyn and Bacon.

Barber, B. (1963) 'Tension and accommodations between science and humanism', *American Behavioral Scientist* 7: 3–8.

Basalla, G. (1967) 'The spread of western science', *Science* 156: 611–22.

Behrens, C. A. (1989) 'The scientific basis for Shipibo soil classification and land use: changes in soil-plant associations with cash cropping', *American Anthropologist* 91: 83–100.

Berlin, B. (1972) 'Speculations on the growth of ethnobotanical nomenclature', *Language in Society* 1: 51–86.

Bloor, D. and Barnes, B. (1996) *Scientific Knowledge: A Sociological Analysis*, Chicago: University of Chicago Press.

Boster, J. S. and Johnson, J. C. (1989) 'Form and function: a comparison of expert and novice judgments of similarity among fish', *American Anthropologist* 91: 866–88.

Burtt, E. A. (1967) *The Metaphysical Foundations of Modern Physical Science*, London: Routledge and Kegan Paul.

Chalmers, A. F. (1982) *What is this Thing Called Science?*, Victoria, Australia: University of Queensland Press.

Cobern, W. W. (1991) *World View Theory and Science Education Research*, NARST Monograph No. 3, Manhattan, KS: National Association for Research in Science Teaching.

—— (1995a) 'Belief and knowledge: unnecessary conflict in the science classroom', in F. Finley (ed.) *Proceedings of the History and Philosophy of Science and Science Teaching*, Vol. I (pp. 222–32), Minneapolis, MN: HPSST.

—— (1995b) 'Science education as an exercise in foreign affairs', *Science and Education* 4: 287–302.

—— (2000) 'The nature of science and the role of knowledge and belief', *Science and Education* 9 (3): 219–46.

Collingwood, R. G. (1940) *An Essay on Metaphysics*, London: Oxford University Press.

Corsiglia, J. and Snively, G. (1997) 'Knowing home: Nisga'a traditional knowledge and wisdom improve environmental decision making', *Alternatives Journal* 32: 22–7.

DeLoria, V. (1995) *Red Earth, White Lies: Native Americans and the Myth of Scientific Facts*, New York: Scribner.

Desmond, A. and Moore, J. (1991) *Darwin – The Life of a Tormented Evolutionist*, New York: Warner Books.

Driver, R., Leach, J., Millar, R. and Scott, P. (1996) *Young People's Images of Science*, Buckingham, UK: Open University Press.

Fuller, S. (1991) *Social Epistemology*, Bloomington, IN: Indiana University Press.

Garrard, G. and Wegierski, M. (1991) 'Oh Canada? An essay on Canadian history, politics, and culture', *The World and I* 6: 589–613.

Geertz, C. (1973) *The Interpretation of Culture*, New York: Basic Books.

Gernet, J. (1993–1994) 'Space and time: science and religion in the encounter between China and Europe', *Chinese Science* 11: 93–102.

Gieryn, T. F. (1983) 'Boundary-work and the demarcation of science from non-science: strains and interests in professional ideologies of scientists', *American Sociological Review* 48: 781–95.

——, Bevins, G. M. and Zehr, S. C. (1985) 'Professionalization of American scientists: public science in the creation/evolution trials', *American Sociological Review* 50: 392–409.

Grinnell, F. (1987) *The Scientific Attitude*, Boulder, CO: Westview Press.

Guba, E. G. and Lincoln, Y. S. (1989) *Fourth Generation Evaluation*, Newbury Park, CA: Sage.

Hawking, S. W. and Penrose, R. (1996) 'The nature of space and time', *Scientific American* 275: 60–5.

Hesse, M. (1980) *Revolutions and Reconstructions in the Philosophy of Science*, Bloomington, IN: Indiana University Press.

Hodson, D. (1993) 'In search of a rationale for multicultural science education', *Science Education* 77: 685–711.

Horton, R. (1994) *Patterns of Thought in Africa and the West*, Cambridge: Cambridge University Press.

Horwood, R. H. (1988) 'Explanation and description in science teaching', *Science Education* 72: 41–9.

International Council of Scientific Unions (ICSU) (1996) *Proposed ICSU Programme on Capacity Building in Science*, Batavia, IL: ICSU.

Johnson, M. (ed.) (1992) *Lore: Capturing Traditional Environmental Knowledge*, Ottawa, Ontario: Dene Cultural Institute, International Development Research Center.

Kawagley, A. O. and Barnhardt, R. (1998) *Education Indigenous to Place: Western Science meets Native Reality*, ERIC ED426823, <http:www.ankn.uaf.edu/EIP.html>.

——, Norris-Tull, D. and Norris-Tull, R. A. (1998) 'The indigenous worldview of Yupiaq culture: its scientific nature and relevance to the practice and teaching of science', *Journal of Research in Science Teaching* 35: 133–44.

Ladrière, J. (1977) *The Challenge Presented to Cultures by Science and Technology*, Paris: UNESCO.

Laudan, L. (1983) 'The demise of the demarcation problem', in R. Lauden (ed.) *The Demarcation between Science and Pseudo-science*, Vol. 21 (pp. 7–35), Blacksburg, VA: Virginia Technical Center for the Study of Science in Society, Working Papers.

—— (1996) *Beyond Positivism and Relativism*, Boulder, CO: Westview Press.

Linden, E. (1991) 'Lost tribes, lost knowledge', *TIME* 138(12): 46–56.

Lord, E. (1958) 'The impact of education on non-scientific beliefs in Ethiopia', *Journal of Social Psychology* 47: 339–53.

Loving, C. C. (1991) 'The scientific theory profile: a philosophy of science models for science teachers', *Journal of Research in Science Teaching* 28: 823–38.

—— (1998) 'Cortes' multicultural empowerment model and generative teaching and learning in science', *Science and Education* 7: 533–52.

Lyotard, J. F. (1995) *Toward the Postmodern*, Atlantic Highlands, NJ: Humanities Press.

Matthews, M. R. (1994) *Science Teaching: The Role of History and Philosophy of Science*, New York: Routledge.

McKinley, E. (1997) 'Science education from the margins: the uneasy selfhood of a post-colonial woman', paper presented at the annual meeting of ASERA. Adelaide, Australia: ASERA.

National Academy of Sciences (1984) *Science and Creationism: A View from the National Academy of Sciences*, Washington, DC: National Academy of Sciences.

Needham, J. (1969) *The Grand Titration*, London: George Allen and Unwin.

Nelkin, D. (1983) 'Legislating creation in Arkansas', *Society* 20(2): 13–16.

Ogawa, M. (1995) 'Science education in a multiscience perspective', *Science Education* 79: 583–93.

Overton, W. R. (1983) 'The decision in McClean *v*. Arkansas Board of Education', *Society* 20(2): 3–12.

Owens, V. S. (1983) 'Seeing Christianity in red and green as well as in black and white: propositional truth is not the whole truth', *Christianity Today* 27(13): 38–40.

Sagan, C. (1996) *The Demon-haunted World: Science as a Candle in the Dark*, New York: Random House.

Smith, M. U. and Scharmann, L. C. (1999) 'Defining versus describing the nature of science: a pragmatic analysis for classroom teachers and science educators', *Science Education* 83: 493–509.

Smithsonian Institution (1997a) *Case Study: Ingrid*, South Berlington, VT: Annenburg/CPB Math and Science Collection.

Smithsonian Institution (1997b) *Case Study: Donna*, South Berlington, VT: Annenburg/ CPB Math and Science Collection.

Snively, G. and Corsiglia, J. (2001) 'Rediscovering indigenous science: implications for science education', *Science Education* 85: 6–34.

Stanley, W. B. and Brickhouse, N. W. (1994) 'Multiculturalism, universalism, and science education', *Science Education* 78: 387–98.

Tempels, P. (1959) *Bantu Philosophy*, trans. C. King, Paris: Presence Africaine.

Van Sertima, I. (1984) *Blacks in Science: Ancient and Modern*, New Brunswick, NJ: Transaction Books.

Warren, D. M. (1991) *Using Indigenous Knowledge in Agricultural Development*, World Bank Discussion Paper No. 127, Washington, DC: The World Bank.

—— (1997) 'Conservation of indigenous knowledge serves conservation of biodiversity', *Alternatives Journal* 23: 26–7.

3.4 Marginalization of socio-scientific material in science–technology–society science curricula

Some implications for gender inclusivity and curriculum reform

Gwyneth Hughes

Science–technology–society (STS), environmental and feminist movements over the past three decades, combined with developments in the philosophy and sociology of science, have increasingly placed science curricula under scrutiny. On the one hand, science education is deemed to be out of touch with society, leaving pupils poorly equipped to deal with a complex modern world of scientific and technological controversy; on the other hand, science education is considered elitist, perpetuating under-representation of certain groups in science (Driver *et al.* 1996; Fensham 1993). Feminist critics of science, for example, have argued that the power embedded in masculine discourses of science reproduces the subordination of women and that the lack of women in science is one outcome (Harding, S. 1986, 1991). Providing science curricula with a social context by inclusion of STS issues in the curriculum has been viewed both as a means of promoting socio-scientific awareness of the social, political and economic dimensions to science and as opening up science to females and excluded or disadvantaged ethnic and class groups. Following early controversy, STS has now gained recognition and some science syllabuses have been adapted and redeveloped with one or more of these aims in mind.

One such example is the Salters' Advanced Level Chemistry course in the United Kingdom, which purports to teach scientific knowledge, laws and theories using applications and integral social context as a focus. This chapter draws on a study of Salters' chemistry (Hughes 1998) to argue the assumption that an STS curriculum will make science more relevant and inclusive is by no means straightforward.

Using a concept of the curriculum as discursively constructed, that is constantly under negotiation and interpretation, I demonstrate how the socio-science content of such an STS syllabus can be marginalized in three related ways. First, the language and structure of syllabus texts allow devaluation of socio-science with respect to abstract scientific principles. Second, socio-science is either omitted from the classroom and teaching practices or else appears only in peripheral activities. Finally, students' narrow interpretations of applications of science mean that they are not receptive to socio-scientific discourse; they appear to be strongly influenced by the marginalization of social context in course documentation and classroom activities.

I next explore how teachers, schools and curriculum bodies help to shape the construction of post-16 science as an entry to higher education and scientific professions for a mainly male elite. This gatekeeping is achieved by a perpetuated symbolic association of 'hard' abstract science and its frequent disassociation from the social world of human subjects with the masculine, and 'softer' socio-science, and also biological science, with the feminine. Because gender is asymmetric – that is, masculine and feminine are not equal and opposite – feminine aspects tend to be devalued and regulated to maintain the status of physical science and its teachers. Prevailing masculine cultures in science are thus difficult to challenge.

Although the inclusion of STS relations in the curriculum has been identified as a possible strategy for countering the symbolic masculinity of decontextualized science, the association of STS with the retention of girls in science is problematic. I also argue that gender equality approaches that perpetuate an essentialist relationship between gender and science risk increasing, rather than decreasing, the power and influence of gendered binaries and hierarchies. Essentialism in STS curriculum reform can therefore be counterproductive.

A science-from-issues approach to teaching may be founded on good intentions to improve inclusivity in science, but when socio-science is kept on the margins in texts and classroom practices, and when the gendering of the science curriculum is continually reinforced, the full potential of an STS approach cannot be realized. The chapter concludes that educators need to acquire greater awareness of their roles in marginalizing socio-science and in reinforcing gender binaries so that they can begin to develop the strategies for making inclusive science education work in practice.

STS and science education reform

The label STS appears to be a broad umbrella term for material that examines the interface between science and the social world. It can either be taught alongside science or integrated into science courses. There is a range of ideas about what might be included: naming applications of science, addressing history, philosophy and sociology of science, and a socio-scientific approach that aims to address areas of contemporary economic, social and political concern, such as in health or the environment (Ziman 1994). STS may be viewed as part of the curriculum in its own right or as a supplement to the real science curriculum.

Aikenhead (1994: 55) gave an overview that encompasses the two extremes: STS as taught completely separately from science, as in *Science and Society* (UK, Association for Science Education) or as short, optional, add-on material for science courses to make them more appealing – for example, *Science and Technology in Society* (SATIS; UK, Association for Science Education). Curricula have also been developed which Aikenhead categorized as 'science through STS' which are thus different from specialist STS courses. The introduction of STS into the Australian Victoria Certificate of Education is one such example. However, interpretations of science through STS vary: STS may be viewed as merely a vehicle for delivery of conceptual science content or the STS context may be included as a worthwhile subject for study alongside the concepts. Salters' science courses, discussed below, appear to take this latter approach.

Two main arguments support STS on educational grounds. First, the need to 'encourage interest in the interaction between Science, Technology and Society' (Solomon 1993: 51) is assumed to be essential to good science teaching and technological awareness (Macaskill and Ogborn 1996). A consideration of STS is described repeatedly as being necessary for wider public understanding of science and active citizenship (Driver *et al.* 1996; Jenkins 1994a, 1994b; Millar 1997). Second, the world of science is alien to many students (Costa 1995) and there is much received wisdom in science education, backed up by mainly US research, that STS improves both pupil interest and enjoyment of science (Aikenhead 1994). Giving science a social and cultural context has thus formed part of the agenda for equal opportunities in science, especially concerning multiculturalism and, to some extent, anti-racism (Dennick 1993; Krugly-Smolska 1995; Reiss 1993). Similarly, it has been assumed that inclusion of STS is especially important for the motivation and retention of girls (Fensham 1993; Harding, J. and Sutoris 1987; Sjoberg and Imsen 1988), although a more recent study by Solomon (1994a) pointed out that males and females are similarly motivated by STS.

However, whereas arguments for the educational benefits of STS in the wider sense have gained increased significance in a climate of declining pupil numbers in science education at higher levels, there are concerns raised about the more socioscientific approaches. Inclusion of socio-scientific content in the formal curriculum has not occurred without a struggle; for example, there have been epistemological debates about teachers revealing political bias (Ziman 1980). Presenting an objective position clearly is difficult when addressing areas of contemporary controversy, such as the use of genetically modified organisms. Fensham (1988) also pointed out that science teachers frequently are specialized and do not have the background in sociology, politics and economics that socio-scientific debate can demand. In addition, they can face unfamiliarity when dealing with controversial material, where several viewpoints require consideration, as constructivist debate is absent from a pure science discourse to which they are more accustomed.

Detailed research on the relationship between STS and conventional science education is limited even in the United States, where inclusion of STS is well established at the college level (Schoneweg Bradford *et al.* 1995: 356), but some themes have emerged. The problem with separate courses focusing on STS is that they contain little science content and often are not accorded the same formal assessment status as 'science proper' (Solomon 1994b). This means STS is viewed as separate from abstract science content and possibly even as a distraction. When STS is diffused into science curricula, Fensham (1988) indicated that the most usual approach is to add on a brief social context within a rigidly prescribed science content in restricted topic areas, rather than to reposition science into a social, economic, political and moral context. However, the more recent Salters' curriculum development project appears to address the latter concerns and deserves a closer examination.

Salters' Advanced Level Chemistry

Salters' courses aim to contextualize the teaching of science through an integrated applications-led approach. In keeping with the STS rationale, the compilers aim not only to motivate students to study science through making it more contextual and socially relevant, but also to provide students with a more authentic view of science and to contribute to wider public understanding of science. They offer evidence that the Salters' approach increases the numbers of students who continue with the subject (Campbell *et al.* 1994). However, using Salters' Advanced Level Chemistry as an example, I shall demonstrate how the socio-scientific content, in particular, is open to interpretation. First, here is some background on the course.

Some degree of STS reference is usually present in post-16 syllabuses in the United Kingdom, but the Salters' Advanced Level Chemistry syllabus document (Oxford and Cambridge Schools Examination Board 1996) goes beyond sprinkling in a few token applications, because it aims to present chemical principles through a socio-scientific context. To achieve its aims, the course is divided up into units and each unit is described as having two components:

- A storyline providing the context within which chemical ideas and skills are developed. Each storyline is self-contained and worth studying in its own right.
- Activities of many kinds, including laboratory practical work, but also group discussion, data analysis, applications of information technology (IT), and so on (Oxford and Cambridge Schools Examination Board 1996: 17).

Use of the term *storyline* in science, with evocations of fiction and the telling of subjective, unconstrained tales, contrasts markedly with conventional views of curriculum science as factual and rigid in its rules and formulations. Thus, the storyline marks Salters' as atypical and potentially contentious. The defensive statement 'and worth studying in its own right' hints at author awareness of this.

The storylines are presented as units with titles that signify context, such as 'The Polymer Revolution', 'Developing Fuels' and 'What's in a Medicine?' Two course texts are provided: *Chemical Storylines* (University of York Science Education Group 1994a), which contains socio-scientific material, and *Chemical Ideas* (University of York Science Education Group 1994b), which provides the abstract theory and principles. Teaching of the Salters' course is then based on a series of activity booklets that are linked to the textbook content. Some of this course material includes student activities based on exploration of socio-scientific areas, such as investigating the development of a drug or the relative merits of different energy sources. Thus, the problem of the lack of STS resources for teachers has at least begun to be addressed.

A study of the effectiveness of the Salters' Advanced Chemistry approach was carried out at a post-16 college (Hughes 1998). Two groups of students and their two teachers were observed for nine months, course documentation was examined, and the students and teachers were interviewed about the importance of STS content in the course.

The study viewed the curriculum as more than a framework for teaching, a set of teaching materials and list of topics that should be covered. A curriculum is made and remade through a process of contestation and struggle between individuals and social groups with differing views on its purpose (Carr 1993). Thus, not only curriculum content, but also its discursively produced meanings as well as practices were examined in the curriculum study.

Curriculum as discourse

The term *discourse* has multiple layers of meaning. At the simplest level, a discourse is any form of talk or writing, any use of language. However, post-structuralists after Foucault refer to discourse as a regulative body of ideas and knowledge that delimits the kind of questions that can be raised and governs the construction of meaning. As such, discourses are constitutive. Foucault defined discourses as:

> … practices that systematically form the objects of which they speak. Discourses are not about objects; they do not identify objects they constitute them and in the practice of doing so conceal their own invention.
>
> (Foucault 1974: 49)

From such a perspective, science curricula become a set of competing, often contradictory, and constantly changing discourses on what counts as science and how it should be taught in the classroom. Science curriculum discourses do not describe classroom practices but produce them, while always being subject to local and temporal variation. Dominant discourses emanate from and circulate within research establishments and governments, as well as educational institutions, and generate human subjects who have hegemonic control over what counts as science and who decides how science should be experienced in schools and colleges. That is not to say teachers and students do not play a part in constructing science education discourses; their part in reaffirming and resisting science education discourses is also crucial (Lakin and Wellington: 1994).

Discourses are constantly undergoing reproduction and reconstruction at the microlevel of texts, talk and classroom interaction. Fairclough (1992) argued that close reading of written and spoken texts gives insight into both dominant and subordinated macrolevel discourses that are in operation. Thus, discourse analysis of interview transcripts and syllabus documents, as well as observation of lessons, addresses different levels of curriculum discourse production to build a picture of science curriculum discourses in operation.

In the discussion that follows, I consider the relationship between socio-scientific and abstract science curriculum discourses in three interrelated domains: in syllabus texts; in classroom discourses and practices; and, finally, in both teacher and student interpretations of their curriculum. In each case, discourses of science education as concerning abstract principles are dominant, whereas socio-scientific discourses are subordinated.

The syllabus: devaluation of socio-science through language and structure

I have described how the Salters' chemistry course superficially presents a science-from-issues approach. However, a more detailed interpretation of the syllabus document reveals how socio-scientific content is devalued and constructed as marginal with respect to abstract scientific principles.

First, the use of language marginalizes all socio-scientific references. For example, the course content states that candidates should be able to:

> *describe* the formation of oxides of nitrogen in internal combustion engines; (-)
> *show awareness* of the work of chemists in improving fuels and in searching for and developing fuels for the future.
>
> (Oxford and Cambridge Schools Examination Board 1996: 20, my italics)

The terms in italics are repeatedly used in similar contexts throughout the document. These different prefixes can be read as signals for the amount of learning required for the examination; clearly, one would have to recall more information for description of scientific processes compared to showing awareness of applications. The difference in emphasis can be made visible by exchanging the terms *show awareness* and *describe* and noting how the relative importance of the statements alters accordingly.

Second, socio-scientific content is constructed as optional because the syllabus is presented in two styles, labelled A and B. Part A is organized by units that follow the storylines and the applications-based theme of the course. Subsections entitled 'The Polymer Revolution' (p. 23) and 'What's in a Medicine?' (p. 25), clearly signify this. In contrast, Part B organizes the content by abstract chemical principles with unit titles such as 'Atomic Structure' and 'Structure and Bonding' (p. 37), which would be familiar to anyone reading a more conventional chemistry syllabus. This alternative structure, in which the socio-scientific content almost disappears, means the syllabus can be read in a manner that minimizes any socio-scientific basis for the course.

Thus, both language use and the organizational structure of the syllabus text give the reader the opportunity to view the socio-scientific aspects of the course as being of lesser importance than the abstract chemical principles. But is the organization of teaching materials to give teachers and students the opportunity to neglect socio-scientific issues consistent with what happens in practice? A closer look at the curriculum in action indicates that there is such consistency and that the ambiguous messages of the syllabus text reinforce rather than challenge dominant science curriculum discourses.

Classroom discourse: marginalization of socio-scientific content through timing and lesson structure

Most lessons observed in the study consisted of teacher-directed activity to help students understand abstract chemical principles. Although applications of chemistry and its social context were introduced through reading aloud sections from *Chemical Storylines,* these lessons contained little or no follow-up activity to address socio-scientific issues that might arise. The two teachers, who were generally enthusiastic about Salters', complained that many of the socio-scientific activities were lengthy and had to be omitted because of time pressures. The unfamiliarity and difficulty of STS content for both teachers and students, and the lack of training and expertise in discussion of complex issues, could also partly explain the ready marginalization of STS. However, neither time pressures nor lack of STS experience provide sufficient explanation; there are plenty of time-consuming and conceptually difficult areas in chemistry that do not receive such treatment. Moreover, even on the rare occasion when socio-scientific content was the focus of learning activities, the abstract chemical principles still took a clear priority over contextualizing science, demonstrating the persistence of an underlying abstract/contextual hierarchy.

An example of this marginalization of socio-science in the classroom was observed in the teaching of a unit entitled 'Developing Fuels'. The teaching material for the unit is consistent with the Salters' discourse of providing an applied context for chemistry. It presents a scenario for comparing different fuels using chemical, environmental, political and economic debates on the relative merits of each. The unit contains an activity in which students are asked to give presentations evaluating the potential of a given fuel. This activity was arranged for the final lesson of term and was not formally assessed, signalling a lack of importance for socio-scientific issues. In addition, the fact that the lesson was structured around a break functioned to marginalize socio-scientific content relative to that of abstract science.

Most of the students gave presentations that contained chemical facts with some reference to applications and environmental concerns, but they did not address social or political issues. The extract from field notes below describes how the teacher attempted to remedy this situation.

After the break the teacher informed me she had planned a plenary discussion of the socio-scientific issues raised, and she explained that this would be an opportunity to compensate for the students' narrow perceptions of science. She began by giving encouraging feedback on the presentations verbally and attempted to initiate discussion on the relative merits of the different fuels. However, the attentiveness of the students had dwindled, and the discussion that followed involved a small number of students and did not last long. Several students had coats on and two students stated that they had expected to go home early. Afterwards, the teacher confessed that she was not pleased with the students' responses to the plenary discussion. She stated that students enjoyed the social context but were not prepared to put in the same effort here that they would for chemical equations.

(Hughes 1998: 118–9)

Because the lesson was planned as an end-of-term final lesson, a common time for frivolities, and was atypically student-led, it was marked out as different, fun and less serious. Lack of assessment could also signal diminished importance. Although students initially took the performance aspect of their presentations seriously, after the break, the formal structure dissolved and the pressure to perform was off. As the term drew to a close, the lesson and its content were no longer marked as significant and the majority lost interest. Whether or not students were interested in this kind of discussion activity, they interpreted this section of the lesson as unimportant.

The lesson structure reproduced an STS linear hierarchy that prioritizes scientific theory, then technological applications, and finally, social and political questions. The important initial activity, student presentations, focused on the abstract principles with some reference to the production of fuels. The discussion of social and political implications was secondary, unplanned and spontaneous, resulting in an inversion of the original Salters' aim to present the chemical theory from the issues.

Thus socio-scientific discourse was marginalized through the timing and structuring of the lesson, reinforcing the students' initial tendency to prioritize abstract science. Further interviews with students confirmed that many of them viewed applications of science in a narrow way and did not interpret the course as having a contextual basis.

Students' interpretations of socio-scientific curriculum discourse

A socio-scientific approach that considers wider social, political and economic aspects of science requires students to think as citizens. However, when these students gave accounts of applications and social context, they drew on localized private experiences, rather than on their social position in the public sphere, suggesting that wider perspectives were unfamiliar or underdeveloped.

Students were asked which aspects of their science courses addressed the social applications of science. The term *applications* was interpreted in a variety of ways, but was often associated with personal relevance and enjoyment of biological science, in particular. A male student who studied chemistry, biology and English after dropping physics was also asked for his subject preferences. He placed biology first:

Male Student 1: Mainly because biology just has a certain appeal about it, 'cos with chemistry it's all very well, knowing about esters and hydrolysis and all that, but you can't really practically apply it to any situation. But like with biology, let's say we're learning at the moment about flowers, you can apply that. Like your dad's having to grow his plants, you can say, 'ah ha ha', but that is your fault because you didn't do this. So it's more down to earth 'cos chemistry can be quite aloof. That's what I thought with physics as well, physics was very, very abstract.

(Hughes: 1998: 131)

The student describes biology as having small-scale applications and gives an example of his father's gardening techniques. This is a small-scale individual perspective on the social relevance of science. Chemistry is described as 'aloof' and not applicable to any everyday situation, implying a total lack of recognition of chemical applications and socio-scientific perspectives. Physics is similarly abstract in this account.

When such students did not appear to acknowledge the applications and context of Salters', they were asked directly about use of the text *Chemical Storylines*. Even this did not necessarily trigger recognition of the contextualizing Salters' approach. In the next example, the student, who studied chemistry and mathematics and also expressed preferences for biology, demonstrates this lack of recognition:

Interviewer: What do you think about the *Storylines* book, do you use it?
Female Student 1: I read it sometimes, and you think, oh wow, I didn't know that. It's got loads of interesting facts in it.
Interviewer: So are those related to the environment and applications?
Female Student 1: Yeah but you don't really look at it that way, you think, oh, chemistry. You think experiments, that's all you think.

(Hughes 1998: 131)

The student admits that she finds the *Storylines* book interesting and agrees that these areas of interest are related to the environment and applications of science. At the same time, she constructs chemistry as only concerning experiments, and here she is dismissive, stating 'that's all you think'.

These examples demonstrate that when students have a partial diet of socio-science, they interpret science in their curricula from either an abstract or an indi-vidual social perspective. Like the student who referred to his father's gardening, many students only engaged with applications of science that are connected with their own experience in the private domain; others expressed narrow views of science. The social, economic and political dimensions of socio-scientific debate are not obvious, even in a course like Salters', and clearly require more emphasis if students are to engage fully.

Why was socio-scientific material not given the necessary airing to challenge these students' narrow views of science? I argue next that socio-scientific material is not a neutral set of concepts that can be integrated straightforwardly into science education; it has the potential to upset the gender hierarchies that underpin the construction of science as masculine. Thus, the socio-science issue is linked to the debates on gender and science education, where even the more progressive and aware teachers are faced with some complex dilemmas.

Gender and science education: moving beyond gender binaries

Over the past decade, research on gender and science education has shifted from identifying the social and institutional factors that deter girls from studying physical science to examining the part played by the science curriculum (Bentley and Watts 1987; Byrne 1993; Kelly 1987; Hughes 1997; Parker *et al.* 1996). Feminist critiques of science, which have exposed some of science's undesirable and oppressive practices (Bleier 1984; Harding, S. 1986, 1991; Rose 1994), have informed recent work on gender and science education. This work has continued to address gender and recruitment issues by focusing a more critical lens on the masculinity of science itself. Exploration of the symbolic aspects to masculinity in science, which in turn underpin practice, help emphasize that the gendering of science is socially constructed rather than biologically determined.

The origins of the symbolic masculinity of science can be traced back to the seventeenth- and eighteenth-century enlightenment. As belief in the power of rationality began to supersede dogma and superstition, hierarchical dualistic splits emerged that associated reason/emotion and objectivity/subjectivity with a male/ female divide (Fox-Keller 1992: 16–21). The persistence of gendered dichotomous thinking is evident in contemporary associations of physical science with masculine, hard abstract rationality and human and social sciences with a feminine, more subjective, or softer approach. The abstraction and objectivity of pure science have masculine connotations, whereas a contextual approach is associated with the feminine. Any consideration of STS is therefore readily caught up in these gender hierarchical binaries.

There is increasing agreement that the cultural and symbolic masculinity of physical science, in particular, underpins the schooling practices and beliefs that give rise to gender polarization within the curriculum (Parker *et al.* 1996). For example, authoritative teaching styles, gendered assumptions about ability and excessive competitiveness make science a hostile environment for many female students, whereas male students dominate the classroom and are favoured by teachers (Butler Kahle *et al.* 1993; Kelly 1987; Whyte 1985). Studies have demonstrated how students bring their standpoints on life into the classroom and that female interests and preferred learning styles are not always congruent with an inflexible abstract curriculum (Roychoudhury *et al.* 1995). I have previously argued that these practices which support gender segregation continually reinforce the symbolic masculine associations of science and the accompanying student gender identities, although it is important to emphasize that these gender identities are in no way fixed and predetermined (Hughes 1997).

Recognition of the importance of the symbolic gendering of science has provided a basis for initiatives for gender and curriculum reform. S. Harding (1991) argued that, whereas discourses of reason and objectivity present science as superior to other forms of knowledge, science is as messy, subjective and complex as any other human activity and its assumed gendered status is contestable. Some of the more recent approaches to gender reform in science education are based on reworking socially constructed gendered binaries to counterbalance the masculine attributes of science by feminine qualities. For example: masculine qualities are abstract, quantitative, objective (hard) and value-free; feminine qualities are contextual, qualitative, subjective (soft) and value-laden.

Because the abstract and impersonal approach has been identified as incongruent with girls' interests and identities (Sjoberg and Imsen 1988), action programmes to improve gender equity aim to bring the curriculum into symmetrical balance by shifting from a symbolically masculine curriculum, which values the first qualities listed, to a more feminine curriculum, represented by the second list. Counterbalancing theories and principles with socio-science would seem to meet this equality objective. However, there are some gender traps of which we need to be cautious.

First, much of the research on gender and science education has a tendency to overgeneralize, as it is based on essentialist conceptions of gender. Assumptions that the feminine qualities appeal to girls who are 'switched on' by process-based, co-operative and contextualized learning is supported by evidence (Hildebrand 1996; Vlaeminke *et al.* 1997: 19–21), but the very success of such gender reform perpetuates gender binaries unless claims are tempered with caution.

Notably, in my 1998 study, the small number of students who demonstrated positive engagement with a Salters' socio-scientific discourse were female. In this example, a female student spoke in praise of the course:

> Last year I was at another school doing Chemistry A Level, then I started here. That was the London Board, it wasn't Salters'. I couldn't really relate it to any(thing), it was almost like physics. But then as soon as I started Salters', I loved the course because it just relates everything, like with medicine and then with the atmosphere. Each unit relates it to something so it helps you learn it. I suppose you already have some basic knowledge of it.
>
> (Hughes 1998: 132)

She distinguishes Salters' from another more conventional chemistry syllabus, because it covers areas such as medicine and atmospheric studies; unlike the previous students, she appears to be taking a citizen rather than an individual perspective. The atmosphere unit she mentioned addresses macrolevel social and political issues surrounding ozone depletion.

It would be tempting to conclude that the Salters' course does improve female inclusivity in science. However, motivation through context does not necessarily apply to all females, or exclude males from appreciating contextualized learning. From an anti-essentialist perspective, gender identity is variable and the relationship between feminine attributes and female identities is complex. Too much blanket emphasis on girls preferring a particular style of learning is in danger of reinforcing the very gender binaries that reproduce inequalities (Hughes 1997).

Second, S. Harding (1986) warned that gender is asymmetric, and obtaining a balance through combination of aspects of both masculinity and femininity is therefore not straightforward. She argued that 'central to the notion of masculinity is its rejection of everything that is defined by a culture as feminine and its legitimated control of whatever counts as the feminine' (pp. 54–5). Masculinity is not equal and opposite to femininity; it attracts a higher status. Walkerdine (1988) further explained that rationality and reason are produced through rejection of others, for example, irrationality and lack of control. Symbolically, that subordinated other represents femininity (1988: 99–201). Gender binaries are therefore not only mutually exclusive, but also hierarchical.

The abstract-rational and frequently mathematical version of science that pervades many school curricula is very much a feature of symbolic masculinity. Supposedly feminine subjective qualities must be suppressed and regulated to maintain a masculine status for science. Because the two sides of gendered binaries are not straightforward alternatives, challenges to the dominant discourses of science are likely to be met with resistance.

Gender hierarchies and binaries have implications for STS curriculum initiatives that aim to increase the weighting of socio-scientific material in the course content, whether for educational reasons or to improve inclusivity. Technological applications may have masculine or feminine associations; compare, for example, military and medical applications. However, the socio-scientific discussion is more congruent with the feminine, not only because of its concern with the social world but also because of its association with uncertainty and debate.

I next explore two implications of the underlying gender binaries: first, that socio-science is assumed to deter the best (male) students and, second, that socio-science is given a lower academic standing than abstract science. These two related assumptions provide explanation for marginalization and regulation of socio-science in texts and classroom practices as teachers take up positions as gatekeepers in science.

Teachers as gatekeepers of scientific knowledge: regulation of socio-science to maintain the masculine elitist status of physical science

Teachers are caught up in a tension between education as liberatory and education as a form of social control (Usher and Edwards 1994). They are expected to take on a gatekeeper role to reserve science education for a predominantly male elite who will go on to higher education and science careers (Roth *et al.* 1996). Teachers' positions in discourses of equality and inclusivity conflict with their gatekeeper function on which their professional status and job prospects may depend. A tension between egalitarian rhetoric and gatekeeping is heightened especially by an educational climate in the United Kingdom that is obsessed with examination requirements and standards, producing a precarious balance between promotion of elitist science and science education for all.

Both Salters' teachers expressed egalitarian views on science education and particular support for courses such as Salters' that are believed to empower a wide range of students. Teacher 2 was particularly in favour of promoting chemistry for females, which she felt Salters' did through drawing on potentially socio-scientific topics which might, more usually, appear in biology. Nevertheless, while promoting Salters' for females, she was anxious not to compromise her gatekeeper role through promoting the socio-scientific aspects of Salters'. She voiced concern that:

> Some students do think it's a bit too waffly and bit too involved in society and social issues, and what they feel is they want to learn a body of knowledge and a group of facts. I had a couple of boys incidentally who actually left the course and went to do the traditional London syllabus, they were very, very bright students.
>
> (Hughes 1998: 145)

Here, the abstract scientific 'body of knowledge' is associated with able students and, by implication, the socio-scientific with less academic students. Gender is explicitly constructed as part of this binary, with girls enjoying the socio-scientific context and able male students rejecting it. Note that these essentialist gender stereotypes contrast with the testimonies of students, none of whom expressed dissatisfaction with Salters' because of the social context; indeed, lack of social relevance was the more common complaint.

Teachers' reluctance to foreground socio-science in their teaching may also be related to the uncertain status of socio-scientific knowledge where gender connotations are less explicit. Socio-scientific topics often involve debate, for example, about waste disposal or gene technology. Driver *et al.* (1996: 18) pointed out that disputes often arise over interpretations of data or uncertainties about reliability when moving from the laboratory to a real-world situation. Political, economic or social interests at work are often obvious, and any notion of impartiality in science is easily questioned. This may lead to revelations that scientific explanation is based on theories and models which are tentative and open to dispute. Thus, there is a connection between contextualizing science and epistemology; socio-scientific discourse is associated with constructivist epistemologies, where the socially contested nature of knowledge is recognized (Driver *et al.* 1996; Roth *et al.* 1996). Socio-scientific content, which raises questions about the production and ownership of knowledge, needs to be kept in check within a dominant epistemological framework that maintains a clear division between supposedly objective scientific expertise compared with more speculative forms of knowledge. Use of dismissive terms such as *waffly* as opposed to *facts* clearly illustrates the objective/subjective hierarchy that underlies the regulation of socio-scientific discourse.

The assessment requirements and the importance of grades for both teachers and the majority of students are also significant. Salters' is a typical science course which is largely assessed by examination and most of the questions rely on a discrete and indisputable body of knowledge. Thus, teachers and students, especially the high achievers, are required to focus on these facts and not stray into the realms of uncertainty and debate. The wording of the syllabus text discussed earlier clearly indicated that the abstract science content needs more attention.

While fears of deterring conventional science students and upsetting gender hierarchies in science underlie teachers' emphasis on certainty and reluctance to dwell on the nature of science, concerns about professional status and expertise are also significant. Salters' Teacher 2 divulged her fears about loss of control and teacher status during an informal conversation over lunch, but did not articulate this during the interview, indicating that this might be a sensitive area:

> Teacher 2 worries that science is expected to be factual and if she presents any challenge to this, students will consider her to be an idiot not a proper scientist, or someone who does not know her stuff.
>
> (Hughes 1998: 155)

Her possibly justifiable fear is that, if she deviates from the position of expert who has unquestionable grasp of the facts, students will not respect her as a person, a scientist or a teacher. It seems possible that the gender of the teacher may be a contributory factor; a precarious position as a female scientist could mean that it is all the more important to maintain scientific authority.

Thus, through engagement with the dominant masculine curriculum discourses and rejection or regulation of competing discourses, teachers perform their gatekeeper function of selecting an elite for higher education and scientific professions and, at the same time, maintain their own status as experts. A socio-scientific curriculum, associated symbolically and literally with lack of rigour, subjectivity and female students, can produce both a fear of alienating able male students and a challenge to the teacher authority which the discipline accords. A high-status, masculine science curriculum can only be maintained through regulation and marginalization of symbolically feminine discourses. Progressive and potentially inclusive approaches to teaching science, such as Salters', thus appear severely limited within a framework based on maintenance of a gendered elitist status for physical science.

Even teachers who are explicitly supportive of inclusion of science context and social relevance may be wary of embracing socio-science wholeheartedly and may adopt compromise positions. Such reluctance is to be expected, given the widespread level of uncertainty in educational circles surrounding STS in general, and the more subtle messages that may be signalled through course documentation. Regulating or limiting the socio-scientific content to occasional or end-of-term lessons gives teachers some opportunities to present a human side to scientific processes without detracting from the emphasis on a coherent body of facts that are required for passing examinations and gaining places in higher education. However, when socio-science is the icing on the cake, not an essential basic ingredient, part of a good-quality product but not fundamental to teaching science, dominant discourses of science as an abstract body of knowledge are not destabilized and implicit gender hierarchical binaries are readily reinforced. [...]

References

Aikenhead, G. (1994) 'Consequences to learning science through STS: a research perspective', in J. Solomon and G. Aikenhead (eds) *STS Education: International Perspectives on Reform* (pp. 169–86), New York: Teachers' College Press.

Bentley, D. and Watts, M. (1987) 'Courting the positive virtues: a case for feminist science', in A. Kelly (ed.) *Science for Girls* (pp. 89–98), Milton Keynes: Open University Press.

Bleier, R. (1984) *Science and Gender. A Critique of Biology and its Theories on Women*, Oxford: Pergamon.

Butler Kahle, J., Parker, L., Rennie, L. and Riley, D. (1993) 'Gender differences in science education: building a model', *Educational Psychologist* 28: 379–404.

Byrne, E. (1993) *Women and Science: The Snark Syndrome*, London: Falmer.

Campbell, B., Lazonby, J. Millar, R., Nicolson, P., Ramsden, J. and Waddington, D. (1994) 'Science: The Salters' approach – a case study of the process of large scale curriculum development', *Science Education* 78: 415–47.

Carr, W. (1993) 'Reconstructing the curriculum debate: an editorial introduction', *Curriculum Studies* 1: 5–9.

Costa, V. (1995) 'When science is "another world": relationships between worlds of family, friends, school and science', *Science Education* 79: 313–33.

Dennick, R. (1993) 'Analysing multicultural and anti-racist science education', in E. Whitelegg, J. Thomas and S. Tresman (eds) *Challenges and Opportunities for Science Education* (pp. 139–50), London: Paul Chapman, in association with Open University Press.

Driver, R., Leach, J., Millar, R. and Scott, P. (1996) *Young People's Images of Science*, Buckingham: Open University Press.

Fairclough, N. (1992) *Discourse and Social Change*, Cambridge: Polity.

Fensham, P. (1988) 'Approaches to the teaching of STS in science education', *International Journal of Science Education* 10: 346–56.

—— (1993) 'Reflections on science for all', in E. Whitelegg, J. Thomas and S. Tresman (eds) *Challenges and Opportunities for Science Education*, London: Paul Chapman, in association with Open University Press.

Foucault, M. (1974) *The Archaeology of Knowledge*, London: Tavistock.

Fox-Keller, E. (1992) *Secrets of Life: Secrets of Death: Essays on Language, Gender and Science*, London: Routledge.

Harding, J. and Sutoris, M. (1987) 'An object relations account of the differential involvement of boys and girls in science and technology', in A. Kelly (ed.) *Science for Girls* (pp. 24–36), Milton Keynes: Open University Press.

Harding, S. (1986) *The Science Question in Feminism*, Milton Keynes: Open University Press.

—— (1991) *Whose Science? Whose Knowledge? Thinking from Women's Lives*, Milton Keynes: Open University Press.

Hildebrand, G. (1996) 'Redefining achievement', in C. Gipps and P. Murphy (eds) *Equity in the Classroom: Towards Effective Pedagogy for Girls and Boys* (pp. 149–73), London: Falmer.

Hughes, G. (1997) 'Not the end of the line: new directions for gender and science education', in D. Thompson (ed.) *Science Education in the 21st Century* (pp. 77–96), Aldershot: Arena.

—— (1998) 'Gender, power and resistance in post-sixteen science education: the production of student subjectivities within competing curriculum discourses and practices', PhD thesis: University of East London.

Jenkins, E. (1994a) 'Public understanding of science and science education for action', *Journal of Curriculum Studies* 26: 601–11.

—— (1994b) 'HPS and school science education: remediation or reconstruction?', *International Journal of Science Education* 16: 613–23.

Kelly, A. (1987) 'The construction of masculine science', in A. Kelly (ed.) *Science for Girls* (pp. 66–77), Milton Keynes: Open University Press.

Krugly-Smolska, E. (1995) 'Cultural influences in science education', *International Journal of Science Education* 17: 45–58,

Lakin, S. and Wellington, J. (1994) 'Who will teach the "nature of science"? Teachers' views of science and their implications for science education', *International Journal of Science Education* 16: 175–90.

Macaskill, C. and Ogborn, J. (1996) 'Science and technology', *School Science Review* 77: 55–61.

Millar, R. (1997) 'Science education for democracy: what can the school curriculum achieve?', in R. Levinson and J. Thomas (eds) *Science Today: Problem or Crisis?* (pp. 87–101), London: Routledge.

Oxford and Cambridge Schools Examination Board (1996) *Chemistry (Salters')*, 9663 GCE.

Parker, L., Rennie, L. and Fraser, B. (1996) 'Introduction and overview', in L. Parker, L. Rennie and B. Fraser (eds) *Gender, Science and Mathematics: Shortening the Shadow* (pp. xi–xv), Dordrecht: Kluwer Academic.

Reiss, M. (1993) *Science Education for a Pluralist Society*, Milton Keynes: Open University Press.

Rose, H. (1994) *Love, Power and Knowledge: Towards a Feminist Transformation of the Sciences*, Cambridge: Polity.

Roth, W.-M., McGinn, M. and Bowen, G. (1996) 'Applications of science and technology studies: effecting change in science education', *Science, Technology, and Human Values* 21: 454–84.

Roychoudhury, A., Tippins, D. and Nichols, S. (1995) 'Gender-inclusive science teaching: a feminist-constructivist approach', *Journal of Research in Science Teaching* 32: 897–924.

Schoneweg Bradford, C., Rubba, R. and Harkness, W. (1995) 'Views about Science–Technology–Society interactions held by college students in General Education Physics and STS courses', *Science Education* 79: 355–73.

Sjoberg, S. and Imsen, G. (1988) 'Gender and science education: 1', in Fensham, P. (ed.) *Questions and Dilemmas in Science Education* (pp. 218–48), London: Falmer.

Solomon, J. (1993) *Teaching Science, Technology and Society*, Milton Keynes: Open University Press.

—— (1994a) 'Learning STS and judgements in the classroom: do boys and girls differ?', in J. Solomon and G. Aikenhead (eds) *STS Education: International Perspectives on Reform* (pp. 141–54), New York: Teachers' College Press.

—— (1994b) 'Conflicts between mainstream science and STS in science education', in J. Solomon and G. Aikenhead (eds) *STS Education: International Perspectives on Reform* (pp. 3–10), New York: Teachers' College Press.

University of York Science Education Group (1994a) *Chemical Storylines*, Oxford: Heinemann Educational.

—— (1994b) *Chemical Ideas*, Oxford: Heinemann Educational.

Usher, R. and Edwards, R. (1994) *Postmodernism and Education*, London: Routledge.

Vlaeminke, M., Mckeon, F. and Comber, C. (1997) *Breaking the Mould: An Assessment of Successful Strategies for Attracting Girls into Science, Engineering and Technology*, London: Department of Trade and Industry.

Walkerdine, V. (1988) *The Mastery of Reason: Cognitive Development and the Production of Rationality*, London: Routledge.

Whyte, J. (1985) 'Girl friendly science and the girl friendly school', in J. Whyte, R. Deem and M. Cruickshank (eds) *Girl Friendly Schooling* (pp. 77–92), London: Methuen.

Ziman, J. (1980) *Teaching and Learning about Science and Society*, Cambridge: Cambridge University Press.

—— (1994) 'The rationale of STS education is in the approach in science education', in J. Solomon and G. Aikenhead (eds) *STS Education: International Perspectives on Reform* (pp. 21–31), New York: Teachers' College Press.

Part 4

Researching science education

Eileen Scanlon

The two chapters in this part are concerned with the nature of science education research. Both have a broad focus. One deals with the topic of science education research itself and the other considers, in particular, work being undertaken in one area – environmental education research.

Edgar Jenkins discusses research practice and policy in science education focusing on the question 'what counts as research in science education?' He discusses the differences between the European and American traditions in a number of ways. One of these is the different balance of work between the pedagogic/curriculum tradition and the empirical/theoretical tradition. He also notes the recent focus on school-based studies of children's conceptual understanding. He also draws distinction between research as improving action and the other uses of research to increase the capacity of the system to recognize, understand, frame and address problems that deserve attention. He concludes by raising questions to be considered about the past impact and future conduct of science education research.

Susan Barker presents an account of the relationship between science and environmental education. She also highlights the range of methods being used in environmental education research projects. These are used to study environmental knowledge and understand environmental attitudes. She summarises some current findings in this area and reports recommendations that the future of environmental education research should adopt a broader empirical focus, a deeper level of empirical investigation and longitudinal studies in future. She argues that a key future direction for the work should be a focus on understanding learning and the role learners play.

4.1 Science education

Research, practice and policy

Edgar W. Jenkins

In 2002, the first article in a special issue of the *School Science Review* devoted to research and practice in science education began with the question 'Does science education research count?' The short answer, according to the author is 'No'. His 'slightly more considered response' was '*not as much as it should*' (Lock 2002: 13). In this chapter, I pose a different and prior question, namely '*What counts as research in science education?*' and, in response, offer a commentary upon the range, quality, purpose and usefulness of the work that has been done.

Any personal account of research in science education is necessarily selective and it runs the risk of presenting a misleading account of events and developments in individual countries and education systems. There are, for example, major differences in the social, political, cultural and economic contexts within which research in science education is organized, institutionalized and conducted within Europe and North America. These lead not only to different levels of research funding but also to somewhat different expectations of, and confidence in, the research outcomes. Nonetheless, the task is worth attempting if it succeeds in helping the reader bring a scholarly scrutiny to bear upon an activity which, like research in education more generally, has become the focus of substantial criticism in recent years.

A relatively new field of activity

Perhaps the most obvious point to make about research in science education is its relative newness, especially within Europe compared with the USA. No European country can claim a long tradition of work in this field, although there is often a much longer history of scholarly study of some other aspects of education, notably in didactics and the history of education. There are also many examples of research undertaken in the first half of the twentieth century that can be properly located within science education, although much of this has been the work of isolated individuals, ad hoc commissions or government committees. More significant has been the absence of recognized communities of research workers within science education that have come to distinguish the current research endeavour. In the United

Kingdom, for example, it was the second half of the 1960s that saw the first professorial appointments in science education. This development owed much to the attempts to introduce and support large-scale reform of the school science curriculum and it helps to account for the present location and profile of much of the research currently undertaken. The same decade brought the publication of new journals devoted to science education and the introduction of postgraduate courses and doctoral degrees in science education in a number of UK universities and polytechnics. Elsewhere, for example in Israel, Italy and the Scandinavian countries, it might be more appropriate to look at the 1970s for the origins of science education as a field of research. Small numbers of researchers began to investigate a variety of aspects of science education, their work sometimes being undertaken within Science Education Groups or Centres, some of which were set up with direct government funding and having quite specific research and development priorities. Collaborative work within and, increasingly, between such groups and centres, became more common and the appearance of the *European Journal of Science Education* (now the *International Journal of Science Education*) in 1979 reflected the need for a non-American outlet for the expanding body of research being undertaken in Europe and elsewhere. The first volume of *Studies in Science Education*, an international research review journal, appeared in 1974 and the 38 volumes so far published provide promising material, not only for researchers but also for anyone who wishes to chart the fortunes of science education as a field of research.

The relative newness of research in science education in many countries prompts three comments. First, it suggests a need for some caution in assessing the contribution that such research might reasonably be expected to make to educational policy or practice. This comment is considered further below, although from a somewhat different perspective. Second, it stands in marked contrast to the much longer, and very different, history of science education research in the USA. The various Curtis *Digests of Investigations on the Teaching of Science,* covering research in the USA from as early as 1906 to 1957, reflect a research tradition that was almost exclusively quantitative and empirical in its methodology and largely empiricist and positivist in its psychology and philosophy (Boenig 1969; Lawlor 1970). Third, newness necessarily entails substantial and important diversity. Such diversity is found, for example, in the topics chosen for investigation, in the assumptions made, in the methodology used, in the institutional or departmental location within which the research is undertaken and in the research and professional backgrounds of the researchers themselves.

All these features are evident in the research literature of the past few decades. It is a research literature that has burgeoned, with new journals in paper or electronic formats, an increase in the number of issues per volume of existing journals and, in some cases, an increase in the number of papers published in individual issues.

Diversity in research in science education

It is difficult not to be impressed by the wide range of topics that researchers in science education have chosen to investigate in the last thirty or so years (see, for example, Fraser and Tobin 1998 and, for a wider perspective on issues relevant to science education, Jasanoff *et al.* 1995). They include work related to teachers, students, schools, museums, the print and broadcast media, textbooks, educational technology, information and communication technologies, pedagogy, curriculum, assessment and evaluation. Within each of these fields, diversity is compounded. For example, few fields, if any, have ignored gender issues, although only a handful have attempted to accommodate a wider international perspective, particularly one that attends to the cultural experiences of girls and women in the developing world. As Malcolm has noted with respect to science education research in South Africa, 'research is only partly about techniques … it is also about asking questions fitted to the specifics of local culture, resources and development' (Malcolm 1999: 138).

Globally, the bulk of the research has been concerned with science education at school, rather than at college or university level, and with formal, rather than informal or non-formal settings, although in each case, change is evident. In the UK, for example, the Royal Society of Chemistry has recently published a journal entitled *University Chemical Education* and the research interests of those working in interactive science centres, museums or exploratories have found an outlet in such journals as *Public Understanding of Science* and the *International Journal of Science Education*, as well as in longer-established and more general museum publications. Broadly speaking, there has been much greater emphasis upon learning than upon teaching and teacher education (Fensham and Northfield 1993), although this, too, is changing.

Also in evidence are perspectives drawn principally from philosophy, psychology and sociology, although other disciplines, including history, anthropology and economics, are also represented. In general, secondary science education has had more attention from researchers than that at the elementary or primary levels, although this is much less true of the USA than for most other countries. This position is also changing rapidly as education systems in many parts of the world make science a compulsory component of the schooling of young children.

Until recently, comparative research studies in science education have been relatively rare. Science education was not singled out for attention in the earlier work in the qualitative and hermeneutic tradition that dominated comparative research in education for the first half of the last century. The second half of that century brought a shift towards more quantitative work supported by a range of qualitative studies. Here, the emphasis has been on correlating 'outcomes', notably student achievement, with a range of 'inputs' such as student characteristics or teacher quality, or with mediating 'processes' such as the form, content and structure of, and the emphases within, the science curriculum and the teaching methods employed (Schmidt *et al.* 1997; Stevenson and Stigler 1992). The First and Second International Science Studies were undertaken in 1970/2 and 1984, respectively, under the auspices of the International Association for Educational Achievement. More recent comparative work includes the Third International Mathematics and Science Studies (TIMSS) and the OECD Programme for International Student Assessment (PISA). For a review and commentary on these comparative studies, see Shorrocks-Taylor and Jenkins (2000).

Constructivism

In the past two decades or so, the science education literature has been dominated by research findings concerned with children's understanding of natural phenomena and it has become almost impossible to escape some reference to 'constructivism' among the papers published in the principal research journals. There is no doubt that constructivist views of learning represent the most marked psychological influence on science education in recent years, although this is more evident at the level of discourse than practice and at the primary rather than secondary level. Research attention has been directed principally at children's understanding of such concepts as mass, acceleration, chemical change, gravity and evolution. Inter-disciplinary concepts that characterize many of the public discussions of science in the media, e.g. biodiversity, sustainable development and various measures of personal or environmental risk, have been almost entirely neglected.

It would be interesting to speculate about the factors that have encouraged and continue to sustain constructivism as a progressive educational orthodoxy and to relate these to the wider social and cultural shift commonly associated with post-modernism. In the present context, however, it may be appropriate to make three points. First, a powerful influence of this kind upon educational theory and practice is not new. In the early years of the twentieth century, all students of education stepped to the tune of Herbart's (Adams 1897) five steps. In the USA, behaviourist assumptions about learning prevailed until the 1950s, when the ideas of Piaget, Ausubel, Novak and others gained influence, initially among the research community. Today, science education may be said to have discovered 'situated cognition', the 'zone of proximal development' and 'multiple intelligence', although other perspectives, notably those drawn from studies of artificial intelligence, expert thinking and language acquisition, should not be overlooked. Second, it is the dubious privilege of each new wave of learning theorists to rewrite the history of how science used to be taught to suit its own current agenda. Much constructivist writing about teaching and learning seems to have little that is good to say about how science was allegedly taught before constructivist ideas came to the fore. In addition, some constructivist writing is prone to presenting that which has been commonplace for many years as new and revelatory, although the opacity of constructivist writing sometimes obscures this point.[1] Third, as befits an orthodoxy, commentaries critical of what might be called educational constructivism were, until recently, in relatively short supply (Matthews 1998).

Despite the role that constructivism has come to play within science education research, there remain many aspects about which there is disagreement at a fundamental level. Over time, there have also been shifts in the focus of attention of those working within this broad field. Early exploratory work, followed by replication studies, gave way in the 1980s to something of an emphasis on how students' ideas about a range of natural phenomena might be changed. Today, there is an interest in how students acquire these ideas, together with a greater understanding that 'alternative' and scientifically incorrect models of several natural phenomena are adequate for many everyday purposes, a view borne out by research in fields as different as the public understanding of science (Layton *et al.* 1993*),* psychology (Lave 1988) and the nature of practical (Holzner and Marx 1979) and professional knowledge (Wilson *et al.* 1987). For some critics (e.g. Matthews 1998, 2000), constructivist perspectives on teaching, learning and the nature of knowledge are linked with philosophical concerns about relativism and the standing and authority of science and scientific knowledge in a world where both are seen to be under assault. The associated debate is plagued by the variety of meanings that the term constructivism has now come to bear (Jenkins 2000).

Constructivism aside, the diversity that characterizes science education research is not without its problems. Research and related expertise can be spread too thinly, especially in smaller education systems, and there is a danger that where researchers in science education talk past each other, they will address no one save themselves. The emergence of science education as a field of research in its own right has served to demarcate researchers from practitioners, i.e. those who teach science in classrooms and laboratories, and, in some instances, from curriculum developers. In some contexts, science educators are conventionally distinguished from science teachers, the former commonly having left the classroom for a research-based academic career and the latter, until recently, occasionally reduced to little more than objects of study. Once committed to an academic career, researchers in science education are subject to the powerful pressures at work within universities which prioritise publication in scholarly journals over curriculum or other initiatives designed to improve the quality of teaching and learning in schools.

The question of standards

Any debate about the standards of research in science education is likely to be just as fraught as that which surrounds the issue of standards within other contexts, e.g. school effectiveness and student achievement over time. Without engaging in that debate here, it is clear that, in a number of countries, questions are already being asked about the quality of educational research in general and about its relevance to policy and practice. These questions, in turn, prompt several others. Who undertakes educational research and in which institutions is it located? How are researchers trained and who sets the research agenda? Is there any evidence that educational research has enhanced the learning that takes place in schools, colleges, universities and other educational institutions? In what ways does educational research influence policy and in what ways might it realistically hope to do so? Does educational research represent 'value for money'?

Although not specifically directed at research in science education, one influential commentator in the UK claims to have detected a considerable amount of 'frankly second-rate educational research which does not make a serious contribution to fundamental theory or knowledge'. Moreover, it is 'irrelevant to practice … uncoordinated with any preceding or follow-up research … and clutters up academic journals that virtually nobody reads' (Hargreaves 1996: 7). A subsequent enquiry by the Office for Standards in Education (Tooley with Darby 1998) identified four broad areas of concern, relating to partisanship, research focus, methodology and non-empirical research. The last of these was said to hint at:

> a game of 'academic Chinese whispers' ... as researchers lifted summaries of controversial positions from the descriptions of other researchers, without apparently any need to consult the primary sources to discover what authors had really said or meant.

> (Tooley with Darby 1998: 74)

The concern about the quality of educational research in the UK was mirrored in a second survey that focused attention on research relating to schools (Hillage *et al.* 1998). This concluded, among much else, that there was 'widespread concern about the quality of much educational research' and that the research effort was 'predominantly supply (i.e. researcher) driven' (ibid: x, xi). In Scotland, the Minister for Children and Education claimed in 2000 that 'Too much education research is weak, unsubstantiated and value-laden' and lacked 'basic scientific values' (Anonymous 2000: 6).

These judgments relate to the general educational research endeavour within the United Kingdom. They have not gone unchallenged (e.g. Bassey 1996; Gray *et al.* 1997; Hammersley 1997) and they have led to attempts to explain and defend what research in science education 'has to say' about practice (e.g. Monk and Osborne 2000; Taber 2000). Nonetheless, it would seem unwise not to ask whether any of the strictures about quality and purpose have a wider international applicability to research in science education. Janiuk, for example, has suggested that some research in chemical education within Europe is not of a 'sufficiently high standard ... regarding methodology and application of the ... results' and that this 'constitutes a serious problem' (Janiuk 1999: 49).

Science education: what sort of research domain?

I do not claim that this is a comprehensive review of the research literature in science education, much of which, it needs to be acknowledged, is published in languages other than English. Even so, it is perhaps just possible to identify two rather different traditions in the research undertaken in this field in the past half century or so. At the risk of over-simplification, these can be described as pedagogic/curriculum and empirical/theoretical. Such a categorization has some parallels with Psillos's three 'modes for approaching science education' (practical, technological and scientific) (Psillos 2001) and with Bishop's approach to classifying research in mathematics education (Bishop 1992).

The pedagogic/curriculum tradition

The primary focus of the pedagogic/curriculum tradition is the direct improvement of practice, practice being understood here as the teaching of science. Improved learning is assumed to follow from improved teaching and the evidence for improved teaching is to be found in such issues as enhanced student enrolment, motivation, attendance or achievement. It is rarely sought in terms of an increased level of job satisfaction for the science teacher. There may be some modest questionnaire or other form of evaluation, but there is usually no grand theoretical underpinning, and it is the practitioners themselves, i.e. the science teachers, who require and offer judgement about improvements in their practice. Such improvements cannot be transferred in some simple way to other classrooms, laboratories or teachers, so that there is no simple transferable prescription for 'best practice'. Ideas, however, can be shared and, if judged appropriate, adapted for use in a different context. The work is close to the classroom, lecture hall or laboratory, and its points of reference are how to make some aspect of science more up-to-date, more interesting to students and effective and relevant for them as a learning experience. On a day-to-day basis, it might be described as an incremental improvement of practice or, somewhat less charitably and to the extent that teaching can be reduced to a technology, as 'technological tinkering'. On a larger scale, the pedagogic/curriculum tradition underpinned the major secondary science curriculum projects of the 1960s which, for the most part, offered science teachers advice, guidance and examples on the basis of materials tried out in classrooms and laboratories.

The empirical/theoretical tradition

The empirical/theoretical tradition in science education research, always more evident and strongly supported in the USA than in Europe, is much more theoretically-grounded. It has undergone important theoretical shifts in the past thirty years, with qualitative studies increasingly augmenting longer-established quantitative approaches. Quantitative empirical work is historically associated with positivism and the generation of the 'objective data' presumed necessary to understand and influence an assumed educational reality, close familiarity with which lies at the heart of the pedagogic/curriculum tradition. While such shifts reflect an increased recognition of the complexity and subtlety of the processes involved in teaching and learning, they also owe much to the failure of a traditional empirical approach to 'deliver the goods', i.e. to raise the standards of learning generated by education systems. Today, there is a richer, although still very limited, understanding of the complexity of teaching and learning and of the interactions involved in teaching science in classrooms and laboratories. It remains a struggle for many researchers in science education to enter successfully the practitioner's world and to develop general strategies that are effective in enhancing students' learning.

How distinct are these pedagogic/curriculum and empirical/theoretical traditions within science education, given that there is often some common membership of the associated communities? Any temptation to establish rigid boundaries should be resisted. Consider, for example, the *Project for Enhancing Effective Learning* (PEEL) in Australia (Baird and Northfield 1992) and the *Cognitive*

Acceleration through Science Education (CASE) initiative in the UK (Adey and Shayer 1994). Each involved teacher–researcher collaboration and was based upon the application of ideas derived principally from cognitive psychology.[2]

Nonetheless, the differences are significant, especially within the Anglo-American community of researchers. They are evident in the journals in which the research is published, the institutional or departmental location and academic background of the researcher, and the conferences that he or she attends. Using chemical education as an illustration, there are those who teach chemistry in schools, colleges and universities and who publish papers in this field. However, for the most part, they would see themselves principally as teachers, not researchers, and their chosen outlet for publication is likely to be a professional journal (e.g. *School Science Review*), rather than one committed to publishing primary research (e.g. *International Journal of Science Education*). Typically, they are not members of the American, Australian, British or other national or international Educational Research Association, but of professional organisations concerned with science teaching or science itself. They are more likely to be found at meetings such as the Annual Meeting of the Association for Science Education (ASE) and the International Conference on Chemical Education (ICCE) than at the annual meetings of the British or American Education Research Associations or their counterparts in other countries. Parallel accounts can be given for research in physics and biology education. In the case of physics and physics education in Europe, for example, Vincenti has referred to a 'communication gap between ... two communities' who often live in separated academic institutions, adding that

> ... researchers in physics education are obviously interested in the problems of education as a research field, which may possibly produce results applicable in ... teaching ... , while the physicists consider teaching as an activity for which research is scarcely relevant.
>
> (Vincenti 1999: 97)

Notwithstanding this judgement, the distinctions drawn above are perhaps much less securely grounded outside the Anglo-American science education community than they are within it. This is partly because of the importance within the wider European tradition of didactics, a term that lacks a precise English equivalent and which sometimes leads to seemingly insuperable problems of communication and translation. To an English audience, any reference to the 'didactics of a discipline' is commonly associated with a rather direct and authoritative style of teaching rather than having anything to do with the grammar and syntax of a scholarly discipline and how it may best be taught in the interest of the students. One consequence of this difference between Anglo-American and wider European traditions may be that, within many European countries (although not the UK), rather more researchers in science education work within, or in close association with, academic science rather than education departments and thus remain in closer contact with developments in the parent scientific discipline. Dialogue between educational researchers within, and others outside, the didactic tradition, is long overdue (Hopmann and Riquarts 1995). For insights into 'didactics', see Menck (2000), Bayrhuber (2000) and Fensham (2001).

The science education research community and science

The underlying issue here can be approached, at least indirectly, by asking whether, in broad terms, researchers in science education and professional practising scientists think in similar terms about science and its educational functions. For those science education researchers working within the pedagogic/curriculum tradition (and certainly most of those engaged in school science curriculum development a generation or so ago), the question would have made little sense. But matters have changed and just how far this is so became evident when several distinguished science educators were invited to respond to an action plan for capacity building in science, produced by a committee under the chairmanship of Nobel Laureate, Leon Lederman, for the International Council of Scientific Unions (ICSU). Lederman described the responses in the following terms:

> Whew! We authored a plan for improving science education and reaped a harvest of philosophical reactions ranging from post-modernism to authentic anti-scientism to accusations of favouring a world government in which narrowly trained scientists (gasp!) make policy decisions, no doubt favouring the military–industrial complex.
>
> (Lederman 1998: 130)

For Lederman, scientific knowledge might be described as true, objective and universal: any suggestion of, for example, feminist or a uniquely 'African' science would be nonsense. In contrast, for many of the responding science educators, each of these adjectives is open to question. The science education research community (although, for reasons indicated above, not all of it) is deeply involved with issues stemming from fundamental questions about the nature of science. It has been quick to claim that some feminist and historical scholarship, together with work in cognitive psychology and the sociology of knowledge, has important implications for science education. The result has been a burgeoning science education literature that challenges, or even rejects, the view of science held by most of the scientific community and opens up new approaches to pedagogy and to the form and content of the science curriculum. Regrettably, this literature has not always done justice to the views of those who challenge some of the more radical and postmodern perspectives upon science and science education. For example, to argue for a greater appreciation of 'other ways of understanding' the natural world is an entirely legitimate undertaking. To argue that science courses should be redesigned to accommodate such 'other views' is quite another matter and raises a different set of issues. From another perspective, those who have made disciplines such as ethics and philosophy their life-long scholarly business, might sometimes be surprised at the ease with which some science educators choose to draw upon them, despite lacking any relevant formal training.

The debate prompted by the ICSU report also raises the question of where authority for the form and content of school science curricula might lie. Historically, the content of school science courses has required the support of the academic scientific community, although the various mechanisms by which its authority was mediated and exercised within different educational systems are culturally and historically contingent. At the start of the new millennium, this academic voice remains important, but there are others that now clamour for attention. Thus, Atkin *et al.*, writing of developments in the USA, comment that 'The newly influential players in determining what is to be taught to today's students include, increasingly, the public at large, scientists outside academia, and teachers themselves' (Atkin *et al.* 1997: 70). Although the other players to whom Atkin and his colleagues refer are evident in other countries, it is by no means clear how effective a contribution they are, or will be, able to make to curriculum reform. What is perhaps beyond doubt is that the school science curriculum has become contested territory to a degree that has not been evident since the mid-nineteenth century. Such contestation sits more than a little uncomfortably alongside the attempts in many education systems to promote national standards or levels of attainment within school science education.

Science education research: what is it for?

> At the University's Christmas party, a porter ... said ... 'that's what you educa-tional researchers get up to, isn't it, trying to make schools better places for people like me?'
>
> (Tooley with Darby 1998: 7)

The view that research in science education is principally, or even exclusively, about improving practice has a long history and it is strongly influenced by the empirical tradition that dominated such research in the USA throughout the twentieth century. One of its contemporary manifestations is the search for 'evi-dence-based practice' or 'warranted practice', but its antecedents lie in an essen-tially nineteenth-century belief in a 'science' of education which presents the solution to educational problems as a matter of gathering objective and empirically tested evidence. It is a belief that still underpins much research in science education.

Arguably, this is not so much a naive or mistaken view of many educational problems as one that is unhelpfully narrow and that prioritises research among the various means for improving professional practice. The narrowness is of various kinds, stemming, on the one hand, from a neglect of other kinds of research in science education that are not concerned directly, or only very indirectly, with improving practice and, on the other, an over-technical and instrumental approach to teaching and learning. A somewhat more generous view of research in science education is that it is concerned with that which 'critically informs ... judgements and decisions' in order to 'improve action' (Bassey 1995). This broader perspective has the merit of accommodating a number of strands of research in science education that are all too easily overlooked by an over-emphasis upon the teaching and learning of science in the classroom and laboratory, e.g. science education and economic development, sociological perspectives on science curriculum reform, philosophical, historical and policy-related studies. Yet, even in this more generous definition, educational research has to be justified by reference to 'improving action'. A somewhat different perspective is provided by Nisbet. Reviewing fifty years of research in science education in the USA, he has argued that the function of research in science education is to sharpen thinking, direct attention to important issues, clarify problems, encourage debate and the exchange of views, and thereby deepen understanding, prevent ossification of thinking and promote flexibility and adaptation to changing demands (Nisbet 1974). Its purpose, if it must have one beyond its intrinsic worth, is to increase the capacity of the education system, especially that concerned with science education, to recognize, understand, frame and address problems that deserve attention, rather than provide unequivocal answers to questions concerned with such matters as pedagogy, standards or teacher quality. Nisbet's case rests ultimately upon a historical understanding of science education research as a mode of thinking. It reflects a view of science education research that is different from that of research in the physical sciences and in most of the research in science education that continues to dominate the conferences of Education Research Associations in different parts of the world. Sharing Nisbet's views does not make scholarly inquiry in science education less worthwhile or important. It does, however, entail a different view of the relationships that might be expected to prevail between research, policy and practice in science education from those often assumed in the past.

Relating research, policy and practice

The relationships between knowledge and its dissemination and use have been studied from a variety of perspectives for the best part of a century (e.g. Bernstein 1971; Gadamer 1981). Within the context of education, the issues involved have attracted the attention of a number of leading scholars (e.g. Eisner 1991). It is clear that the outcomes of research in science education constitute only one of several influences, and rarely the most important, upon policy and practice. Indeed, from the perspective of the policy-maker, educational research in general seems to leave much to be desired. Tomlinson and Tuijnman, writing in 1994, judged that, in the USA, 'Educational research has yet to win acceptance on the basis of its contribution to the resolution of policy conflicts or to the improvement of educational practice or decision-making' (Tomlinson and Tuijnman 1994: 15). Of ten government departments in the Netherlands studied up to 1982, the use made of research was lowest in the Ministry of Education and Science (van Oijen 1994: 90). In 1998, Hillage and his colleagues, writing about research on schools in England and Wales, concluded that 'the actions and decision of policy-makers and practitioners are insufficiently informed by research'. They add that, where research has addressed policy-relevant and practical issues, it tended to be small-scale, failed to generate reliable and generalizable findings, was insufficiently based on existing knowledge and thus incapable of advancing understanding, and lacked interpretation for a policy-making or practitioner audience (Hillage *et al.* 1998: xi).

These concerns, which to varying degrees are common to all education systems, pose several questions. What assumptions do policy-makers, practitioners and researchers share about the nature of research in science education and the contribution it might reasonably make to meeting their respective needs? For the researcher, the answer is relatively clear. Research is about producing knowledge and that is what researchers set out to do. The research culture, however, is different from that of either the policy-maker or the practitioner, where interest lies principally, but not exclusively, in practical knowledge that underpins decision-making or action. This difference is not simply a reflection of the nature of much educational research and the institutional and functional separation of the producers and consumers of knowledge that it entails. Different types of knowledge are also involved. As Huberman has expressed it 'the universes of research and of practice seem to march to different drummers' (Huberman 1994: 46).

Huberman's comment is indicative of a more general difficulty, namely that knowledge generated within one system for one set of purposes cannot normally be readily transferred to another designed to serve different ends. Policy-makers have often, and sometimes necessarily, responded to this difficulty by espousing so-called 'quick and dirty research', much of which is concerned with data gathering and most of which is never published. It serves immediate or short-term rather than long-term needs and is unlikely to meet the criteria demanded for more scholarly work. For their part, researchers have responded by developing strategies that encourage or require the involvement of practitioners, typically teachers working in schools. As an example, action research involves self-reflection by science teachers upon their own working practices, sometimes with the assistance of others. However, many of those working within the empirical/theoretical tradition of research in science education are likely to be sceptical of, or unsympathetic towards, the democratic, participatory nature of action research with its fusion of inquiry and change and the rejection of positivist notions of objectivity and 'truth'.

Some concluding questions

Writing in *Studies in Science Education* in 1993, Atkin and Helms argued that it was time 'to raise the visibility of various options in science education and the reasons for them' (Atkin and Helms 1993: 19). Perhaps the time is right for a similar exercise, *mutatis mutandis,* for research in science education. What should be the priorities of the science education research community and how are these best determined at an individual, institutional, regional, national or international level? Is it unreasonable to expect a programme of research in science education to be both deeply grounded theoretically and of immediate use to practitioners or policy-makers?

To what extent can research in science education be said to have advanced in, say, the last thirty years? To the extent that there have been advances, why has the impact on practice commonly been so small as to be almost negligible, even in a field such as 'constructivism' where the level of investment has been high?

Where might the balance lie between fundamental and applied concerns? This question can be posed in more particular forms. To what extent should the research agenda in science education seek to address the immediate or short-term concerns of legislators, policy-makers or teachers, rather than address more fundamental questions that *may* be of longer-term significance for policy or practice? To what extent are the issues addressed by researchers in science education taken too readily as 'givens' rather than as historically, culturally or socially contingent?

What do teachers, policy-makers, legislators, parents and students want from research in science education? What do they expect and what do they *get*? What can researchers in science education, in each of the broad fields of interest, confidently expect to *deliver*? In sum, what is research in science education *for*?

Notes

1 Matthews (2000: 499) offers some examples of what he refers to as 'constructivist speak', e.g. conceptual ecology (ideas), dialogical interactive processes (discussion) and verbal discourse (speaking).
2 The two initiatives also resonated with wider political shifts in a number of countries to draw practising teachers more closely into the process of raising standards or even, as in England and Wales, to give them direct responsibility for research, including access to and control of, research funding.

Acknowledgement

Parts of this chapter appeared in an article in Volume 35 of *Studies in Science Education*. I am grateful to the Editor for permission to draw upon some of this earlier work.

References

Adams, Sir J. (1897) *The Herbartian Psychology Applied to Education*, London: Isbister.

Adey, P. S. and Shayer, M. (1994) *Really Raising Standards: Cognitive Intervention and Academic Achievement*, London: Routledge.

Anonymous (2000) 'Research body must adapt to survive', *Scotsman* 29 March.

Atkin, J. M. and Helms, J. (1993) 'Getting serious about priorities in science education', *Studies in Science Education* 21: 1–20.

Atkin, M., Kilpatrick, J., Bianchini, J. A., Helms, J. A. and Holthuis, N. I. (1997) 'The changing conceptions of science, mathematics and instruction', in S. A. Raizen and E. D. Britton (eds), *Bold Ventures*, Vol. 1 (pp. 43–72), Dordrecht: Kluwer.

Baird, J. R. and Northfield, J. R. (eds) (1992) *Learning from the PEEL Experience*, Melbourne: The Editors.

Bassey, M. (1995) 'Creating education through research', paper presented to the British Educational Research Association, Edinburgh, September 1995.

—— (1996) 'We are specialists at pursuing the truth', *Times Educational Supplement*, 22 November.

Bayrhuber, H. (2000) 'State of art of biology didactic research in Europe: an overview', in M. Bandiera, S. Caravita, E. Torracca and M. Vincenti *Research in Science Education in Europe* (pp. 7–14), Dordrecht: Kluwer.

Bernstein, R. J. (1971) *Praxis and Action*, Philadelphia: University of Pennsylvania Press.

Bishop, A. J. (1992) 'International perspectives on research in mathematics education', in D. A. Grouws (ed.) *Handbook of Research on Mathematics Teaching and Learning* (pp. 710–23), New York: Macmillan.

Boenig, R. W. (1969) *Research in Science Education, 1938 through 1947*, New York: Teachers' College Press.

Eisner, E. (1991) *The Enlightened Eye: Qualitative Enquiry and the Enhancement of Educational Practice*, New York: Macmillan.

Fensham, P. J. (2001) 'Science content as problematic – issues for research', in H. Behrendt, H. Dahncke, R. Duit, W. Gräber, M. Komorek and A. Kross (eds) *Research in Science Education: Past, Present and Future* (pp. 27–41), Dordrecht: Kluwer.

—— and Northfield, J. R. (1993) 'Pre-service science teacher education: an obvious but difficult arena for research', *Studies in Science Education* 22: 67–84.

Fraser, B. J. and Tobin, K. G. (eds) (1998) *International Handbook of Science Education*, vols, Dordrecht: Kluwer.

Gadamer, H. G. (1981) trans. F. G. Lawrence, *Reason in the Age of Science*, Cambridge, MA: MIT Press.

Gray, J., Goldstein, H. and Kay, W. (1997) 'Educational research and evidence-based practice: the debate continues', *Research Intelligence* 59: 18–20.

Hammersley, M. (1997) 'Educational research and teaching: a response to David Hargreaves' TTA lecture', *British Educational Research Journal* 23(2): 141–61.

Hargreaves, D. H. (1996) *Teaching as a Research-based Profession: Possibilities and Prospects*, London: The Teacher Training Agency (mimeo).

Hillage, J., Pearson, R., Anderson, A. and Tamkin, P. (1998) *Excellence in Research on Schools*, London: Institute for Employment Studies, DfEE.

Holzner, B. and Marx, J. H. (1979) *Knowledge Application: The Knowledge System in Society*, Boston: Allyn and Bacon.

Hopmann, S. and Riquarts, K. (eds) (1995) *Didaktik and/or Curriculum Studies*, Kiel: IPN.

Huberman, M. (1994) 'The OERI/CERI Seminar on educational research and development: a synthesis and commentary', in T. M. Tomlinson and A. C. Tuijnman (eds), *Education Research and Reform: An International Perspective* (pp. 45–66), Washington, DC: OECD Centre for Educational Research and Innovation/ US Department of Education.

Janiuk, R. M. (1999) 'The state of the art in research in chemistry education', in M. Bandiera, S. Caravita, E. Torracca and M. Vincenti (eds), *Research in Science Education in Europe* (pp. 49–56), Dordrecht: Kluwer.

Jasanoff, S., Markle, G. E., Petersen, J. C. and Pinch, T. (eds) (1995) *Handbook of Science and Technology Studies*, London: Sage.

Jenkins, E. W. (2000) 'Constructivism in school science education: powerful model or the most dangerous intellectual tendency?' *Science and Education* 9(6): 577–98.

Lave, J. (1988) *Cognition in Practice: Mind, Mathematics and Culture in Everyday Life*, Cambridge: Cambridge University Press.

Lawlor, E. P. (1970) *Research in Science Education, 1953 through 1957*, New York: Teachers' College Press.

Layton, D., Jenkins, E. W., MacGill, S. and Davey, A. (1993) *Inarticulate Science? The Public Understanding of Science and Some Implications for Science Education*, Driffield: Studies in Education.

Lederman, L. (1998) 'Forum: The ICSU Programme on Capacity Building in Science', *Studies in Science Education* 31: 71–91 and 'A response', *Studies in Science Education* 31: 130–5.

Lock, R. J. (2002) 'Does science education research count?' *School Science Review* 84(307): 13–18.

Malcolm, C. (1999) 'Inside the square and outside', *Studies in Science Education* 33: 134–40.

Matthews, M. (1998) *Constructivism and Science Education: A Philosophical Examination*, Dordrecht: Kluwer.

—— (2000) 'Editorial', *Science and Education* 9(6): 491–505.

Menck, P. (2000) *Looking into Classrooms: Papers on Didactics*, Stamford, CT: JAI Press.

Monk, M. and Osborne, J. (eds) (2000) *Good Practice in Science Teaching: What Research has to Say*, Buckingham: Open University Press.

Nisbet, J. (1974) 'Fifty years of research in science education', *Studies in Science Education* 1: 103–12.

Psillos, D. (2001) 'Science education researchers and research in transition: issues and policies', in H. Behrendt, H. Dahncke, R. Duit, W. Gräber, M. Komorek and A. Kross (eds) *Research in Science Education – Past, Present and Future* (pp. 11–16), Dordrecht: Kluwer.

Schmidt, W. H., Raizen, S. A., Britton, E. D., Bianchi, L. J. and Wolfe, R. W. (1997) *Many Visions, Many Aims: A Cross-national Study of Curricular Intentions in School Science*, Dordrecht: Kluwer.

Shorrocks-Taylor, D. and Jenkins, E. W. (eds) (2000) *Learning from Others: International Comparisons in Education*, Dordrecht: Kluwer.

Stevenson, H. W. and Stigler, J. W. (1992) *The Learning Gap. Why our Schools are Failing and What we can Learn from Japanese and Chinese Education*, New York: Summit.

Taber, K. (2000) 'Should physics teaching be a research-based activity?', *Physics Education* 35(3): 163–8.

Tomlinson, T. M. and Tuijnman, A. C. (eds) (1994) *Education Research and Reform: An International Perspective*, Washington, DC: OECD Centre for Educational Research and Innovation/US Department of Education.

Tooley, J. with Darby, D. (1998) *Educational Research: A Critique*, London: Office for Standards in Education.

van Oijen, P. M. M. (1994) 'Changes in the relationship between educational research and policy: the case of the Netherlands', in T. M. Tomlinson and A. C. Tuijnman (eds) *Education Research and Reform: An International Perspective*, Washington, DC: OECD Centre for Educational Research and Innovation/US Department of Education.

Vincenti, M. (1999) 'Physics education and physicist: two communities apart?', in M. Bandiera, S. Caravita, E. Torracca and M. Vincenti (eds) *Research in Science Education in Europe* (pp. 73–95), Dordrecht: Kluwer.

Wilson, S., Shulman, L. and Richert, A. E. (1987) '150 different ways of knowing: representations of knowledge in teaching', in J. Calderhead *Exploring Teachers' Thinking*, London: Cassell.

4.2 Science education and environmental education

Susan Barker

Orr (1992) believes *all* education is environmental education so can we interpret this to mean that all science education is environmental education? In this chapter, the relationship between science education and environmental education is explored and some research that underpins the ethos of environmental education is presented.

The word 'environment' is very much part of our daily vocabulary, yet it is a complex scientific reality that is perceived differently by each one of us. The perception of our environment stems from an analysis of the objective elements (physical, chemical and biological components of the environment) and subjective elements (psychological, emotional needs and attitudes) of the surroundings in which we live. Science is historically rooted in an understanding of the objective elements, with many early biologists, physicists and chemists observing and exploring the environment as part of scientific endeavour and advancement. Moreover, ecology, which emerged out of natural history, is now a fully fashioned science with a rich array of principles and concepts, observations, experiments and models (McIntosh 1985). This view is disputed by di Castri and Hadley (1986), who highlight lack of rigour, weak predictive capability and failure to harness modern technology as shortcomings. Despite these criticisms, ecology, which is very much a study of the interrelationships within our environment, clearly adheres to the principles and definition of science (Wali 1999). As such, it is an interface between environmental education and science education. With today's increasing global environmental problems, ecology, and science generally, play a critical role in providing a foundation of knowledge that is precise, rigorous and sophisticated, and science education plays an important role in public understanding of the issues. Environmental education, however, has a much broader remit than science education; it is more than just the study of the environment and its scientific aspects and more than the communication of knowledge. The relationship between science education and environmental education has been controversial. Part of the tension stems from the fact that knowledge of scientific facts is not enough and there is a recognition of the gap between knowledge and pro-environmental behaviour (Kollmuss and Agyeman 2002). Public awareness and concern about environmental issues emerged in the 1960s over pesticide use, with the publication of *Silent Spring* in

1962 by Rachel Carson (Carson 1962). It has progressed to cover major global issues such as climate change and more specific issues affecting local communities. In order to bring about change, pro-environmental behaviour and inculcation of positive environmental attitudes, values need to be recognized and skills developed to help tackle these issues concerning environmental quality. It is questionable, despite having much to contribute to environmental education in terms of contexts, concepts and ideas, whether science education, in its current form, can fully meet these needs, with ethics being a key divergent point. Ethical issues are often at odds with scientific agendas and science educators face a dilemma about how to address ethical issues in a science setting (Andrew and Robottom 2001). Indeed Andrew and Robottom (2001) argue for the consideration of environmental ethics in scientific environmental studies and this might help to address the tension between the two disciplines.

Environmental education – a cross-curricular theme

Environmental education does not have an absolute or fixed definition and is considered by many to be a process rather than a discipline, but it emerged as a study of the environment within the sciences. It then went on to develop into an interdisciplinary field which considers the environment in a holistic way and embraces the skills, knowledge and values needed to make sense of the world and to contribute constructively and ethically to a future characterized by uncertainty and change. A cross-curricular approach to environmental education, where it is embedded in a wide range of subjects across the curriculum, is now a widely accepted strategy applied throughout the world in formal education. This is partly due to logistical issues in delivering another subject in a crowded timetable and is much criticized by Van Matre (1990) for fragmentation and lack of coherence in an approach that he regards to be 'supplemental, piecemeal and disconnected'. Van Matre (1990) gives a good analogy of asking how an airline pilot learned to fly. If the answer was a little bit of instruction in maths, some in history and some in language/arts then would you stay on board the plane? Whatever the approach or definition, there is a general consensus that environmental education has three dimensions: cognitive, behavioural and ethical, and these are addressed within a wide range of contexts and settings.

Education for sustainable development

The concept of sustainable development arose in the late 1980s, when it became clear that development and environmental conservation were two issues with reciprocal affect. This issue was discussed by the UN World Commission on Environment and Development (WCED 1987), under the Chair of Gro Harlem Brundtlant. The resulting report, *Our Common Future*, highlighted the need for development and environmental conservation to be considered together and thus the concept of sustainable development was born:

The development that meets the needs of the present without compromising the ability of future generations to meet their own needs.

Development + Conservation = Sustainable Development

(World Commission on Environment and Development 1987)

Sustainable development is the fundamental challenge that all societies face if we are to avoid long-term damage to the Earth's basic life-support systems. The Rio de Janeiro 'Earth Summit' in 1992 led to new education initiatives in many countries and a growing interest in 'education for sustainable development' (ESD). In the UK, for example, the government set up a Sustainable Development Education Panel to provide strategic advice to the Departments of Environment and Education. As a result, teaching about sustainable development in schools is now compulsory in four subjects – science, geography, design and technology, and citizenship. One of the aims of the curriculum is to secure pupils' commitment to sustainable development. The definition of ESD in the National Curriculum for schools in England is:

> Education for sustainable development enables people to develop the knowledge, values and skills to participate in decisions about the way we do things individually and collectively, both locally and globally, that will improve the quality of life now without damaging the planet for the future.
>
> (Qualifications and Curriculum Authority 1999)

The roots of education for sustainable development are in environmental education and development education, thus interdisciplinary and holistic approaches are fundamental. However, Scott (2002) argues that there can be no single way of learning about sustainability and that there are persuasive practical and philosophical grounds for supporting learning through subject disciplines where teachers can explore such issues with both subject coherence and professional confidence. So, science and science educators will continue to play a crucial role in ESD. However, a key question is 'do we need to be informed by science in order to take action or change behaviour?' Environmentalists have, for a long time, taken direct action based purely or partly on a love of the natural environment (Kollmuss and Agyeman 2002).

Science and environmentalism

As science has provided us with evidence to help us understand our natural environment, it probably offers the strongest justification for the adoption of pro-environmental behaviours and policies (Ashley 2000). Pepper (1996), however, describes science as an 'unreliable friend to environmentalism'. The relationship between science and environmentalism, like that between science education and environmental education, has been uneasy and partly rests on interpretation of the precautionary principle (Harremoées *et al.* 2002)and the thesis that science is value-free (Ashley 2000). Science is rather conservative through its use of the scientific method and the need for sound evidence. For many environmentalists, a respect and love of the natural environment is sufficient enough reason to take direct action regarding environmental problems when scientific evidence is inconclusive. An understanding of risk and scientific uncertainty is seen as an essential element of citizenship education for a sustainable society. Ashley (2000) believes that environmental education must 'understand the limits of science and appreciate the fact that scientists are moral agents who face ethical dilemmas in their work'. Ashley (2000) further argues that science education can move forward as a key partner of environmental education. His views are endorsed by Bishop and Scott (1998), who believe that science, despite being dismissed by many environmental educators, has a significant role to play within environmental education, particularly through the achievement of scientific literacy and capability, both of which seem fundamental to an understanding of science, environmental issues and their interrelationship.

The status of environmental education, whether it be environmental education per se or education for sustainable development, has risen over the last few years and has evolved into a discipline (or process!) critical to achieving a more sustainable economy and society. Science still plays an important role in environmental education despite the evolution from apolitical scientific environmental studies to more political activities within education for sustainable development.

Research in environmental education

The need to evaluate environmental education experiences has driven environmental education research, which is rapidly expanding in size and diversity. There are a number of comprehensive reviews of the current position: Hart and Nolan (1999) present a comprehensive methodological review and Rickinson (2001) provides a complementary review of environmental education learning research as related to learners and learning in schools. An earlier review by Leeming *et al.* (1993) analyses a number of research articles that have attempted to demonstrate changes in environmental knowledge, attitudes and behaviours. They conclude that a large part of the research findings is limited because of experimental design and data analysis and only a few of the studies demonstrated changes in environmentally relevant behaviour. They recommended that researchers need to be more sensitive to the importance of rigorous designs that include meaningful control groups, controls for expectancy effects, use of reliable and valid-dependent measures, follow-up data and appropriate unit analyses.

As a consequence of the interdisciplinarity of environmental education and its increasingly political role, research in environmental education reflects this evolution. Traditionally, science education in the UK has tended to focus on the cognitive dimension rather than the affective and therefore may contribute little in this respect. Rickinson (2001), however, demonstrates that the established literature on environmental education does have a science education focus (environmental knowledge, environmental attitudes and environmental learning outcomes) with emerging themes having more sociological and political dimensions (perceptions of nature, experiences of learning, learner's influences on adults).

Environmental knowledge and understanding

Constructivist approaches to science education have had a great influence on environmental education. Current research and teaching in this area is often underpinned by a constructivist approach, which recognizes that:

> both individuals and groups of individuals construct ideas about how the world works. It is also that individuals vary widely in how they make sense out of the world and that both individuals and collective views about the world undergo change over time.
>
> (Novak 1987: 349)

Many environmental educators using constructivist approaches to teaching start their activities with eliciting information about current understanding by participants and this information lends itself well for use in research. Thus, a large proportion of environmental education research examines the very conceptions and understandings that individuals bring with them to environmental education experiences or that they have afterwards. Indeed, research into learner's environmental knowledge provides us with the majority of the empirical evidence shown in the literature and much of it has a strong science education influence. The key areas of research are:

- factual knowledge about environmental phenomena
- understanding and misunderstanding of such phenomena
- sources of environmental information.

Data tend to be generated from surveys/questionnaires with evidence derived from fixed and open-response questions. A series of papers by Leach *et al.* (Leach *et al.* 1995, 1996a, 1996b) presents such an approach to elicit information about children's understanding of ecological concepts. The authors emphasize how inherently difficult such concepts are for all students and their data help to inform teaching styles and curriculum development, particularly within science. This is in stark contrast to more interdisciplinary environmental education research where the applicability to school settings is sometimes questionable (Rickinson 2001). Dillon and Scott (2002) consider that, in appealing to constructivist discourse on learning, we will neglect other aspects that may be as, or even more, relevant to environmental education.

Draw and write technique

The ability of respondents to read and write very much limits the age at which questionnaires can be distributed and thus pupils of secondary school age and above are the usual subjects. With younger children, a 'draw and write' technique (Williams *et al.* 1989) can elicit information about their environmental knowledge, views and attitudes. Children are given verbal prompts and asked to draw in response to them. The drawings often require some limited writing, although facilitators will record verbal comments from the children where such skills are limited. This research method was developed within health education and therefore, much of the research where it has been used has been in this field, although there are some examples with environmental aspects, e.g. the link between the sun and skin cancer (Hughes *et al.* 1996; McWhirter *et al.* 2000).

The use of children's drawings, together with semi-structured interviews, provided Shepardson (2002) with qualitative data on children's understanding about insects, where he found that these are juxtaposed to those of a scientific perspective.

Drawings in questionnaires

Summers *et al.* (2001), when examining scientific understanding of environmental issues by teachers, used drawings of complex environmental issues within questionnaires to elicit responses to true/false questions. A methodological innovation in this research was the use of benchmarks to judge understanding. As in other similar research, widespread misconceptions about the science of environmental issues were evident.

Measuring environmental attitudes

Attitude research is a major area in environmental education as attitudes influence behaviour. Fishbein and Ajzen (1975) define attitude as 'a learned predisposition to respond in a consistently favourable or unfavourable manner with respect to a given object' (p. 6). They break the definition into three components: attitude is learned; it predisposes action; and such action or behaviour is generally consistent. Attitude is evaluative in nature, for instance to pollution or wildlife, and such evaluations are based on beliefs. It is much more difficult to measure environmental attitude than environmental knowledge, and getting the right answer means developing a scale that is valid and able to measure the attitude in question accurately. There are many scales available that attempt to measure aspects of people's attitudes toward the environment – attitudes toward wildlife, pollution, habitat, are just several examples. The model for these scales tends to be the 'New Environment Paradigm Scale' (NEP) developed by social scientists Dunlap and Van Liere in 1978. The paradigm emphasized environmental protection, limited industrial growth and population control, and the twelve-point scale was developed to measure this mind set.

The new environmental paradigm scale
(after Dunlap and Van Liere 1978)

- We are approaching the limit of the number of people the earth can support
- The balance of nature is very delicate and easily upset

- Humans have the right to modify the natural environment
- Humankind was created to rule over the rest of nature
- When humans interfere with nature, it often produces disastrous consequences
- Plants and animals exist primarily to be used by humans
- To maintain a healthy economy we will have to develop a 'steady state' economy where industrial growth is controlled
- Humans must live in harmony with nature in order to survive
- The earth is like a spaceship with only limited room and resources
- Humans need not adapt to the natural environment because they can remake it to suit their needs
- There are limits to growth beyond which our industrialized society cannot expand
- Mankind is severely abusing the environment.

Agreement or disagreement with these statements constitutes acceptance or rejection of the NEP. At first glance, this seems rather a simplistic way of measuring environmental attitude, but Dunlap and Van Liere tested this scale against a range of other measures of environmental attitude and behaviour in order to achieve construct validity. In order to obtain validity, they went through the following processes:

1   operationalized – or explicitly defined – what they meant by the NEP and how they were going to measure the NEP;
2   worked with a panel of experts who approved of the content of their scale;
3   used two separate population samples – an environmental group sample and a general public sample;
4   used several scales to measure environmental attitude;
5   theorized how their scale would work in relation to the other scales and with the different population samples – in other words, what kind of data they would expect to get;
6   established that the data actually supported their theory and predictions.

They found a high degree of correlation, and subsequent testing has led most researchers to agree that the NEP scale is a valid measure of environmental attitude, although most questioned whether a paradigmatic shift has indeed occurred or is occurring.

Fieldwork and environmental attitudes

Research into attitudes to fieldwork has a clear science education focus, as fieldwork has long been a traditional teaching technique in science and, indeed, also in physical geography. Students are taken outdoors to investigate aspects of the environment and thus their education is placed in a real-world context. There is concern about the demise of fieldwork within science education (Barker *et al.*

2002) and consequently, there is an increasing amount of research into the impact of such fieldwork with regard to knowledge, attitudes and behaviour. The use of rating scales is the predominant research tool, with Likert scales most widely used to measure attitudinal change. A Likert scale usually consists of a series of attitude statements that are clearly either positive or negative, on a 5-point scale. A wide range of scores is achieved by having respondents report the intensity of an attitude. Bogner (1998) used a Likert-type scale on pre- and post-test questionnaires to determine the influence of outdoor education on long-term variables of environmental perspective. For example:

Statement	1 strongly agree	2 agree	3 unsure	4 disagree	5 strongly disagree
Words such as *nature* and *life* have become much more important to me.					

Bogner found that changes in environmental knowledge, attitudes and behaviours are crucial goals for environmental education and so are appropriate criteria for programme evaluation (Bogner 1998). Indeed, Bogner has gone on to conduct several large-scale studies in Europe to measure environmental perception of young people using similar research methods (Bogner and Wiseman 1999, 2002; Bogner and Wilhelm 1996). Knapp and Poff (2001) conducted a similar piece of research, i.e. pre- and post-outdoor education experience. This differed from that of Bogner in that it took a qualitative approach, with data generated through exploratory interview and data were analysed using an interpretative phenomenological approach. They found that interactive environmental activities in an outdoor programme had a significant impact on student environmental attitudes and that passive instruction had little impact on retention of environmental knowledge.

Attitudes and behaviours

Another type of rating scale is a semantic differential scale. A scale of this type consists of a series of bipolar adjective pairs (e.g. good–bad, beneficial–harmful) listed on opposite sides of a page, with seven spaces in between. The attitude object is identified at the top of the scale and may be a word, statement or picture. The respondent is instructed to evaluate the attitude object by placing a mark in one of the seven spaces between each adjective pair. Development of semantic differential scales stems from the use of Fishbein and Ajzen's (1975) theory of reasoned action to investigate science-related attitudes. This is particularly important in the field of environmental education where pro-environmental behaviour is a clear objective. In their theory, Fishbein and Ajzen (1975) suggest that attitude measures should focus on a person's attitude toward a *behaviour* rather than on the person's attitude toward particular *objects*. That is, instead of asking about students' attitudes towards the environment, teachers or researchers should assess their attitudes toward *learning* about the environment.

Such scales have some advantages over Likert scales in environmental education as they clearly help differentiate between attitudes and behaviour.

Bogner and Wiseman (1997) examine a variation on this method (association tests) for evaluating an outdoor ecology education programme, with great success. As an evaluation tool, they found it rapid and appealing to participants and thus useful to the teacher.

Kobella (1989) outlines efforts to develop and test Likert and semantic differential attitude scales and this study has led to the following conclusions:

- Attitude instruments provide us with a convenient means of assessing behaviour. The only true reason for studying attitude is its relationship to behaviour;
- Without reliable and valid measures of attitude, assessing attitude change is impossible;
- Attitudes toward science cannot adequately predict nor provide a satisfactory explanation of science-related behaviours;
- The prediction of behavioural intention, and hence behaviour, is improved when the elements of the attitudinal and behavioural intention variables are calibrated at the same level of specificity as the behavioural criterion;
- The use of semantic differential scales based on the theory of reasoned action is preferred over Likert scales for the prediction and understanding of behaviour and the assessment of the effects of persuasion.

Phenomenographic research

Phenomenography looks at how people experience, understand and ascribe meaning to a specific situation or phenomenon (Marton and Booth 1997). It is becoming increasingly used as a research tool in education. Marton and Booth (1997) suggest that there is a relationship between how people experience a situation and how they act in that situation.

> To make sense of how people handle problems, situations, the world, we have to understand the way in which they experience the problems, the situations, the world, that they are handling or in relation to the way they are acting
>
> (Marton and Booth 1997: 111)

For environmental education this is crucial, as finding out the different ways in which people experience or understand the environment is related to the ways in which they then act. Loughland *et al.* (2002) are pioneers with this research method in environmental education where they categorize student conceptions of the environment through descriptions of salient characteristics and their variation. The sources of data are written descriptions of how students experience a phenomenon. For example, students were asked to respond to the statement: 'I think the word environment means ...', etc. The variation within the whole group's responses was analysed, with a general conclusion that the majority of young people see the *environment* as an object. This has great implications for environmental education since, if an object view is taken, then it may seem unnecessary to them to take any responsibility for the environment.

Key messages from the literature

Rickinson (2001) provides a useful synopsis from the evidence base of recent research around the world:

- *students' environmental knowledge* low levels of factual knowledge and poor understanding are commonplace with science particularly poorly understood;
- *students' environmental attitudes and behaviours* generally positive environmental attitudes are evident;
- *students' learning outcomes* learning outcomes can be changed by certain environmental education programmes;
- *students' perceptions of nature, experiences of learning and influences on adults* young people perceive 'nature' as natural living things with minimal or no interference and as a relatively static entry.

The main implications for our current knowledge base from research are that, although there is considerable evidence in the literature, it is difficult to translate this into policy or environmental practice (Rickinson 2001). People come to environmental education with a whole host of existing environmental and educational perspectives and these need to be taken into account. As Payne (1998) points out:

> Environmental educators would do well to consider learners' views about 'nature' and the 'environment' ... . Without an adequate understanding (of such views) teachers may find themselves promoting a view, or experience of nature that has a lot, little or nothing to do with children's daily living circumstances.

Rickinson (2001) makes clear recommendations for the future of environmental education research:

- broader empirical focus be adopted
- deeper level of empirical investigation
- longitudinal as opposed to cross-sectional studies be prioritized.

The current evidence base provides a solid foundation for future research, but there are two key challenges. One is to move beyond a concern with simply evaluating environmental education programmes or establishing information about students' environmental characteristics towards genuinely seeking to understand learning and the role learners play in this process (Rickinson 2001). The other key challenge is to make progress towards addressing the environmental and social problems faced by the world. The current evidence base provides a bewildering mixture of often-contradictory guidance and advice, and Scott and Oulton (1999) argue for realization of different types of environmental education, which can be shared and evaluated. In this context, environmental education is no different from science education. Indeed, environmental education is uniquely placed to offer science education a range of perspectives on knowledge and situated learning that assist those in the science education movement who wish to challenge existing orthodoxies (Dillon and Scott 2002). Gough (2002) argues on pragmatic grounds for a new, mutually beneficial relationship between science education and environmental education, where science becomes more culturally and socially relevant and environmental education uses science to underpin its objectives and provide it with a legitimate place in the curriculum.

References

Andrew, J. and Robottom, I. (2001) 'Science and ethics: some issues for education', *Science Education* 85(6): 769–80.

Ashley, M. (2000) 'Science: an unreliable friend to environmental education?', *Environmental Education Research* 6(3): 269–80.

Barker, S., Slingsby, D. and Tilling, S. (2002) *Teaching Biology outside the Classroom. Is it Heading for Extinction?*, Field Studies Occasional Publication 72, Shrewsbury: Field Studies Council.

Bishop, K. and Scott, W. (1998) 'Deconstructing action competence: developing a case for a more scientifically-attentive environmental education', *Public Understanding of Science* 7: 225–36.

Bogner, F. (1998) 'The influence of short-term outdoor ecology education on long-term variables of environmental perception', *Journal of Environmental Education* 29: 17–29.

—— and Wilhelm, M. G. (1996) 'Environmental perspectives of pupils, development of an attitude and behaviour scale', *Environmentalist* 16: 95–110.

—— and Wiseman, M. (1997) 'Association tests and outdoor ecology education', *European Journal of Psychology of Education* XII: 89–102.

—— and Wiseman, M. (1999) 'Towards measuring adolescent environmental perception', *European Psychologist* 4(3): 139–51.

—— and Wiseman, M. (2002) 'Environmental perception of French and some Western European secondary school students', *European Journal of Psychology of Education* XVII: 3–18.

Carson, R. (1962) *Silent Spring*, Boston: Houghton Mifflin; Cambridge, MA: Riverside Press.

di Castri, F. and Hadley, M. (1986) 'Enhancing the credibility of ecology: is interdisciplinary research for land-use planning useful?', *Geojournal* 13: 299–325.

Dillon J. and Scott, W. (2002) 'Editorial perspectives on environmental education research in science education', *International Journal of Science Education* 24(11): 1111–7.

Dunlap, R. and Van Liere, K. (1978) 'The New Environment Paradigm: a proposed measuring instrument and preliminary results', *Journal of Environmental Education* 9: 10–19.

Fishbein, M, and Ajzen, I. (1975) *Belief, Attitude, Intention, and Behaviour: An Introduction to Theory and Research*, Reading, MA: Addison-Wesley Publishing.

Gough, A. (2002) 'Mutualism: a different agenda for environment and science education', *International Journal of Science Education* 24(11): 1201–15.

Harremoèes P., Gee, D., MacGarvin, M., Stirling, A., Keys, J., Wynne, B. and Guedes Vaz, S. (2002) *The Precautionary Principle in the 20th Century*, London: Earthscan.

Hart, P. and Nolan, K. (1999) A critical analysis of research in environmental education, *Studies in Science Education* 34: 1–69.

Hughes, B. R., Wetton, N., Collins, M. and Newton Bishop, J. A. (1996) 'Health Education about sun and skin cancer: language, ideas and perceptions of young children', *British Journal of Dermatology* 134: 624–9.

Knapp, D. and Poff, R. (2001) 'A qualitative analysis of the immediate and short-term impact of an environmental interpretive program', *Environmental Education Research* 7(1): 55–65.

Kobella, T. R. Jr. (1989) 'Changing and measuring attitudes in the science classroom', *Research Matters – to the Science Teacher* (8901), <http://www.educ.sfu.ca/narstsite/publications/research/research.html>.

Kollmuss, A. and Agyeman, J. (2002) 'Mind the gap: why do people act environmentally and what are the barriers to pro-environmental behaviour?', *Environmental Education Research* 8(3): 239–56.

Leach, J., Driver, R., Scott, P. and Wood-Robinson, C. (1995) 'Children's ideas about ecology 1: theoretical background, design and methodology', *International Journal of Science Education* 17(6): 721–32.

——, Driver, R., Scott, P. and Wood-Robinson, C. (1996a) 'Children's ideas about ecology 2: ideas found in children aged 5–16 about the cycling of matter', *International Journal of Science Education* 18(1): 19–34.

——, Driver, R., Scott, P. and Wood-Robinson, C. (1996b) 'Children's ideas about ecology 3: ideas found in children aged 5–16 about the interdependence of organisms', *International Journal of Science Education* 18(2): 129–42.

Leeming, F. C., Dwyer, W., Porter, B. and Cobern, M. (1993) 'Outcome research in environmental education: a critical review', *Journal of Environmental Education* 24(4): 8–21.

Loughland, T., Reid, A. and Petocz, P. (2002) 'Young people's conception of environment: a phenomenographic analysis', *Environmental Education Research* 8(2): 187–97.

Marton, F. and Booth, S. (1997) *Learning and Awareness*, Mahwah, NJ: Lawrence Erlbaum.

McIntosh, R. P. (1985) *The Background of Ecology: Concept and Theory*, New York: Cambridge University Press.

McWhirter, J. M., Collins, M., Bryant, N. M., Wetton, N. and Newton, B. J. (2000) 'Evaluating "safe in the sun" a curriculum programme for primary schools', *Health Education Research: Theory and Practice* 5: 203–17.

Novak, J. D. (1987) 'Human constructivism: towards a unity of psychological and epistemological meaning making', in J. D. Novak (ed.) *Misconceptions and Educational Strategies in Science and Mathematics*, Proceedings of the Second International Seminar, New York: Cornell University.

Orr, D. W. (1992) *Ecological Literacy: Education and the Transition to a Post-modern World*, New York: New York Press, New York State University.

Payne, P. (1998) 'Children's conception of nature', *Australian Journal of Environmental Education* 14: 133–53.

Pepper, D. (1996) *Modern Environmentalism. An Introduction*, London: Routledge.

Qualifications and Curriculum Authority (QCA) (1999) *The National Curriculum for England*, London: QCA.

Rickinson, M. (2001) 'Learners and learning in environmental education; a critical review of the evidence', *Environmental Education Research* 7(3): 207–320.

Shepardson, D. P. (2002) 'Bugs, butterflies, and spiders: children's understanding about insects', *International Journal of Science Education* 24(6): 627–43.

Scott, W. (2002) 'Education and sustainable development: challenges, responsibilities, and frames of mind', *Trumpeter* 18(1), <http://trumpeter.athabascau.ca/content/v18.1/scott.html>

Scott, W. A. H. and Oulton, C. R. (1999) 'Environmental education: arguing the case for multiple approaches', *Educational Studies* 25: 89–97.

Summers, M., Kruger, C., Childs, A. and Mant, J. (2001) 'Understanding the science if environmental issues: development of subject knowledge for primary education', *International Journal of Science Education* 23: 33–53.

Van Matre, S. (1990) *Earth Education a New Beginning*, West Virginia: The Institute for Earth Education.

Wali, M. K. (1999) 'Ecology today: beyond the bounds of science', *Nature and Resources* 35(2): 38–50.

World Commission on Environment and Development (WCED) (1987) *Our Common Future; World Commission on Environment and Development*, Oxford: Oxford University Press.

Williams, D. T., Wetton, N. and Moon, A. (1989) *A Picture of Health: What Do you Do that Makes you Healthy and Keeps you Healthy?*, London: Health Education Authority.

Index

eBooks – at www.eBookstore.tandf.co.uk

A library at your fingertips!

eBooks are electronic versions of printed books. You can store them on your PC/laptop or browse them online.

They have advantages for anyone needing rapid access to a wide variety of published, copyright information.

eBooks can help your research by enabling you to bookmark chapters, annotate text and use instant searches to find specific words or phrases. Several eBook files would fit on even a small laptop or PDA.

NEW: Save money by eSubscribing: cheap, online access to any eBook for as long as you need it.

Annual subscription packages

We now offer special low-cost bulk subscriptions to packages of eBooks in certain subject areas. These are available to libraries or to individuals.

For more information please contact webmaster.ebooks@tandf.co.uk

We're continually developing the eBook concept, so keep up to date by visiting the website.

www.eBookstore.tandf.co.uk